By Water and Rail

A History of Lake County, Minnesota

by Hugh E. Bishop
for the Lake County Historical Society

Lake Superior Port Cities Inc.

First Edition: October 2000

5 4 3 2 1

Published by
LAKE SUPERIOR PORT CITIES INC.
P.O. Box 16417
Duluth, Minnesota 55816-0417
USA 888-BIG LAKE (244-5253)

Publishers of *Lake Superior Magazine* and *Lake Superior Travel Guide*

Library of Congress Cataloging-In-Publication Data

Bishop, Hugh E., 1940-
By water and rail : a history of Lake County, Minnesota / by Hugh E. Bishop for the Lake County Hisotrical Society. – 1st ed.
p. cm.
Includes bibliographical references and index.
ISBN 0-942235-48-7 – ISBN 0-942235-42-8 (softcover)
1. Lake County (Minn.) – History – Anecdotes. 2. Lake County (Minn.) – Biography – Anecdotes. I. Lake County Historical Society (Minn.) II. Title.

F612.L3 B5 2000
977.6'76 – dc21 00-062989

Printed in the United States of America

Editing: Paul L. Hayden, Konnie LeMay
Design: Matt Pawlak
Printing: Sheridan Books, Chelsea, Michigan

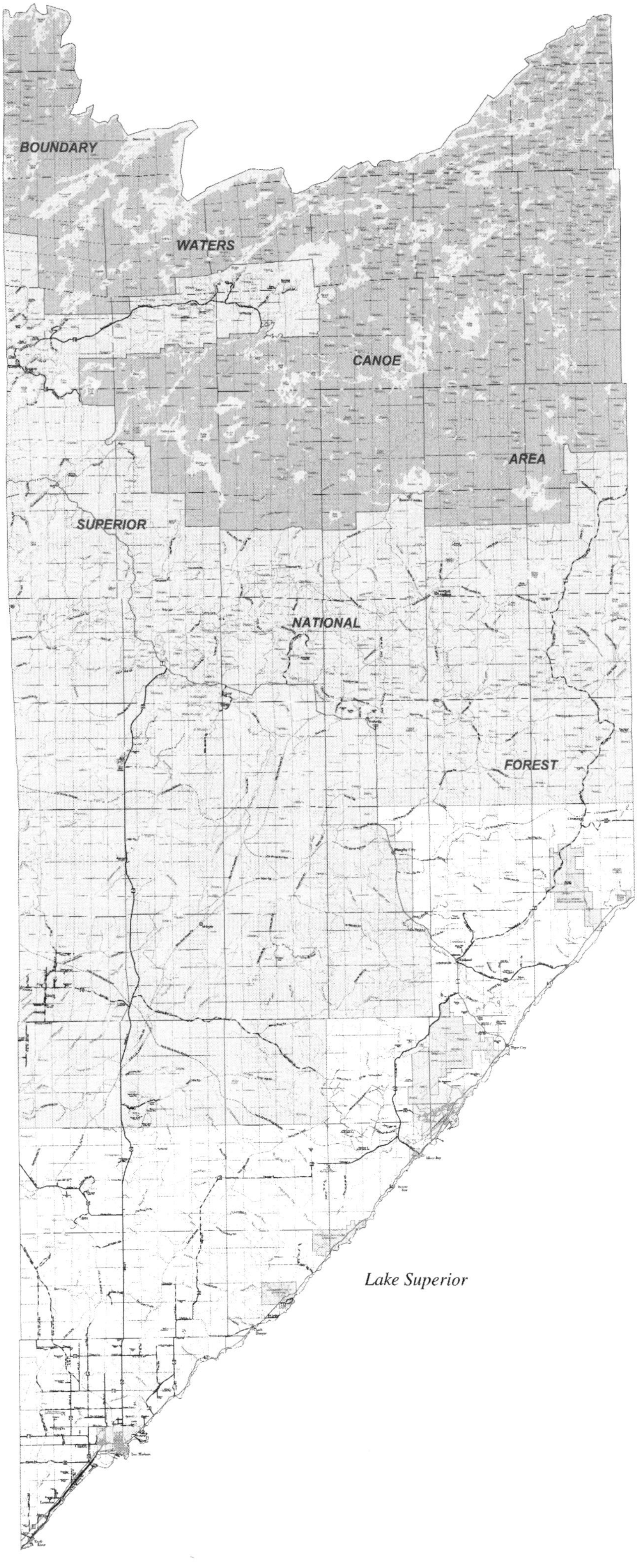

BOUNDARY WATERS CANOE AREA

SUPERIOR NATIONAL FOREST

Lake Superior

Dedicated to the early settlers of Lake County who made all of the history possible and the five generations of the LaBounty family in Lake County.

911 Map of
Lake County, Minnesota.
COURTESY LAKE COUNTY

Introduction

Stretching from Lake Superior's cool waters to the international boundary with Canada and from Ely-Winton on the west to Little Marais and Cook County on the east, Lake County, Minnesota, constitutes an enormous project for anyone seeking to document its history. In addition to encompassing a huge area, the county has experienced a wide variety of development in several phases – some of which were gradual and others that almost seemed to drop from the sky.

With that said, the history of Lake County is also the story of persistent folks willing to invest their money, effort and lives in the tough work of opening a trackless wilderness and maintaining themselves on often inhospitable land.

Yet the story of those folks' struggles is really the history of this area. The fact that Lake County exists today testifies to their success at overcoming obstacles and sustaining their families.

Third-generation Lake County resident Roy LaBounty deserves the credit for this book becoming reality. His dream of recording the past and his generosity produced it. Without that vision, and the monetary support he provided, this book could not have come into being. He also contributed valued information as a member of the committee that oversaw the production of this book.

Although this volume highlights the history of the several communities that make up Lake County, there are a number of local area history books that have been a major source of information. They are frequently cited in the text and are also noted in the endnotes and bibliography. Those local historians deserve a good deal of credit for documenting their community's history and devoting the time such a project demands. We thank them for everything we've learned from their efforts and recommend that readers obtain a copy of these histories to round out our somewhat synopsized versions. Most are now only available at local libraries, since they have been sold out by the sponsors and private owners are reluctant to loan them out.

The bulk of the photographs that illustrate this book come from the Lake County Historical Society archives and carry no credit line. Photos from other sources are individually identified with the name of the contributor or collection. But our search for illustrative materials revealed that the archival collection of the LCHS is very good until about 1950, when the record becomes considerably less abundant.

Having said that, we encourage anyone with photos in family collections to contact the LCHS and offer to donate them to the permanent collection. Often, one person's unidentified or uncherished picture will be recognized and used by someone who is looking for just that image.

We need to especially note the huge contribution of the members of the oversight committee for this book. Alf Sandvik, Patricia Reed, Roy LaBounty, Jon Anderson and Chele Maloney, later joined by Bill Johnson, endured more than a year of meetings, loaned their personal copies of books, memoirs and other materials, reviewed more than 125 pages of draft text, offered advice, encouragement and suggestions, conducted research on specific topics and provided the actual information for many of the stories contained in this text.

In addition, a special thanks to all of the people who contributed their own stories in the form of videotaped interviews. Although some were at first hesitant at the idea of appearing on tape, their stories are an integral and interesting addition to this book and the LCHS archives.

Finally, for you the reader, we appreciate your interest in this book and hope you find it interesting and useful. As noted earlier, there are other, more specific reference materials about local areas and we were hard pressed as to what information from those sources to use in this volume. Having to keep the length of this overview within reason, we regret that many interesting and fun stories from those works had to be omitted or severely shortened. Luckily, they are still available with a bit of added effort.

Hugh E. Bishop

Table of Contents

Behind the Glaciers

Throughout history and prehistory in northeastern Minnesota, enterprise of one type or another has dominated human activity. From the collection and distribution of particularly desirable types of rock or native copper for toolmaking to the mining of minerals on a more colossal scale, logging, commercial fishing, recreational pursuits and daily commerce, this frontier provided the opportunity to thrive and obtain wealth for those willing to assume the risks involved. The opportunities offered also seemed to find the right entrepreneurs at exactly the right moment to take advantage of an endeavor.

While historic accounts only begin in about 1670, they note the widespread presence of native people throughout the Lake Superior region. In addition, recent archaeological efforts have unearthed artifacts that seem to show that humans were in this region significantly earlier than had previously been thought.[1]

Indeed, increasing evidence along Lake Superior's shoreline indicates that people were living here from very shortly after the last glacier receded and may have even occupied some exposed lobes of land during the latest glacial epoch. Archaeologists have documented Paleo-Indian tools and other artifacts at sites in northeastern Minnesota that date to a period from 7,500 to 9,000 years ago.

Since glacial recession is usually dated at about 10,000 years ago and glaciation would have disturbed and reduced nutrient levels in the soil and water, these people would have inhabited an area in which vegetation likely consisted of shrubby, pioneering species like tundra vegetation, wetland grasses and forests of

mixed species like jack and red pine, willow and dwarf birch. These pioneer people were apparently hunters who depended upon large upland animals like moose, caribou and bison, but lived in what appear to have been seasonal locations near rivers and lakes where fish would also serve as a food staple.

At that time, Lake Superior was brimming with glacial melt water and the waterline was considerably higher than it is today. The sites where these early people lived along the lake are, therefore, well above and inland from the current shoreline. While little is known of their lifestyle, they undoubtedly used waterways in their travels, since many of the larger tools found from that period appear to have been used in making dugout canoes, which predate the introduction of birch-bark canoes by later cultures.[2]

It is not known if these early Paleo-Indian people were pushed out or were assimilated by the several prehistoric cultures that followed. There is a considerable body of evidence that all of these prehistoric cultures used tools and ornamental/ceremonial items fashioned from stone, copper, shells and other materials that came from considerable

distances, leading archaeologists to conclude that there was an extensive trading system operating in North America long before European people first arrived for their fur trading purposes. That conclusion is borne out by archaeological excavation of the large burial mounds of the slightly later Laurel culture in the Canada-Minnesota boundary area, which documents sea shell ornaments that came from as far away as the Pacific Ocean and the Gulf of Mexico.

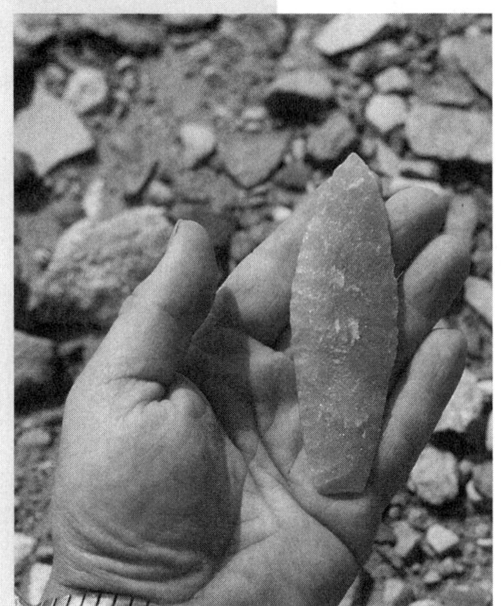

To archaeologists, stone tools have life and character that tell a great deal about the people who fashioned them. Tools found at sites like McDougall Lake indicate the presence of people in northeastern Minnesota shortly after the last glacier receded about 10,000 years ago. LAKE SUPERIOR MAGAZINE

In addition to stone tools attributed to the original Paleo-Indian people, copper artifacts have been found mixed in with stone tools at some sites. It's possible, therefore, that these earliest inhabitants were the first miners to work the rich native copper deposits of Isle Royale and Upper Michigan. The copper would not only be useful in fashioning their own tools and ornamental/ceremonial items, but is known to have provided a valued trading commodity for hundreds of generations of humans before white culture moved in. Artifacts of native copper from these midwestern sites have been found in a huge territory of North America, again attesting to the widespread trading system maintained by these people.

At some point, the Blackduck culture succeeded or absorbed the Laurel people and was in turn driven northward out of Minnesota by the incursion of the Siouan people of the Mississippian culture, which began about 1000 A.D.

Although it is doubtful that they built permanent settlements in this area, by about 1500 the Sioux people held sway over a large area of the Midwest, including nearly all of Minnesota, but were soon challenged by the eastern Algonquian tribes – particularly the Ottawa, Huron and, especially, the large Ojibway tribal group, which had established a more or less permanent hold on the seasonal fishing and communal site at what is now Sault Ste. Marie, Michigan, at the eastern end of Lake Superior. From that point, the Ojibway pushed west to become dominant in the entire Lake Superior region. Among a number of Lake Superior north shore locations that the Ojibway people visited regularly during the year was *Wasswawinig* – "the place to spear fish by moonlight" or "to fish with torches," which would later be named Two Harbors.[3]

By the time the first French traders and missionaries arrived at western Lake Superior in the 1660s they found a situation in which bloody territorial skirmishes were relatively common between the Sioux and Ojibway people, particularly on the western end of the lake, where the Ojibway had only recently begun their efforts at conquest.

The traders needed the natives to supply furs and this squabbling over domain hardly promoted ideal trade conditions. As much as possible, the traders attempted to intercede and keep the Indian people tending to the trapping business. One of the primary objectives of Daniel Greysolon, Sieur du L'hut, when he visited western Lake Superior in 1678 and 1679 was to establish a lasting peace between the warring tribes.[4]

Since they had encountered and traded with the whites first, the Ojibway likely brought more modern weapons and other gear to the strife that eventually drove the Sioux out of the woodlands – or it may simply have been that the Ojibway were more accomplished in woodland settings than the Sioux, who had migrated into these northern areas from the warmer, prairie environment to the south and west.

For whatever reason, by the early 1700s, the Ojibway people dominated the northern forest lands. Living a seasonal, nomadic lifestyle, they moved about in fairly small groups to take advantage of the best locations for fishing, hunting, gathering and maple sugaring. Some of their more frequently visited sites were La Pointe and, somewhat later, Fond du Lac (the first trading post of that name was located on Connor's Point in present day Superior, Wisconsin). Grand Portage, Minnesota, became headquarters for important trading operations of the North West Company and, later, the succeeding American Fur Company.[5]

There are records from the mid-1700s onward by several diarists about trading posts along the Grand Portage voyageur route in northern Lake and Cook counties and it is certainly true that the rest of Lake County's wilderness would have yielded significant tonnages of beaver, fisher, marten, mink, otter, weasel and other pelts for commerce, although there is little record of early trading posts beyond those noted on the voyageurs' route through the Boundary Waters.

In 1823, Dr. John Bigsby, a member of the commission to explore and establish the international boundary between the United States and Canada, recorded that there was a Hudson's Bay Company post at Basswood Lake on a highland near Inlet Bay and Prairie Portage. There are later reports of an American Fur Company post on Hoist Bay of that same lake that also supplied traders at Fall, Burntside, Vermilion and Shagawa lakes. The Hudson's Bay post used sled dogs for the trader/voyageurs doing business in a large area surrounding the post.[6]

About 40 years later, R.B. McLean reports in his memoirs that during an 1861 trip on the Grand Portage boundary waters route to take charge of a trading post at Lake of the Woods, he stopped at trading posts on Mountain, Saganaga and Basswood lakes, Lake Vermilion and Lac La Croix on the old voyageur route. By that late date, the posts were all owned by H.H. McCullough, who also operated the post at Grand Portage.[7]

It's probable that each of the 1861 posts described by McLean was located at a site that had become traditional during the earlier era, but it's also true that the tribal people who trapped in Lake, Cook and St. Louis counties during the heyday of fur trading were certainly capable of making the relatively short trek to the North West Company's large post at Grand Portage. Many would likely have preferred that exciting community as their residence during the annual rendezvous there, as well.

For about 200 years of first French, then British control of the territory, the hardy class of French-Canadians known as voyageurs pushed the frontier ever farther west, entering that distant land through the Grand Portage/Boundary Waters

The workhorses of the fur trade in northern Minnesota and lower Canada were the voyageurs, shown here portaging on the Boundary Waters route from Grand Portage to their inland fur trading areas. Several fur trading posts were established in the northern area of Lake County.
HOWARD SIVERTSON FROM *THE ILLUSTRATED VOYAGEUR*

passageway that provided waterborne access to virtually the entire northern and western region of the continent. The North West Company maintained its trading territories in the Midwest by using the traditional voyageur route through the Great Lakes, Grand Portage and the inland waters accessible from the Pigeon River westward. Necessarily, the North West Company employed a large number of voyageurs to paddle the canoes, carry the freight, erect the forts and trading posts and to generally do the labor required by such a far-flung enterprise.

By contrast to North West, Hudson's Bay Company operated from primary supply posts on Hudson Bay, pushing its traders south and westward and shipping its furs directly to England by the easier salt-water route through the bay and across the Atlantic Ocean.

Modern canoeists quickly find that the Boundary Waters voyageur route is no piece of cake. Even without the voyageurs' 90-pound packs of furs or trade goods, the many portages in the northern area of Lake County will challenge even veteran paddlers. The voyageurs, starting at the nine-mile "grand portage" near Lake Superior, moved tons of freight over this uneasy route. With 180 pounds or more on their back, they would trot off up the portages, dropping their loads after a quarter to a half mile and returning for another mule-sized load.

Once the portage reached navigable waters, the entire load of goods would be quickly transferred back into the canoe and the voyageurs would resume their paddling. Maintaining a steady rhythm of 45 to 60 strokes a minute, accompanied by lively songs, they would push ahead for upward of an hour, before a pause would be called by the steersman. A *pipe*, the designation given to these rest stops, would be smoked and the pace resumed. One diarist estimated that the voyageurs paddled 57,000 strokes during a day, which began at about 3 a.m. and ended at 9 p.m.[8]

While the French and English fur traders and the voyageurs were virtually the only white people in this area from the mid-1600s until the mid-1850s, the North West Company that dominated the Lake Superior trade from about 1775 was relocated in 1803 from Grand Portage, Minnesota, to Fort William, Ontario (what is now Thunder Bay), under terms of the Treaty of Paris that settled Revolutionary War hostilities between England and the United States. The North West Company would also shortly be taken over by Hudson's Bay Company.

The British traders continued to operate on both sides of the ill-defined border between Canada and the United States, despite the fact that northeast Minnesota was now definitely established as United States territory. The only issue was the exact location of the international border, which was not finally settled until 1842, when the Webster-Ashburton Treaty sealed the Pigeon River and the traditional voyageur route through the Boundary Waters as the boundary. By that time, the fur trade had declined to a mere shadow of its previous importance.

But Congress had put a stop to cross-border trading when it passed legislation in 1816 barring any further incursion into this country by foreign traders. John Jacob Astor's American Fur Company had already effectively taken over the former English and French operations at Grand Portage and La Pointe, Wisconsin, and had also located a major new "Fond du Lac" post in the area of western Duluth that bears that name today.

After Astor's company charter expired in 1833 and Astor withdrew from it, the Lake Superior division would be reorganized as a new American Fur Company in about 1835 and would prove to be the pioneer in commercial fishing when it established major fishing posts as a source of secondary revenue at Grand Portage, Grand Marais and Isle Royale, with lesser outposts on the north shore and a fishery headquarters at La Pointe. The company maintained major warehouses at each of those sites and at Sault Ste. Marie and Detroit, Michigan. Although the catch from this early effort was prolific and yielded 3,000 or more 200-pound barrels of salted fish each season, the company only lasted for about seven seasons before the exploitation of the new fishery depressed prices in the fish market and the company failed.

It would not be until about 1880 that commercial fishing again became important in the Lake Superior economy, although most early settlers did depend on fish as a staple in their diets.[9]

MINNESOTA TERRITORY Showing the ORIGINAL COUNTIES

The Territory of Minnesota was considerably larger than the state, taking in more than half of what would become North and South Dakota. Northeastern Minnesota was all designated as Itasca County from 1849 until 1855. MINNESOTA HISTORICAL SOCIETY PRESS

When the Territory of Minnesota was established in 1849, Itasca County was formed and included all of the area of northeastern Minnesota from Lake Superior's shoreline to a straight north/south line from the headwaters of the Mississippi River to just west of Lake of the Woods, bounded on the south by the easterly flowing Mississippi. Those lines remained until 1855. The Territory of Minnesota stretched from Lake Superior and the present boundaries with Iowa, Wisconsin and Canada westward nearly halfway across the present states of North and South Dakota to the Missouri and White Earth rivers.

Although all of northeastern Minnesota was part of the new territory, the entire north shore was also designated as "Indian Territory" and settlement or exploration were forbidden from the border of Wisconsin to the Canadian international boundary. That would not change until the Treaty of La Pointe was signed in the fall of 1854 and ratified by Congress in early 1855.

When the north shore was opened to white settlement, interest in mineral exploration in these rocky lands was high – leading to a rush of landlooking prospectors backed by investors from all over the world. Copper was the principal objective, but the landlookers were disappointed in that effort. A financial panic in 1857 followed by the Civil War effectively ended this first rush of settlers to the north shore.

In 1855, Itasca County was divided into three counties, with a much reduced Itasca to the west, Doty in the middle and Superior on the east. After only five days, the names of Doty and Superior were changed to Newton and St. Louis, with St. Louis being the present Lake and Cook counties. On March 1, 1856, that area was renamed Lake County and the

St. Louis name was moved westward to more correctly name the county that includes the St. Louis River and Bay. These territorial names remained when the State of Minnesota entered the Union in 1858.[10]

A Beaver Bay townsite was platted on the eastern bank of the Beaver River in 1856 by W.H. Newton, Jessie Ramsey and Thomas Clark II. Clark and Newton were major figures in the earlier development of Superior, Wisconsin. German-speaking settlers arrived at the mouth of the Beaver River in 1856 and the Wieland family sawmill became important in the pioneering settlement that became Beaver Bay. These pioneers were successful in establishing permanent roots on the western side of the river, giving Beaver Bay the distinction of being the oldest continual settlement on Minnesota's north shore. Beaver Bay also served as the first county seat of Lake County.

It would be 1874 before Cook County was officially separated from Lake County, but it took until 1882 to form a county board of commissioners that would organize that governmental subdivision – meaning that Beaver Bay remained the seat of government for the entire north shore, assessing taxes and administering all aspects of the laws.

The village of Two Harbors was officially platted in 1885 with a population of 550. A year later, the townsite on Agate Bay became the county seat and was incorporated as a village on March 9, 1888.

Meanwhile, A. DeLacy Wood founded the *Two Harbors Iron Port* newspaper in 1887 and persuaded the county board to designate his paper to publish all legal advertising. This almost guaranteed financial success and he would also establish Cook County's first newspaper, the *Grand Marais Pioneer* in 1891, retaining ownership of the *Iron Port* and giving him, in effect, a monopoly on north shore news and advertising. During his career as a tramp newspaper man, Wood is credited with starting 48 newspapers in the Upper Midwest, even though he died before 60 years of age.[11]

Although the building of Charlemagne Tower's Duluth & Iron Range Railroad in 1883-84 established a new town on Agate Bay and the first shipments of iron ore from the Tower mines to Agate Bay in 1884 assured the success of the settlement, the 74-mile railroad also opened interior land to settlement. It was only a matter of a year or two before families settled in along the railroad and, about a decade later, a wave of pioneering families were locating in the Brimson-Toimi area and other inland locations along the rail line. Meanwhile, hardy fishermen and their families had been settling along the lakeshore from Knife River to the Canadian boundary, using whatever the land and lake would yield to scratch out their livelihoods.

While the companies that were headed and financed by Charlemagne Tower were successful in opening the Lake Vermilion mines and Duluth & Iron Range Railroad, Tower's influence was to be shortlived. After completing the railroad connection from the Iron Range to Duluth by building the lakeshore line in 1886, thus qualifying for more than 600,000 acres of land grant property, Tower was forced to sell his controlling interest in the railroad and mining properties to a syndicate of (primarily) Chicago financiers a year later. Those investors, in turn, would fold their interests into the huge United States Steel Corporation, which was formed in 1901

Life Along the Beaver River

Surveyed in April 1856 and registered later that summer by Thomas Clark II of Superior, Wisconsin, Beaver Bay sprang to life as a platted townsite east of the Beaver River. It was actually first inhabited from November 1854 until February 1855 by Antoine Ambul, Henry Schutte and R.B. McLean, whose memoirs of this early period on the north shore have been widely quoted. Before the March 1855 ratification of the 1854 Treaty of La Pointe by Congress, three "preemptor" cabins 14 feet by 16 feet by six logs high were thrown together by McLean and his companions on the site in an effort to establish a claim on the property and the water power of the Beaver River for the townsite's proprietors, Clark, Justus Ramsey of St. Paul and W.H. Newton of Superior.

Clark's familiarity with the site preceded his official plat by about 18 months, for McLean recorded that he, Clark and two other men took an October 1854 "sneak preview" trip up the north shore to Grand Marais and that on the return trip "Mr. Clark made a thorough examination of the water power on Beaver River and decided that there was plenty of power there for a sawmill, if there were timber enough back in the country to warrant building one.

"We camped there for the night and (the next morning) Clark and myself took our packs and followed the valley for several miles back from the lake. There was a large body of white pine along both banks of the river, enough to keep a mill running for a number of years."[1]

Clark's field notes from that exploration also noted good meadowland with red top and meadow grass growing in sand and gravel soil. Saying that he saw little poor land in the two days in the area, his diary also noted "a fair show of copper – 100 to 150A."

While the exploration and earliest occupancy of the site was undoubtedly illegal, having occurred before the early 1855 Congressional ratification of the treaty that allowed whites to visit or settle on the north shore, Clark no doubt felt he had good reason for his precipitate actions. Development and speculation in townsites had proven highly profitable in many other areas where treaties opened native lands to settlement – including the townsite of Superior that served as the jumping-off place for the later exploration of northeastern Minnesota.

And it's probably no coincidence that, by the time the plat was officially filed in 1856, about 20 German and Swiss immigrants had already begun to resettle there from their homes in Ohio.

Christian Wieland, one of the five brothers who were generally recognized as being leaders in the early Beaver Bay community, was described by his nephew Henry as "an architect and surveyor,"[2] and as a "civil engineer" by another nephew, Fred.[3] He is known to have worked with Thomas Clark in Toledo, Ohio, and followed Clark to the city of Superior in 1854, where a plat map dated that year for the eastern division of the city is signed by Clark as the county surveyor, with a notation, "the plat and notes made by C. Wieland, Deputy County Surveyor."[4]

As an associate of Clark, Christian undoubtedly heard office discussions between Clark and McLean about the

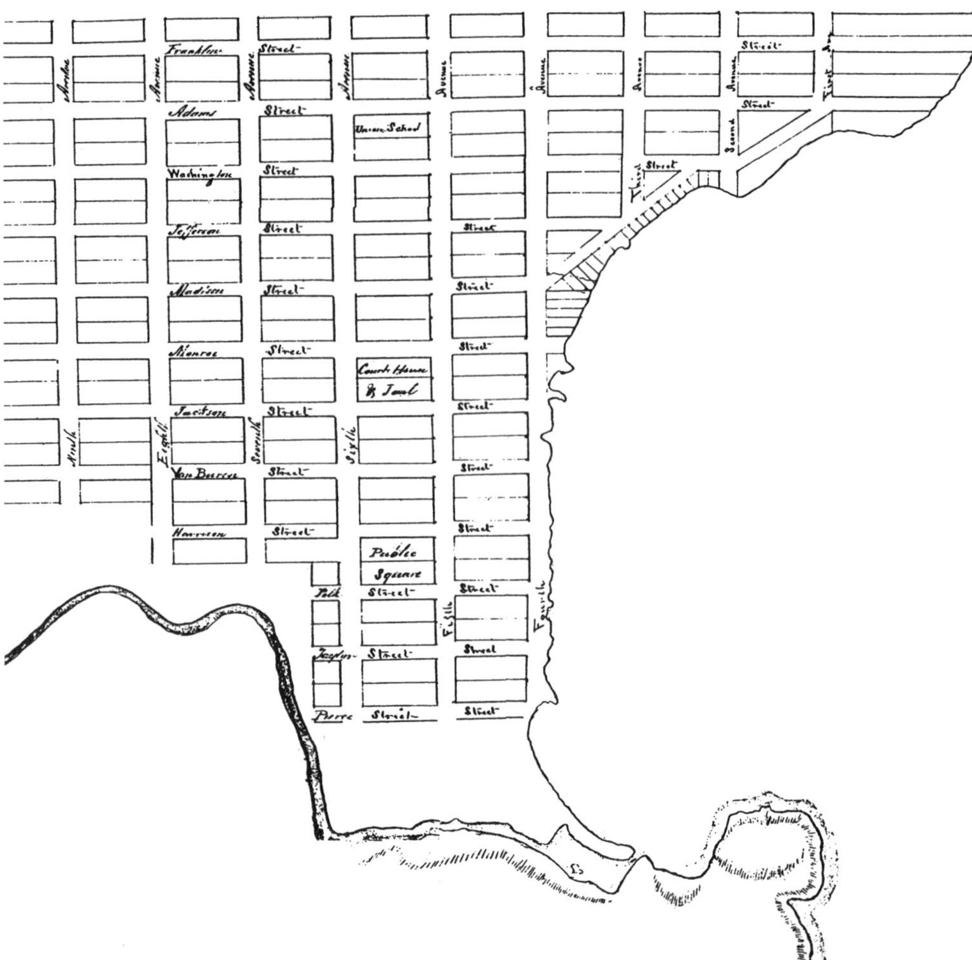

Although Thomas Clark surveyed and platted a townsite on the east bank of the Beaver River, the Swiss and German settlers who first occupied Beaver Bay chose the west bank for their homesites.

Facing page: *A 1911 postcard view of Beaver Bay shows rapacious logging was well under way in the area by that point.*

water, timber, agricultural and mineral prospects that had been found at the Beaver River during the 1854 prospecting trip. Christian also likely knew of the preemptive claim that had been established on the site for Clark and his partners by McLean and his 1854 companions.

Christian may have even expressed interest in the site to Clark, because his older brother, Henry, had let him know that the Wieland family would be moving away from Perrysburg, Ohio, where Henry and their three younger siblings, Ernst, Albert and August, were operating a tannery they built there in 1849. Their father had owned a successful tannery in Germany, but ownership of the property passed at his death to the oldest son, Karl. He, in turn, paid cash to each of the others for their share of the inheritance and the non-heirs immigrated to America.

The Wielands' Ohio business was apparently quite successful in its early days, buying hides from and selling leather to the German, Swiss and Dutch farmers who settled in the surrounding countryside. However, the prevalence of "ague," which is variously named in reminiscences as yellow fever, cholera or malaria, killed many settlers and was so pervasive that many others simply fled. With business deteriorating, the Wielands chose to dispose of the tannery and move to an area with a healthier environment.

After learning of his brothers' plans to flee Ohio, Christian undoubtedly passed along his inside information about Beaver Bay to his brothers. By that time, he had enough experience in this region to be able to assure them that this northern climate would be a healthy place to raise families.

The Ohio Wielands began making plans to migrate to the spot that Christian recommended. Although McLean's memoir makes no mention of any trace of copper at the site and Clark's observance was rather casual, Henry P. Wieland Jr. said in a short 1933 history, "It was the mineral prospect of the north shore of Lake Superior that induced the Wielands to select Beaver Bay as their future home. Copper was the great possibility."[5]

In his memoir, McLean is quite specific in identifying copper traces at Knife River, Clifton, the French and Sucker rivers, noting that each of those locations was preemptively claimed in 1855 for the copper ore, but he makes no mention of copper in his description of the Beaver River site, where he, Ambul and Schutte were told by Clark "to build and hold possession for Jessie (Justus) Ramsey of St. Paul, W.H. Newton (a partner in founding and platting of Superior) and Thomas Clark, who were to be the proprietors. We built two cabins to hold the water power and one to hold the townsite." Having thus established rights for the townsite proprietors, the three preemptors walked back to Superior in February 1855, after the ice was sufficiently thick on Lake Superior.

Once the Treaty of La Pointe opened the area, Ramsey, Newton and Clark were in no apparent hurry to establish the townsite, for it was not until an emergency trip by rowboat in early April 1856 to obtain a supply of flour from the trading post at Grand Portage that McLean recorded finding Clark and three other men surveying a townsite on the east side of the Beaver River. "We left one barrel of flour with them: the others we brought to Superior and divided among those who were most in need of it."

The arrival at Beaver Bay of the Wielands and several other families aboard the steamer *Illinois* in June 1856 is widely documented, landing there "with their horses, cattle and other stock," but it's also reported that a party of men was sent there to clear land, plant crops and locate areas for pasturing livestock and making hay before the June arrival of the eastern contingent.[6]

Although the townsite platted by Clark was on the eastern side of the river, the Wielands established their community on the west side, with John Gilomen claiming a 160-acre homestead where Clark's townsite was surveyed.

Henry P. Wieland Jr. says of those early days, "All the people lived in log huts. The floors were natural, one good thing about them being that the ladies did not have to scrub them. At first, they sawed boards by hand with a large handsaw. The shingles for the roof of the huts were all split by hand, using a broad ax and shaving them smooth with a drawknife."

The log structures that McLean and his 1854 companions erected to secure the water and townsite rights may have provided the first shelter for these settlers but, six weeks after their arrival, Reverend James Peet of Superior stopped there several days and recorded that within eight miles there were 13 men, two women and eight children, two shanties, seven houses and 12 acres of cleared land, four of it in crops. He also estimated seven miles of roads and 12 tons of hay curing for winter fodder, with hopes of 50 to 100 tons.[7]

Though Peet's road estimate is contradicted by a later surveyor's report, which listed four miles, Henry P. may support Peet. He recalled, "Father took a homestead about five miles up Beaver River. The location was known as West Beaver Meadow. Uncle August took a homestead about two and a half miles up the river." If a trail were cleared to the

Carl Tate on Wood Cutting

As noted by H.P. and Fred Wieland in their memoirs of Beaver Bay, the efforts of young people were important in the well-being of early families.

In a memoir written sometime after his 1961 retirement, Carl Tate (originally the family name was spelled Tett) vividly remembered woodcutting in the early 1900s as a crucial task he and brother Hugo undertook.

"Woodburning stoves furnished the heat and were fueled by birch trees cut down in the nearby forest, hauled to the front yards, sawed into suitable lengths and split into suitable sizes. Hugo and I became quite active at an early age in the stove wood business. Pa (stepfather Joe McGregor Jr.) provided the needed tools – a crosscut saw and two double-bitted axes.

"When two persons are involved in cutting down a large tree, one works right-handed and one works left-handed. Hugo, being older, took the right-handed spot and I was left with the left-handed one. The work consisted of notching the tree with the axes in the direction in which we wanted it to fall, then using the saw to finish the job. In time, swinging an axe and pulling the saw handle left-handed became second nature.

"After the logs were hauled to our front yard, usually Hugo and I converted them ▶

homesteads of Henry Sr. and August, it would have accounted for a sizable portion of the seven miles that Peet reported.

Names that H.P. remembered in the first contingent of settlers were "John Gilome (variant spellings appear to stem from the anglicizing of the family's French surname, Guillaume), Tis(c)her, Nicklar, Shaw, Christ Dome and a few others whose names have slipped my mind."[8] In her extensive research for *Beaver Bay, Original North Shore Village,* Jessie C. Davis discovered variations between two lists: one showing "the Gilomen, Tischer, Zimmerman, Niggler (likely H.P. Wieland's "Nicklar") and Gronowalt families, and a Mr. Shaw," while another list showed Christian Tome (H.P.'s "Dome"), G. Reichert, A. Schwab and others.[9] Davis also says, "While these names occur in the first census of 1857, many of the original families seem to have left after a few years" and Henry P. and Fred both point out in their memoirs that many of the original Swiss farmers soon moved on, disappointed that agricultural prospects were considerably less optimistic than they had hoped. Their departure was also likely hastened by the financial panic of 1857, which began to be felt on the frontier in 1858 and then deepened when the Civil War began in 1861.

But as some left, others arrived. The names of Jacob and Andrew Hangartner do not appear on the first lists, but show up on the 1860 tax list, although a short, undated family history records them as arriving at Beaver Bay in 1861. Andrew would depart the settlement in 1870 and settle at New Ulm, but Jacob put down deep roots on his homestead along the river and he and his descendants hold the distinction of the longest continuous residency of the early families at Beaver Bay. In Beaver Bay's first wedding, Joseph Betzler, a name not in the first manifests, married Rose Giloman in 1869 and Adam Burr married Henrietta Piper (shown as Pieper in some sources) in 1870. Neither Burr nor Piper show in the 1856 listings, although the wife of August Wieland, the youngest of the brothers, was Louisa Piper of Sheboygan, Wisconsin, and their marriage apparently also took place in the early 1870s. As might be expected, relatives and in-laws of the pioneers joined them later. For example, Charles Hohly was not in the early lists, but shows up in the 1860 census as sawyer at the Wieland mill. Christiana Hohly was Ernst Wieland's wife and her father, Dr. Karl Hohly, was the only physician to ever try to practice medicine in Beaver Bay.[10]

These early years were tough. In Fred Wieland's "Reminiscence," he says, "That first winter they had no vegetables, not even potatoes, and some of them, my mother among them, got the scurvy … when I was born they did not expect me to live on that account."

Having arrived with everything they believed they would need to pioneer a new land, the settlers were undoubtedly disappointed to find growing seasons that barely spanned three months and, as Fred noted in his memoir, might have frost every month of the summer in inland locations. In addition, very little of the soil was prime cropland, despite Thomas Clark's first observations. Even making hay was mainly confined to inland areas where enough silt had accumulated in beaver ponds to form the occasional open meadow.

By H.P. Wieland's account, "The only food there for years was potatoes and fish, with a rabbit or a partridge once in a while – not to forget wild ducks and passenger pigeon. I know many days that we had fish and potatoes for breakfast, potatoes and fish for dinner and the leftovers for supper. There was always plenty of milk. Bread was a luxury; fruit out of the question, but we were all healthy and contented. The first years, there was a doctor (Karl Hohly) at Beaver Bay. He could not make a living, so he moved to Superior City. After that, people at Beaver Bay got along splendidly without a doctor."

After Dr. Hohly left Beaver Bay, Christian's wife, Pauline, and Henry Sr. are credited in several sources as being a competent and successful medical team for settlers in the area. Several instances of successful treatments are related in memoirs, including one in which a workman suffered burns when a blasting fuse exploded in his face. Henry and Pauline applied continuous cold packs to the burns for 36 hours and the workman healed with only a couple of minor scars to show for his mishap.

Cold water also figured in their ministrations to Henry's wife, Rosina, when she contracted typhoid fever. Immersing her in the Beaver River for a period of hours, the medical team was heartened to see her make a complete recovery.

Henry Jr. stated in his memoirs that there were abundant moose and caribou in the area, but white-tailed deer and wolves did not appear until about 1871. Hunting and trapping during the winter provided some meat for the table and pelts to sell – bringing in the only cash most of these new inhabitants would have the first few years – but the Wieland memoirs all agree that the white settlers were inept at hunting and trapping. It was usually the Ojibway people, who settled in Beaver Bay within a couple of years after the white settlers arrived, who occasionally provided the Germans with game such as rabbits, caribou, beaver or bear meat to break the monotony of their fish and potato diet. The natives also made maple sugar in the spring, which they swapped or gave to the pioneers.[11]

In his memoir, Fred Wieland noted that a sawmill powered by a 30-foot, overshot water wheel was constructed in 1859 by J.J. Hibbard and his brother, who had already constructed their own steam powered sawmill on Burlington Bay. This first Wieland mill was located at the second falls of the river, about where the highway bridge is today. This early up-and-down reciprocating saw would produce a bit more lumber than was needed for home construction so, ever the entrepreneurs, the Wielands established markets in Michigan for the excess lumber. The first shipment was bartered for flour, salt pork and other supplies and taken to his home port by Captain John G. Parker of Ontonagon, Michigan.[12]

Since bartering didn't prove satisfactory to them, the Wielands bought the schooner *Charley* in the mid-1860s to move their lumber and other products to the various mining locations in Upper Michigan. The "faithful old tub" did its job admirably for about 15 years, despite wrecks at Grand Marais, Michigan, and Madeline Island, Wisconsin, before finally being broken up by a northeaster as the schooner attempted to tie up at the dock in the Beaver River on May 10, 1881. During its working life, the schooner called at virtually every port across Lake Superior, carrying Wieland lumber to Michigan's Upper Peninsula and the Copper Country mines, Duluth, as well as Port Arthur/Fort William and Silver Islet in Canada – although the latter destinations added 100 miles to the *Charley*'s itinerary to obtain clearance to enter the Canadian ports from the U.S. government offices in Duluth.[13]

Although its primary duty was delivery of lumber to customers, return trips frequently found the little ship laden with goods needed at Beaver Bay or with other cargo destined for delivery en route to its home port. After the final 1881 wreck, the Wielands bought the steam barge *A.H. Morrison*, which H.P. credited as being a great improvement over the sailing schooner.

That the enterprising and industrious pioneers were soon producing more than was needed for survival is recorded in the November 3, 1870, *Duluth Tribune*, which noted: "The schooner *Charley* came in for the last time for the season today, then goes into winter quarters ... with 15 barrels of potatoes, 100 head of cabbages, two barrels of sauerkraut, one barrel of native raspberry wine ... all consigned to Wieland Brothers, Minnesota Point." Presumably, some of that cargo was winter provisions for the Wielands involved in the family's general store and lumber yard that was opened in 1869 at that location, but some was also destined for sale to other Duluthians.

Although a vast improvement over the large hand saw that was first used to cut lumber for homes, it soon became apparent that their crude, straight-bladed sawmill would not long support an ongoing commercial operation. More modern equipment with circular saws was built in the 1860s and was later powered by Leffel water turbines of varying horsepower that were purchased in the 1870s.[14]

In addition to the original sawmill, the H. Wieland and Brothers Lumber Company is shown in some sources as including the Henry Wieland and Brothers lath and shingle mill, Henry Wieland and Brothers family sawmill, a tannery and, for a short while, a grist mill to grind grain into flour. Although all the brothers seem to have been somewhat equal partners, as the oldest brother

▶ into stove length size. This was done after school hours, mostly Saturdays. (There were only eight grades at Beaver Bay school, so the boys would have been something like 12 or 13 years old.)

"Pa did the splitting. In the early spring, Hugo and I piled the stove wood into neat piles. It seems we never lacked for chores of some kind. I recall there were times when I was so anxious to move the job along that I would work at it during school recess. Our house was only one block from school.

"A few families solved the wood problem by holding a 'wood bee.' There would be a group, in teams of two, sawing logs in stove length chunks. Another group, not as many, would split the chunks in pieces for the stove. Then there was the kitchen staff who always supplied refreshments. The entire year's supply of wood was prepared for use in a single day.

"Pa took pleasure in offering Hugo and me as a sawing team at wood bees. He would take pains in sharpening the saw and no one could do it better than he. Since Hugo and I had worked so much together with the crosscut saw, we always were the number one team.

"We felt pretty good about our performance, for which I think Hugo, with his strength and endurance, was mainly responsible."[15] ▲

The original bridge over the Beaver River was engineered and built by Christian Wieland, who first interested his brothers in settling at the site and would be a major force in the community until his sudden death in 1880 at age 56.

Henry Sr.'s name was apparently used in all the lumber businesses, with his brothers' involvement noted secondarily.

By 1869, the family had accumulated 3,000 acres of pine land and were well situated to provide major supplies of lumber from their Beaver Bay operation. Their method of obtaining desired land was explained by Fred W. in his 1934 memoir and provides an interesting look at the casual attitude toward land at that time.

"Land was usually bought with soldiers' scrip or Sioux scrip (in other references also called 'half-breed scrip'). The soldiers got scrip instead of cash. That scrip called for so many acres of land – 40, 80 or 160 (acres) or more – and could be placed on vacant government land anywhere. Most of the soldiers sold their scrip for what they could get for it. Speculators bought most of it and then resold it to people who wanted to buy government land. Scrip could sometimes be bought as low as 50 cents per acre.

"When our folks wanted more pine land, they would buy some of this scrip and send it to Washington with an order for what land they wanted and, as soon as the receipt (he may mean 'patent' here – see next sentence) came back saying that the land had been entered in their name, they could go ahead and cut the pine. Sometimes when they had their logging roads near a nice bunch of pine, they would send in the necessary scrip to cover it and, when the receipt came back stating that the land had been entered in their name and that the government deed or patent would be forwarded in due time, they would go ahead and take off the timber. Sometimes, they had the timber all taken off before the patent came along and then they would just let the lands go for taxes, as it was of no value after the timber was off."

Such land dealings may also have been involved in another venture in which the Wielands were involved. Fred W. states, "Our folks were the first white men who discovered iron ore in northern Minnesota. The Indians brought in specimens from near Greenwood Lake. After our folks had gone out and explored it, they cut a winter road through from B.B. to Greenwood and brought in several hundred pounds of iron ore.... Then they got some other people interested and a company was formed that bought some 9,000 acres of iron land.... The iron was a very high grade magnetic ore, but it contains titanium, which makes it worthless.... They never got anything out of it."[16]

And land acquisition, logging and sawmilling were not the only enterprises in which the industrious Wielands invested. They operated the general store in the community, had the government contract to carry mail between Superior and Grand Portage, traded for furs and operated lumber yards at various times in Duluth, Hancock, Michigan, "Prince Arthur's Landing," Ontario (now Thunder Bay), and Moorhead, Minnesota. After a fire destroyed much of Marquette, Michigan, in 1868, many "*Charley*-loads" of lumber were sold to rebuild that city. Shortly thereafter, the Silver Islet mine was another market that consumed a good deal of Wieland Co. lumber for homes and as mining timbers to extract the fabulous vein of silver discovered there in 1868.

In addition to his involvement in the family's several business interests, the ever-energetic Christian Wieland served as Lake County auditor, acting postmaster, the first and thereafter an occasional school teacher, clerk of the school board for North Shore School District #1 in 1865, and was also a regular Sunday School teacher, but was apparently so tone-deaf that there was no singing in his classes. He engineered and built the original bridge over the Beaver River and often contracted as surveyor, engineer or the builder for various civic or government projects.

Christian's apparent restlessness, expertise as a surveyor and as a wilderness guide also led to numerous exploratory expeditions to the interior, which were important in later exploration of metal-bearing rock formations by Henry Eames.

Although state geologists were disappointed to find no gold, Christian pointed out sizable areas of iron ore deposits that disrupted his use of a magnetic compass on the eastern Mesabi Iron Range. He disagreed with the opinion of the geologists that iron in the formation was too low-grade to be of value. Christian's opinion went unheeded in official circles and his early death in 1880, at age 56, prevented him from seeing the vindication of his opinion about the value of Minnesota's iron ore.[17]

Although Christian and Pauline enjoyed about as much success as pioneers could expect, one yawning gap disrupted their happiness – they had no children.

In his memoir, Henry P. says, "From the time the Wielands settled at Beaver Bay, brother Charles never was home.... Aunt Pauline insisting on adopting (him), father and mother consenting. Consequently he never was home with us."[18]

And Charles wasn't the only child to fall under Pauline's care. In her investigation of census records, Jessie Davis found that the 1857 census done by R.B. McLean listed four children in Christian and Pauline's home, with no explanation of who they were – much like we will see later, when four "unexplained" Sexton children are enumerated by McLean at Agate Bay in this same census. In the 1860 census, Davis reports that three children (Charles Christian, Paul F. and Henry P.) of Christian's brother Henry were counted in Christian's home – but Henry Sr. and his wife, Rosina, were inexplicably listed as having no children.

No explanation for this discrepancy has been found and none may even be necessary, in light of Henry Jr.'s note.

Pauline Wieland wanted children – so badly that Henry Sr. and his wife took pity and agreed to adopt-out their eldest son to Pauline and Christian – and it seems quite natural that other Wieland nieces and nephews would be welcome to stay in her home at any time, certainly including Charlie's younger brothers and, later, sister Elise, who was born in 1861. It was also true that parents traveling to Duluth or other destinations would be absent for extended periods and likely left their younger children with one or another of the other families during such trips. Childless Pauline likely reveled in such opportunities to dote on Wieland children.

Although only about 20 people were landed in the first party, the census of 1857 enumerated 59 "foreign born" people on the north shore, most of them in Beaver Bay. By the 1860 census, 62

Mary MacDonald: A Wee Bit of Energy

Remembered by Patricia (Lorntson) Reed as a bundle of energy with many interests, Mary (Castner) MacDonald arrived in Beaver Bay in the summer of 1915 to visit her sister, Mrs. Florence (John) Slater, who had taken a job as a school teacher in the village in 1909. The laid-back nature of Beaver Bay would never again be quite as bucolic.

"Mary Mac was a little woman, maybe four-feet nine-inches in height, and a bit buxom," Pat remembered. "Her husband, Hugh, was a tall lanky fellow, so they made a kind of comical looking couple."

While visiting her sister, Mary was offered a job as school teacher at the Lax Lake School. Since that job paid $75 a month and the job in Albert Lea for which she already had a contract paid only $50, she wiggled out of the previous contract and settled into the northland, teaching 16 kids at Lax Lake and staying at the home of Mr. and Mrs. John Waxlax. She and Hugh were married a year later and settled on a farm between Beaver Bay and Lax Lake.

"I think her mother, Mrs. Frank Castner of Minneapolis, was involved in a hotel or something in the cities and she prodded Mary to start building a lodge when the highway was being built in the 1920s. "By the time Highway 61 came through ▶

The Henry Wieland Sr. home would later be occupied by the Wagner and Slater families. Note the cupola, which some sources say was used occasionally to hang a lantern as a beacon for the Charley, *the family's wide-ranging lumber schooner.*

residents were named in the town, but the panic of 1857 was blamed for many of the earliest families leaving the area before that census was taken.[19]

Everyone was expected to contribute to the well-being of the community and most were multi-talented. John Gilomen, for example, used the leather tanned at the Wieland tannery to make shoes, boots and other leather goods for the pioneer families. The leather was also fashioned into the belts that powered sawmill equipment.

Even children pitched in. Fred and Henry Jr. both tell stories of children who in one way or another were instrumental in capturing game or furbearing animals, protecting the homesteads or contributing to their family and community.

Indeed, Henry recalled that in 1868 he was posted with only a small dog for company at a family trading post on Greenwood Lake, where he was to stay several months and trade with the natives for furs. Obviously, young people were expected to work and were given responsibility, since Henry Jr. was only 15 years old at the time he was posted at this lonely task. He did not return home until Christmas, a chilly time for a teen-ager to make a 25-mile-or-more trek through the wilderness with a good-sized load of furs.

In his memoir, Fred W. remembered working as a 13- or 14-year-old with his Uncle Albert at the family's first Duluth store and lumberyard operation when it was opened in 1869. Doubtless he got his exercise, since there was no dock at the yard just north of where the Duluth Ship Canal would be channeled two years later. The *Charley* was anchored as near shore as possible and lumber was pitched into the water, gathered by hand into rafts of perhaps 25,000 board feet, towed to shore and stacked on the beach above the high water mark.

The early establishment of a general store at Beaver Bay was recorded by the July 1, 1856, *Superior Chronicle* as a welcome customer for the Superior merchants, who had already noted "the disposal of a large quantity of goods and supplies at wholesale, consigned to A. Wieland, Beaver Bay."

Since this news item was published within weeks of the arrival of the pioneers, it's obvious that at least some of the logistics of settlement had already been worked out and that Albert was to be the merchant for the community.

Albert's general store not only supplied goods to the settlers, but the natives came in regularly to trade pelts for goods they needed. They would not, however, negotiate until several pipeloads of the good tobacco that Albert supplied were smoked. Out in the bush, they eked out their tobacco supply by mixing in the bark of red willow that they called *kinnikinnick*. Often on longer outings, they ended up smoking nothing but the bark, so Albert's pure tobacco was especially prized as a prelude to trading.

His nephews note in their memoirs that Albert was also appointed as postmaster shortly after the settlers arrived. Later, Albert served as captain of the *Charley* for several years – a position requiring navigational skills not only at sea, but also in the ports, where prices of the lumber were negotiated. As already noted, Albert was also appointed to head the family's first Duluth lumberyard and store.

The 1880 death of Christian may have been a cataclysm to the other members of the family, since their stay at the historic settlement ended within three years of his burial. The Wieland Lumber Company had accumulated upward of 3,000 acres of timberland in the 25 years after their arrival at Beaver Bay but, by 1880, the elder members of the family had begun to drift away. Henry Sr. and wife, Rosina, had moved to what is now Thunder Bay, Ontario, in 1875 to tend to lumber sales in that area. Later they made their way to Duluth, having deeded their Beaver River homestead in 1876 to Henry Jr., who later maintained lumber sales for the company in the Thunder Bay area. Eventually, even the second-generation Wielands left the settlement, most settling first in Duluth, before scattering to other locations across the country.

In 1877, Ernst sold his share of the lumber business and opening a tannery in Duluth. Although no longer a partner in Wieland Lumber Co., he did continue to provide business to the firm, buying hemlock bark for his tanning operation along the south shore in Michigan and receiving shipments of that bark in Duluth aboard the *Charley*. The tannery was located in Canal Park and was torn down after 17 years of operation. Ernst built an apartment building on the site, which is described as a block north of the ship canal on South First Avenue East.

In 1883, the Wieland timber interests were sold to Gibbs and Mallett, a Ludington, Michigan, lumber firm. Fred W. Wieland remembered in his narrative that the estimated 55 million board feet of timber brought $1 per thousand, meaning the sale netted the family $55,000. He also states that the stumpage was resold 10 years later for $10 per thousand and was estimated at 75 million board feet.

The four brothers surviving Christian's 1880 death all died within a period of about two years of each other: Henry Sr. in 1897 at age 75, Ernst and Albert in 1898 at ages 72 and 70 respectively and August in 1899 at age 69.

But the departure of the Wieland family members from Beaver Bay hardly spelled doom to the settlement, for by that point a number of hardy individuals had put down roots deep enough to keep them prospering at the village. Perhaps chief among them was Jacob Hangartner, who was one of the earliest arrivals at the townsite and had a homestead about a mile up the Beaver River that remained in the family from his arrival in 1861 until Reserve Mining Co. bought it (and a great deal of other property) when that company was being built.

That Jacob had to be tough and adaptable to prosper through the early years goes without saying, but his wife, Elizabeth, also tells a chilling story displaying her own personal fortitude. In a letter written in 1929 for the then upcoming diamond jubilee of the city of New Ulm, Minnesota, Elizabeth Hangartner, nee Zimmerman, tells of her family's part in the Sioux uprising of 1860 near New Ulm.

Having first settled at Beaver Bay in 1856-57, John and Mary Zimmerman and their five children found it necessary to leave the settlement within a year or two, "taking our oxen and belongings and mov(ing) to New Ulm." The family claimed land on the Minnesota River in southwestern Minnesota near what is today the city of Franklin, where John was able with great effort to build a house and begin farming. About three years later, the story turned tragic, as factions of the Sioux nation turned against the white settlers.[20]

In Elizabeth Hangartner's own words, "Early one morning, a man came to our house and said the Indians were shooting down the town of Agency (no longer

▶ *town, the Beaver Bay Lodge was ready and would house and feed many tourists and construction workers through the years."*

While the diminutive businesswoman would hardly intimidate by size, her way with words and demand that her instructions be followed to the letter were enough to predominate in almost any situation.

"Mary never minced words. She didn't back down from anyone and stood up to the biggest of them," Pat recalled of her friend.

Like most other kids in the area, little "Patsy" Lorntson learned hard work at an early age, starting to work for Mary Mac as a second grader for a dime per after school session.

"Her sister Florence lived right next door to the school and Mary would call her and ask her to send me up to the lodge after school," Pat remembered. "I made beds, washed pitchers and bowls and emptied the chamber pots that were in each room because there were only two real bathrooms. I worked many summers and falls, cleaning and serving meals. Mary was demanding, but she was always teaching. If you didn't do a job the way she told you, it meant that you hadn't been listening when she told you what to do."

As described by Pat, until the early 1960s the Beaver Bay Lodge dominated the hillside on the upper side of the highway where ▶

shown on maps, but presumably located on or adjacent to the Lower Sioux Indian Reservation). Father was not home at the time, but was helping one of the neighbors make hay. Later a half-breed came across the river and warned us to go away, for the Indians were breaking loose. When father got home, he took his oxen team and necessary belongings and started for the Fort (Ridgley). My brother, John, also drove a neighbor's oxen team. We went about a half-mile with the oxen teams past the first neighbor when we met two Indians. When they saw us, they clapped their hands together and gave the 'Indian War Whoop.'

"There was a man that ferried people across the river that father knew well. He came to tell father that the Indians were shooting, but on his way was killed. We found him with a little dog sitting along side of him.

"We went about a half-mile farther, while passing a farm house, two Indians ran out. They stopped the oxen and told father they were going to shoot him. My father insisted on giving the Indians the oxen and belongings, but they said that they were going to shoot all the men and boys, so they could not farm anymore. My mother, who was blind, told the Indians to shoot her, as father could take better care of us children. Meanwhile, more Indians, including the chief, came and immediately killed father, who was sitting in the wagon along side of mother. Frightened, my brother, John, who was driving the other oxen team, ran for shelter. But in doing so, he was shot three times in the back and fell headlong into the creek. Godfrey (another brother) started to run for the woods when he was shot and dropped right near my father.

"Our blind neighbor woman went to get her money from the wagon, which was in a cigar box. The Indian chief saw this. He quickly came to her and began pulling at the cigar box, but she would not give it up. He held his hatchet ready to split her head when my sister Mary told her to let go. He broke the box with his hatchet and put all the silver and gold in his long tobacco pouch. It just about filled the pouch, which was a foot long. He took a penny and threw it at the blind woman's head, which I picked up later for a gold piece."

Noting that her brother Sam escaped being murdered because he was wearing a dress and the Indians mistook him for a girl, Elizabeth Hangartner goes on with the chilling story. "During this excitement, the oxen ran into the woods with the wagon and that was the last I saw of them. Tired and fatigued, we kept going toward

Mrs. Jacob (Elizabeth Zimmerman) Hangartner was one of the first arrivals at Beaver Bay, but her family soon abandoned their homestead there and moved to southwestern Minnesota, where disaster struck.

the Fort. When we were half way up a long grade, an Indian on a pony came and drove us back to the farmhouse. At this time, I was carrying the blind woman's 3-year-old child. Being overloaded, I was a little behind and the Indian lashed me with his whip. I yelled at the blind woman to take the child, so she did. As we were all in the house, the Indian looked all over, including the pantry, for matches, but could not find any. Their intentions were to burn us up. Mother told us to run out, if you see that they are going to burn us, because being shot was a much easier death than being burned. They told us to stay there until tomorrow morning. I said to the Indian, 'We have nothing to eat,' in their language. He told us he would bring enough to eat the next morning, so we wouldn't be hungry again.

"Two other Indians came and asked me who shot those three persons. I told them that it was the Indians and he said it was too bad. They asked me if I wanted something and I said, 'I would like a drink of water.' The Indian asked for a dish. I went into the pantry and gave one to him. He went down to the creek and got some water. He warned us to go away and not stay there any longer. In a short while the soldiers came. There were 60 of them in all. The Indians that were left were hiding in bushes along side the road and shot at the soldiers as they went by. One of the men that was amongst the soldiers had a stove pipe hat and a bullet went through his hat. He only laughed and said to us, 'That devil thought I had a long head.' He picked up his hat and ran for his life to catch the rest of the soldiers. This man told us to walk toward the Fort and so we did. He made the Fort before us and returned with a team of horses to our aid. As we reached the Fort, it was almost dark. Supper surely tasted good, as we had had nothing to eat all day."

Elizabeth Hangartner goes on to say that the following day the soldiers placed whiskey in an outbuilding and the Sioux warriors crowded into that house to get the fire water. The soldiers from the fort then latched the doors and burned the building.

"You ought to have heard the noise they (the Sioux) made," she wrote. "That in particular, I shall never forget."

The uprising died within a matter of days and the widow, Mary Zimmerman, and her three surviving children first went to New Ulm, then moved to St. Paul. Mary died within about 18 months and her brother, Mr. Tischer of Duluth, brought the orphaned children, Sam, Mary and Elizabeth, to live at Duluth, where Elizabeth Hangartner says, "A family by the name of Merritts, whose children had interests in the iron ore mines of the Arrowhead Country, kept me until I got married."[21]

As noted by Henry Wieland Jr., the Tischer family had also been early Beaver Bay residents, but apparently moved about the same time as the Zimmermans. Tischer Road and Tischer Creek in Duluth bear the family name, and Zimmerman Road north of Duluth is also presumably named for Elizabeth Hangartner's family.

With the fortitude shown by such ancestors, the descendants of Jacob and Elizabeth Hangartner would survive longer at Beaver Bay than any other of the earliest settlers, with grandchildren and great-grandchildren still living in northeast Minnesota.

Legend of John Beargrease

Sometimes, a legend is built through centuries of oral history that gradually embroiders the factual material into a mythic fabric. In the case of the legendary Ojibway mail carrier and north shore resident John Beargrease, the legend was earned by dint of diligence and prompt delivery of mail that kept the pioneer residents along the north shore in touch with the outside world.

The son of Chief Beargrease, who showed up with three wives at Beaver Bay within a year or so of the Germans who settled there, John undoubtedly shared his childhood with some or all of the Wieland and other children in the settlement. By the time he was grown, he was known to have developed major skills in hunting, fishing and sailing on Lake Superior, for it is recorded that he served at times as a pilot on the Wieland Brothers Lumber Company schooner *Charley* as it wended its lumber-laden voyages far and wide around Lake Superior.

But it would be his reputation for delivering mail as a contract mail carrier along the north shore that would endure and place him firmly among the legendary characters of this area.

▶ the Beaver Bay city complex is now located. The property consisted of the three-story main building that housed several guest rooms, a summer and a winter kitchen, a library and a dining room with a large fireplace that seated 35-40 people. In addition, there was a large L-shaped cabin with nine guest rooms and there were several other smaller cabins for guests. In addition to travelers and construction workers, deer hunters were a large part of the autumn business at the lodge.

While her business was a huge complex for its time, it would be her activities relating to the several school systems in Lake County that insured that her name continues to be remembered.

"Mary really worked very hard for the consolidation of the many school districts on the north shore. After that was accomplished in the early 1930s, Mary Mac was the first woman board member ever elected to the school board and served for three terms," Pat recorded.

Although she died of cancer in 1959, her intense interest and efforts in north shore education were enshrined in 1962, when the Lake Superior Independent School District dedicated the new elementary school at Silver Bay as Mary MacDonald School.[22] ▲

John Beargrease with his wife and children. John arrived in Beaver Bay with other Ojibway friends and family members within a year or two of the landing by white settlers. His diligence in delivering the U.S. mail along the difficult north shore earned him praise during his lifetime and legendary status after his death in 1910 from pneumonia contracted when he helped rescue another mail carrier caught in a storm on the lake.

John began making the mail run from Two Harbors to Grand Marais and back in 1887. From that point until sometime in 1890, he hiked, sailed, rowed or drove his dog team in all weather conditions to get the mail through. It would be his prowess as the driver of his three-dog team, however, that would endure in the modern age when his name was adopted for the John Beargrease Sled Dog Marathon along the north shore. It is also reported that it was his success in using a team of horses in delivering mail that persuaded the Lake County board to upgrade a crude trail system which eventually led to construction of Highway 61.

But John was more than a legend. He was a man who had the respect of his Indian and white neighbors at Beaver Bay and was known to be willing to challenge the shifting conditions of Lake Superior, testing thin ice, rowing or sailing in rough waters and pushing himself and his animals to keep to the schedule for mail delivery.

Some records indicate that he gave up the rigors of the mail contract in 1890. His history then becomes a bit less clear, but seems to have included a period of employment on the ore docks at Two Harbors. He is reported to have moved to Grand Portage in about 1900 and died there of pneumonia after suffering exposure while rushing to the aid of a mail carrier whose boat was caught in heavy seas in Grand Portage Bay. His burial took place in the Native American cemetery in Beaver Bay.

However, the former mail carrier obviously continued the migratory lifestyle practiced by his ancestors, for Elise Sonju Williams states in her memoir published in *How We Remember, Stories and Recollections of Finland, Minnesota's First Century* that her parents settled in Finland in 1903 and that her family first met Beargrease and his family in October 1905 at Little Marais and became friends with him.[23]

From her memoir comes one of the few eyewitness accounts of the famous mail carrier whose legend lives on in north shore folklore and reinforces his prowess as a woodsman, hunter and Lake Superior traveler.

"A few days (after that first meeting), we saw smoke up on the hill (above the

Sonju homestead in Finland).... (Mother) was boiling potatoes for dinner and she took two potatoes, wrapped them in her apron and ran up the hill in the rain with four kids trailing behind her.

"My mother handed John Beargrease the potatoes. He felt them and said, 'Dinner time.' That became the beginning of a good friendship. He came hunting with his dog team.... When he got a deer he always gave us part of it. Sometimes the whole family stayed overnight.

"One time he came with his gun. He had no bullets and asked my mother if she had some .22 bullets. (She) happened to have two. He took my mother's .22 pistol (she was a good shot) and went out into the woods and got a deer. It was snowing heavily. They brought the deer right into the house and skinned it right on the floor in front of where I was. I was very ill with a stomach ache and I'll never forget the smell of that raw meat in front of my bed."

Although the smell of fresh game may have nauseated the young Elise, it was no doubt welcome provision for the family's table and also marks the depth of friendships that developed between the indigenous Ojibway people of the north shore and the white settlers who moved into their traditional hunting and gathering territory along Lake Superior.

Establishing Agate Bay

Thomas Sexton, taken from his obituary in the May 18, 1908, DULUTH NEWS

Thomas Sexton

Not much of a place, really – a 14-foot-by-16-foot cabin thrown together by Thomas Sexton and two companions in the summer of 1855, standing in the wilderness rising gently out of Agate Bay. But this boreal vantage point drew Sexton back again and again for fishing, hunting or simply sitting near the water to watch as increasing boat traffic proved that Duluth/Superior was becoming an important shipping center. Even though he left regularly to work at whatever gainful employment might come his way, he would hold onto and return to this spot for nearly three decades.

Credited as the first dwelling in Two Harbors, Thomas Sexton's Agate Bay cabin was east of what is now Van Hoven Park, in the vicinity of the northeast corner of the bay where Whiskey Row would later rear its disreputable head. The few early references to Sexton all list his "home" as Agate Bay, making it seem that this small house was his primary abode, even though he was frequently absent from it.

And "home," or even "cabin," may be a bit generous in describing this Agate Bay habitation, if we are to take the word of Henry P. Wieland Jr., the son of one of the five Wieland brothers who pioneered at Beaver Bay. In his 1933 memoir, Henry recalled having "put up at Mr. Thomas Saxton's (sic) home at Agate Bay" in June 1876. With tongue in cheek, he says, "The house at that time was a very modern home, kitchen, dining room and parlor all in one room, with one bed. Mr. Saxton was not at home, but we just made ourselves at home for the night. In those days, nobody living along the lake shore had a lock on their doors. Anyone who happened along in need of shelter or food was welcome to the premises and there never was anything taken except food, if there was any.

"After supper, Mrs. August Wieland (his aunt) inspected the room (and) came to the conclusion that spring house cleaning had not been done, preferring to sleep with her son on the beach under our boat."[1]

While fragmentary references to Sexton are found in several sources, the most complete picture is contained in two published biographical sketches done nearly 25 years apart (examined a bit later) and in the May 18 and May 19, 1908, obituaries published by the *Duluth Evening Herald* and the *Duluth News*.

Little enough is recorded about Sexton, but one detail in the references is curiously consistent – that being the inconsistent spelling of his surname. As noted above, the Wielands apparently knew him as **Saxton** and he is listed with that spelling in a couple of other references. Perhaps it was merely that less attention was paid to the niceties of spelling in those days or the spelling may have been confused by the fact that there was a rather large and prominent early Duluth family headed by "Commodore" Horace Saxton at that time.

Whatever the reason for confusion, the correct spelling of his last name is amply clarified by the Lake County Historical Society's collection of documents entitled "Early History, Volume 2," which contains a typewritten transcript of an interview, which must have been recorded in about 1950, conducted with 96-year-old Charles Saxton (a son of the Commodore) of Duluth on this subject. Judge William E. Scott of Two Harbors did the interview and transcript, accompanied by William F. Lawrence, Lake County clerk of court and one of the first two white children to arrive in Two Harbors in 1883.

"Scott: Did you know Thomas Saxton who formerly lived in Two Harbors?

"Saxton: Yes, but his name wasn't Saxton: it was Sexton – Tom Sexton.

"Q: Were you related to him?

"A: No, I was not. We were of two entirely different families.

"Q: Did you know him well?

"A: Yes, I knew him very well as a boy....

"Q: Were you ever up in Two Harbors in the early days?

"A: Two Harbors? You mean Agate Bay?...

"Q: Were you ever in Agate Bay?

"A: Yes, three or four times...." (Here Scott determines that Saxton's first visit was in about 1868-69, when he would have been 14 or 15 years old.)

"Q: Who was living at Agate Bay at the time?

"A: Just Tom Sexton. He was the only one there and lived in a shack.

"Q: What part of the Bay did he have his shack on?

"A: Towards the north end of the Bay.

"Q: What did Agate Bay look like then?

"A: There was nothing but brush and woods – poplar, birch and balsam and spruce.

"Q: Any pines?

"A: Yes, there were some nice pines growing there, too."

At this point, William Lawrence verified that when he arrived as a young boy at Agate Bay, pines grew all along the shoreline.

Although there is little doubt that he was born in Ireland of parents who were listed as Irish, Scott's interview with Saxton calls into question the assumption that Sexton was actually of Irish descent.

"Q: What kind of a man was Thomas Sexton?

"A: Oh, he was a big, heavy-set man – a Scotchman who talked with a decided brogue."[2]

With immigrants arriving in the United States in large numbers during his youth, it's likely that Charles Saxton would know the difference between various brogues. It is also true that a large number of Scottish and English people did adopt Ireland as their homeland in the 18th and 19th centuries. Certainly, Charles Saxton's physical description of Thomas Sexton is borne out by the photograph published with his obituary in the May 18, 1908, *Duluth Evening Herald,* showing a husky, slightly jowly, goateed gentleman of perhaps 55 years of age staring intently off to the left.

Interestingly, Charles Saxton's references during Scott's interview are the only ones in which the familiar "Tom" is used. All others refer to Sexton by the full, formal "Thomas," which may imply that acquaintances treated him with more than common respect.

That he was a substantial citizen of Duluth can be inferred from the fact that his pallbearers included Alfred and Napoleon B. Merritt (two of the "Seven Iron Men" of Mesabi Range fame) and Camille Poirier (the creator and patent holder for the Original Duluth Pack). Also, while newspapers printed photos sparingly in those days, a sizable photo accompanies his obituary, which notes that "hundreds visited his home yesterday to take a last look at their old friend," according to his funeral announcement on May 19 in the *Duluth News.*

In his memoir written shortly before he died in 1922 and in the 1857 state census that he conducted and compiled, it's apparent that Superior pioneer R.B. McLean had a good deal of contact with Thomas and he verifies the Sexton spelling, stating that in the spring of 1855, "Thomas Sexton, Peter Larkins and a man named

Grady located at Agate Bay, now called Two Harbors … Antoine Ambuhl, Nick Arn and myself were at Beaver Bay."

McLean's recollections have been widely quoted and verified by historians and other scholars for more than 75 years. As the recorder of the first census taken on the north shore in 1857, the first postmaster of Beaver Bay and the first contractor to deliver mail from Superior to Grand Portage, his recollections carry the authority of having witnessed early north shore history up close.[3]

Robert McLean was an eyewitness and his 1920s memoir records much of the earliest history that can be found about the north shore. As an early explorer, an original "preemptor" at Beaver Bay, the first mail carrier and recorder of the 1857 census, his record is a valued resource to anyone seeking the history of this area.

The Minnesota Historical Society's handsome leather-bound *History of the Upper Mississippi Valley* (page 696), published in 1881, is the earliest of two biographies of Sexton, stating: "Thomas Sexton, one of the early settlers of this region, was born in Ireland in 1825. His family came to Canada when he was an infant, and in 1854, (he) removed to Ontonagon County, Michigan, where our subject was engaged in the (copper) mines for one winter. Then coming to Superior City, Wisconsin, he was employed for a time in bridge building and removed to Agate Bay, Minnesota, where he engaged in mining and fishing till the spring of 1881. He now makes Duluth his headquarters and is at present engaged as commissary with the surveying party on the proposed railroad route from Duluth to Winnipeg (Manitoba, Canada). Mr. Sexton still owns a homestead at Agate Bay."[4]

Exactly what Thomas "mined" from Agate Bay or what a "commissary's" duties entailed with the Duluth and Winnipeg Railroad Company survey crew is unexplained by this source. Presumably, a commissary would be involved in supplying food and other goods to the crews, so Thomas had evidently gained the trust of the early D&W Railroad investors.

A partial clarification of the sketchy 1881 information is contained in a more encompassing biography in the 1905 *Commemorative Biographical Record of the Upper Lake*, published in Chicago, Illinois, pages 149-150, a typewritten duplicate of which appears as page 69, Lake County Historical Society archival "Early History Volume II."

This latter source corroborates most of the information of the earlier biography, but adds considerable detail subsequent to 1881 and, instead of 1854, dates his arrival on Lake Superior as 1853: "in which year he came to the Head of the Lakes on the steamer *Sam Ward.* After spending a few days at Superior he went to Ontonagon and secured employment as engineer in (the Forest) copper mine. The following year, he came to the Head of the Lakes and made a 'claim' on the site now occupied by the Duluth post office, but abandoned it because he thought there were too many rocks and mosquitoes in the locality.

"His next location was in Two Harbors, where he made a 'claim' in 1855…. His home was at Two Harbors until 1882, though much of his time was spent (working) in the copper country."[5]

Thus, the "mining" referred to by the 1881 sketch was apparently done in Michigan's copper range, which might help explain the 1881 reference to him as a "commissary," since early investors in the Duluth & Winnipeg Railroad consisted of businessmen from Minnesota and Michigan, and Thomas seems to have had solid connections in both areas by 1881.

The first R.L. Polk Directory for the City of Duluth (1883-84) shows the address of Thomas **Saxton** as "s.s. (ie: south side) Fourth St., 1 (house) East of Sixth Ave. E.," which is commercial property in the general vicinity of St. Mary's and Miller-Dwan medical centers today. Those are the only facts provided about him by this source, but the 1905 sketch fleshes out this information, telling us that, after selling the bulk of his Agate Bay property in 1882, he bought lots on East Fourth Street in Duluth and put up a number of houses, "which yield him a nice income. His own home, built in 1888, is a modern and comfortable residence…."

The 1882 dating shown above for the sale of 150 acres of his Agate Bay property may have been the point at which the deal

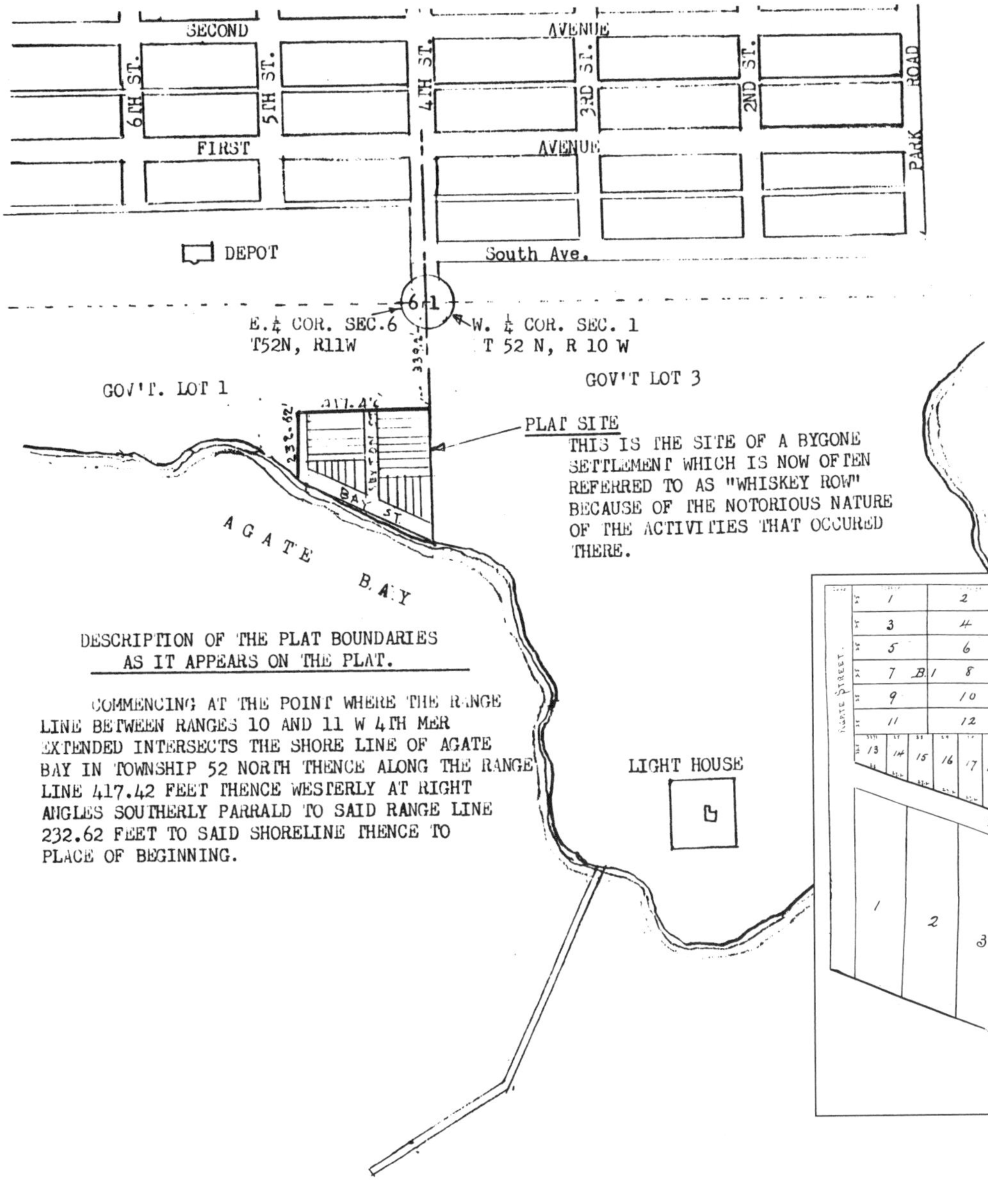

SECOND AVENUE

FIRST AVENUE

6TH ST. 5TH ST. 4TH ST. 3RD ST. 2ND ST. PARK ROAD

DEPOT

South Ave.

E. ¼ COR. SEC. 6
T52N, R11W

W. ¼ COR. SEC. 1
T 52 N, R 10 W

GOV'T. LOT 1

GOV'T LOT 3

PLAT SITE
THIS IS THE SITE OF A BYGONE SETTLEMENT WHICH IS NOW OFTEN REFERRED TO AS "WHISKEY ROW" BECAUSE OF THE NOTORIOUS NATURE OF THE ACTIVITIES THAT OCCURED THERE.

BAY ST.

AGATE BAY

DESCRIPTION OF THE PLAT BOUNDARIES
AS IT APPEARS ON THE PLAT.

COMMENCING AT THE POINT WHERE THE RANGE LINE BETWEEN RANGES 10 AND 11 W 4TH MER EXTENDED INTERSECTS THE SHORE LINE OF AGATE BAY IN TOWNSHIP 52 NORTH THENCE ALONG THE RANGE LINE 417.42 FEET THENCE WESTERLY AT RIGHT ANGLES SOUTHERLY PARRALD TO SAID RANGE LINE 232.62 FEET TO SAID SHORELINE THENCE TO PLACE OF BEGINNING.

LIGHT HOUSE

This map shows the location of Thomas Sexton's last four acres of Agate Bay property, which became the site of the earliest businesses established in the city.

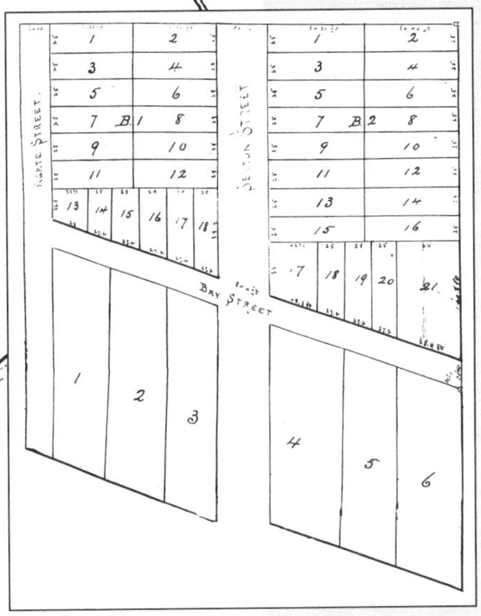

Agate Street

Sexton Street

Bay Street

The actual plat of Thomas Sexton's townsite of Agate Bay crowded 39 lots on the four-acre site. Whether Sexton received any rent for the land is unknown, but the fact that he went to the expense to plat it makes it seem likely there was some form of payment to the pioneer owner.

with the agent for the railroad was struck, since the Scott manuscript that was cited earlier states that the deed for the property is actually dated April 4, 1883.

Some geologists of the time theorized that the rich veins of native copper found in upper Michigan dipped under the lake and would also be found on Minnesota's north shore and McLean's memoir suggests that all of the earliest north shore settlers, including himself and Sexton, were agents of a group of investors who believed in the theory that huge deposits of copper awaited discovery. Those investors wanted trustworthy representatives to be settled as "preemptors" on any land where that fabulous lode of copper might be found.

That Sexton's shack on Agate Bay was first built to establish a preemptive claim for later purchase is almost certain, since McLean's reference to the occupancy in the summer of 1855 was included in his remembrance of the rush to the north shore by speculators, prospectors and "preemptors" just after the area was ceded by the Lake Superior Ojibway tribes to the United States in the 1854 Treaty of La Pointe. McLean documents many such dwellings along the north shore built during that rush – some even having been built surreptitiously in the fall of 1854 before the treaty was ratified in early 1855.

A clause in the treaty permitted white people residing in the territory to buy the land they occupied at the minimum price and such a "preemptive claim" – the occupation of a site to establish prior rights to the land – could be established

simply by building a "house ... 14 by 16, with a good roof."

Though no mansion, Sexton's shack did at least meet the implied meaning of the specifications, whereas some less scrupulous land claimants skirted the law by placing a 14-by-16-inch shingled box on a claim.

Saying that he went to work early in August 1854 for the proprietors of Superior on an engineering party led by chief engineer Thomas Clark II, McLean states, "I found that my associates on the work were preemptors, some of them hired preemptors. As I became better acquainted with the people, I found they were nearly all preemptors. What conversations I heard around me all turned toward copper and copper claims."

Admitting to making an early and illegal exploration for copper in September 1854 with John Parry, "an old miner and explorer," to the Lester River, Clifton, French River, Smith's Creek and the Sucker and Knife rivers, McLean writes that Parry told him during the trip that the investors for whom they were working included R.B. Carlton, George and William Nettleton, Vose Palmer, W.H. Newton, an Indian agent named Major John Watrous, Ben Thompson and Major Hatch of St. Paul and others.

Parry is quoted as saying, "They have organized a company and, as soon as the treaty has been signed, they will put some men onto the places which I select, to hold them for the company."[6]

Although Parry and McLean did not get as far as Agate Bay on their pre-treaty trip, McLean's later reference to Sexton, Larkin and Grady's presence there was in a listing of 1855 preemptors at the locations selected by Parry on their trip.

The "preemption" explanation for Sexton's 1855 residence at Agate Bay fits in with the fact that he moved to Superior just prior to the exploratory rush into northern Minnesota, after working at a copper mine in Ontonagon, Michigan, where his 1908 obituary states, "a happy accident secured for him a position as engineer ... at what was then a princely salary of $1,200 a year."

While there is no clue as to the nature of that "happy accident" and no record that Thomas had the background to serve as a mining engineer, it is a fact that, at the time, Ontonagon was the largest commercial center on Lake Superior, was a major center for copper mining and was home to many investors who became wealthy in the Michigan copper boom and who kept close watch on the Minnesota situation. The fact that he had served a year in a position of authority in a copper operation likely gave him credibility with the investors in the Carlton syndicate.

Despite the fact that Sexton occupied the Agate Bay site sporadically from 1855 onward, the 154.18-acre parcel that he later purchased was first patented to a Mary Snow under terms of the 1855 Military Land Grant Act and was signed by Abraham Lincoln sometime after he took office in 1861. An eastern widow of a veteran of the War of 1812, Mary obviously never intended to use the land and assigned it to John D. Howard of Superior, Wisconsin, who sold the parcel to Thomas Sexton in 1863 for $145 – giving him full rights to any future profits that ownership might yield.

In addition to the preemptive cabins built in 1854 at Beaver Bay and in early 1855 at Agate Bay, other Summer 1855 settlers at Lake County locations that McLean specifically mentions were at Knife River, where John Parry, John Scott, John Gatheres and Alex McIntire and his wife were set up, and at Encampment, where he says King S. Mead and a man named Ward had a snug cabin. Although the Agate Bay site showed only traces of copper, the copper deposits at Knife River were promising enough that Parry established a small mine there, which was abandoned only when it became clear that the copper was not of the rich Michigan variety and that it would not be a profitable operation. Later, copper would be mined inland from the lake during the 1920s.

McLean's implication that most of these settlers were hirelings of speculators is again apparent when he notes that manpower was recruited from the entire region in the autumn of 1855 to work on crews building a military road from Superior to the state line and to survey the Lake Superior and Mississippi rail line from Superior to the St. Croix River.

He says, "Myself and two men were called from Beaver Bay to go on the (railroad) survey," implying that someone had direct authority over their activities.

The same call for workers had Mead and Ward leaving Encampment and Sexton, Larkins, Grady and two other men temporarily abandoning Agate Bay to work on the military road.

In 1856, McLean notes Lake County "townsites" at Beaver Bay, Burlington, Encampment, the mouth of the Stewart River (Marmota), Knife River and nearby Buchanen in St. Louis County, where a U.S. Land Office was set up.

Of particular interest in June, he notes the landing of the five Wieland brothers with their families and other German-speaking settlers at the Beaver Bay townsite with their horses, cattle and other belongings, stating that the Wielands purchased the townsite from Clark, Newton and Ramsey in June 1857, and also records 1857 townsite plats in Lake County at Gooseberry, Split Rock and Little Marais.

McLean also briefly notes the 1857 arrival at Burlington Bay of Captain John J. Hibbard and his brother Ashley and their families with equipment for a steam-powered sawmill. Hibbard's autobiographical account of this period was published in the August 11, 1939, *Duluth Free Press*, and adds the name of L.A. Hill "and wife" to the list of new Burlington Bay arrivals.[7]

Hibbard corroborates the memory of Fred W. Wieland, another son of the Wieland pioneers, who remembered in a 1934 letter to his cousin, Ernest A. Schulze, that Hibbard was hired as the millwright to build the Wieland family sawmill (1859). Wieland makes no mention of Hibbard's own, earlier mill 20 miles west, but Hibbard states, "We raised the mill before the hard times of 1857 came on, and in the summer of 1858 finished the mill and sawed 150,000 (board) feet of lumber," adding that L.A. Hill had left the scene in the fall of 1857, "being discouraged by the hard times."

Apparently, 1858 was the only year that any significant amount of lumber was produced at the Burlington Bay mill, for Hibbard notes continued fishing and other

Construction of the No. 1 ore dock at Agate Bay was under way early in 1884, but the collapse of the clay footings forced workers to hurry completion of the No. 2 dock to receive the first iron ore on July 31, 1884. The notation of 1882 on the photo likely is in error.

A large steam-powered sawmill was erected by the Duluth & Iron Range Railroad at the corner of 1st Avenue and 7th Street, turning out a large amount of timber used in dock and railroad construction.

activities at the site, but makes only one mention of later lumbering, saying he went inland six or seven miles looking for oak timber and was caught by a tornado that nearly killed him and left a swath of downed pine six miles long by 300 yards wide.

Interestingly, in view of his five years of intermittent occupancy and activity at the site, Hibbard makes no mention whatsoever of Sexton or the Agate Bay cabin in his memoir, but does state, "My brother left in the spring of 1860 and from that time until 1862 my nearest neighbor was six miles away," leaving the impression that he did not know Thomas Sexton, who must have been absent during that entire two-year period. Indeed, the lack of any mention of the Agate Bay pioneer, whose shack was not much more than a pleasant stroll from Hibbard's mill, seems puzzling, since there were so few people along the shore that any habitation within miles was likely to be known. The Agate Bay shack must have been plainly visible from the lake, which Hibbard regularly traveled from Burlington to Superior, and the Wielands were obviously accustomed to using the cabin as an overnight stop on their trips to Duluth-Superior.

It's possible, of course, that Hibbard and Sexton simply didn't hit it off, but Hibbard's notation of the hard times of 1857-59 is a more likely reason that he may not have known Sexton. McLean reports, "The panic of '57 was a hard blow to the settlers on the north shore. During the summer and fall of '58, Agate Bay was abandoned. J.J. Hibbard and family were the only ones at Burlington, the townsite at Gooseberry was abandoned.... Those at Little Marais left.... During the summer of '59, Encampment had a few fishermen in fishing season, Stewart's River, Flood's Bay and Silver Creek were deserted.... Beaver Bay was the only permanent settlement from Duluth to Grand Portage and it continued to be the only one until the arrival of the railroad."

We know that Sexton was definitely missing the last two sailing seasons of Hibbard's occupancy, for his obituary states that in 1861-62 he worked on the steamer *Seneca* under Captain Whalin, plying between Copper Country and Duluth.

He was for certain located at Agate Bay when Hibbard arrived in 1857, for the census report of the north shore done by McLean in October of that year enumerates he and four Sexton children on a page headed "Township 52 Range 11" and his occupation is rather cryptically shown as contractor. Ireland is shown as the birthplace for all five of them and, although his age is obscured, he would have been 32 years of age. The

three girls and one boy with him are listed as being 18, 17, 13 and 11, respectively – far too old to be his children. The form did not ask his marital status, but all evidence indicates he was unmarried and McLean apparently knew Thomas by that time and surely would have enumerated a wife, if one existed.[8]

Who, then, were these Sexton children enumerated at Agate Bay in 1857? Younger siblings visiting their big brother? The biographies agree that his parents immigrated to Canada in 1826 when he was an infant. The 1905 biography states that he was the oldest of 13 children, so the children at the shack could certainly have been younger sisters and a brother. But, if so, McLean's listing of their birthplace as Ireland is in error – and his recordings are generally considered reliable and accurate – although we've already noted that he wrongly enumerated the parentage of Wieland children in this same census.

Whatever the children's lineage and reason for being with him at the site in 1857, by the time Thomas bought the land in 1863, the girls, Esther, Martha and Jane, were 24, 23 and 19, respectively, and at least the elder two could certainly have been married. The boy, Joseph, was 17 and old enough to be in college, working or, if he lived in the United States., serving in the Civil War, which was raging by that point.

We are told in the 1905 biography that a quarter of a century after the 1857 census named the mystery children, Sexton married Amelia Murphy (nee Lemke, and alternately spelled Emelle in one source), a widow, in 1882 and her name appears jointly with his on the 1883 document deeding a small parcel of land in Whiskey Row, but is absent from the deed for the 150 acres of his Agate Bay property purchased for the railroad in 1882.

From these few available facts, Thomas Sexton was in his prime when he arrived at Agate Bay and, even though he was frequently absent from the site for periods of work, the enterprising Sexton obviously kept referring to Agate Bay as his home.

Whether Agate Bay ever really served as his permanent home is a question, but all references to his occupancy are matter-of-fact and would seem to indicate that he, at least, viewed the site as his home and frequently returned to it until he sold the last of it to the Duluth & Iron Range Railroad in 1887.

The fact that he bought the land means Sexton obviously found this cool, nearly bug-free shoreline much more to his liking than his previously mentioned Duluth claim. He would also likely know the value of the timber as clearly as did George C. Stone, the Minnesota agent for Charlemagne Tower, who pointed out to his employer that the stumpage on land he was acquiring for harbor purposes in the early 1880s would approximate 2 million (board feet) and "is valuable to us all of it and worth to us if we build docks, etc., fully $3 to 4 per M (thousand board feet) where it stands."[9]

A few smaller logging operators were harvesting timber from the mid-1850s onward, the most successful being the Wieland mill at Beaver Bay, but development on the north shore was slow in coming after that first rush of prospectors and speculators were disappointed. It would be 1882-83 before the railroad brought in and set up its sawmill to produce lumber on the site of its construction. Thus, the D&IR became the first of what would be a rush of large logging companies about a decade later.

While Sexton's location likely was a bit lonely, especially in the earliest period, Thomas does seem to have been "neighbors" with other Irish settlers, since the entry just prior to that for the Sextons in the 1857 census is John and Ellen Maron (Moran?) and three children, listed in the same township and range as Sexton and those mystery children at his cabin. All but the 6-year-old (youngest) Maron child were born in Ireland and John Maron was a carpenter. McLean's mention of "a man by the name of Grady" also was likely of Irish lineage and, in the early 1880s, George C. Stone mentions another nearby Irishman with annoyance, reporting that negotiations to buy three harbor lots from a "rough uncouth Irishman" named O'Grady were not going well, saying that the owner refused to sell "at any price." Whether Stone's O'Grady and McLean's Grady were one and the same person remains a question.[10]

If he were out fishing on a quiet day in 1858, Thomas could undoubtedly have

heard the far-away chuff-chuff-chuff of the steam engine as the Hibbards' sawmill produced the 150,000 board feet that John J. mentioned in his reminiscence. If he wanted some company, a short hike over the forested hillside or an easy paddle around the rocky point would get him to their location, but J.J. Hibbard's failure to mention him makes that contact seem unlikely. It's more likely that he left sometime after the October 1857 census was taken and simply didn't return until after the panic of 1857 or the Civil War was over.

In the vernacular of the time, "down" was the direction one traveled from Duluth to Grand Portage, so a few miles "down" the shoreline lay Flood's Bay, where the logger of that name had his sawmill. Miles farther, Encampment had sporadic settlers and farther still would have him at Beaver Bay.

"Up" the opposite direction, Knife River/Buchanen attracted early prospectors. A settlement of copper miners lingered there until it was proven unprofitable. For a short period, Buchanen had a government land office and the north shore's first and only newspaper, the *North Shore Advocate,* which would have provided some diversion from humdrum life.

A day's paddle or sail fetched him to Duluth, an interesting location that seemed to double in size every time he visited in these early years. It was here that he would settle after selling the railroad 150 acres of his property in 1882, while holding onto four acres of the lakeshore at the northeast corner of Agate Bay. The $4,000 paid to him by William C. Sargent of Superior was invested in Duluth property and Thomas undoubtedly later heard that the harbor land was immediately turned over to Charlemagne Tower and Samuel Munson, the eastern financial partners who seemed to actually believe in the iron ore near Lake Vermilion that George Stuntz had been talking about for years with anyone who'd listen to him.

In Scott's earlier cited interview with Charles Saxton about Thomas, Saxton remembered, "After his real estate (the 150-acre parcel) was sold, as I have been told, he lived at the old Wicklund Hotel (in Duluth). He married while he was staying at this hotel and later had a family of four children."

The four acres of Agate Bay land that he held onto were located on the shoreline between what would be a southerly extension of Fourth and Fifth streets. The parcel was platted and registered in March 1884 as "Agate Bay, Lake County, Minnesota, Thomas Sexton Proprietor." Although the lakeshore meandered inland from east to west and cut about 185 feet from the southwestern edge of the property, the plat squeezed 39 lots into the two small blocks that were bounded on the west by Agate Street and divided in the middle by Sexton Street, with Bay Street following along the lakeshore eastward from the D&IR commercial dock at the west end of the property. At its peak, Whiskey Row was reported to have 22 saloons, several hotels and other businesses in 1883.

Having realized a profit of more than $25 an acre on the larger portion of his land, this four-acre vantage point gave Thomas a front row seat from which to

The sidewheel steamer Dove *made regular runs from Duluth-Superior to Agate Bay, bringing workers, freight and other needed material to the worksite.*

The schooner Niagara unloaded the first boatload of steel rails for the D&IR in 1883, as John Wolfe and Company started building the rail line.

observe activity as Charlemagne Tower launched the development of the Vermilion Iron Range and the Duluth & Iron Range Railroad – first with the 1882 arrival of surveying crews that were led by a young engineer named William A. McGonagle, then the full-blown boom as the 68-mile railroad was being built in 1883-84.

As the only land in the townsite that was not controlled by the railroad, Sexton's four-acre waterfront property was ideal as the site of the iniquitous "Whiskey Row" that roared to life when all of this railroad and harbor construction began in 1883.

Although it is not directly recorded that he gained income from rental or other payments from the unsavory establishments, it's likely at this point of his life that he had learned to drive a hard bargain and knew the value of his remaining land in the midst of all this railroad-building activity and money. It's also likely that a lifetime spent in frontier settings meant that he understood boomtown economics and wanted a piece of any action that might take place here, on "his" bay.

From his home in Duluth, it's almost certain that he would continue visiting his Agate Bay property to watch over any business there and, no doubt, marvel at all the activity, as shiploads of horses and men, rails, barrels of railroad spikes and blasting powder and a myriad other materials were unloaded at docks butting the shore just off his property. Where once it had taken him a full day of rowing or sailing to travel from here to Duluth, the many ships now calling regularly at his harbor made the trip a matter of hours.

And every trip brought changes. The forest that had grown on his land was being logged and turned into lumber for all of the construction that was taking place. A large, modern sawmill went up on the site of what is now First Avenue and Seventh Street, just a stroll from the site of his cabin. If he were present at the site, he would surely have been on hand in 1883 to watch the *3-Spot*, the railroad's first locomotive, chug off the barge that was towed to the relative safety of Agate Bay through heavy winds and seas by the tug *Ella G. Stone*, which then nudged and nosed the scow into place against a dock fitted with rails to accommodate the new locomotive and other rolling stock that was arriving.

With but four acres of his original property remaining in 1883, Sexton may have reluctantly agreed to sell one final piece of his land to Jasper S. Daniels and James Dingwall, who were undoubtedly businessmen intent on opening some type

Hastily constructed railroad buildings sprung up on the shoreline of Agate Bay during the construction period, with most of the business places located east of the railroad properties in what was known as Whiskey Row.

of enterprise on Whiskey Row. Daniels and Dingwall's names also appear as signatories to the survey on the plat map of the Agate Bay townsite, apparently making them the only other property owners. For three booming, rip-roaring years, this "town" continued as the site of wide open, continuous activity, unchecked by any moral or legal authority – until the whole place burned to the ground in 1885.

In his biography of Charlemagne Tower entitled *Iron Millionaire*, author Hal Bridges certainly expresses the conviction that Sexton had proprietary interests in Whiskey Row, stating that Tower's agent, "(George C.) Stone succeeded in buying all (of the land on both bays in Two Harbors) except four acres owned by a hard fisted individual named Saxton, who preferred to keep his land and crowd it full of saloons. It quickly became a trouble spot. Two Harbors already had its share of saloons, which (company president Charlemagne) Tower Jr. remarked were 'the natural outgrowth of every western town....' But Saxton's land provided a special haven, entirely beyond the control of the iron company officials, and on it flourished a parasitic community entirely devoted to the business of relieving laboring men of their pay."[11]

Since Bridges had access to personal and business correspondence by early railroad and other company officers, it's apparent that those papers led him to believe that Sexton's land acquired the name of "Hell's Four Acres" and that Sexton was an accomplice, if not an outright investor in the collection of saloons and bawdy houses known as Whiskey Row. Bridges neither acknowledges Sexton's long ownership of the land, nor the fact that the pioneer of Agate Bay was apparently a trusted contractor or employee of the D&IR during this period.[12]

But Sexton's obituary states that soon after gaining his earlier mentioned position as commissary for the Duluth & Winnipeg Railroad, "he was placed at the head of the commissary department of the Duluth and Iron Range road, where he remained until his property interests in this city (Duluth) required too much of his time," also noting that Sexton was regarded highly by his acquaintances, especially the older residents of Duluth.

Circumstantial evidence would indicate that he was tough and shrewd enough to reap a harvest from even the worst shysters who set up shop on his land, but the fact that he became commissary for the D&IR would seem to belie Bridges' assessment that Sexton's connections to Whiskey Row were construed by his neighbors or by the D&IR officials as anything but honorable. The obituary note is a bit hazy on the location of his job with the D&IR commissary, but seems to have been at company offices in Duluth, while likely requiring some presence at Agate Bay as well.

If, indeed, he was employed by the railroad and visited Agate Bay/Two Harbors in these early days, he would certainly have been witness to and could take as much pride as did Charlemagne Tower Jr. in developments here. In a letter to his father, Tower Jr. said the activity was "a fine sight ... two great vessels discharging cargo in our own dock, with a steam lighter there lifting rails out of their holds and all the busy multitude that one sees at active sea-port towns. I began to see the results of our labors and they were good."[13]

On visits, remembering the quiet and peace he'd known at Agate Bay, Thomas no doubt shook his head ruefully, as hundreds of workmen came and went during the construction and early months of railroad and dock operation – their respite being the refreshments and relaxation available at one or more of the establishments bellowing with life on his "Hell's Four Acres." By this point, the longtime settler undoubtedly rejoiced in the fact that his once-wild property on Agate Bay was destined for great things in the world of industry.

The Sextons finally relinquished the last of their Agate Bay land to the railroad in 1887 for $20,000, a princely sum for such a small acreage at a time when miners and laborers earned considerably less than $2 a day – but the high price undoubtedly reflected the resolve of the railroad company that Whiskey Row would not rise from its ashes on his property – whether or not he had been actively involved in that development.

By the time he sold the last of his land, Two Harbors was a thriving city and, in 1888, replaced Beaver Bay as the county seat of Lake County. Although Whiskey Row was gone, new commerce was springing up in the form of retail stores, groceries, hotels and boarding houses, druggists, eateries and, yes, a few taverns.

As a 62-year-old man of means, Sexton must have taken satisfaction from the fact that the site that drew him back again and again had more than justified his investment and faith in it. With sales of well over $24,000 and the profits invested in Duluth property and a "modern and comfortable" Duluth residence for Amelia and their family in 1888, he kept busy in business and no doubt found it pleasant to rub elbows with other successful Duluthians. Here, the 1905 biography effuses of its then 80-year-old subject: "retired from active

The 3-Spot kept busy moving work crews and materials from the shores of Agate Bay to the ever more distant work on the railroad in late 1883 and 1884.

labors, Mr. Sexton is enjoying the results of his successful business career. His means have been acquired by honorable industry and good management, and he is esteemed by all his associates, whether in business or private life."

Thus, his history at the homestead that grew into a major shipping port on the Great Lakes comes to a happy ending. But, even as this earliest "longtime" settler fades from the scene – his $1 per acre payment increased by more than 5,000 times for the last four acres – he remains just elusive enough to cause frustration. What was it about this site that kept his interest for more than 30 years? Why is there nothing in his own hand recording his early years here? What exactly was his role relating to Whiskey Row?

Indicating that he died the afternoon of May 17, 1908, the newspapers said, "Death, the doctors say, was primarily due to senility. Mr. Sexton had been in a comatose condition for many hours before the end came. The fact that he had lived in Duluth for a period extending over more than a half century made him a very familiar figure in the city, and he was particularly well known and well liked among the older residents."

Interestingly, the longer obituary published May 18 in the *Duluth Evening Herald* makes no mention of his connection to Two Harbors, Agate Bay or the fact that his property was the source of his later comfortable circumstances, although the *Duluth News* did make brief mention of that fact.

His wife, Amelia (shown as Emelle in the 1908 *R.L. Polk City Directory* listing her as Thomas's widow), was a native of Soldin, Germany, and was first widowed in 1879, having borne two children who died in infancy with her first husband, Richard Murphy. She was obviously considerably younger than her husband's 57 or 58 years when they married, since four children are listed as Howard, Thomas H. Jr., Florence and James. The family was reported to attend the Congregational Church, but the Duluth records for that denomination going back to 1870 show no listing of a Sexton membership nor any record of a Sexton marriage, funeral or christening ceremony having been performed. The funeral notice, however, states that the funeral was held May 20, 1908, in the family residence at 616 E. Fourth St. (Duluth) with "Rev. Alexander Milne of Pilgrim Congregational Church officiating." Burial was at Forest Hill Cemetery on Woodland Avenue.

Meanwhile, the fate of Sexton's Agate Bay, the new city of Two Harbors, its iron ore railroad and harbor had long since been finagled out of the hands of Charlemagne Tower Sr., an elderly financier from Pottsville and Philadelphia, Pennsylvania. Tower followed his dream for the iron ore mines and railroad, carefully planned for and almost single-handedly assured the financing of this highly successful and profitable new enterprise – though never set foot in Minnesota.

"Down the shore," the durable, hardworking settlers at Beaver Bay continued to nurture the oldest continuous settlement on Minnesota's north shore, even though the entire Wieland family had drifted away before the first iron ore arrived at Lake Superior in 1884 or the county seat had been wrested from Beaver Bay in 1888 by the upstart city on Thomas Sexton's Agate Bay.

CHAPTER 4

Building the Iron Range

Charlemagne Tower was, perhaps, the most significant contributor to the development of this part of the country. This story is a creative adaptation of facts contained in Hal Bridges' book Iron Millionaire: The Life of Charlemagne Tower *published in 1952*[1] *and David Walker's* Iron Frontier *from 1979.*[2]

Charlemagne Tower

Of course, it would be money, Charlemagne Tower Sr. said to himself, lifting his eyes from the ledger on the desk to gaze out the window of his Philadelphia offices. There was no possible doubt that he and his new enterprise were in trouble. Even the crisp autumn sunlight failed to lift his sense of impending gloom on this November 11, 1884.

It always seems that I have to worry about money, even after I thought I had my fortune and could forget that worry.

As far back as he could remember, money had been the objective of all his years of work in the law and in his personal life, but lack of money had been the bane of his life for much of that time. Having pinned his hopes of attaining an unassailable fortune on the legal work required to amass and perfect titles on Pennsylvania coal property in the fabulous Schuylkill basin, he had devoted more than two decades of his law career to the tedious processes of clearing liens and mortgages from the title to 11,000 acres of coal land in the name of the Alfred Munson family of Utica, New York. Half of the value of that property was to be his fee for the labor he expended and, in 1871, he had achieved the unimaginable – selling the entire estate for $3 million and splitting that sum with the heirs of Alfred Munson, who had died in the midst of the great enterprise.

Having worked his entire lifetime to amass that fortune, had he now foolishly sunk it like some wild-eyed speculator into a series of holes in the ground and a railroad across 68 torturous miles that started in a forest above the icy water of Lake Superior and ended at a tiny hamlet of miners in northern Minnesota?

It's the absolute worst time for a financial panic and a drop in the iron market. With our railroad built and chugging through the swamps and forests from our mines to our own harbor at Agate Bay – with sizable docks waiting for our ore to begin moving when shipping resumes next spring – ore that we're already digging out of the mines and stockpiling and which we're paying the costs on right now – **now** *– with more than 60,000 tons of rich blue and silver iron ore laying unsold on the docks in Cleveland – now – with proven iron ore and railroad properties in which we've invested everything we own – now we're in trouble because the market dropped out from under us.*

And he *had* invested everything that he owned – something like $1.75 million – everything, in fact, owned by his wife, Amelia Malvina, his only son, Charlemagne Jr., and the inheritances he had always planned to give his daughters and their families. The entire future for all of them now hung in the balance.

In his 70s when he undertook the construction of his Minnesota Mining Company property at Lake Vermilion and the Duluth & Iron Range Railroad to haul the ore to Agate Bay, Charlemagne Tower Sr. faced one final crisis before success was assured.

Always money – and now again, I'm face-to-face with grim facts – he reflected to himself, looking again at the stacks of correspondence from his son, from George C. Stone, his chief agent in Minnesota, his mining superintendent Elisha C. Morcom and scores of others involved in the massive project of building a railroad and harbor, opening mine pits on the iron ore land and shipping the first season's ore to market – a market that dropped out of sight the moment they offered the ore.

The letters documented the enormous effort and planning that had gone into his enterprise. From the logistics of keeping a steady flow of needed materials and supplies at the worksite to winter temperatures that seemed fantastically cold, this project had consumed nearly all of his attention the last four years, not to mention the huge investment of capital funds.

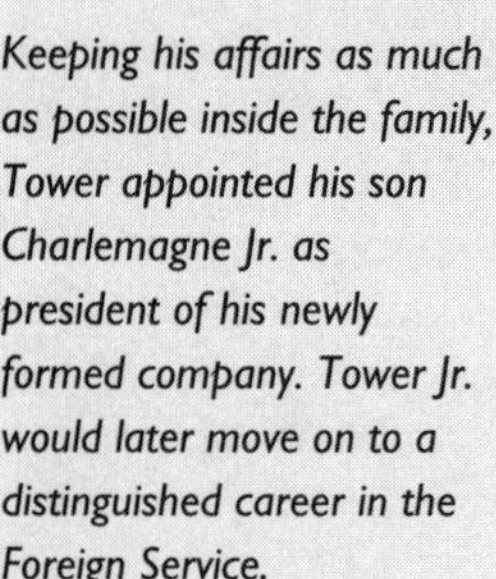

Keeping his affairs as much as possible inside the family, Tower appointed his son Charlemagne Jr. as president of his newly formed company. Tower Jr. would later move on to a distinguished career in the Foreign Service.

Until the past few weeks, the letters and telegrams from Minnesota had been unfailingly confident and optimistic. The mines on the Vermilion Iron Range were producing thousands of tons of rich iron ore each month. John Wolfe, the contractor on the railroad, had put on more than 1,400 workers to meet the July 31 deadline to finish the railroad. The first trainload of ore had been dumped into the new dock on Agate Bay that same day. Ships had loaded 62,000 tons and delivered it to Cleveland, where it now lay on the docks, no buyer coming forward when it was offered for sale.

Just the very worst time for the iron market to collapse, he repeated to himself.

Of course, he had looked in the face of ruination before: first as a young man, when the distillery and farm left to him and the family by his successful father plunged into bankruptcy; then, again, in his maturity as an investor in stocks and bonds and as a director and lawyer when Jay Cooke's Northern Pacific Railroad enterprise went busted. But those disasters were well in the past, when he was a younger, more vigorous man. Now – now, in his old age, his own carefully amassed fortune was completely invested up in that Minnesota wilderness and was insufficient to pay the overhead of keeping this new iron range up and operating until the ore began to sell.

"Just when we have everything in hand and running like a clock, he heard himself repeat. *A few months of good sales would have carried us…."*

He dropped into his chair and again faced reality in his carefully maintained balance sheets. Ely Brothers – the best iron ore salesmen in the world – had sold barely half a thousand tons of the 62,000 tons of Vermilion hematite that was shipped from Agate Bay that late summer and fall. At a cost of about $4 a ton delivered to Cleveland, the price they had received barely covered the cost of mining and shipping that ore, certainly leaving nothing to apply against the costs on the remaining unsold tonnage. More than 61,600 tons went unsold and, although he knew there would be a ready market for the ore someday, who knew how long this depression might last?

He needed nearly a half-million dollars immediately to keep his own investment and that of his family and the other investors secure.

Looking at his own shakily written tally of every expense of his business and private life, Charlemagne Tower Sr. knew to the penny where the millions had gone during the past three years of land acquisition, harbor and mine development and construction of the 68-mile railroad from Agate Bay to Tower, but could point to but one instance where his careful planning and caution had failed him – that being the drop in the market.

Over a lifetime, he had learned that the business of mineral speculation needed a cautious, steady, conservative head, learning his lessons from Alfred Munson, whose wealth was increased substantially by Charlemagne's tireless endeavors on behalf of the Munson family. His own fortune was intimately associated with that of the Munson family, first with the senior Munson and, after his death, with Alfred's son, Samuel

Alfred, who became Charlemagne's partner in the Vermilion project, as well as an old friend – now also dead. The death of the elder Munson was to be expected after a full lifetime, but Samuel's death from heart problems and Bright's disease was sharper because it came in the exhilarating early stages of acquiring property and planning their development of the Vermilion Iron Range in northern Minnesota.

If Sam had lived, there would be no problem – he ruminated. *He was as committed to this enterprise as I am and his investment in our partnership would certainly have carried us through any problems. These others who agreed to come in with me have just not carried their share of the financial burden. Even now on the edge of disaster, and knowing that I have exhausted my funds to keep this enterprise moving along, I first have to raise $200,000 to move Breitung to put in $150,000 – almost exactly four-tenths of the money we must have and matching his four-tenths interest in the business.*

The headlong pace of this emergency reminded him of the first hectic days of the Civil War when he was scurrying to raise a company of three-month volunteer soldiers in Pottsville to join the Pennsylvania Regiment. Even though he was 52 years old and certainly could have avoided service, he felt obligated as a former militiaman to lend his experience to the war effort. He signed up 160 volunteers for what would become two companies of militia. Long hours had resulted in an excellent group of volunteers, one company of which he led as a captain.

Within a week he had recruited the men, obtained essential supplies for them, put his considerable business affairs in Pottsville in order and boarded a train with his troops to join the regiment. Although they would only see combat in a single skirmish at Williamsport, Maryland, he emerged at the end of the three months of service with a reputation as an excellent military leader and was prized as a speaker during subsequent recruiting rallies. Later, as provost marshal in the Pottsville area, he devoted long hours of work and worry to maintaining law and order and establishing a fair system of drafting soldiers, after conscription became the hated means of obtaining troops for the Union Armies.

On the other hand, the financial gravity of this situation really was closer to his frantic efforts in 1871 to finalize a sales agreement for the 11,000 acres of coal holdings held by the Munson estate, half of which were to be his. A former legal colleague, Franklin B. Gowen, was the president of the Reading Railroad and had expressed a serious interest in purchasing the coal land, but was scheduled to leave for England while the deal was being finalized.

Fearing that the Reading would find sufficient coal elsewhere during the time that Gowen was overseas, Charlemagne determined to complete the deal before the railroad's president slipped away. Chasing Gowen by train from Utica to Philadelphia to New York City, he caught up with him at his hotel at 6 a.m. Charlemagne commenced negotiations, continuing them on the carriage ride and on the dock right to the moment when Gowen needed to board the ship for England. They reached agreement that sealed a $3 million sale of the 11,000 acres of Pennsylvania coal property. Thus did his 23-year coal-land acquisition effort turn his meager previous fortune into his lifelong dream of being a bona fide millionaire.

Richard Lee was married to Charlemagne Tower Sr.'s daughter, Deborah, and was named chief of engineering for construction and operation of the Duluth & Iron Range Railroad.

All of that was small comfort at this point, however, for his millions of dollars of assets had long since been spent or were now tied up as security for notes he'd already made.

After Samuel's death, the entire Munson fortune had passed into the hands of his widow, Cornelia (Catlin) Munson, and Helen Elizabeth Munson Williams, Samuel's sister, both of Utica, New York. Helen Williams had earlier invested $100,000 in Charlemagne's Minnesota Iron Company and the two widows had been approached by a third party a few weeks ago, asking for a loan to

George C. Stone carried George Stuntz's story of a fabulous deposit of iron to Philadelphia, where he convinced Tower to look further into the matter. He became Tower's chief agent in Minnesota when Tower decided to move on the iron properties.

support Charlemagne's mining and railroad enterprise. The widows had regretfully refused, saying they did not consider the venture a wise investment, even though they had the highest esteem and concern for their old friend's dilemma.

Charlemagne knew their concern for him was genuine and the length of time that it had taken them to turn down the request for the loan surely indicated that their decision was painful, yet he was now in dire straits and looked again at the latest letter from his son Charlie, urging him to visit Helen Williams in Utica personally and to appeal to her to rescue him – not as a matter of business, but as a lifelong friend – using whatever company assets were necessary to obtain the funds that would allow the company to continue operating and insure that other financial sources would come forward with needed cash.

After painful hours of arguing with Charlie's reasoning, Charlemagne had telegraphed Mrs. Williams asking permission to visit her. Her response had been cool, but she did consent to see him.

Charlemagne Sr. now roamed his offices restlessly, rehearsing the pleas he would voice tomorrow in the parlor of Helen Williams.

Knowing her to have an acutely bright business sense, he carefully formulated responses to every conceivable argument she might raise, planning this meeting as carefully as he would prepare for an important court case – this meeting being, perhaps, the most important negotiation in a lifetime of plea bargaining, arguing cases and doing a wide range of legal maneuvering.

He was sure that his pleas would move her to loan him the $200,000, but he was also aware of that sharp-eyed attention to business detail that he'd discovered over the years they'd known and done business together. Having planned and taken every precaution to obtain title and maintain strict control over every aspect of this Minnesota endeavor, it was particularly galling that now he would certainly be placing sizable portions of his holdings into someone else's hands, for Helen Williams would certainly demand solid collateral, once he won her over and convinced her to help.

Turning away from the heavy concerns facing him, Charlemagne Tower Sr. went about his usual routine of locking and securing his offices. His mind dwelt on his dear son, his darling oldest daughter, Deborah, whose husband, Richard Lee, was the chief of engineering for the railroad – all so far away in that small, cold Minnesota community called Duluth and all now desperate for cash with which to cover outstanding bills and the payroll for the hundreds of workers employed in the mines at Tower.

Charlie knew as well as anyone the pressures under which his father labored, but being on the scene, his letters lately had begun to convey an increasing sense of desperation as expenses piled up and the stream of money from the east became a trickle. He alluded to credit problems that loomed if bills were not paid. George Stone, Charlemagne's chief Minnesota agent, confirmed these dire forecasts and was using every trick in his considerable repertoire to sustain the company's good credit and maintain enough cash in hand to cover critical needs.

Operating on Charlemagne Sr.'s own instructions, and against his own advice to shut down the mines to conserve cash and credit after the market failed to buy their early shipments, Charlie kept the ore flowing during the shipping season and continued mining at the end of the 1884 shipping season, stockpiling ore at the mines in expectation of improvements in the 1885 market.

That was my decision to make, Charlemagne told himself. *I want to be*

able to meet any sales that the Elys make as soon as possible, but first we need to resolve this shortage.

His bed this night was far less comfortable to his aging body than usual and he tossed, memories arising from the nightmare days when his friend, Jay Cooke, suffered his business failure. Despite his own scurrying activities to protect and enhance the Tower Family investments and keep the Northern Pacific Railroad solvent, while serving on the NP board of directors from 1873 to '79, Cooke's bankruptcy had left an impression of ruin that he now feared might be his own fate.

NO, he told himself in the darkness. *Helen Williams is a good woman and will put up the money, if I plead with her face-to-face. Our families are as close as kin and she knows the part I played in the making of their fortune. She will help, if I make it a personal appeal, and then I shall see what she demands for security. I have no choice in that matter and will have to give what she asks, because Charlie and the rest of them need cash up there in the wilderness. Besides, how bad can any terms be, when our need is so desperate?*

The idea of a five-hour train ride, the end of which was begging with hat in hand, did not come easily to the old man. He traced his fingers through the thick white beard and wished for the sleep that would soothe him. Slowly, the strain of the past weeks eased and he did, in fact, find himself waking from a short nap at dawn. He would need to look his best and represent his position in as sympathetic a way as possible. He took special pains with his preparations, retying his necktie to perfection and ensuring that his dark suit and topcoat were brushed to a fare-thee-well.

After a light breakfast and the ride to the station through drizzling rain, he obtained his ticket, stood at the platform a moment, still disquieted by the craven nature of this trip, but squared his hat and boarded the train.

The heavy smell of coal smoke – "the smell of prosperity," Alfred Munson used to call it – lingered in the car as the train left the depot, but dissipated as they rolled out into the country. He opened his satchel and took out papers he wanted to review. He knew that Helen Williams and her sister-in-law had received a full and laudatory accounting of his enterprise and financial state, but did not want to trust her memory of that accounting – even given her sharp eye for business. In the midst of his review, his eyes grew heavy and he napped for a number of miles as the train chugged toward Utica.

"Come in, sir," urged Mrs. Williams' maid when he knocked on the door. Handing over his hat and topcoat, he was greeted from the parlor door by his old friend, who bemoaned the dampness of the day.

He inquired if the weather gave her any special health problems. In her recent letter refusing the loan, she had mentioned neuralgia, dyspepsia and failing eyesight as the reasons her response was slow in being posted.

"Only a bit more pain than usual, but I've nearly gotten used to it. It seems the older we get, the more we tolerate, even though we grow weaker with each year – but you, old friend, must have already observed that."

He retrieved his satchel and followed her into the parlor, where a fire warmed the air.

"We are very sorry to hear of your difficulty," the widow stated, coming immediately to the point and squinting through her steel-rimmed spectacles to observe his reaction. "I hope you know that our refusal has nothing to do with our affection for you and your family."

Captain Elisha Morcom was the supervisor of the mining effort at Tower, recruiting 350 men, women and children from Quinnesec, Iron Mountain and Vulcan, in the older mining ranges of upper Michigan. His winter caravans moved the families from Duluth to the newly built Tower in three-day journeys in March 1884.

The open pit of the Breitung Mine loaded the first trainload of iron ore from Minnesota on July 31, 1884, amid celebration and a native powwow. Thomas Owens was engineer on the No. 8 locomotive that pulled the trainload of ore and a carload of VIP passengers on the trip.

He nodded and, knowing that it would be best to strike quickly, said, "Yes, yes, I certainly know that, but I must immediately tell you that I've come to you as a last resort. I've exhausted my own funds and sold off all my securities to keep this venture going. We've been to every banking and investment firm we've ever dealt with, and a couple I'd have preferred not dealing with, but sufficient money just isn't available. This entire venture will collapse and I'll be bankrupt, unless I can secure at least $200,000 immediately. You hold my own future and that of my family in your hands."

As he spoke, growing anxiety spread across her face and he lowered his eyes to the carpet to avoid that pained expression.

"But surely there is someone you've overlooked?" she queried.

He shook his head, leaning forward and allowing his hands to sink between his knees in as humble a pose as his long years would allow. "I assure you, we've approached everyone whom I consider to be scrupulous. I have one promise of help, but first I must raise the $200,000 I mentioned. I also estimate that we'll need additional funds of about $150,000 next spring, when shipping resumes and interest comes due on some of our bonds."

He looked back into her face. The look of concern had deepened as he spoke.

"Poor fellow," she said, leaving her sympathy at that.

"As Shoemaker & Co. told you in our first solicitation to you, everything is in good order with the mines and the railroad and harbor. They're just humming along and our ore has proven to be very good, but the market dropped just when our success was in sight. We shipped more than 62,000 tons last year and if Ely Brothers had been able to place it, even at the low prices at which they offered it, we'd have taken in about $345,000 for our work last season. Unfortunately, they couldn't sell the ore, there was no revenue and our ore is laying in Cleveland waiting for a customer."

She nodded. "Mr. Shoemaker's letter was quite positive and concise and we are convinced that what you've built out there will be a success. But we have already put $100,000 into the business and we also believe we sacrificed Samuel's share when we sold it to you after his death for only $20,000. I am not inclined to put more money in at this time."

Thus, she introduced the beginning of the serious discussion, and he allowed more than a pause to elapse. "Please understand that I am not here to speak from a business standpoint," he said slowly. "I come to you now as one old friend to another, begging you to help me. You speak of Samuel's share of our venture and I'd just remind you that he believed in this thing as strongly as I do. It would have been my dearest dream that he were here to share this great undertaking and I have no doubt at all that he would have been that strong partner that I have not been able to find elsewhere – for this was his dream, too. Unfortunately, I have not been able to find another partner with his personal and financial integrity and must resort to begging friends to save me from collapse."

Again he paused and her eyes remained on him. His throat tightened. "I'm nearly worn out by all of this and, to make matters worse, I must tell you that I cannot guarantee your previous investment, if we do not receive your assistance now. Without those funds, our enterprise will certainly collapse and all of the investors will suffer loss."

Her eyes blinked behind the steel-framed glasses. He cleared his throat and continued. "Every move I've made in this venture has been done with caution and prudent management, just as Samuel and I laid it out at the start, but no caution and no prudence could have avoided the sort of ore market we found this year. Nobody wanted ore and what did sell went for less than cost. Maybe worst from our standpoint, our ore was new to the market and the furnacemen didn't trust it. It will prove itself very soon, but that will only benefit you and me and our other investors if we keep the company sound."

She made no move to respond and he sat in silence, his eyes straying to the window, where rain continued to spatter in windblown patterns. Glancing back to her, he recognized her frown as a mixture of concentration and vexation.

"You put me in a *very* uncomfortable situation," her voice inflecting the "very," making it sound almost as a curse. "We refused your request for a loan only a week or two ago for business reasons, but I agreed to see you today because of my long regard for you. Now you seek to impose on that regard by asking me for money, then threatening the loss of my earlier investment, if I do not provide it."

The glasses caught the firelight, deflecting his attempt to catch her eye. "And you ask for money without so much as a mention of how you intend to secure the loan. What am I to have that would insure I can get my money back at some point before I die?"

Here at last was the hard-eyed business person he knew as Helen E.M. Williams.

"It is no threat that I make to you, but an absolute fact," he dared contradict her. "Insofar as security for your money, I am prepared to do whatever is necessary to satisfy you, within reason. I am well enough acquainted with your affairs to know that the funds I seek are well within your means and I am so confident in the future of this business that it is of little concern to me if I leave here with less-than-favorable terms, if only you consent to lend me the money needed."

Her eyebrows arched and a smile brightened the creased face. "That's hardly the Charlemagne Tower that I know, nor the one who taught me so much about business and investment!"

"And I only hope I may not rue that instruction," he replied, allowing his own smile to flicker. The hard bargaining had begun, but on as genteel a note as either of them could wish.

She wasted little time, demanding that he divulge and explain to her every item of an adverse nature to the companies. Thus passed more than hour, as he pointed out, first, the immediate debts, then the need to cover future payrolls and other daily costs and, finally, the structure of interest payments on bonds and other investment capital coming due in early spring of 1885. He also explained the agreement by which his sometimes reluctant and difficult partner, Edward Breitung, a mining man from Negaunee, Michigan, would throw $150,000 into the company, if the Towers raised $200,000.

At the end of this lengthy examination, she observed, "You come seeking $200,000, but that will not be adequate, will it?"

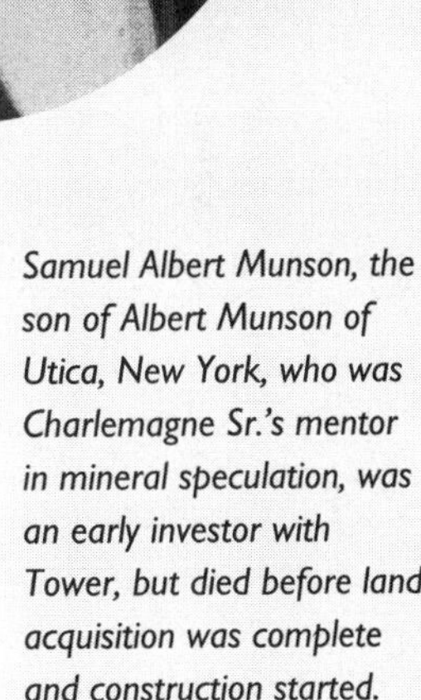

Samuel Albert Munson, the son of Albert Munson of Utica, New York, who was Charlemagne Sr.'s mentor in mineral speculation, was an early investor with Tower, but died before land acquisition was complete and construction started.

Two Harbors Ore Dock #2 46 pockets on one side.
Steamer Hecla + Schooner Ironton taking 1st Cargo
August 1884, also piling being driven for dock one
to the left; the point in the distance was only Harbor
protection at that time.
Hecla Tonage 1427. Tons
Ironton Tonage 1391. Tons
Breitung ore
Loaded aug 18-19-1884.

The first shiploads of Vermilion Iron Range ore were loaded aboard the steamer Hecla *and its schooner tow, the* Ironton, *in early August 1884, but only 500 tons of the first season's production of more than 60,000 tons could be sold to steel mills.*

Again clearing his throat, he agreed. "It will not float us completely free, but it will get us to the point where we maintain our good credit, meet our most immediate obligations and can assess the market next year."

A frown scowled across at him. "If I am to be your salvation, I do not care to have you beating around the bush. Tell me what you believe will carry you to the point of success and then, perhaps, we can discuss terms."

The brittle tone reminded him that Helen Williams was a proud woman, with just enough temper to give her piquancy.

"I'm counting on an early surge in ore demand next year to help us out," he stated, still facing her scowl. "With my faith in that market, I mean to make this as easy on you as possible, but it would give me a great comfort if you found it comfortable to lend a total of $300,000."

Her frown slowly relaxed and she leaned back against the cushions of the settee. "And what am I to have as my assurance?"

"I will place in your hands our railroad bonds with a face value of double the amount of the loan," he said, reaching into his bag and drawing out a packet of carefully prepared documents signed by his own hand. It had pained him deeply to contemplate placing the valued securities in another's keeping, but he had no other choice. Helen Williams was not only his last hope, she was also a hard bargainer. As he put the documents together yesterday, he told himself he had to make this transaction as attractive as possible to her. Surely, bonds worth twice the loan would entice her, especially since she knew his misfortune was bad timing and not a lack of anything needed to make his business run smoothly.

Her eyes rested on the papers he held out to her, then rose to meet his gaze. "What will I do with bonds from a company that you totally control? If I am making this loan as a personal matter, then I want your guarantee that I can demand payment from you personally at any time.

And I will also have interest that is well above what is paid on investments that I consider to be more secure than this one."

He maintained his composure, though her speech disturbed and somewhat saddened him. He was offering what he considered to be gilt-edged securities as collateral for the loan and she had so little regard for them that she preferred a promissory note. Or did she merely mean to place him in a position where everything he owned would be confiscated, if the loan went into default?

After hesitating, he nodded and said, "Very well, I shall give you my personal note, payable on demand. Can we agree on nine percent per annum as suitable interest?"

"No, I believe 15 percent is what I have in mind."

Shocked, he immediately said, "My dear Mrs. Williams, you can't be serious! That's – that's quite out of the question. I could manage 10 percent, but five points above that is usury."

Her smile was bright and her eyes again squinted as she said, "You, old friend, are the one asking for money, but when I name my terms you have the nerve to call me a usurer. I do not take that kindly."

"But surely not 15 percent," he protested. "That's double the rate that bankers receive."

"You cannot get the money from a banker or you would have already done so."

Again nodding, he said, "But I come to you with $600,000 worth of valuable bonds as security. Our railroad is already built and has hauled more than 60,000 tons of ore. And our mines are producing high grade ore at this very moment. We have built towns and populated them with our workers and our harbor has already loaded more than 30 shiploads of our ore. Surely, you can give a more reasonable rate, in light of all of this."

Suddenly her giggle sparkled in the afternoon gloom. "Dear, Dear Mr. Tower! First you accuse me of usury and now you call me unreasonable. What am I to do?"

She paused, then said, "Very well. I cannot very well refuse you, but I want a bonus of $10,000 in cash and you may have the money at 12 percent per annum. I will hold your bonds as assurance on the loan and you will give me your personal pledge to pay me upon demand."

He sensed that she was making her final offer and, his hand shaking, he again held the papers out for her signature. This time, she took them and placed them behind a cushion on the settee. Seeing his pained expression at this casual handling of papers he had so laboriously drafted, she said, "Don't worry yourself, Mr. Tower. You are a very good instructor and I will handle these papers with extreme care, but first my own lawyer will review them."

He allowed himself a brief smile, then returned to the business at hand. "If you could telegraph Joseph Shoemaker and Company informing them of our agreement after you are satisfied these contracts are in order, I will take care of any other necessary documents and mail them to you within the week."

She looked tired and he suddenly realized that he, too, was exhausted. His restlessness of the night before had evaporated with the realization that his enterprise was now secure and he wished only to return to his home and find needed refuge in sleep.

Taking leave of Mrs. Williams, he sank heavily into his train seat and let it rock him gently. When he repaid her, would Helen Williams continue to feel that an old friend had taken advantage of her? Or would she simply conclude that she had made a wise investment? The money, of course, would be repaid and her exorbitant interest rate and cash bonus would be absorbed as an added expense of doing business, just as his bookkeepers factored every other expense from labor to coal costs and bond interest into the cost per ton of ore – but what would she and her family think of him in the meantime? A huge piece of his pride had been sacrificed this afternoon and the only remedy was to completely and honorably overcome this financial embarrassment at the earliest possible date.

The questions nagged at him as the evening gloom settled over the landscape. Yes, his personal appeal to Mrs. Williams had procured the desperately needed cash and would procure an additional $150,000 when Breitung met his part of the agreement. But when and where would the next emergency strike – and who or where could he turn to then? Helen Williams and her family had been his last resort and they were no longer a stopgap, if the market failed to recover next spring.

Occasional dim lights passed the window and his head nodded against the glass. He had so much to do, yet a torpor made it impossible even to think of it. He would spend tomorrow recovering and

Shortly after completion, the D&IR office, hotel and warehouse at Agate Bay were equipped with wooden sidewalks to provide mud-free access. In a note at the bottom of this picture, Thomas Owens said that W.A. McGonagle was the engineer in charge and that Owens was the carpenter who built the sidewalk.

attack the needed documents after that. So long as Helen Williams' bankers notified Shoemaker of the arrangement in a reasonable period, his immediate duty was done and the paperwork could wait. His most immediate concern was getting a message off to Charlie that all was again well. Yet, even that could wait, he decided, as the train pulled into Philadelphia.

He had no way of knowing at this moment that his financial troubles, and the resulting humiliation he felt, were largely momentary and that by the end of shipping season in the fall of 1885, his glorious enterprise would have produced and shipped more than 225,000 tons of ore at prices of $5.75 or more a ton. Despite the costs of land acquisition, building and development, interest on debt and the near slide into receivership, the company bootstrapped itself to the brink of prosperity after little more than 12 months of operation, finding enough cash in November 1855 to liquidate a $150,000 loan by a Chicago banker to tide the company through its near-insolvency.

But, Charlemagne Sr. would also suffer a setback this year in the form of a light stroke that resulted in slight paralysis, from which he did recover, but which would force him to cut back his workday of 10 to 16 hours a day to four hours, at the end of which he was frequently exhausted.

Nonetheless, on February 12, 1886, he was particularly elated to pay Helen E.M. Williams in full for her 1884 loan, recovering his precious railroad bonds and canceling that personal promissory note to her. Later that year, the Duluth & Iron Range Railroad would complete the rail line from Two Harbors into Duluth, thus qualifying for a land grant of more than 600,000 acres that could be selected anywhere in the state. Having spent long years and many dollars to secure the land grant pledge assigned to the original Duluth & Iron Range Railroad investors, this was particularly satisfying, since he had earlier found sale of such tracts to be a profitable sideline to his investment in Northern Pacific stocks and bonds.

Within three short years, the Minnesota Iron Company that Tower had personally planned, paid and begged for was ranked by the trade journal *Iron Age* as the third largest mining company in the United States.

But in this moment, as the exhausted old man debarked in the Philadelphia train

station, he also had no way of knowing that the Duluth & Iron Range Railroad, its docks and harbor, and the Minnesota Iron Company properties would be out of his control within a span of only three years.

Tower was basically forced out of his own company by a syndicate that was headed by Henry H. Porter, a self-made Chicago millionaire. His partners included John D. and William Rockefeller of Standard Oil, Marshall Field of the Chicago retail firm of the same name, farm machinery manufacturer Cyrus McCormick and Jay C. Morse of Union Steel Company, a longtime and astute investor in iron ore properties in Michigan and Wisconsin.

Porter's group first obtained 25,000 acres of iron property near the lands owned by Tower's Minnesota Iron Company, then threatened to build a competing railroad to serve the mines they intended to develop there, unless Tower sold them his railroad. Next the group uncovered evidence of irregularities in land acquisitions by Tower's company and threatened a lawsuit over ownership issues, which they claimed were based on fraudulent preemptors and homesteaders. And such was undoubtedly the case, for George C. Stone had carefully placed "settlers" he trusted on the land and manipulated the selection of George Stuntz as the government surveyor of the iron property, saying he was on "the best of terms" with Stuntz, the surveyor general and the local land office. "I can manage them all," he had assured his employer.

Later, ownership of some 2,000 acres of valuable ore land was cancelled by action of the U.S. Land Office after a finding that title to the claims had been patented to preemptors or homesteaders who were paid to take residence and were, therefore, fraudulent.

Samuel Ely, the ore sales agent for Minnesota Iron Company, had earlier advised Tower to sell the railroad to a national railroad company to avoid the possibility of competition, but the Towers spurned his advice. Their mines were successful, the railroad gave them cheap transportation and their profits from their operations were now considerable and promised to grow in the future.

By 1887, however, despite his reluctance to part with any part of his glorious enterprise, Charlemagne Tower was 78 years old, had suffered the paralytic stroke, from which he only partially recovered, and really had no stomach for what he knew would be a protracted battle defending his land titles – not to mention fighting a railroad war simultaneously. Charlemagne Jr. wanted to stand and fight, but Edward Breitung, Tower's partner, had died the previous March and Charlemagne Sr. heeded George C. Stone, who warned him they were facing a "strong and unscrupulous crowd. We have got to make the best deal we can and get out."

Perhaps part of his decision was also based on the fact that the mines at the Tower end of the D&IR were as deep as open pit methods would take them and the company was faced with buying expensive new equipment to take the mining effort underground.

The exact set of circumstances that led to his final decision will probably never be fully known, but Tower began serious negotiations with the Porter group in April 1887 and signed the final papers turning over the entire operation on June 14 in Philadelphia for what has been reported as $6 million in certified checks and $2.5 million in cash, a sum the *New York Times* described as "the largest transaction in the way of a cash sale that has ever taken place."

Several sources agree that Tower's deposit of the $2.5 million in cash caused a flurry in the eastern money markets from Philadelphia to New York City.

Even with his fortune renewed and again securely in his own hands, Charlemagne ruefully told his cousin, "I did not want to sell … I had to … because it was necessary for (Porter) to control and manage the whole Minnesota Iron Company."

In his resignation from the board of directors, the senior Tower asked the new board to keep his son as an executive of the company. Charlemagne Jr. did serve for a short time as president of the railroad, but resigned within a few months of his father's sale – although he continued on the executive committee until 1889.

Henry H. Porter of Illinois Steel, a syndicate of powerful investors, engineered the takeover by his company of all the Tower properties in 1887. The largest cash transaction to have taken place to that time, Tower invested $500,000 of his new wealth back into the syndicate.

After re-organization of Tower's company into the Minnesota Mining and Railroad Syndicate, investment, acquisitions and a healthy market resulted in the company purchasing its own boats, as well as furnishing large cargoes for boats from other fleets.

And Charlemagne Sr. did not totally sever his relationship with the companies he had founded, for he was one of only six investors who bought $500,000 or more of a total of $10 million in share that Porter solicited from 81 subscribers for the reorganization of the company into the Minnesota Mining and Railroad Syndicate. Tower and Porter also remained on friendly terms and Porter praised Tower in testimony before the U.S. Senate as the single person who opened the Minnesota Iron Ranges, saying, "I doubt if there are three men in the United States who could have done it and would have done it; and, from the experience I have had with railroads – and I have been connected with them from my boyhood – I should just as lief have bought a ticket in the Louisiana lottery as to have undertaken that job (building the D&IR line to Tower)."

Moving quickly, the new group of investors applied for a security listing on the New York Stock Exchange in 1888, listing assets of more than $8.25 million in real estate, $4.4 million in D&IR securities and $2.28 million in ore, supplies and receivables. A total of $14 million in capital stock was issued and a profit of $473,873 shown in that statement.

Also in 1888, the first ore from the Chandler Mine at Ely was shipped over the expanded railroad and loaded on ships at Two Harbors. From 1892 onward for 60 years, the combined mines of the Vermilion Range sent more than 1 million tons of iron ore a year down the track to the docks at Two Harbors – with the exception of eight years, two of which were the panic years 1893 and '94, when the Merritt Brothers lost control of their mines and railroad to interests that also included the Rockefellers.

But Charlemagne Tower Sr. was not to see most of these events, for he suffered a stroke in July 1889 and died five days later. Having never set foot within 500 miles of his grand enterprise, he could envision it only through maps and the eyes of his son, daughter and son-in-law and other agents who were on the scene when the frenzy of development was under way and reported that activity to him.

And his dear son, Charlie, who commanded most of the activity of those early years, was destined to go on to a distinguished career in the U.S. Foreign Service, serving first as minister to Austria-Hungary from 1897-99 and later as ambassador to Russia and Germany, accumulating a total of 11 years as a foreign diplomat.

CHAPTER 5

Day to Day Near the Lake

By the late 1880s, the skyline across Agate Bay was filling as an expanding workforce required homes, retail stores, churches, schools and other structures. Smaller boats anchored off the eastern shore probably indicate that commercial fishing was well-established in the area.

The following is not intended as a definitive examination of the Two Harbors area, which is contained in Two Harbors – 100 Years: A Pictorial History, *published in 1984. Rather, these are highlights of events that are discussed in greater detail in that earlier volume.*

There is no doubt that the center of life in the settlement that became Two Harbors was the railroad and dock facilities that Charlemagne Tower Sr. single-mindedly dreamed of and built. Here were the jobs that provided income. From company offices, the work schedules were issued that dominated every facet of life. Ships coming and going brought coal to fire steam engines and heat homes, taking away the rich iron ore that paid the wages.

The company sold the land on which the original homes and early businesses were built, parceling it as much as possible to those who would put down permanent roots. It is reliably recorded that the elder Charlemagne Tower took personal responsibility for the earliest development of the town, specifying "wide streets, public squares, a reliable water supply and the complete elimination of real estate speculation."[1]

It is also recorded in the several community histories in Lake County that many settlers in other areas also looked to Two Harbors for employment, where jobs on the railroad and the docks provided income to tide the scattered settlers through hard times or to purchase needed machinery or other items they couldn't otherwise afford. Four men of the Waxlax family, for example, homesteaded land in 1897 on what would become Lax Lake and worked a number of summers on the railroad to save enough money to bring the rest of their family to America. Anselm Johnson remembered that Two Harbors later provided his mother, Emma, the oldest Waxlax daughter, work as a cook at Dallberg's Boardinghouse until she married Fred Johnson and they took up a homestead on Lax Lake.

Construction of Dock No. 1 was started in 1883, but work stopped when clay footings shifted and part of the structure gave way. Dock No. 1 would be completed and put into use in 1885, while Dock No. 2 was hastily completed in time to load the first iron ore to leave Agate Bay on the steamer *Hecla* and the tow schooner-barge *Ironton* in early

By 1898, the D&IR had constructed and opened the original Two Harbors YMCA Clubhouse at First Avenue and Seventh Street, providing recreation and athletic events for employees and the public.

August 1884, assisted by the wooden tug *Ella G. Stone.*

Four more wooden docks would be constructed by 1907 to handle the increasing iron ore traffic as Vermilion Range mine production grew and the Mesabi Range became productive after 1894. The docks consumed millions of board feet of lumber, but rather quickly deteriorated from the heavy traffic they sustained. In 1907, the first concrete and steel ore dock in the United States was erected at Agate Bay and proved to be far more durable than its predecessors.

By the end of the 1884 shipping season, the D&IR's 11 new locomotives and 350 ore cars had delivered 62,122 tons of high quality ore to the dock for transfer to vessels. By 1888, after Charlemagne Tower sold his mines and railroad and the mines at Ely began development, nine more locomotives and 200 ore cars were added to the rolling stock, along with 226 other freight cars.

Through the later 1880s and 1890s, tonnages of ore delivered to the docks steadily increased, hitting the 1.2 million long ton mark (a long ton equals 2,240 pounds, a standard weight in shipping and iron ore production) in 1892, a bit more than 4 million long tons in 1900 and about 8.3 million tons in 1910. That number would jump to an average of 8.5 million tons through the next decade, with some yearly fluctuations, but a total tonnage of 85 million tons.

An extension of the D&IR into the Mesabi Iron Range in the mid-1890s to compete with the Duluth Missabe and Northern built by the Merritt family had proven to be a good business decision, with upward of half the ore delivered to Two Harbors coming from the Mesabi Range by 1899.

Obviously, World War I spurred the demand for iron ore, although the first year that the D&IR handled more than 10 million tons occurred in 1913, prior to the United States taking an active role in those hostilities. At that time, the most modern ships carried only 8,000 tons, meaning that the iron port had to load upward of 1,200 boats during the seven- to eight-month season to ship the 1913 production. Although a couple of other years totalled 10 million or more tons, it would be 1940 before tonnages remained above that figure on a sustained basis, with 1953 holding the record for Two Harbors ore delivery at 21.33 million tons.[2]

The earliest businesses sprang to life as Whiskey Row on the four acres of lakeshore that Thomas Sexton retained when he sold 150 acres to the Minnesota

Iron Company in 1882. The early flush of construction wages attracted proprietors of businesses seeking quick profits in the various "shanties" serving as hotels, saloons, boardinghouses and other businesses in that area but, when Whiskey Row was destroyed by fire in 1885, other businessmen were already developing a downtown that would prove more enduring than Thomas Sexton's platted Agate Bay townsite.

From the very beginning, the railroad was active in developing amenities in the city, having built the Lakeview Hotel in 1883 as a boardinghouse for its workers, as well as a hospital operated by Dr. William Alden. Later, the company would also pretty well singlehandedly establish and provide support for the YMCA Clubhouse that became a center of community life on the corner of First Avenue and Seventh Street. Camp Francis House on Lake George in the Brimson-Toimi area would be an offshoot of the YMCA and was also supported generously by the railroad.

Meantime, as the railroad and docks began operating in 1884-85, good wages led to homes being built, an expanding population, a bit extra to establish savings accounts and a relatively stable economy. Builders were hard pressed to keep up with the demand for new structures and many residents solved that problem by doing their own carpentry, rather than wait on or pay a contractor. Most of the homeowners worked for the railroad and wanted to be within walking distance of their worksite, so many homes were built on narrow lots to provide space for more homes in the downtown area.

The Village of Two Harbors was officially platted with a population of 550 residents in 1885, the year that Whiskey Row burned, adopting a name that reflected the fact it was bordered by Agate and Burlington bays. A year later the D&IR Lake Line connected Two Harbors to Duluth, making for easy and comfortable travel from Tower and other points along the way. Passenger service had been established between Tower and Two Harbors immediately after that rail line was completed, but travel beyond Agate Bay was by boat until the Lake Line was completed. The area served by the D&IR then had direct connections to the national railroad system and freight moved easily into and out of northeastern Minnesota's first and, at that time, only operating Iron Range and its iron port.

March 9, 1888, would see Two Harbors incorporated as a village. Village officers were elected a month later. A few months earlier, in October 1887, Charlemagne Tower had sold his companies to the Chicago syndicate of investors headed by Henry H. Porter that operated first as the Illinois Steel Company and later as Federal Steel of Chicago. The new owners quickly developed new mines in the Ely area of the Vermilion Iron Range and for more than a decade continued to invest in and expand the Duluth & Iron Range Railroad and its Minnesota Mining Co. iron ore properties. The future of the Two Harbors iron port was bright and First Avenue was lined by stores and wooden sidewalks to make shopping in those stores easier and more comfortable.

Joining Charlemagne Tower's original Soudan Mine at Tower, the newly opened Chandler Mine at Ely began shipping ore in 1888, after a 21-mile extension of the mainline was pushed in from Tower. Four other mines would shortly be producing at Ely as part of the syndicate's properties.

The syndicate followed the iron ore body of the original shallow open pit mines at Tower underground, also acquiring mining rights on a number of properties on the Mesabi Range after ore was discovered there in the early 1890s. It built 58 miles of rail into that mining district from Allen Junction through Aurora to serve mines at Biwabik, McKinley, Sparta, Gilbert, Eveleth and Virginia – despite the fact that the Duluth Missabe & Northern was also operating in that general area. The syndicate would also invest in its own fleet of ships to deliver ore to its mills and other customers.

H.R. Bishop was appointed president of the railroad at the first meeting of the

J.L. Greatsinger served as president of the D&IR from 1892 until the giant consolidation of the steel industry that resulted in the birth of United States Steel in 1901. His term in office was marked with dramatic change and increases in ore tonnages, as the Mesabi Range became active after 1893.

Construction of the Two Harbors Lighthouse began in 1891 and the dedication occurred in April 1892, with Charles Lederle as head lightkeeper. Three keepers were normally assigned to this important navigational aid on Agate Bay and the busy seaway south of Two Harbors.

***Above:** All was not work for the sturdy tug* Ella G. Stone, *which served at Agate Bay from 1883 until the 1896 arrival of the* Edna G. *This party was probably a group of company officials or VIPs who decided to do some shooting in the wilderness surrounding Two Harbors.*

board after the 1887 acquisition from the Towers by Illinois Steel. He would serve in that capacity until late 1891, when M.J. Carpenter assumed that role, serving jointly as head of the D&IR and the Chicago & Eastern Illinois, also an Illinois Steel property. Carpenter's D&IR tenure lasted only a matter of months, with J.L. Greatsinger serving locally as general manager and succeeding Carpenter as president before the end of 1892.

With increasing boat traffic coming and going at Agate Bay, it was determined that a lighthouse was needed as an aid to navigation. Construction of the Two Harbors Lighthouse began in 1891 and the light was commissioned and lit in April 1892. Although less than 50 feet (49 feet 6 inches) from the base of the tower to the peak, its location provided another 30 feet of elevation to make the light visible for a considerable distance to welcome ships to the burgeoning port – as well as guide homebound fishermen and navigators sailing in the shipping lanes between Wisconsin's Apostle Islands and Duluth-Superior. Charles Lederle is credited as the first Two Harbors lightkeeper. There were normally three keepers assigned at the light.

The Two Harbors Light continued to be operated by the U.S. Lighthouse Service until 1939, when the U.S. Coast Guard took over that duty and remained on the site until 1982, when the light was automated. By 1990, the Lake County Historical Society (LCHS) gained access to the keepers' residences and began restoring the facility, using period pieces when available. That work continued as funding could be found and in August 1999 ownership of the property was officially transferred by the government to the LCHS.

The gush of iron ore coming down the D&IR from the Vermilion and Mesabi Iron Ranges would be an essential ingredient in the expansion of the United States throughout the last decade of the 19th century and the entire 20th century, but the nature of the iron ore business had changed dramatically by 1900. Consolidations, mergers, takeovers and a rash of business re-arrangements had resulted in the entire steel and iron business being held in fewer and fewer hands, as Henry Porter of the Chicago syndicate had foreseen when he forced Charlemagne Tower Sr. to sell his northeastern Minnesota holdings to the Chicago syndicate.

Based on the growth and investments made, the iron mines and railroad were obviously highly profitable for the Porter syndicate throughout the late 1880s and 1890s and Two Harbors grew to about 1,225 people by the end of the '90s.

But changes blew in the business winds. In 1898, Illinois Steel was the heart of a merger that forged the Federal Steel Company, an integrated steel manufacturer that came into existence with the backing of financier J. Pierpont Morgan. Specifically, it was formed to compete with the huge Carnegie Steel Company. As fashioned by Morgan, Federal Steel purchased or merged with other companies to acquire all of the natural resources and facilities needed in the steel business, including the Minnesota iron mines, the D&IR and a sister railroad, the 180-mile Elgin, Joliet & Eastern Railway that circled the Chicago area and served the Federal steel mills scattered there.

This state of affairs was to be shortlived, however, for in 1901 Federal Steel would become a basic component in the consolidation that resulted in United States Steel Corporation. Included in that massive consolidation was the huge complex of Carnegie Steel mills, mines and shipping interests and several smaller steel companies.

Perhaps most significant to the local scene, Morgan's merging of assets also included all of the Mesabi Iron Range ore assets and the Duluth, Missabe and Northern Railroad obtained by John D. Rockefeller when he acquired the bulk of the Merritt family interests after the panic of 1893 threatened the family with bankruptcy. With this huge list of assets, U.S. Steel Corporation was the world's first billion-dollar corporation – organized, financed and chartered by J.P. Morgan in New Jersey in 1901 as a completely self-contained steel producer.[3]

Initially, such boardroom manipulation had little effect on day-to-day life on the local scene. Hundreds of workers worked on the tracks, ore docks, rolling stock, coal dock, shops and other facilities needed to keep the iron ore railroad and shipping port running like a clock.

By the time that U.S. Steel was chartered, the population of Two Harbors had risen to more than 3,000 people, largely on the foundation of jobs offered by the railroad and docks. No matter that many of those jobs existed only during the summer shipping season, for the wages were steady and would tide over those who used a bit of discretion in their finances. For those who were less careful with their money, there was winter work in the nearby lumber camps or on the "Alger Line" – the railroad that came to life as the Duluth & Northern Minnesota at Knife River in 1898 and hired the D&IR to deliver logs from D&NM's Knife River rail yard to the Duluth sawmill. Since logging was heaviest in winter and ore haulage in summer, a number of railroaders found year-round employment, joining the D&NM after the D&IR laid up ore shipping for the winter season.

Two years before the establishment of Federal Steel, the D&IR had taken possession of a snappy new tugboat to move boats around in Agate Bay and the surrounding waters of Lake Superior. The 1,000-horsepower steam-powered tug was christened the *Edna G.*, named for the

For all but two years of its working life, the tug Edna G. labored in the harbor at Agate Bay. During World War I, the federal government took over the tug and moved it to the East Coast for the war effort. The distinctive whistle of the jaunty little tug was recently rebuilt by a group of volunteers and can occasionally be heard around town.

D. & I. R. TUG, EDNA G.

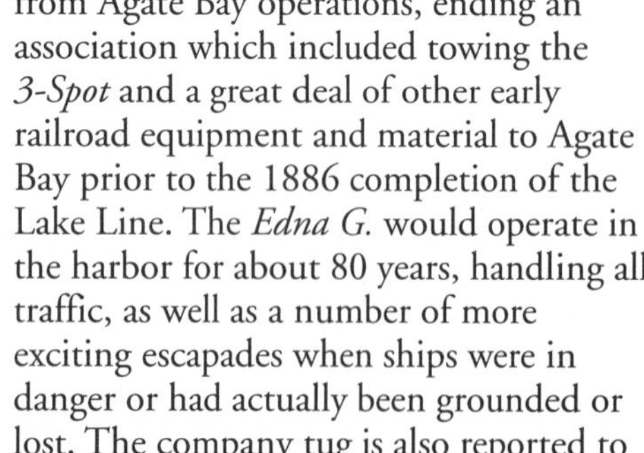

That Two Harbors was a busy and important shipping center is evident in this 1907 photo of the waterfront and harbor, with five whaleback steamships awaiting loading to the right and the infrequently idle coal unloading facilities on the left.

daughter of company president Jacob L. Greatsinger, who headed the railroad when the tug was ordered and delivered.

As observed by a ship-savvy reporter for the *Cleveland Plain Dealer* of May 23, 1896: "The tug is a revelation in tug building. She was built for work at Two Harbors in heavy weather and for the use of officials of the road which owns her. Consequently, she presents a great combination of strength and elegance."

Once the new tug arrived and proved itself in service at Agate Bay, the venerable wooden-hulled *Ella G. Stone* was removed from Agate Bay operations, ending an association which included towing the *3-Spot* and a great deal of other early railroad equipment and material to Agate Bay prior to the 1886 completion of the Lake Line. The *Edna G.* would operate in the harbor for about 80 years, handling all traffic, as well as a number of more exciting escapades when ships were in danger or had actually been grounded or lost. The company tug is also reported to have helped out many fishermen caught on the lake by bad weather.

Through the years, with the exception of 1917 to 1919, when it was pressed into federal wartime service on the East Coast, the *Edna G.* was a workhorse on the Two Harbors waterfront, pushing and tugging a wide variety of ships into or out of dockage, providing occasional search and rescue for lost and damaged craft and attending to other tasks required to keep a long line of ore boats moving efficiently through the harbor.

After U.S. Steel Corporation absorbed the mining, railroad and dock assets in 1901, Francis E. House, who had previously served as general manager of the Bessemer and Lake Erie Railroad, was selected to succeed Greatsinger as president of the D&IR and held that position for 25 years – until his sudden death on April 3, 1926. He would also serve as federal manager of both U.S. Steel railroad operations (Duluth Missabe & Northern and the D&IR) during World War I. In the 28 months of federal control, William McGonagle, who was president of the DM&N, also presided over the D&IR – thus extending his on-again, off-again contact with the D&IR from its earliest days, when he was head of the surveying party that laid out the original right of way.

House's name was enshrined shortly before his death by Camp House on Lake George in Brimson-Toimi. He is also credited with the rescue and preservation of the historic *3-Spot* locomotive, which had been rented to the Scott Holsten Lumber Company for a logging operation north of Two Harbors for a year or two before being sold in 1899 to the Alger-Smith Duluth & Northern Minnesota Railroad. The jaunty little 2-6-0 engine became D&NM *No. 2* and served the Alger line for many years as both a construction and a log hauling locomotive, but ended up being abandoned when the company closed down.[4]

After House died, he was succeeded by Horace Johnson, who presided over the D&IR until 1930, when the D&IR was leased and operated jointly with the DM&N. A 1938 merger of several U.S. Steel-owned rail properties in northeastern Minnesota ultimately formed the Duluth Missabe & Iron Range Railroad – just in time for increased ore shipments demanded as European nations entered World War II. The joint operation of the two railroads during the Great Depression saved U.S. Steel considerable overhead. The merger would later prove to be a major reason that the railroad was able to meet demand for the iron ore deliveries that sustained the Allied effort in the war.

For a number of years by the time the *Edna G.* was delivered to Agate Bay in 1896, commercial fishing had been a vital part of the local scene. Scores of families earned some or all of their income from the nets set by hardy fishermen, who seemed able to work in the most bitter weather to bring in their catches. A line of fish houses ringed the eastern edge of Agate Bay and were scattered regularly along the entire north shore. The railroad and SS *America* hauled tons of fish a week from the fish and freight docks to Duluth. From there, the catches were shunted all over the country.

A bit later, when relatively good highways came to the area, trucks became important in the movement of fish but, in the interim, the *America,* the railroad and, a bit later, a number of smaller freight boats referred to as the Mosquito Fleet allowed fish to be shipped to whatever market was offering the best price.

Although prices for Lake Superior fish fluctuated greatly, the catches yielded

Tugging the Heartstrings

The late Ebner Anderson served as one of four stenographers working in the D&IR Railroad offices upstairs at the Two Harbors Depot from his high school graduation in 1926 until 1933, when he took employment in the county Welfare Department.

He laughed as he remembered one windy day taking dictation in superintendent Thomas Owens' (whose affectionate office moniker was T.O.) office. He glanced up to spot the tug Edna G. coming off the lake with a small fishing boat in its downwind protective lee.

"I stopped T.O. and said, 'You might want to see this, T.O.,' as I pointed out the window behind him. He turned in his chair and a big smile came over his face as he watched the Edna G. escort the little fishboat into the safety of the harbor. He turned back to me and said, 'Wasn't that a nice show, Ebenezer?'

"All I could do is smile and agree, because he was so enthused about anything the railroad did and was a very good boss – even though he never could remember my name."[5] ▲

enough income to keep a substantial number of fishermen working into the last quarter of the 20th century, when the last of the fish houses remaining on Agate Bay in the mid-1980s were burned under fire department supervision to make way for improvements and a new public boat landing on lands adjacent to Agate Bay.

During this period of growth in Two Harbors, a number of communities had sprung to life, as settlers claimed homesteads or bought logged-over land, cleared fields and made other improvements.

Henry Clark is credited as being Silver Creek's first settler in 1890 in a short unpublished manuscript by Campman "Campie" Anderson. Two years later, Clark would be joined in the area by Charles Carlson and Oliver Olson in 1892 and by L.C. Anderson, Campie's father, in 1893. By 1896, a schoolhouse had been constructed, with 10 students enrolled. The Town of Silver Creek was organized in 1906 or 1907, when the earlier settlers had been joined by perhaps 20 or 30 other homesteaders.[6]

Despite glowing praise in the booklet *Two Harbors in 1910,* agriculture in most of Lake County never attained the success that the boosters promised, but a few areas would prove profitable for farmers.

North of the iron port, Waldo had attracted scattered settlers when the area was first opened by the railroad and the area was fairly well populated by about 1905, as farming there proved to be somewhat more successful than in other Lake County settlements. Settlers were also moving into the Knife River and Clover valleys where farming proved to be relatively successful. Many other areas of Lake County, however, became known for their "rock farms." Each of the outlying settlements had one or more schools to educate the children of those communities.

To the west of Two Harbors, Larsmont came to life as a small settlement somewhat after the D&IR passed through with its Lake Line. The three Thompson brothers, Teodore, Tollof and Louis, had arrived and started fishing before the D&IR line was built, setting up at Thompsons' Landing about a quarter mile east of the Larsmont School perhaps as early as 1883-85. Ted Wahlberg remembered that the Thompsons told him that when they

In 1923, the D&IR rescued the 3-Spot locomotive from abandonment by the Alger-Smith Lumber Company, rebuilt and renovated the historic engine and put it on display as a reminder of the important role the 3-Spot played as the first locomotive purchased by the company. The sleigh used by company officials during construction work was also dedicated during the Veteran Employees celebration.

first settled on the lakeshore, they would see large canoes packed with furs being paddled to Duluth by natives. Three or four days later, the canoes would be headed back up the shore, presumably bound for Grand Portage.[7]

Although Larsmont was a rocky site, a number of families settled in, cleared land and raised crops to supplement the income that most earned from fishing. The same was true farther west at Knife River, where the promise of copper first attracted early settlers who then abandoned the site after the copper proved unprofitable in the late 1850s. (A short history of Knife River is contained in the chapter on Logging and the Alger-Smith railroad operation at Knife River.)

Much like the area west of town, Castle Danger attracted fishermen like the Lind brothers, Tom and Dan, and their families who arrived from Norway and were settled in on cleared land by 1900. Ole Wick likely preceded the Linds and is credited by lifelong resident Richard Stone as being perhaps the most successful farmer in the Castle Danger area. Although the origin of the area's name is shrouded in the mists of time, Stone believes the legend that a ship with the word "castle" in its name foundered on the reef near the shore and the location was named for that ship.

In the early days of Castle Danger, Agnes (Lind) Thorngren was born at her parents' homestead in 1902 and remembered in an untitled, undated manuscript that her family planted huge gardens with "rows about a half mile long" that she and her 11 siblings had to tend. The autumn herring run meant that men were busy pulling nets, dressing and packing fish, so the women and children were generally the workforce. Fall found them picking potatoes, rutabagas, carrots, cabbages and other hardy crops that were stored in the root cellar for the winter. A herd of cows kept them busy after school and there were always other chores when nothing more urgent pressed in on them – including knitting and sewing many of the clothes that kept them warm in winter.

With that as her childhood background, it's little wonder that Agnes was quickly hired at an early age to work at the Beaver Bay Club after it was

Although farming is usually a difficult, labor intensive occupation in Lake County, a number of early farms found that sheep did pretty well on the cutover land and also provided a dual source of income from both their wool and as slaughter animals.

Facing page: *By 1890, the downtown area of Two Harbors was taking shape, as this photo of an August 3 celebration illustrates. The two larger buildings behind the "Commercial Hotel" were the home of W.N. Moulton, an early merchant, and the office building of the D&IR.*

founded in 1919 and found the work there rather pleasant. She also enjoyed going to occasional dances in the Beaver Bay Town Hall on Saturday evenings during her summer job, but had no contact with her family during that time, since her father had to row his skiff to take her there and bring her home.[8]

Castle Danger is credited as being the site of the first cabin resort in Minnesota, after Emil Edisen built a single rental cabin in the early 1900s and called his new venture Camper's Home Resort. It was located on the site that later became Star Harbor Resort and is now Grand Superior Lodge and Resort. Edisen had originally settled in the Split Rock River area, but burned out there. He continued to add cabins to his resort in succeeding years. The business had 24 rustic cabins in the 1930s. Some other settlers also offered rental cabins in the area. In about 1928, Edisen established the Edisen Cafe, which is still operating (in a new location) as the Rustic Inn. Edisen also operated a store that served the needs of locals, as well as the tourists who were increasingly traveling Highway 61 to visit the north shore after the highway opened in 1924.

Life in most of the outlying settlements followed pretty much the same routines – work long hours, hope for good crops and decent prices for produce and try to be prepared for anything that might come up. In some of these outlying communities, men traveled to work on the docks or railroad in Two Harbors, while others farmed during summers and worked at winter

Ted Wahlberg's Larsmont Memories

"I was one of seven babies born in Larsmont in 1919. There were only 11 or 12 families in the area then, so seven babies were a lot in one year. An old-timer told me there were so many of us born that year because the railroad started running the Ely Highball the year before that and it left Duluth at 10 at night. The engines would really bark going up the Larsmont grade at about 11 o'clock and woke all the folks up. You know the rest of that story," laughs T(h)eodore "Ted" Wahlberg, who notes that the "h" in his first name was appended by his first grade teacher, but that the name that appears on his birth certificate is the righteously Swedish "Teodore."

Ted also notes that merely getting to the little schoolhouse where the teacher worked was a chore for a 6-year-old, since his parents' homestead was a mile and a half up the hill from the school and the road was not snowplowed until 1937.

"Naturally, with so few families living in the area, we all knew one another and looked after each other," Ted said. "The first thing every one of the women would ask was, 'How's your mother?' because the women did so much work on the farms. If one of them was sick or was about to have a baby, other women would drop off food to help the family."

Most of the men in Larsmont fished, but Ted says it was common for them to also hold jobs and nearly everyone had specialty skills, like the Hill brothers with their boatworks or shoemaker John Sjoblom, who turned many pairs of worn-out leather boots into pack boots by sewing an inexpensive rubber shoe onto the salvaged leather tops.

Fire – of the forest, home and chimney varieties – was a constant threat for the early settlers and Ted's parents experienced both a home fire and several encounters with forest fires.

Their home burned the autumn before he was born in December 1919. A bit earlier, their homestead narrowly missed being consumed in the forest fire of 1918 that burned a huge area of northeastern Minnesota. The fire roared through the crowns of trees heading northeast past their farmstead, but the wind switched to the northeast and blew the fire back the way it came, subjecting the burned area to a second attack. Although his parents' farm was spared, a neighbor lost his barn and haystacks and the whole countryside was blackened by the fire.

Ted says the neighbors trooped to help his parents after their home burned, taking up a collection of whatever money they could contribute, donating pieces of furniture or other household items and volunteering labor to rebuild the home. Charlie Hill had a sawmill and gave his father all the lumber he could haul on a sleigh. Another neighbor hitched his horses up with Ted's father's team to pull an extraordinarily heavy load of lumber to the building site. Within a couple of months, a new home sheltered the family from the winter's blast – just in time for Ted's birth.

"That's just the way things were done in those days. You helped one another out, tried to look after each other and you always had time enough to stop and visit or have a cup of coffee with neighbors."[9] ▲

logging operations for their livelihood. Few of these early folks managed to save much more money than they needed to buy their families the shoes and what few other items they did not make themselves – yet the memoirs of their children are nearly all upbeat and relate stories of happy times along with those of hard work and less pleasant memories.

Meanwhile, business in Two Harbors continued to expand. One of the earliest, The Big Store, was founded in 1883 and became a major "department store" after 1888, when John and E.H. Schreiner bought the business, which was located in the center of First Avenue at the present site of the American Legion club. In that era, the store reportedly ordered wares by the carload and had its own narrow gauge railroad to deliver the goods to the store.

Another longtime major business was established in 1893 with the organization of the Scandinavian Cooperative Mercantile Company, the original stock being sold only to those of Scandinavian origins. Later, that stock policy would be amended to include anyone wanting to buy shares. The business became the largest commercial building in the city, which currently houses J&J Lumber Company. It was remodeled as the New Scan Store in 1957, but apparently didn't last long after that. The building is reported as the original site of Don & Bill's IGA prior to 1968, when owners Don Carroll and Bill Young moved their business into the building at 501 Seventh Street. That grocery would, in turn, close in the 1990s and the building was taken over for use as the Bumper to Bumper Auto Parts store.

National Tea Company operated for many years at 623-625 First Avenue until 1957, when the store was moved to the north side of Seventh Avenue between Fifth Street and State Road 2. In 1982, the company constructed a new building on the southeast corner of State Road 2 and Seventh Avenue, but sold out to Super One a year later. That company moved the operation to the west end about 10 years later.

Through the years, numerous other variety stores, a dime store, grocers, meat markets, specialty clothing stores, numerous barbershops, several pool halls, taverns or saloons, hardware and other retail outlets were almost always successful in Two Harbors, where railroad wages fueled the economy and shoppers found virtually anything they needed in their hometown.

Restaurants, in particular, proved to be an important and seemingly symbolic source of civic pride. One of Two Harbors' earliest cafes, the Delmonico, was operated

Roy LaBounty on Farming

Born and raised five miles out of Two Harbors on a farm in Waldo, Roy LaBounty says he's thankful for that rural background, which gave him plenty of opportunity to work in mechanics, which he loved.

"We raised purebred Holstein dairy cattle, tested them carefully for production and then sold the proven cows to big dairy farms," Roy remembers. "We sold milk and cream to creameries and also had chickens and sold eggs.

"There was always something that needed to be fixed on the farm and that's how I got the experience to build machines that we used when my brother Clarence and I were logging in the Isabella area after World War II and in my own contracting business later on. The grapple I built for my contracting business is the product that made LaBounty Manufacturing possible, but it was growing up on a farm that got me interested in mechanics and where I learned how to make things work."

With this farm-based and business background in the use, maintenance and building of equipment, Roy went on to patent 24 designs for machinery in seven or eight product lines that made his company the world leader in building specialized attachments for use in the construction, demolition, recycling and material handling industries.[10] ▲

Opened in 1923 by the Amundson family, the Rustic Inn was a favorite eating place throughout its 35 years of operation. It was located where Harbor Point Apartments now stand in Two Harbors.

by Charles Colby and William Ray, the town's first African-American businessmen and possibly the first black residents. Their establishment lasted only from 1893 to 1895, although Colby, who was born as a slave in the state of Virginia, baked and served apple pie to President Calvin Coolidge when he visited Minnesota's Iron Range by train in 1928.

Several other eating establishments took root through the years and were longer lasting, establishing the reputation of the city as a good place to dine. Among the better known of these restaurants was the Rustic Inn, which was operated from 1923 to 1958 at Third Avenue and Park Road (present site of Harbor Point Apartments) by the Amundson family. It was a special favorite of Duluth visitors on Sundays, when "Ma Amundson's" chicken dinners were featured on the menu. The New Life Cafe on First Avenue was opened in 1920 by John Huliares and ran until it was annexed by Falks Drug Store, which has since become Wings by the Bay. A number of the cafe's wall murals are said still to exist behind a false wall in the store.

On Seventh Avenue, Oscar's Restaurant operated from 1929 until 1974, when it was sold and renamed the Harbor House. That establishment, in turn, was remodeled and became Black Woods Grill and Bar in the mid-1990s. The site of the present Judy's Cafe has long been a restaurant location, reaching at least as far back as the Golden Gate Cafe in the 1940s.

In 1889, a bank that became known as the Sellwood and Burke Bank was founded. Named for the major stockholders, Joseph Sellwood and Dean Burke, the name was changed to the Bank of Two Harbors in 1897 and became Commercial State Bank in 1908, operating under that name until May 2000, when a switch to a national charter forced a name change to The Lake Bank.

Meantime, the First State Bank of Two Harbors had been chartered in 1902 and was renamed First National Bank of Two Harbors when it was re-organized under a national bank charter. Northwest Bancorporation bought the bank in 1929, maintaining controlling interest as the name changed to First Northwestern National Bank in 1983, then Norwest Bank and, ultimately, Wells Fargo.

Two Harbors Federal Credit Union was organized in 1948 as Two Harbors Co-op Federal Credit Union and was

open only to members of the Two Harbors Co-op Association. The charter was amended in 1965 to allow membership by the general public.

And, while commercial establishments provided goods and services, others were focusing on more esoteric needs of Two Harbors citizens.

Soon after the settlement at Agate Bay started, A. DeLacy Wood arrived in town and established the *Iron Port* newspaper in 1885, later changing the name to *The Twin Port* and, in 1890, the name *Iron News* was adopted for his enterprise, following reorganization after an irate customer destroyed the job press. Meanwhile, competitors came and went, but Wood had persuaded county officials to use his publication for legal advertising, giving him a virtual lock on the success of his venture. He also established the first newspaper in Grand Marais a few years later, retaining ownership in Two Harbors for some period. Wood was credited by his son with the creation and sale of 48 frontier newspapers during his 60-year lifetime.

Wood's was not the only newspaper in town, for the *Iron Port Advocate* is reported to have been publishing in 1890 and the *Iron Trade Journal* came to life in 1897. In 1909, the latter newspaper merged with the Two Harbors *Iron News* to become the *Two Harbors Journal News*. Two years later, the *Iron Port Advocate* was also apparently merged with the *Journal News*. This publication continued unchallenged until August 5, 1920, when a new owner changed the name to the *Lake County Chronicle*, after absorbing the *Two Harbors Socialist*, which operated from 1915-1919. In August 1930, publisher Clarence Hillman again changed the name of the paper, this time to the *Two Harbors Chronicle*, claiming that was what people called the paper anyway. In 1935, the "gray, boring looking" paper included a color comics section that was a favorite with many readers.

But even that inspiration by the newspaper did not spell the end of competition, for the *Two Harbors Times* was born in 1941 and a lively debate between the two newspapers ensued as each accused the other of unethical or questionable practices. Providing lively reading for three years, the war of words ended in 1944 with the merger of the two newspapers as the *Two Harbors Chronicle and Times*, which would eventually consolidate with the *Silver Bay News* in 1974 to form the *Lake County News-Chronicle.*

In 1997, the longtime ownership of the newspaper by the Williams family of Spencer, Iowa, ended when Murphy McGinnis Media added the *News-Chronicle* to its Up North Network of publications and a bit later also bought the *Cook County News-Herald*, thereby acquiring both of the successors to A. DeLacy Wood's pioneering north shore newspaper ventures.

And, while the newspaper battles waxed and waned in the community, other facilities were being erected to educate, amuse and fulfill residents' desires for mental stimulation.

In 1896, the first half of what would become Hiawatha School was completed on Third Avenue and, by 1902, a high school had been built to serve the older kids on the site where the present high school stands. The new high school boasted a library of 200 volumes. A number of country schools had also been scattered throughout the county to serve their communities.

Churches were some of the earliest established organizations, with the First Presbyterian Church being organized in 1887. Its first building at Third Avenue and Sixth Street was dedicated in 1888. Holy Ghost (now Holy Spirit) Catholic Church was the second parish in Two Harbors, served by the legendary missionary priest Father (later Monsignor) Joseph Buh from his parish in Tower.

After the Village of Two Harbors was incorporated in 1888, public services were implemented as technology made them practical. Lodges and other organizations were being organized and the D&IR Clubhouse was completed in 1900, providing space for entertainment, exercise and lodging. The Carnegie Library was built in 1908, replacing the first library that had been established in 1897 with a collection of 481 books. The library had always been popular and the new edifice made it even more of a favored stopping place.

Two years before the Carnegie Library was built, the Grand Opera House opened at the corner of First Avenue and Fifth Street to bring a bit of high culture

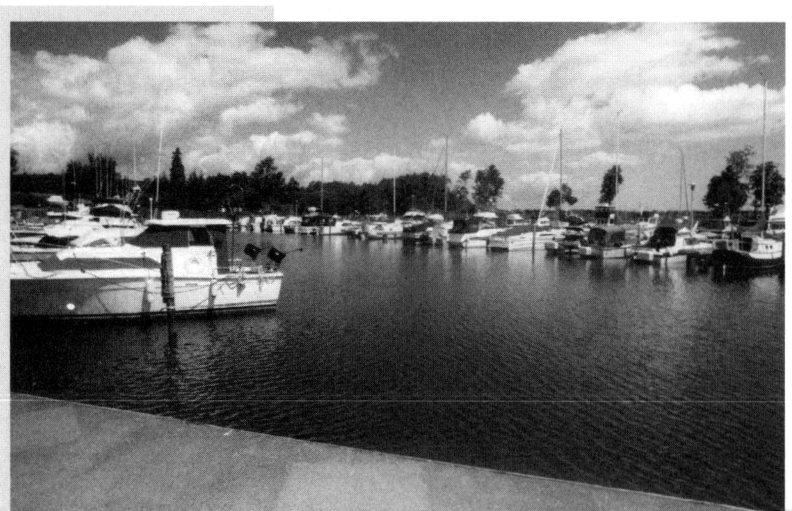

Knife River Marina.

to the city. For the thirsty and, perhaps, less culturally inclined, there were also reported to be nine saloons, a pool hall and a liquor store in town during some of this early period.

The city built an electric light plant in 1899-1900 and a new-fangled doodad called the telephone had been installed by the railroad as early as 1894 in the Tower-Soudan area. In 1895, a line was strung to connect the company's Duluth and Two Harbors offices. By 1896, a small switchboard was installed in the superintendent's office at Two Harbors,

Marina, I'll Never Stop Saying Marina

Son of Knife River pioneers Peter and Katrina Bugge of Knife River, Wesley Bugge remembers that he and Arnold Salakka were manning skiffs to set and pick nets around Larsmont and were rowing their heavily loaded skiffs back to Knife River when a sudden wind hit and swamped their boats. They swam to shore, rescued their boats, but lost their load of herring to the sea gulls.

Though only 16 years of age, Wesley and Arnold were good-sized boys and managed to be accepted for the Civilian Conservation Corps, serving in the Sawbill Camp and helping erect the fire tower at Kekekabic Lake. When the tower was finished, Wesley was called home to haul fish and would later serve in the Navy during World War II, where he had another boat go down under him – this time a Naval destroyer that was blown up in the Pacific.

Perhaps those two experiences, coupled with the memory of the so-called Armistice Day storm that wrecked a substantial amount of the fishermen's gear and shoreline property on November 11, 1940, spurred Wesley to join the effort to develop a safe harbor at Knife River.

"After the storm in 1940, we wanted a safe harbor and had a meeting of lakeshore fishermen at Shorecrest Supper Club to talk about setting up good harbors of refuge on the north shore. After the war, Kenny Ojard, Joe Liberty, Randy Loining, Tim Luukenen and I were picked as a committee to do the harbor," Wesley remembers. "There was a big area at the third sand beach that belonged to Ole Roske and we managed to get it pretty cheap. We sold enough shares to cover the cost of the land and drove pilings into the beach, dug out the area behind the pilings and it worked good as a harbor for the fishermen for a number of years.

"When the fishing pretty well died out in the 1960s, all of us who had shares in the harbor agreed to give the property to the county to develop the marina, with the agreement that a cove would be built that could be used by the fishermen, so that they wouldn't be mixed up with the recreational boaters.

"That plan is still in place and the two fishermen who are left at Knife River, Kenny Hanson and Mark Torgerson, are still using the cove. The rest of the harbor is set up real well as a full service marina and it's worked really well."

But, while the harbor became a reality in the late 1940s, Wesley lost all of his fishing nets in a storm in 1946. He went to work on the DM&IR Railroad, doing a bit of fishing out of the Knife River harbor on the side, but the fishing ended in 1956 and the railroading ended with an accident in 1972 that left him disabled.

He has since recovered from the disability, went on to care for the Knife River Rest Area on Highway 61 and has watched the growth of sport fishing with interest.

Like many old-timers in Knife River, he decries the loss of fishing in both Lake Superior and the river.

"The river fishing hasn't been the same since the DNR blew the beaver dams out. It was always good steelhead and trout fishing, but now you're lucky to even get a bite, let alone catch a nice fish," he says. "Fishing on the lake is a little better than it was a few years ago, but I think they planted way too many of the salmon. Those big salmon have almost done away with smelt and we used to take tons of smelt. Now, it isn't worth putting out nets for them.

"It's too bad, but today Kenny Hanson, Mark Torgerson, Walter Sve at Split Rock and the Midbrodts up at Silver Bay are the only fishermen I know of that are left on the north shore.

"It's a thing of the past, and now Knife River seems to be a place where retirees live. There are many nice lake and retirement homes in Knife River now, but almost nobody's making a living from the lake."[11] ▲

making communication possible all along the railroad, after the railroad strung wires on the poles that already carried the company's telegraph wires and connected Duluth and Two Harbors to Biwabik, McKinley, Tower and Ely.

Adopting this new communication device into its business was a natural for the company, which took pride in using all the latest equipment, but they could find no one willing to operate or maintain the system to provide telephone service in the communities along the railroad. So the D&IR went into the telephone business in 1900 as the first and only railroad to furnish public telephone service in its service area. From a system serving 13 D&IR phones in 1900, the system grew to include several hundred customers by 1910.

While it would have preferred not to be involved in such sideline businesses, the D&IR/DM&IR often found it was the only entity in the largely undeveloped area that could take the lead in many such projects. The telephone operation was a convenience to the railroad and, when the company provided wider service to the communities it served, that sideline operation became a profitable business – much as the expansion of the iron ore railroad into logging transportation was proving to be at about the same time.

Through the years, the telephone company grew and handled not only local calls, but served as the long distance switching station and carrier connecting a number of rural "farmer" systems like Brimson-Toimi, Silver Creek, Segog, Homewood, Waldo, Palmers and others to one another and to Duluth.

A good portion of the success and the history of the company was presided over by manager Michael H. Brickley, a Spanish-American War veteran who joined the D&IR Telephone and Telegraph Department in 1903. Shortly afterward, he was named manager and later was picked as superintendent. Active in civic affairs as well as the business, he served as mayor of Two Harbors for 21 years, first being elected in 1923. He held his high profile position with the D&IR phone company until his death in 1949 at age 67.

By 1914, the company switchboard service included all of the north shore, after the Fenstad family loaned $1,000 to establish the Lake Shore Rural Telephone Association that tied Grand Marais to the "farmer line" in the Silver Creek community, which connected to the D&IR Telephone Co. exchange. (See Fenstad family history in Chapter 8.)

To the present time, the telephone system that was somewhat reluctantly started by the D&IR is intact and providing service to a large area of Minnesota's Arrowhead. From Knife River to Castle Danger and from Two Harbors to Brimson-Toimi, Palo-Markham, Aurora/Hoyt Lakes, Tower-Soudan and the Ely areas, the original exchanges established with the D&IR still operate. Continental Telephone Corporation (CONTEL), operating as Gopher State Telephone Co., bought the telephone system from the DM&IR in 1962 and upgraded the system to provide dial service in 1963. In 1973, Gopher State assumed the name of CONTEL, its larger parent corporation, which eventually merged with GTE in the early 1990s. In August 2000, GTE sold all Minnesota telephone holdings to Citizen's Communication, a Verizon company.

Although the company once had upward of 90 employees, local facilities were gradually shut down in the later 1980s and 1990s. Today, only a handful of maintenance people are employed by the telephone company in this area, but it's common to bump into people almost anywhere who worked there in some capacity.

Meanwhile, shortly after the establishment of rudimentary telephone service in Two Harbors, a new company was incorporated to mine and process the corundum that was reported to be located near the mouth of the Baptism River west of the Fenstad family homestead at Little Marais.

Corundum is a hard, abrasive aluminum oxide that was used in the manufacture of whetstones, grinding wheels, sandpaper and other abrasive products. Only one profitable corundum mine existed in North America at the time, that being in northern Ontario, Canada. Since abrasive products depended on a limited supply of corundum, flint, garnet or emery (a less pure form of corundum), the abrasives market was receptive to any new source of these minerals.

Henry S. Bryan is credited as having the first automobile in Two Harbors and being a founder of 3M Corporation. His attractive bungalow home was turned into the Bryan House Bed & Breakfast on Third Avenue.

Corundum is rated next to diamonds in hardness. Rubys and sapphires are two of its transparent varieties that get more attention, but prices for the abrasive forms had skyrocketed as demand for corundum and emery doubled from 1897 to 1901. The industrial age needed better methods and products for polishing, scouring and sharpening metal, glass and wood. Corundum was in short supply.

By April 1901, a group of Duluthians had incorporated as Minnesota Abrasives Company to mine corundum, with stock offered to the public at $10 a share. One of the founding partners in that firm, Ed Lewis, was the first to report lodes of the mineral on the north shore. In August that same year, Henry S. Bryan, Hermon W. Cable and a Job Dodge of Two Harbors traveled "down the lake" from Two Harbors to investigate the corundum mining possibilities on a property owned by Bryan near Little Marais. Nothing further is heard of Dodge in this regard, but within a year Bryan and Cable had teamed up with Dr. J. Danley Budd, William A. McGonagle and John Dwan to charter the Minnesota Mining and Manufacturing Company to exploit north shore corundum deposits.

All of the chartering officers of 3M were prominent in the Two Harbors area. Bryan was the chief of motive power for the D&IR Railroad, had served as an early village president and was on a number of civic boards and organizations. Cable was a leading merchant who started his own meat market in 1891 and also had a number of civic accomplishments to his credit. Budd was the leading physician in Two Harbors, operating his 50-bed hospital and serving as county coroner, as well as chief surgeon for the D&IR.

As perhaps the most prestigious partner in the corporation, McGonagle was a well-known pioneer in the Two Harbors area, having arrived at Agate Bay as a 20-year-old engineer in charge of the 1881 surveying crew that laid out the right of way of the D&IR. A year later, he supervised the laying of the first rails in Agate Bay and was present on the tug *Ella G. Stone* when the *3-Spot* was delivered in stormy seas in July 1883. When 3M was chartered, McGonagle had recently moved from the position of assistant chief engineer of the D&IR to become assistant to the president of the Duluth Missabe & Northern. Both railroads were owned by U.S. Steel by that time and McGonagle would be named vice president of the DM&N in 1902, assuming the presidency of that railroad in 1909 and, as noted earlier, serving as president of both lines under federal operation during World War I. He would take on the additional responsibility as president of both the D&MN and D&IR in 1930, after a lease arrangement allowed that joint operation. Within months of becoming head of the joint operation, he died on August 2, 1930.

For various reasons, three of these four founding members of 3M would eventually drop from involvement in the company because they had other, more pressing responsibilities or feared the company's increasing indebtedness would destroy their other assets.

The fifth member of the "corundum company" was the only one who would see the company's affairs through the long haul and, thereby, achieve financial success from his early investment.

John Dwan was a native of Sanilac County, Michigan, arriving in Two Harbors in 1891 to open a law office. Apparently a speculator by nature, the 41-year-old lawyer dabbled with a wide range of investments, while also working long hours in his profession. He served as a representative for 14 insurance

companies, as the village attorney for $150 a month and a volunteer fireman at $2 per fire. On the civic side, he served on the library board, was a charter member of the Two Harbors Commercial Club and would be a prominent member of the Minnesota State Fair Board later in his life.

The 3M Company began with wild optimism, but limited capital. Shortly after 3M was founded in the upstairs of John Dwan's law office at 113 Poplar Street (now the 3M Museum on Waterfront Drive), the company was offered ownership of the earlier chartered Minnesota Abrasive Co., which was foundering, and 3M purchased it by trading stock in 3M.

Hermon Cable, a tireless worker who had never met a job he couldn't handle, became general manager of the mining and crushing operation at "Pickwick Bay," which was rather quickly renamed Crystal Bay, the name it bears today. He personally cut trails, traveled back and forth between Two Harbors and the minesite by boat, horse or snowshoes and supervised the building of the plant and installation of equipment.

Underfinanced, the company borrowed $5,000 at seven percent interest from the Bank of Two Harbors in October 1903 and another $5,000 in December of that year to tide them over. Finally, on January 21, 1904, the first stone was crushed at the new plant, but there was no means of shipping it to the railroad at Two Harbors in the winter season – short of horse and wagon on miserable, snow-clogged trails. In desperation, Dr. Budd and Cable took Budd's fine team of matched mares and hauled a small load of the dressed mineral to the railhead. The company made its first (and last) bulk sale of a ton of "corundum" in March 1904.

Having successfully opened the quarry and crushed and shipped minerals from the Crystal Bay site, the future of the 3M company was hardly secure, for the presumed corundum would ultimately prove to be unsatisfactory. To add insult to that injury, an artificial abrasive material, Carborundum™, had entered the market and proved to be a suitable substitute for the more expensive mineral abrasives that were being used at the time.

Nothing the company tried paid off and debt continued to plague every action. At an August meeting, the board had formed a committee to study the possibility of making its own abrasive products. The only major conclusion of the committee was that Duluth would be a logical site for such a plant. By November, the usually cheerful, herculean Hermon Cable tendered his resignation from the board of directors, although the board tabled that resignation and Cable would ultimately continue his activity and investment in the company until his death.

Through November 1904 the board met weekly. Bryan, Budd, McGonagle and Dwan paid employee wages from their own funds and Dwan worked out agreements with creditors to extend the terms of some notes that were due. Dwan and Cable also went on the road to try and sell 6,000 additional shares of stock, offering one free share for every two that were purchased. Even this incentive failed to raise the hoped-for money.

The company was sinking and the proud, successful men who founded it were embarrassed when 3M stock dropped to a point that two

John Dwan worked tirelessly in civic and governmental affairs, as well as maintaining a busy law practice and insurance business. He also invested in numerous projects like 3M.

Bottom: *Dr. J. Danley Budd operated his own hospital and was a respected physician when he invested in the early 3M company. He would later withdraw from activity in the company, but held onto his stock.*

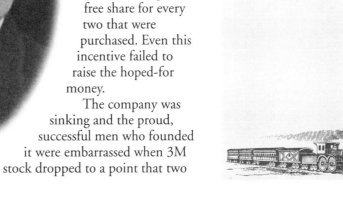

The Crystal Bay plant built by 3M.

shares were needed on the "barroom exchange" to buy a shot of rotgut whiskey.

At this point, an angel was needed and fate produced the right people at just the right time. Edgar B. Ober, a freight agent for a major railroad from St. Paul, had been an early investor in the company, putting up $5,000 early in 1903. He had followed the misfortunes of 3M for two years by the time he determined that the company had to get into the manufacture of its own abrasive products. He also knew that, unfortunately, the company was broke and would need a minimum of $14,000 just to pay debts that were due. If he did not act, he stood to lose his $5,000 investment. He contacted an affluent and influential St. Paul acquaintance, Lucius Pond Ordway, and convinced him that the company had a future in the production of sandpaper.

Ober outlined a plan whereby Ordway would put up the necessary capital to retire debt and maintain running expenses, obtaining 60 percent of the company's assets, which consisted of 285 shares of the earlier acquired Minnesota Abrasives Company and 222,846 shares of 3M stock. By the end of his meeting, Ober had Ordway's backing. The agreement also committed Ordway to loan the estimated $25,000 needed to equip a sandpaper manufacturing plant and supply needed working capital as required. An expert in the manufacture of sandpaper was also brought into the agreement.

The deal was signed by May 1905 and control of 3M passed from the local board to Ordway and Ober. Bryan and McGonagle, whose railroad duties took most of their time, retired from the board and sold their stock in the company for 15 cents a share. Dr. Budd also retired from the board, but retained his shares in the enterprise. Ober was elected president, Ordway as first vice president, Hermon Cable as second vice president and John Dwan remained as secretary. D.D. Smith of St. Paul was elected as treasurer.

All of these arrangements were based on the belief that the corundum at Crystal Bay was a valuable asset. The company was hardly out of trouble, but at least the founders were now debt-free and 3M seemed assured of capital when the need arose. Still, even Ordway's backing was strained, as the costs mounted to more than $200,000 at the new sandpaper factory in Duluth. Then came the realization that the Crystal Bay corundum was not, in fact, the abrasive mineral at all. It was nearly worthless, yet the mineral, mine and crushing plant would continue to be listed as assets on the company's books for a number of years afterward.

By 1909, the fledgling company had deduced that, not only were its mineral holdings on the north shore of questionable value, but the humid climate along St. Louis Bay in Duluth was not conducive to efficient drying of the glues that fixed the "sand" on the sandpaper. Drying ovens were not yet available or practical in solving this humidity problem. Also, since none of the principals of the company was located in Duluth, with Ordway, Ober and Smith in St. Paul and Cable, Budd and Dwan located in Two Harbors, the directors had little loyalty to the city where the original factory operated.

John Dwan had always urged that 3M maintain some business connection with its birthplace in Two Harbors, but Lucius Ordway and his board members had equally strong loyalties to St. Paul, where Ordway was widely known as a civic leader and booster. On August 20, 1909, Hermon Cable died of Bright's disease and John Dwan lost a valued colleague in his effort to maintain some 3M presence in Two Harbors. Apparently John Cable, Hermon's son, did not share his father's loyalty to Two Harbors, although he would continue his father's presence and stock ownership in the company and served on the board of directors for many years.

The company headquarters did officially remain in the boardroom above John Dwan's law office on the corner of Poplar Street (Waterfront Drive) until 1916 but, increasingly, all of the company activities except the occasional board meeting focused first on Duluth and would shortly be moved to St. Paul. In June 1916, the final chapter of the Crystal Bay mining endeavor was written, when a newly constituted board approved the sale of all the company's Crystal Bay machinery, equipment, tools, timber, dock and beach gravel for conversion of the plant into a lathe and sawmill. Although none of the mineral there had been used in the company's sandpaper from about 1910 onward, the company agreed to hold onto ownership of its "mineral" properties at Crystal Bay and Carlton Peak in Lake and Cook counties.

The board voted to move its factory to St. Paul and that was accomplished in 1910, a year after Cable's death. Thereafter, Budd and Dwan would commute to St. Paul for company meetings. In 1916 Budd divested all but 3,382 shares of his stock in the now promising endeavor. Dwan would maintain his position as secretary and legal counsel to the company and lived to see the start of the success of the company during World War I. He remained a director in the enterprise until his death on October 10, 1920, while attending to Minnesota State Fair Board business in Detroit, Michigan.

Held in high esteem by both the 3M Company and fellow Two Harbors residents, John Dwan's death was the first in the city to be observed by flags flying at half-mast and business being suspended for his large funeral. His son, John C., was elected to replace him on the 3M board in November 1920 and he would serve in that capacity through more than 35 years of phenomenal growth, profitable operation and development of dozens of innovative new products that more than fulfilled the senior Dwan's early investment and his years of hard work and faith in the

Hermon W. Cable and William McGonagle ***(bottom)*** *completed the original board of directors and investors in 3M. McGonagle would withdraw and sell his shares in the company, but Cable remained active in the company and on the board until his death in 1909, when son John assumed his father's position with the company.*

company for which he drafted the original charter.

Of the 3M north shore mining properties on Crystal Bay and Carlton Peak, 40 acres were sold to Rudolph Illgen for an early tourist resort at the site of Illgen City. Another 40 were donated to the state for Baptism River State Park (now part of Tettegouche State Park) in 1947. The remainder was later donated to The Nature Conservancy, which in turn gave the state the entire acreage at Crystal Bay when Tettegouche State Park was formed. The Conservancy would also contribute the parcel of Carlton Peak land for inclusion in Temperance River State Park. One additional parcel at Kennedy Landing east of Crystal Bay remains in Conservancy ownership.[12]

The years of Minnesota Mining and Manufacturing Company's early struggle was a period in which Two Harbors experienced increasing prosperity and expansion, as the investment by U.S. Steel continued to improve and upgrade their properties. As heavier rail, bigger more powerful locomotives and improved ore cars and other freight equipment became available, they were incorporated into the operations.

World War I, of course, produced a frenzy of ore shipping. Tonnages on the D&IR remained high through the five years that the war influenced the markets. More than 45 million tons were shipped through Two Harbors from 1916 to 1920, with an additional 515,800 tons going directly by rail to steel mills. At the same time, the D&IR's sister U.S. Steel railroad, the Duluth Missabe & Northern, was carrying more than double those tonnages.

The war saw a good many men from Two Harbors reporting for duty and 17 of those servicemen gave their lives in that conflict.

Demand for iron ore dropped in 1921 and the D&IR experienced nearly a 50 percent decrease in traffic. Despite the 1921 tonnage drop, the dock crew established a record of 16½ minutes to load 12,507 tons aboard the *D.G. Kerr*, which spent only 19 minutes in port to receive the record-setting load of ore. Legend says that two tugs were used during the loading to steady the ore boat against the face of the dock as the ore crescendoed down the chutes into the hold, but the accompanying photo seems to show that was not the case.

After the 1921 drop in tonnage, the iron ore market rebounded for the remainder of the 1920s and the D&IR maintained tonnages in the range of 5

Fastest loading time on record

Although demand for ore dropped in 1921, the dock crews loaded 12,507 tons of ore into the D.G. Kerr in a record setting 16½ minutes. The ship was reported to have spent only 19 minutes in port during the loading.

Facing page: *On the July 31, 1934, 50th anniversary of the first trainload of iron ore, Albert Headley and Thomas Owens were on hand to reminisce about the early days. Owens was engineer of the train. The park where the iron ball still sits is named for him. Headley had been a supervisor for the railroad during construction and later operations. The iron ball was constructed by members of the Carlstrom family, who discovered that the ore used was extremely hard and difficult to shape.*

million to 6 million tons a year. In fact, the future appeared bright enough that the company added three new heavy duty Baldwin steam locomotives in 1923. But that market turned downward to 3.3 million tons in 1931 and went totally into the dump in 1932, when a total of 410,714 tons were shipped from Two Harbors. That tonnage was so paltry that ore trains were discontinued and ore cars were simply added to regularly scheduled freight trains. The tug *Edna G.* was also shuttered during that year, leaving crewmen to seek other work to support their families.

By that time, the D&IR was being jointly operated by the Missabe in a lease arrangement. Upon the August 2, 1930, death of William McGonagle, Charles E. Carlson became president and held that position until he retired in 1944. The savings in overhead from joint management of the two railroads persuaded U.S. Steel that a merger into a single corporate entity was a wise move.The merger was finalized in 1938, when ownership of the D&IR was taken over completely by its sister line to the north and west – which had already been renamed the DM&IR after absorbing the Duluth-based Interstate and Spirit Lake Transfer railways that were also owned by U.S. Steel Corp.

To commemorate the two original companies, the rail line built by the Merritt family to connect their Mesabi iron mines to Duluth was named the Missabe Division, while the railroad built by Charlemagne Tower from Two Harbors northward to his mines was called the Iron Range Division.

Through the remainder of the Great Depression, ore tonnages on the jointly operated railroads did increase to nearly 10 million tons in 1933 and steadily climbed through the mid- and late 1930s, although only the momentary excitement of the merger offset a dismal tonnage figure of 8 million tons in 1938.

The tonnage of ore increased dramatically in 1939, jumping to 18 million tons as Europeans turned to the American steel industry to bolster their arsenals in the face of World War II. By 1940, the railroads serving the Mesabi and Vermilion Iron Ranges were experiencing a frenzy of activity, as 28 million tons of ore passed through Two Harbors and Duluth. Those tonnages would continue to increase throughout the war effort and the first of the giant Baldwin Works Yellowstone class of locomotives (Mallets) arrived in Two Harbors in the spring of 1941. Eventually, eight of these giants would work from the Two Harbors yards, hauling more than 9,000 tons of ore per trip.

But lines in a corporate ledger hardly tell the real story of the 1930s, for a one-industry town like Two Harbors was particularly prone to the vagaries of that industry. The downturn in the steel industry forced layoffs and cutbacks that sapped the resources of many families.

From the earliest days, roads have always been important in Lake County. In 1923, when the new lakeshore highway was opened, it was cause for celebration, even though long sections went unpaved for a while. Here, a Model A Ford traverses the recently blasted and graded Silver Creek Cliff leg of what became known as the International Highway (now Highway 61).

Roads: The Ties That Bind

From the very beginning, a great deal of private and governmental effort has been expended in building the system of roads to connect the various communities scattered widely through the sprawling expanse of Lake County.

From mere trails hacked through the wilderness in order to backpack supplies to remote homesites, the townships, county and state spent upward of 60 years of labor and investment in road development by the time that Alfred Sandvik went to work for the county Road and Bridge Department. He remembers that most county roads had been improved with gravel surfaces, but that a number of them were still narrow, winding trails.

From the time he was hired in 1948 as a member of both the county survey crew and the road crew until his retirement as county engineer, Alf says the county was involved in almost continuous construction work to upgrade and improve the approximately 350 miles of roads that the county maintained and/or snowplowed.

"As the county got more gas tax money, we were able to do more work, of course, but we never had what I'd call a huge project," Alf recalls. "In 1967, the Silver Rapids Bridge was one of our bigger contracts at about $250,000, which was a lot of money then. The improvements and paving on the Fernberg Road in the north end of the county from the county line to Lake One was also a big improvement. Before, it had been a narrow 16- or 18-mile winding trail and now it's a wide, paved road."

To maintain the network of roads, the county kept one employee (later two) in Fall Lake Township east of Ely and hired seasonal workers as necessary. Five employees worked on the crew based in Finland and the remainder of the employees worked out of Two Harbors – although crew members were temporarily assigned to work projects out of their normal work districts.

He notes that the county also has jurisdiction over two large unorganized territories where townships either disbanded or were never formed and that necessary roads in those large areas were also the county's responsibility. Although the population in that large area of the county tends to be somewhat scattered, those residents depend just as heavily on roads as the more densely populated regions.

"Many of our road projects were done in shorter segments over a few years and we might have more than one at a time," Alf says. "A number of our roads are also County State Aid Highways, which means that both the county and state pay certain costs for those roads."

Saying he has never tried to estimate the miles he traveled as a county employee, he smiles and says, "It would be a lot of miles because Lake County is a big area and you don't always have a road to take a straight line. For example, a trip to the end of Fernberg Road would always be a daylong trip and when we had crews working in that area, we had them stay at cabins and, later on, at motels, because there was no way they could travel back and forth to the job."[13] ▲

When the paved section of Highway 61 west of Two Harbors was opened in 1932, a large contingent of Canadians was on hand for the ribbon cutting ceremony.

As the Great Depression deepened and it became apparent that it was more than a momentary economic blip, various organizations and government agencies initiated relief programs to help people maintain some semblance of an income. Federal, state and county programs provided work for men whose jobs had evaporated in the panic. The Civilian Conservation Corps established 12 camps throughout the area where young men could earn $30 a month, with $25 of that sum going home to their families. The Works Progress Administration was organized to utilize unemployed men in public works projects and many of these, like the Two Harbors High School building, benefited not only the workers but generations of descendants.

It is also remembered by a number of longtime residents that the Lake County Work Farm northeast of Two Harbors provided board and lodging for indigent men and minor law offenders during the early years. With a substantial building site and large fields surrounding the area, the work farm was somewhat of a showplace where occupants worked in a variety of jobs to pay their way. The farm would later be sold to Dean Chicken and, still later, Maynard Johnson eventually turned it into a mink ranch that prospered for a number of years.

In the depths of the Great Depression, the late Ebner H. Anderson, a lifelong resident of Two Harbors who was born in 1908, four years after his father arrived in Two Harbors in 1904, grew tired of waiting for a call-back to a stenography job with the railroad, quitting in 1933 to join the Civil Works Administration of the county Welfare Department as assignment and payroll administrator.

In an interview shortly before his death in March 2000, Ebner remembered making weekly trips to pay workers in Knife River, Finland, Toimi and other locations where county relief crews were employed. Each man could earn up to $100 under the regulations of the program, then had to be laid off. Although he had some protests from workers who received their notices of lay off, he said that the men were generally polite and that most were happy to receive even the small amount of aid that was available.

"The ore trains were pretty much shut down, of course," Ebner recalled. "Some early government programs had men working on the breakwater and the railroad would try to find a day or two of work a week for employees. The Proctor yard operation had what they called an 'extra gang' to do some big jobs on the railroad.

"There was federal relief, state emergency relief and even a feed relief program for farmers, who shipped cattle from all over into the area up by Big Noise corner, where a crew took care of feeding them."[14]

Churches also joined the relief effort for parishioners and one of the more notable of these parish relief efforts occurred at Holy Ghost (now Holy Spirit) Catholic Church, where Father John Zarrilli supervised the enlargement of the basement to house a winter chapel and an auditorium in 1933. The work involved blasting and removal of 500 cubic yards of rock and 100 yards of dirt, without injury to either the building or any parishioner. As a result of this work, some parishioners claimed that Zarrilli preceded the federal government in establishing the WPA.

In a letter to the editor published in the *Two Harbors Chronicle*, Father Zarrilli outlined the success of the project. "Under the main part of the church, we constructed in solid rock an auditorium seating about 300 people, having a stage, clothes room, etc. To do this work, we had to blast 210 times under the church, but not even a piece of plaster was broken. The work was done by our own people at the very peak of the Depression, under a relief plan whereby men received $3 a day from the parish – $2 credit on their past-due pew rent from former years and $1 cash, which came in very handy at a time when a great many people were practically starving. Thus, while the work done was probably worth $7,000 or $8,000, our cash outlay was only a little more than $2,000."[15]

Even with the variety of public and private relief programs that blossomed during the Great Depression, life grew more and more harsh for those whose regular wages were interrupted. Parcels of government land in Lake County were still available for homestead claims and some families like John Gralewski's father and mother opted to move to rural areas and tried to wrest enough food from the land to keep the body and soul of their family together.[16]

Some idea of the vast tonnages of fish shipped from the north shore can be inferred from this photo taken (and probably staged) by William Roleff in the late teens or early 1920s.

John's family moved from Duluth and filed a claim for a 40-acre homestead in the Cramer area in 1932. With several relatives already living in the area, it seemed that they would be able to at least put food on the table, but the hardscrabble life on what can best be described as marginal farmland may have contributed to the ultimate separation of his parents.

The Depression would grind on until the end of the 1930s, but the tonnages of ore being shipped by the newly integrated DM&IR did increase after the low point of 410,000 tons in 1932 and more and more employees were called back to work on the railroad and ore docks. And even in the grimmest of those times, little things remain memorable. Ted Wahlberg remembered that a large bakery in Duluth was getting a lot of bread returned, because all the women baked their own bread to save money. The bakery began to toast their returns and sell large boxes of the toast for 50 cents. "That was great for morning coffee," Ted recalls, "especially if you happened to get a piece of one of the rolls that had jelly on it."

As the railroad rebounded from the Great Depression, workers began to repay debts they had amassed. Income picked up for businesses – many of which had helped tide families through the worst of times by extending credit beyond what might be considered judicious levels. Still, the businessmen knew most of these people from past dealings, knew them to be hardworking and honest and most of the businessmen understood that only a thin line separated a family's faintest of hopes from total devastation. Slowly the jaws of the worst economic disaster in America's history relaxed, but the bitter lessons of the Depression resulted in a resolve by many people to never again be caught without a rainy day fund. A few may have even carried this resolve to the point of miserliness.

Fishing

Wasswawinig, the Ojibway people called it – "The place to spear fish at night by torch light."

Their descriptive name for the Two Harbors area is probably only one of many Lake County locations named and favored by the natives for fishing, but it is a clear indication that the earliest north shore inhabitants regularly visited the area to harvest abundant populations of fish that cruised Lake Superior's shoreline and rivers. The Ojibway probably weren't the first and certainly were not the last to exploit the fish that teemed in the big lake.

Like the aboriginal people, early settlers depended on fish for sustenance, although an earlier attempt at commercial fishing occurred in 1834, two decades before the north shore was opened to white settlement. The American Fur Company operated fishing camps for several years at La Pointe, Wisconsin, Isle Royale, Michigan, Grand Portage and Encampment Island on the north shore and a number of other points on the lake. That fishery was successful in netting and preserving large catches of fish, but failed in the early 1840s because of the distance to and uncertainty of markets.

Following that failed effort, any fishing during the early settlement of the north shore was primarily to put food on the tables of the early settlers. That would change in the 1870s, when a scattering of Scandinavians began to settle on shoreline properties and introduce the efficient fishing techniques they had learned in their homelands. By the 1880s, Booth Packing Company had upward of 150 commercial fishermen on Lake Superior's north and south shores. The company served the fishermen with boats that transported supplies and delivered the catch to market.

The earliest of Lake County's commercial fishermen were surely part of that effort and Knife River is mentioned in several accounts of early commercial fishing – undoubtedly because of its somewhat sheltered location at the mouth of the river and the short distance to deliver fish to the rapidly expanding cities of Duluth and Superior, which provided a ready market by the mid-1870s.

These earliest fishing efforts were likely conducted by seasonal contractors who were spaced regularly at camps along the shores but did not settle as permanent residents. A bit later, the Scandinavian immigrants would establish the homesteads that made up a string of fishing families every half mile or so along the north shore during the heyday of the fishing industry.

While some accounts claim that whitefish and herring were the principal products of these early fishermen, there is some question about when herring first became a major fish commodity. In a biography of Benjamin Fenstad Sr., who arrived in Little Marais about 1890, a *Silver Bay News* article states emphatically, but without attribution, that after Ben Sr. settled and began fishing: "The fish caught by commercial fishermen at that time was the trout. Herring fishing came much later."[17]

Whatever the facts of those claims may be, trout was definitely a staple of the commercial fisherman's livelihood from the very beginning and local fishermen were definitely in the herring business by the peak year of the herring harvest in 1905, when a catch of 146 million pounds was registered by U.S. and Canadian fishermen.

While the early fishermen produced a hefty volume of fish, it was rare that they found themselves with more than a few coins to rub together, for they were usually pinched by a double whammy. They were dependent for supplies and groceries being delivered by the same freight boats that took away their catch. Depending on the price the company was paying at that moment – minus freight charges for delivery of supplies, groceries and the fish they shipped – fishermen would occasionally get a freight bill from the fish company because the check for their fish did not even cover the cost of moving them to market.

Nonetheless, nearly 400 commercial fishermen were noted along the north shore in the early 1900s, setting nets in spring and summer for trout and whitefish and switching to finer mesh nets for the heavy autumn run of herring. Huge catches were occasionally recorded during the herring run, filling the fisherman's skiff to the gunwales and making a long night of work in the cleaning and salting or icing of the catch.

A Rough Crossing

Probably there are as many hardship stories as there were immigrants coming to the New World, but the experience of 18-year-old Norwegian immigrant Ragnvald Sve illustrates that hardships on those passages came in a variety of shapes and styles.

Once Ragnvald received money from his uncle in Alberta to pay ship and train passage to Edmonton, Alberta, Canada, he caught a tramp freighter from Norway to England, where he expected to board a liner for North America. When that ship arrived, however, it had been badly beaten in a storm and had to go into a shipyard for repairs.

Passengers booked for the liner were reassigned to berths on a number of other ships sailing for Canada. Ragnvald was assigned to a Greek freighter. Once under way, he discovered there were only two other people aboard who could speak Norwegian – those being a lady who was returning to Canada after visiting relatives in Norway and her 5-year-old daughter.

After a couple of days at sea, the mother became seasick and stayed in her cabin. When he wanted conversation, Ragnvald was stuck talking to the little girl, which was hardly satisfying chatter.

By the time they landed in Montreal on New Year's Day 1921, the lady had recovered enough to ensure that Ragnvald got on the right train to Edmonton ▶

In his memoir entitled *Wonderland of the Herring Chokers,* Ted Tofte recalled his most memorable herring run as having taken place when he was a boy in about 1916. Herring Choker is fishing slang springing from the fact that the fishermen had to squeeze the fish to remove it without damaging the fine mesh of a net.

In four incredible days of work, his father's operation picked, cleaned and salted upward of 10,000 pounds of fish that involved nearly 24-hour-a-day labor by the entire family to keep up. Even if they received a whopping price like 2 cents a pound for that huge catch, the tally would be $200 – minus freight costs. Out of the remainder would come the wages to pay the two hired hands (most likely a percent of the profit) and the costs for supplies like kegs and salt, as well as the cost of any equipment that may have been lost or damaged. If there were bills pending, the fish company would also likely deduct those payments from the check.[18]

Almost certainly, by the time the transaction was completed, there would be little compensation for the many members of the family who labored long and hard to pick, dress, pack and ship the fish. Years in the future, after gas boats began to be used by fishermen, additional expenses for gas and engine maintenance would have to also be calculated. Seldom did prices rise above 3 cents a pound, but it was common for them to drop to a penny, or less. Little wonder there were few loose coins clinking in the fisherman's pocket.

Not only did fishing pay a little on the light side, the work could be hazardous, as well. Virtually every family involved in fishing has stories of tragedy, near-tragedy or lucky escapes from Lake Superior's infamous storms.

In his *Autobiography of a Herring Choker*, the late Tom Sjoblom, son of early Larsmont settlers/fisherfolk Victor and Sophia, remembered that the

Netting of fish didn't necessarily stop when Lake Superior froze over, as this photo taken at the mouth of the Beaver River shows. Nets would be set under the ice and could result in good catches of fish like the one pictured. The fishermen from left to right are identified as Art Lorntson, Marvin Amundson, Chris Jacobson, John Jacobson, Ed Mattson, Alfred Fenstad, Nick Peterson, L.A. Simonson, Peter Johnson, Oscar Lovold and Frank Thorngren. NORTH SHORE COMMERCIAL FISHING MUSEUM

constant vigilance for sudden storms, early ice chunks and white-out snows added to the misery of working with freezing hands in icy weather while pulling nets in late fall and winter.

Since a three- or four-day nor'easter raised a very real possibility that the nets and other equipment would be damaged or lost, fishermen were always anxious to get out to pick up and repair their nets as soon as possible after the worst of the winds died down. The skiffs were heavy craft that tended to plow the water as the oarsman rowed into the rolling groundswells that followed a big storm – sometimes with ice floes riding the waves. Those rhythmic swells meant that any fisherman who was sensitive to motion sickness was almost sure to get seasick – especially if the herring had been in the nets for a couple of days and were bloated enough to pop as they were squeezed out of the mesh.[19]

Ted Tofte related two incidents attesting to the dangers that storms posed. In the first, his father and two uncles rowed a skiff through stiff northwest winds and crashing seas to save a neighbor, who had lashed his skiff to an anchor buoy to keep from being blown out to sea. Ted reported that they rescued not only the fisherman, but tied his skiff at the back of their boat and brought it to safety as well.

Ted also remembered that his father, Andrew, didn't react quickly enough to an early November 1901 northwest wind, which suddenly blew into a gale that nearly swamped his skiff by the time he grasped the intensity of the storm. He made a desperate effort to tie up to a nearby anchor buoy, but had only gotten a momentary handhold on it before the wind wrenched the boat so powerfully that he had to let go of this last hope and was blown to sea. For the next 24 hours and without heavy winter clothing, he concentrated on keeping the boat from being swamped – maintaining its heading into the wind by rowing and bailing water to keep it afloat.

The storm was so powerful that a good-sized tug, used for log rafting, that was sent out for a rescue effort was forced back and had considerable difficulty returning to the dock. The tug's captain advised Andrew's family and neighbors that there was no way a man in one of those clumsy, cumbersome fishing skiffs could survive in those seas.

Nonetheless, as the wind abated the following morning, Andrew was still afloat in his skiff about midway between Tofte on the north shore and the south shore of Wisconsin. Sensing that he would now be able to make headway on his 25-mile or more journey back to Tofte, he rowed steadily for hours and surprised everyone by being at home when the neighbors returned from Lutsen, where they had gone to vote in the election.[20]

Beyond bad weather, though, other work involved in fishing carried risks. In his book, Tom Sjoblom recalled two particularly hazardous endeavors involved in fishing. The first was the setting of 300- to 400-pound "buoy anchors" for the nets as new fishing areas were opened. Tom's father used large stones from the shoreline,[21] while Ted Tofte indicated that big gunny sacks filled with coarse beach gravel were used by his father.[22]

These buoy anchors were set in the spring and as needed on new fishing grounds during the season. The anchors had lines attached that would hold the nets in place and were marked at each end of a net by a cedar "buoy" pole. Since the anchors cost nothing, no effort was made to retrieve them, but the thrifty fishermen did recover the attached lines at the end of fishing season, using a specially designed knife to cut the ropes.

An especially hazardous aspect of fishing occurred as each buoy anchor was tipped over the side of the boat from a wide slider board. They obviously sank "like a rock" and the attached line could entangle a fisherman or his boat as it was running out, causing certain disaster. Tofte recalled that two brothers in his area lost their lives in this way while setting buoy anchors.[23]

The coming of the gas engine to the fishing trade brought not only welcome relief from the labor of rowing, but the Sjobloms found that by enclosing the cooling system in a waterproof box, they had a place into which wet, frozen mittens could be thrown to be thawed and dried. That worked well, until fish scales clogged the air intakes and the engine overheated, at which point they were again forced to work with wet, freezing hands.[24]

▶ Finding that there was no one on the train who spoke Norwegian, Ragnvald was reduced to gestures in trying to find out the time or any other information he sought.

After five more days of this lack of communication, he arrived in 20-below-zero Edmonton and found his uncle waiting to greet him to his new homeland – in good Norwegian.

His uncle had a team of horses and sleigh waiting and told Ragnvald to climb under the straw in the back of the sleigh to stay warm during the trip to his farm, but Ragnvald was adamant on that point. "No sir!" he told his uncle, "I haven't had anyone to talk to on this whole trip and I'm going to sit right up here with you and make up for those three weeks."

After a couple of years of working on his uncle's farm to repay the passage money, Ragnvald came to Lake County, where another uncle had settled. The look and feel of the area made him feel right at home and he would settle on Minnesota's north shore permanently, first working as a blaster at Silver Cliff while the International Highway (61) was being built. While there, he met his future wife, Ragnhild Jacobson, the daughter of Silver Creek fisherman Julian Jacobson.

"Dad always laughed and said he had to come all the way to America to find a woman with as crazy a name as his," son Walter laughs.

After sailing on ore boats, Ragnvald ▶

It was common to continue fishing right to the time when the lake froze completely over. That meant plowing the skiff through the glaze of early ice. Larger chunks of floating ice were often blown in and created a serious threat. Not only were they dangerous for the boat, but they could also cut lines or drag nets away. Gathering the last of the nets in these conditions always presented challenges, some of which could instantly turn dangerous.

When fishing from skiffs was shut down by ice, some fishermen continued their occupation by setting nets under the ice – if the ice were clear enough to see through. This was done by chopping a hole that tapered from top to bottom in the direction the net would be set. A long pole with a line attached was inserted under the ice through this hole and the pole was "sent" (pushed) as far as possible in the direction the net was to run. The rope played out through the hole and

Ethnic I Been Svenska

The earliest settlers in Lake County were short-term and most likely to have been put on the land by speculators to preemptively claim the land if a deposit of rich mineral were discovered there. By the 1880s, however, settlers came to Northeast Minnesota for what they knew best – hard work, farming and fishing.

As with the rest of America, settlers in Lake County tended to show up in waves of nationalities as political and economic events in the various European nations fostered large-scale emigration first from one nation, then another.

Ranging from the Irish potato famine to a ravenous desire to own land or a desire to avoid governmental decrees like compulsory service in the armed forces of their native lands, immigrants found many reasons for leaving Europe to come to the United States and, in every case, this nation was the beneficiary as each wave of new European arrivals washed ashore here.

In the 1850s, many of the names appearing in memoirs and notes about Lake County have the imprint of the British Isles – with the exception of the Swiss/German settlers at Beaver Bay. By the 1880s, that scenario had changed and the settlers increasingly bore names that marked them as being Scandinavian in origin. Today, there is no question that those of Norse lineage predominate in the modern population.

It's unlikely we'll ever know exactly who the earliest of Lake County's Scandinavian settlers were, but Norwegian born Captain Charles Anderson is recorded as the first settler at Knife River, arriving there in 1869. Mons Jensen is recorded as the earliest fisherman at that settlement, perhaps as early as the mid-1870s. The Thompson brothers, Tollof, Teodore and Louis, of Larsmont may also have a strong claim, since they are recorded as settled in at farming and fishing at Thompson Landing before the D&IR Lake Line was built in 1886.

By the time the D&IR was being built, there were numerous immigrant Scandinavian workers who took construction jobs. Some of them would later continue working on the docks and railroad, but many saw the railroad jobs as temporary, choosing to save a bankroll at those jobs and claim homesteads that gave them the land they so earnestly desired.

And claim land they did. By the mid- to late 1890s, the entire lakeshore was sparsely populated by mainly Scandinavian fishing families like the Fenstads at Little Marais, the Thompsons and Jensens in the western areas of Lake County, Martin and Hannah Lorntson and their family settled in at Beaver Bay, along with numerous other early fishing/farming settlers who put down roots that would last.

By 1910, the Lake Superior fishery had attracted so many of these families that it's said that there was a fish house every half-mile along the lakeshore from Duluth to the Canadian border, and the fishermen extended their fishing territory by rowing their skiffs relatively long distances to set and retrieve nets.

Fishing and farming were not the only endeavors that these intrepid early settlers brought to the area, for they brought a multitude of skills and talents when they arrived on the scene. From craftsmen needed to keep the railroad operating to tailors and shoemakers to clothe the growing population and retail merchants to sell products needed by those families, the port city of Two Harbors drew a wealth of talented people for the opportunities it offered.

The first African-Americans in Two Harbors were likely Charles Colby and William Ray, who operated the Delmonico Restaurant from 1893-1895. It's unknown what became of Ray, but Colby apparently went to work for the railroad, since he made and served apple pie when President Calvin Coolidge made a train tour of the Iron Range in the late 1920s.

Scandinavians brought the idea of cooperatives to Lake County and by the ▶

another hole was chopped and a pusher pole with a nail protruding from the end was used to again send the under-ice pole on its way.

This was repeated until a point was reached equalling the length of the net that was to be set. The pole would be retrieved and the line that had been attached was used to pull the net beneath the ice, where its floats and sinkers would align it properly. Each end was anchored to a pole laid across the outermost holes. Once the tedium of this first set was finished, the net would be retrieved with a rope playing out under the ice from the opposite end, allowing it to be pulled back into place after the fish were removed. Tom Sjoblom noted, however, that it was common for the mesh to freeze in large masses during the interim when it was out of the water, creating difficulty in resetting the nets.[25]

The decrease in fishing during the winter meant that there was time for net

▶ mid-teens of the 20th century a substantial number of cooperative businesses were organized and operating throughout the area. There was little that could not be obtained through these businesses, with membership often restricted to those of Scandinavian lineage in the earlier days they operated. Later, they would be open to anyone who wanted to join the organizations.

In several of the outlying communities, Finnish was the language of record for the early governmental units – that ethnic group being the majority of settlers in places like Brimson-Toimi, Finland and Isabella. (Strictly speaking, "nationality" would be incorrect terminology for Finnish speakers until 1917, when Finland gained independence from Russia.)

German was the dominant language in Beaver Bay until the early years of the 20th century, when Scandinavians had overtaken the earlier preponderance of German speakers. By that point, of course, Beaver Bay's influence over county government had waned and the county seat was firmly located in the railroad town at Agate Bay, with English as the language of record.

Although many second generation Lake County residents clearly remember their parents speaking nothing but the language of their homelands, all agreed that the children of these ethnic parents quickly and easily adopted English and that few children who entered school were delayed by the need to learn English. The early school in Beaver Bay seems to have been the only case where classes were taught in German, but H.P. Wieland stated in his memoir that the books were written in English, which would seem to make for some rather convoluted educational exercises.

Memoirs of early Beaver Bay indicate that the use of German was so prevalent there that the natives adopted and used that language, although the German children also quickly and easily picked up the Ojibway that was spoken by their early school chums and playmates.

Of Native Americans, the earliest memoirs record that there were no "permanent" settlements along the shore in Lake County or in any other area where white settlement occurred.

It is noted, however, that temporary native camps were found in scattered locations for seasonal activities like fishing, maple sugaring or the harvesting of wild rice and berries. It should also be noted that the natives may have covered very large areas in their seasonal migrations, since the family of Chief Beargrease, father of famed mail carrier John Beargrease, showed up more or less permanently within a year or two of the settlers arriving at Beaver Bay in 1856 and there are also notations of a Beargrease occupying a site on Basswood Lake in northern Lake County that still bears that name.

While the immigration patterns of the late 1800s and the climate of northern Minnesota favored those of Scandinavian descent, the early records of the Holy Ghost (Spirit) Catholic Church in Two Harbors show a sizable number of French, Irish and other nationality groups present from the earliest days of the city. Many families with surnames like Shea, Belland/Beland, Griffin, Lassonde, LeClair, LaBounty, Gervais, Dwan, Archdeacon and Croke were present during or shortly after the railroad was built. They would establish their church by the latter 1880s under the religious guidance of the legendary missionary, Father Joseph Francis Buh, and many also held important positions in the business and civic institutions of the growing town, contributing to the mix of cultures that we ultimately see today.

Thus, while those of Scandinavian descent became the more numerous of the settlers, it was a mix of cultures and backgrounds that gave the city an increasing sense of its own potential and of the unique opportunities offered. ▲

▶ married Ragnhild and they moved into a 14-foot-by-18-foot combination home upstairs and fish house downstairs that he'd built on 54 acres of property at Split Rock River, which were purchased on time payments from the agent of a logging company. Ragnvald took up commercial fishing for his living. It would be 1936 and four kids later before they could move out of the cramped quarters above the fish house into their big new home on their property.

Continuing to fish, the Sves built two tourist cabins in 1932, calling that business Split Rock Cabins, and adding eight other cabins as tourism increased. They would offer deep sea charter fishing for a number of years after 1945. On busy days, Ragnvald and sons Leonard and Walter guided three charter boats for visiting anglers on the big lake, but Walter says the charter business died in the mid-1950s when the lamprey devastated the lake trout population.

Walter and his wife took over the business in 1974 and built the tenth and last cabin in 1976. Their son, Erik, is now operating the business and Walter, who worked for 30 years as a carpenter with contractor Richard Stone of Castle Danger, enjoys his "retirement" by continuing to fish commercially, selling fish to local restaurants and residents he knows are looking for the fresh herring he provides.[26] ▲

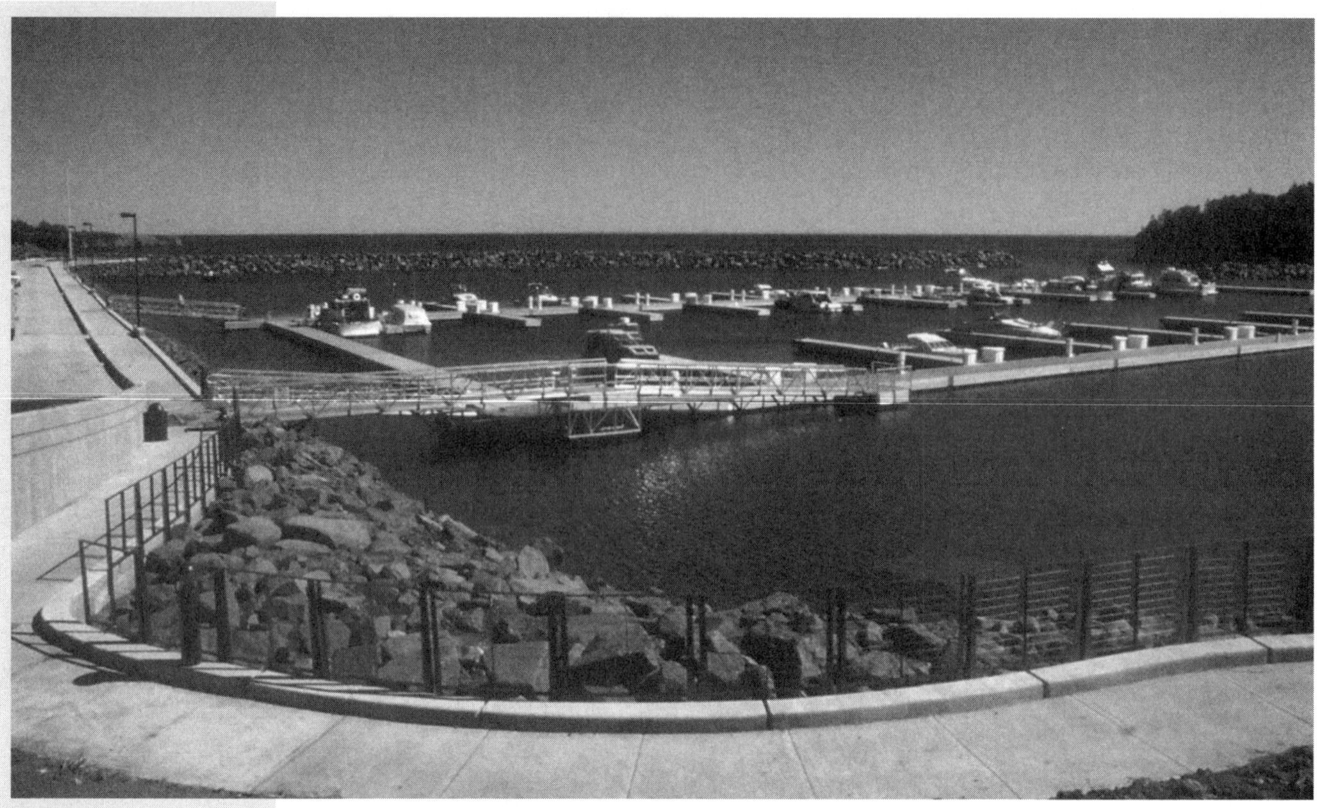

Silver Bay Marina is a second safe harbor refuge that boaters have embraced on the north shore. Opened in 1999, it immediately attracted the praise of the large boating community that uses Lake Superior. Full-service, it offers 61 slips, fuel, water, pumpout and other amenities.

mending, fashioning new sinkers and floats from molten lead and cedar blocks, repairing boats and making other preparations for the next season. There might even be time for an occasional nap to try to catch up on sleep lost during the fishing season.

A common winter chore was putting up ice, which was used in the packing and shipping of fish. The lake provided the ice in abundance, which was cut into chunks with a saw, lifted from the water with tongs and pulled up the bank to the icehouse. Sjoblom says that "kid power" provided a good deal of the muscle for moving and burying the large cakes in sawdust. Their reward was ice cream prepared in a hand-crank freezer the following summer.[27]

After the state highway was completed in the mid-1920s, fisherman were less dependent on boat or railroad shipping to market. Trucks from Sam Johnson, Kemp, Lake Superior, Hogstad or other fish companies made pickups along the highway. It was common to see large stacks of fish boxes awaiting the arrival of the trucks.

The market for fish dropped off in the early part of the Great Depression and a concerted effort was made to find additional outlets for fish – many tons of which were spoiling as the market plummeted. A mission in the Twin Cities agreed to buy a half-ton of herring a week at 2$^1/_2$ cents a pound and pay delivery costs. The fish were distributed in bread lines and provided some income for a number of fishermen – who were likely as poor as those receiving the fish, but with at least a source of food for their families. Fish were also bartered for vegetables, milk and other commodities.

In 1931, commercial fishermen became interested in a cooperative marketing effort being put together by George E. Morrison, editor of the *Two Harbors Chronicle*, Torstein Grinager, Lake County extension agent, and D.C. Dvoracek, a marketing expert from the University of Minnesota. Included in the newly formed Icy Waters Fish Mart of Two Harbors would be cold storage and facilities for preparing fillets and other forms of herring. Marketing efforts convinced Hormel, Walgreen's Drug and Liggett Lunchrooms to distribute the products. Lind Brothers of Castle Danger smoked the first batches to set the standard that Hormel required.

By February 1932, working in a former D&IR storage building, Icy Waters was smoking and shipping up to 1,000 pounds of herring a day, but encountered a glitch when six weeks passed without any appreciable catch of herring by the fishermen.

In July 1932, the North Shore Cooperative Fisheries was chartered and joined Icy Waters in marketing north shore fish to fish buyers. The cooperative also agreed to buy all fishing equipment for the fishermen at wholesale prices. By 1940, 130 commercial fishermen were selling their catches through the two cooperatives, with total sales ranging between $250,000 and $275,000 a year.

The success of the cooperative marketing groups fostered enough confidence that the Knife River fishing community took action to protect their boats and other equipment from a repeat of the damage caused by a March 1939 storm that piled 10 to 15 feet of ice over the shoreline and created havoc with everything in its path.

Although several plans to build a breakwater and harbor were presented at a public meeting, World War II interrupted the plans and local fishermen and other boaters had to wait for peace before taking steps to create a safe haven for boats inside the mouth of the Knife River.

The Knife River Harbor Association was formed, with members buying stock and investing their own time and money in the initial excavation for a safe harbor, with promises of government help. Later, the stockholders agreed to sign over their ownership to the county, which took action to improve the facility to make the marina amenable to recreational boaters, after commercial fishing had declined.

And decline this vital industry did – rapidly and inexorably. The introduction of smelt and lamprey into Lake Superior's waters over several decades – probably exacerbated by the massive tonnages of trout and herring netted by increasingly proficient commercial fishing during that same period – resulted in a decline in the harvests of trout and herring. By 1960, smelt had largely replaced herring as the major commodity of the commercial fishery, although a few commercial fishermen continued to take a few trout and modest catches of herring. In 1978, commercial fishing for trout officially ended, although a few old-timers were "grandfathered" to allow them to keep their licenses to take fish under strict guidelines.

Attempting to maintain a sport fishery, the state and a number of private organizations had been stocking millions of lake trout, brown and brook trout, steelhead, splake and herring, as well as introducing chinook, coho and Atlantic salmon to Lake Superior. At the same time, a lakewide effort was also attacking the lamprey with an arsenal of mechanical, electrical and chemical weapons that appear to have gotten that exotic species somewhat under control. These efforts were rewarded in the late 1970s and 1980s, as sport anglers began to report improved fishing on Lake Superior.

To help sport anglers pursue the increasing stock of game fish in Lake Superior, in 1985 the Minnesota Department of Natural Resources (DNR) undertook a major project to beautify and upgrade facilities at Lighthouse Point in Two Harbors. With the lighthouse beaming over Lake Superior to the southeast and the ore docks jutting out toward the location, this had always been a point of interest in town, but railroad ownership had stymied efforts to make significant improvements. A ramshackle dock that served as a boat launch could be accessed by a steep approach consisting of a couple of rutted tracks, but this was about the only improvement for public use at the site. A string of fish shacks lined the waterline, but had fallen into disrepair as the fishermen abandoned their trade and the buildings.

The DNR negotiated a lease from the railroad to improve the property for public use. The fish shacks were burned as a training exercise for the Two Harbors Volunteer Fire Department. The DNR shifted into high gear, creating a gently sloping approach to an excellent, spacious paved boat launch, landscaping major areas of the previously weedy and potholed grounds, grading and paving a large parking area, installing stairways from the paved parking area to the breakwall and down to the boat launch, placing convenient benches for boat and lake watchers and generally doing whatever was needed to create a major multi-purpose attraction that has become a favorite – not only with anglers, but a wide variety of other visitors and residents.

The completion of the Sonju Walking Trail along the scenic eastern shoreline from Fisherman's Point to Burlington Bay in 1998 added a new aspect of recreation at this historic and ever-changing location.

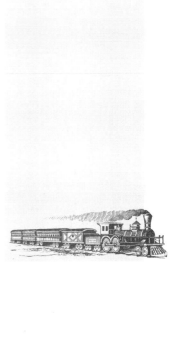

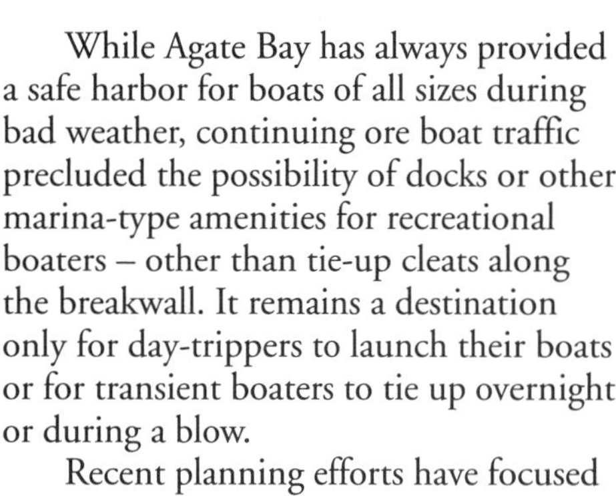

While Agate Bay has always provided a safe harbor for boats of all sizes during bad weather, continuing ore boat traffic precluded the possibility of docks or other marina-type amenities for recreational boaters – other than tie-up cleats along the breakwall. It remains a destination only for day-trippers to launch their boats or for transient boaters to tie up overnight or during a blow.

Recent planning efforts have focused on creating an inland marina in the vicinity formerly occupied by the railroad coal docks and time will tell if these plans come to fruition.

A decade after the 1980s success of the DNR's development at Fisherman's Point, the agency again got involved in creating a major facility for Lake Superior boaters – this time at Silver Bay. Designed to offer not only a harbor of refuge and boat launch, the Silver Bay Marina offers amenities any boater might want.

A joint project of the DNR and U.S. Army Corps of Engineers and an agreement with the city of Silver Bay to manage and operate the completed marina, the project involved moving and placing 92,000 tons of "armor rock" to create a large breakwater. Much of the rock was hauled in a continuous stream of trucks from Babbitt. The full-service facility occupies the original site of a city boat launch just west of Northshore Mining and adjacent to the city's Bayside Park. The Silver Bay Safe Harbor and Marina has seven acres of protected water, 61 boat slips, diesel and gasoline fuel, water, sanitary pumpout and an administration building where arrangements can be made for nearly anything that might be needed or desired by boaters.

Opened in 1999, the Silver Bay Marina was immediately lauded as a major improvement in boating safety and comfort on the north shore.

Today, the lake appears to have regenerated healthy populations of both trout and herring and continues to produce trophy specimens of the salmon that were introduced in the 1970s.

The huge influx of "smelters" that arrived with the frenzy of the spring spawning run from the 1950s until mid-1990s has declined – almost as rapidly as the numbers of this small, tasty fish. Commercial operators that once netted tons of the silvery smelt now find little more than empty nets. Theorists opine that the increasing numbers of large trout and salmon have simply foraged the once-vast population of smelt into grudging balance. As the smelt decreased in numbers, the populations of herring appear to have increased and commercial fishermen again report decent catches – though certainly not the vast production they once enjoyed.

Despite the hardships, low pay, hazards and sudden decline, commercial fishing was a vital industry for nearly a century of this area's history – not only to the hundreds of fishing families along the north shore, but to dozens of area merchants, fish dealers, the customers who ate the fish and dozens of affiliated businesses like Hill Brothers' boatyard in Larsmont, which built many fishing and other craft over the years – including the *Crusader* fishing tug that was christened at Thompsons' Landing at Larsmont in 1937 by Norwegian Crown Prince Olaf. The *Crusader* is now restored and on display at Lighthouse Point.

Other beneficiaries of commercial fishing were the boat and railroad companies that hauled the fish as freight and the companies that manufactured the few pieces of fishing equipment that the fishermen didn't make themselves.

Despite the overall success of the Lake Superior commercial fishery, the cold, wet toil with nets and other gear took its toll on the individual fishermen. Arthritis in the hands and wrists was a common, even likely, result of a fishing career – even for second or third generations like the late Lloyd "Cudda" Johnson, who produced a photograph of three specks on a frozen field of white that was obviously the ice of Agate Bay and the lake beyond.

"That's why I've got these achy hands," Cudda said with a grin, when asked what the picture was. "That's me and my brother pulling our skiff out to pick nets through the ice. We hauled gear in the skiff, but the real reason we took it with us was in case we broke through the ice. If that happened, you jumped into the boat right now, or you'd be a goner."

His eyes returned to the photo. "After a couple of hours out there, you felt like your hands would never get warm again –

and maybe they never did, from the look of them."

Steamin' Ore

Natural iron ore from the Mesabi Iron Range proved to be a particularly interesting product for the Duluth & Iron Range/Duluth Missabe & Iron Range Railroad to handle.

Unlike the Vermilion ore, the rich red hematite discovered on the Mesabi was fine grained and became viscous and sticky when wet – which was the case much of the time. Most of the Mesabi's open pit mines were at least damp, with some being absolute water holes. Adding to the problem in later years, a good deal of the ore was subjected to a washing process. This ore, when loaded into rail cars and joggled and compacted during the 70- to 80-mile trip to Two Harbors, was reluctant to leave the cars under the best of circumstances. After cold weather set in, that sticky situation hardened into a mass of ore that actually froze in the cars.

To get the sticky wet ore from the cars, dock workers called ore punchers would hammer the cars and use long poles to poke and prod the ore through the bottom dump doors into the dock pockets.

When colder weather set in, the dock workers found it necessary to resort to more imaginative measures. Steam was generated in a variety of equipment ranging from the tug *Edna G.* to the ships calling at the port and the locomotives owned by the company. That steam provided the means of thawing the stubborn frozen ore, making it possible to empty the railcars and transfer the ore to waiting ships.

Through the years, the memory of large plumes of steam rising from the railyard and the dock became an indelible part of the colder months of life in Two Harbors, as this vital labor contributed to longer shipping seasons and periods of employment of the railroad employees whose wages largely supported the town.

Prior to World War I, it's doubtful that steaming ore was ever a regular

Ore punchers were employed on the docks to prod sticky ore from the rail cars during warmer weather. As longer shipping seasons came to be common, the wet ore that stuck to the cars in summer turned to an icy mass that had to be thawed before it could be dumped into the dock pockets. Steaming the ore became a common sight on the dock and in the railyard during the cooler season.

Atop the docks, ore punchers had a grand view of the surrounding area, but were undoubtedly too busy getting the stubborn ore out of the cars and dock pockets to really enjoy their vista.

requirement, since the shipping seasons usually closed before seriously cold weather set in. As higher tonnages of ore were required for the war effort, it's likely that this technique was improvised with the resources at hand – steam being the logical means of thawing already wet ore.

Once this means of moving the wet ore in cold weather proved feasible, it remained an institution in Two Harbors – even through the 1950s, when Bill Johnson remembers that many of his late-1950s classmates were excused from high school classes during the end of the year to work steaming ore.

"They were hired just for the end of the season, so their wages came in handy for the holidays," Bill remembered. "Just about everybody in town depended on the railroad in one way or another, so letting the kids go ore steaming was seen as being important to the well-being of the town."

Somewhat later, when the company did substantial upgrading of facilities at Two Harbors, a car thawing facility was added – but even that improvement became almost obsolete when taconite pellets became the predominant product shipped from the docks. Pellets are dry and unlikely to either stick to or freeze in the ore cars.

Logging the North Woods

Using hand tools and horse and manpower, the lumberjacks of the latter 1800s and early 1900s harvested a prodigious amount of white and red pine logs, along with pulpwood and other timber products.

Alger and Knife River

Although timber and lumber were being commercially produced in Lake County from the early 1860s onward, the great logging era in Lake County did not get seriously under way until the 1890s. It was the arrival of the Alger-Smith Lumber Company and the beginning of its Duluth & Northern Minnesota (D&NM) Railroad at Knife River in 1899 that really ushered in the "boom times" of logging on the north shore.

Unlike most other areas where massive white pine logging occurred, northeastern Minnesota's rugged terrain, with narrow rivers rushing precipitously through steep canyons, extraordinarily long, cold winters and uncertain spring runoff all worked against driving logs to market on the rivers. The Sucker, Knife, Stewart, Gooseberry, Split Rock and most other north shore streams/rivers proved to be unsatisfactory water conduits, so this area awaited the development of logging railroads before wholesale exploitation of the pinery began.

Starting in about the mid-1880s, Duluth evolved into a sawmill boom town, as lumber mills of ever increasing production capacity were built. The availability of Lake Superior for transportation for both log rafts to the mills and finished lumber out of the harbor made the city second only to Minneapolis in production of Minnesota lumber products. By 1900, Duluth's western waterfront was literally studded with sawmills and other lumber-related equipment. Several of these mill complexes were capable of cutting upward of 50 million board feet of lumber a year.[1]

A bit farther inland, the less precipitous and more dependable flow of the Whiteface and Cloquet rivers and their tributaries converged with the St. Louis River, providing good waterways for river drives. Cloquet proved to be the handiest place to hoist logs from the St. Louis River, establishing that town as a major logging and wood production site. A fair amount of logs cut in western Lake and northeastern St. Louis counties were driven on that river system when logging was at its peak, but logs cut in the rest of Lake County tended to be delivered to mills using railroad transport.

For differing reasons, therefore, Duluth and Cloquet received a large percentage of the pine harvested in northeastern Minnesota – although a number of large and successful logging companies built roads and railroads to the Lake Superior shoreline, where huge rafting operations moved logs from the north shore to mills in Ashland, Wisconsin, and as far away as Baraga in Michigan's Upper Peninsula.

In time, the logging railroads of various companies crisscrossed nearly all of Lake County, with the Duluth & Iron Range often serving as the connecting link between logging spur lines thrusting

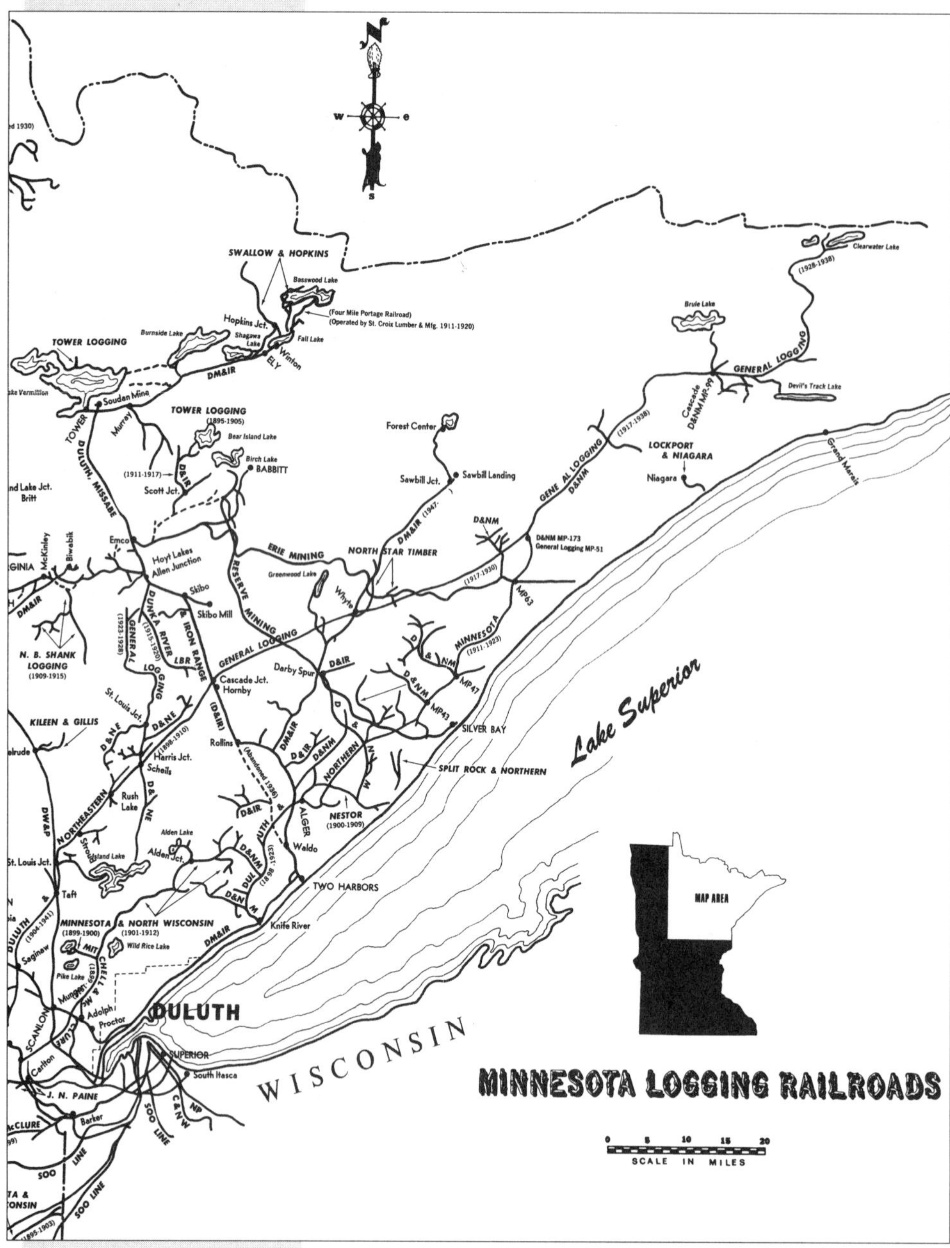

Compiled by Frank A. King.

into the cutting areas and the sawmills in Duluth or Cloquet that produced the lumber. Occasionally, the D&IR also built its own spurs into logging operations, although these tended to be limited to relatively short lines. The exception was the Wales Branch that meandered northeasterly to Whyte and was later extended to Sawbill Landing and Forest Center. Typically, the rail lines into the forest camps were laid quickly, used heavily and then either torn up and moved or extended to new stands of timber farther away.[2]

Today, the vestiges of most of these lines are little more than the unexpected, semi-smooth route through an area. A few scraps of metal or other hardware, an occasional memory by a real old-timer and a few names on maps are all that remain. But, once upon a time, somewhat provincial names like Lax Lake, Maple, Cramer, Cascade, Hornby, Echo Lake, Lenox, Forty Siding and dozens of others along the meandering rail lines meant serious business and the logs from these remote locations kept the trains chugging, the sawmills screaming and the nation's carpenters hammering. Today, most of the sidings and station locations have receded in recognition, bringing wrinkles to the brow of even the old-timers.

With the exception of the DM&IR's Wales Branch from Whyte to Forest Center on Isabella Lake, which was not built until after World War II, all of the logging railroads have been gone from Lake County's forests for 60 years or more. Many of the original grades for logging routes remain in use today as county, state and forest roadways. For example, about seven miles of Highway 4 from Fortythree Creek to the west and north of Lax Lake going toward Finland follow the original mainline route of the Alger-Smith Lumber Company's Duluth & Northern Minnesota Railroad – which provided passenger and freight service in the area from about 1907 onward, while moving tens of millions of board feet of logs each year. Although the highway was moved inland slightly away from the shoreline to allow development on Lax Lake, the railroad grade was adapted for much of this stretch of Highway 4. A fair number of miles of Highway 7 from Finland to Cramer and Echo and Hare lakes are also built on former Alger-Smith rights of way.

As previously noted, logging and lumber production in Lake County began in the latter 1850s, particularly with the Wieland operation at Beaver Bay, the Hibbard brothers' mill on Burlington Bay and the Flood sawmill in the vicinity of Flood Bay, the latter two being rather

Facing page: At one time or another, Lake County had many miles of railroads serving logging companies. For three decades and more, timber products constituted a significant income for the D&IR iron ore railroad as well. FRANK KING COLLECTION.

Left: Not notorious for frills, logging camps were hastily erected near a stand of timber, served the needs of the lumberjacks a year or two and were then either abandoned or the materials salvaged and moved to a new camp site.

shortlived. The Wielands' operation continued for about 20 years, before they sold their timber, sawmills and retail lumber operations to Gibbs and Mallett of Ludington, Michigan, in 1883. Even with that ownership transfer, the heavy, rapacious logging of Lake County's pinery did not hit high gear until the latter 1890s.

An early logging effort by a company called Miller and Gould is recorded in the Castle Danger area, using winter haul roads to move timber from nearby cutting areas to landings on the shore of Lake Superior. Once the ice went out of the lake, the stored logs were formed into rafts and towed by tugs to Duluth sawmills.

Mitchell & McClure Lumber Company, the operator of a huge mill capable of sawing more than 43 million board feet of lumber a year in West Duluth, also logged in the vicinity of Castle Danger and rafted logs from their landings there, recording some 5 million board feet from that operation in 1890. The company later pushed rail lines into Lake County off the D&IR Drummond line between Alger and Highland and built a 13-mile spur eastward from the D&IR that would shortly become part of Alger-Smith's rail operation into the Greenwood Lake area.

In roughly this same mid-1880s period, Scott-Holsten (later: Scott-Graff) Lumber Company was cutting timber along the Knife River and near Two Harbors and an operation headed by Barney Toppurn and another owned by Wheelihan and Potter are both reported to have harvested pine near Castle Danger. The pine cut in all of these logging operations was moved by sleigh and landed on the shore of Lake Superior to be rafted to mills in Duluth during the sailing season, but seldom would such an operation attempt to cut timber more than five miles from the landing.

Because sleigh haulage was the primary means of transportation from forestland to the rafting areas on the lake during this early period and limited the amount of timber that could be harvested,

Sometimes, the camps had a certain majesty, despite their remoteness and crude facilities. Standing in a grove, this unidentified Alger-Smith camp was captured by William Roleff, whose photographic record of the northeastern Minnesota logging era is unparalleled in quality and quantity.

Although railroads made extensive logging in Lake County possible, the day-to-day work in the woods was still done primarily with horses or – occasionally – oxen, which were preferred in wet and swampy areas because their divided hooves would splay and they were less likely to bog down.

Not destined to become one of the monster loads of logs that are more common in photographs, this sleigh is being loaded by Alger-Smith loggers using the traditional technique of horses pulling the logs up a skidway to the top of the load, where the toploader carefully places them.

the rafts might consist of logs from several companies – marked on both ends with a distinctive "brand" of the company where a log originated. This method of identifying logs originated in river driving, since the spring melt floated the logs of every logging operation on a watershed – all heading downstream in a headlong rush of water dammed along its route during spring runoff.[3]

With the 1898 arrival in Knife River of the first locomotive of Duluth & Northern Minnesota Railroad, owned by the Alger-Smith Lumber Company, the stage was set for heavy logging to begin in Lake County's white pine forests.

Prior to moving to northeastern Minnesota in 1898, Alger-Smith was already a major lumber producer and an experienced railroad operator in Michigan's Upper Peninsula, having chartered the 78-mile Manistique Railway in 1886 to move logs, people and freight between the company's timberland in the Seney/Germfask/Curtis area and company's large mill operation at Grand Marais, Michigan.

With huge holdings of timber in northeastern Minnesota by 1897, the company contracted with the Knox interests, which owned a large sawmill complex in western Duluth capable of sawing about 50 million board feet of lumber a year. Alger-Smith established Knife River as the main terminus of the D&NM Railroad operation. From the D&NM Knife River yard, log trains were switched to the Duluth & Iron Range Lake Line for delivery to the mill in West Duluth.

Although most of the timber was moved by rail, the company opened its operations in Minnesota on a somewhat smaller scale, using river drives from camps along the Pigeon River to Lake Superior, where they assembled huge rafts up to five million board feet that were towed to Grand Marais, Michigan, or Duluth by the Alger-Smith tug, *Ada*. An elaborate flume was built to sluice the logs around the High Falls of the Pigeon River and slide them safely to lake level.

But it would truly be the logging and railroad operations based at Knife River that would stamp the company as the bull of north woods.

The D&NM operation began modestly enough, as Joseph Rabey kept up steam while the company's *No. 1* engine was barged from Grand Marais, Michigan, to Knife River in 1898. Rail crews laid several lengths of rail on the beach and Rabey landed the locomotive as a storm was brewing. Crews quickly put down more track to get the engine off the exposed beach and into safer surroundings. That haste was apparently maintained after the storm, for rail crews pushed the mainline 7.5 rugged miles up the Knife River, bridging the river three times in the first three miles. That first year, the D&NM operated with two locomotives and 100 cars that shuttled logs from the forest landings to the Knife River switchyard and thence to the sawmill in West Duluth.

In 1899, the D&NM acquired the former D&IR *No. 3* locomotive (the *3-Spot*), which had been used when the railroad from Two Harbors to Tower was built and was later rented to the Scott-Holsten Logging Company in one of their operations. This relatively lightweight class of engine with its 2-6-0 drive wheel configuration was ideal for logging railroads because it worked well on the less than perfect trackage usually associated with logging.

After being assigned a new number, *No. 2,* the jaunty little engine served the D&NM faithfully for years in railroad construction during summers and log hauls in colder months, but was rather ignominiously abandoned when the D&NM ended operations. The little engine lay untended until a group of D&IR veteran employees salvaged and restored it as a reminder of the important part it played in the development of northeastern Minnesota and the iron industry. Likely, Thomas Owens, the first engineer of the stout little engine and later the superintendent of the D&IR, had a strong hand in that salvage effort, but president Francis E. House also took an active interest in the renovation effort. Alger-Line engine *No. 14* has also been salvaged and restored and serves as motive power for steam train tours that are operated by North Shore Scenic Railroad over the former D&IR Lake Line between Two Harbors and Duluth.

The D&NM eventually put down 99.8 miles of mainline track between Knife River and Cascade (northwest of Grand Marais, Minnesota, and south of Brule Lake) and upward of 350 miles of spurs, branches and other temporary trackage.

The D&IR No. 53 locomotive hauls 66 loaded Russel log cars from the Alger-Smith yards at Knife River to the sawmill at Rices' Point in Duluth.

Busy for more than 20 years, the Duluth & Northern Minnesota Railroad operated by Alger-Smith created a brief boom in Knife River, where the logging railroad turned over its freight to the D&IR for delivery to the Duluth sawmill.

As well as hauling their own logs, D&NM also connected with and moved timber products for other logging operations, as well as serving as a "common carrier" for passengers and freight for much of northeastern Minnesota.

Despite a few river driving operations like those on the Pigeon River, the primary destination for most of the company's logs was its large switching and storage yard at Knife River, where the D&NM transferred the timber onto the D&IR Lake Line. The log trains constituted a major part of the business on the Lake Line for about 20 years, even though the iron ore railroad sometimes imposed an embargo on use of its locomotives for log haulage during the busiest ore shipping seasons.

Whenever possible, Alger-Smith also used the D&IR mainline north from Two Harbors by running spur lines off that track into its logging areas in the vicinity. The timber from these operations would then either be shipped from the docks at Two Harbors or shunted through the D&NM yards to Duluth via the Lake Line.

As the D&NM mainline and spurs snaked north and eastward from Knife River into new stands of timber, Alger-Smith logging camps and convenient landings were built along the rails and used for a year or two, then were abandoned or the materials salvaged and moved to build a new camp in the next cutting area. Because this was an ongoing construction process, with old spur lines being torn up as timber was depleted, the same rail materials were recycled many times in construction of the many spur lines. In fact, when the company found no buyer for its Manistique line after its Michigan timber was exhausted in 1910, it simply moved most of that railroad's equipment and materials to the D&NM and used them here.[4]

Frank "Gunny Sack" Kane, who arrived in the area with the early Alger-Smith personnel from Michigan, was assigned as the boss of one of the earliest logging camps inland on the Knife and would become superintendent of the railroad operation. Uneducated but obviously talented, Kane was remembered as having a reputation as a ladies man, despite the fact that his wardrobe was little better than his nickname might indicate. But, with an expert eye for laying out rail lines, Kane remained important in keeping those rails creeping north and eastward throughout the history of the D&NM and would become

the last superintendent of the line before it was abandoned.[5]

Kane Crossing, about two miles from the townsite, was the site of the lumber camp that Kane first opened for Alger-Smith and was also important in the railroad operation, since inbound trains had to pause there to have brake retainers set on the cars to ensure that trains did not run away on the steep grade down to the yards. It was also the staging area where outbound trains were assembled after the locomotives "doubled the grade," pulling half the empty cars at a time to the top of the rise.

In time, the "Alger-Line," as virtually everyone referred to it (although it would also attain the moniker of the "Gunny Sack Line" because so much of the winter food supply came wrapped in burlap), would employ up to 15 locomotives in its huge operation. It stretched out 99.8 miles of mainline and transported something in the range of 40 million to 50 million board feet of its own pine timber a year for nearly 20 years, while also serving the needs of numerous other companies that set up operations in the vicinity of that mainline. The logging railroad did rent locomotives and other equipment from the D&IR as needed and such rentals were a profitable sideline for the iron ore railroad through the boom years of logging.

That all of this logging and railroad activity required a solid business and financing base goes without saying and General Russell A. Alger and M.S. Smith, the principal members of Alger-Smith Lumber Co., certainly met the qualifications on both counts. With a large central lumberyard in Detroit, the company sold lumber to retail customers or shipped lumber either from that yard or directly from the mill to wholesale customers.

At the time the company moved into Minnesota, General Alger was serving as the Secretary of War under President William McKinley (1897-1901), holding that position during the Spanish-American War.

Having established a Michigan logging operation in 1860 that immediately sank into financial difficulty during the panic that followed the start of the Civil War, Alger enlisted and distinguished himself in the Union Army, rising from the rank of private to that of major general during the conflict. Perhaps his most courageous act occurred as a junior officer, when he volunteered to ride into hostile territory to lead troops who were stranded back to the Union lines. One officer observed as he set out, "That's the last time we'll see Alger," but the young officer returned with the rescued troops and was decorated for the rescue.[6]

Following the war, Alger returned to Michigan and again got involved in the lumber business in the Upper Peninsula, where the Alger-Smith Lumber Co. was organized and operated a huge sawmill at Grand Marais amidst a widespread string

While the Alger-Smith did utilize the most modern equipment available in some of its operations, it was manpower that felled the logs and cut them into the best possible lengths for shipment to the mills.

Drifting downgrade on the approach to Knife River, a D&NM train has easy going to the yard. Outgoing trains, however, had to "double out" the grade on the way out of town, since it rose rather steeply in the first two miles.

of logging camps served by the aforementioned 78-mile Manistique Railroad. General Alger was elected governor of Michigan from 1885-87 and was elected to the U.S. Senate in 1903, following his stint as Secretary of War. He died in 1907 during his term as senator. Alger County in the Upper Peninsula of Michigan is named for him.[7]

Somewhat less public in his activities, Alger's partner, M.S. Smith, was a prominent banker in Detroit and served as president of the overall company. Some speculation is that Smith was primarily the money manager for the operation and took little part in day-to-day decisions.

Although they accumulated millions of dollars from their investment in the massive northern Minnesota operations, like Charlemagne Tower, neither of the partners ever actually visited their Minnesota holdings.

On the other hand, there is ample evidence that John Millen, the president and energetic general manager of the company's railroads, not only visited here, but regularly spent long periods in the Minnesota holdings and is said to have known virtually every employee of the railroad by name and was liked by nearly all of them. Indeed, Ralph Anderson, a youthful hostler on the railroad at the time, remembered that Millen invited him to have lunch in the fancy parlor car used by the Alger-Smith manager.[8]

A business associate of Smith and Alger since 1868, when he worked on a company railroad in Michigan that preceded the Manistique Line, it was Millen's job to get the new Minnesota operations under way.

In 1899, the D&NM rail lines had doubled to 15 miles, with a network of spurs and temporary trackage splayed in a crisscross pattern on the territory inland and north of Knife River. Alger-Smith then continued to extend the mainline eastward every year until 1918, when the decision was made to stop maintaining track, except for emergencies, and close down the entire logging and rail operation. But, as the mainline crept eastward over two decades, hundreds of miles of spurs were constructed to the company's scattered logging camps, which kept a flow of six to eight trainloads of logs a day moving through the Knife River yards.

Through most of its operation in Minnesota, Millen would continue as head of the D&NM. The profitability of the logging operation can be inferred from the fact that he traveled between the company's Michigan and Minnesota operations in a plush, specially built luxury car named the *Grand Marais* for the company's headquarters in Michigan. This VIP car was also used when Millen went on vacation or took business trips in the south, but it must have constituted a particularly incongruous sight to lumberjacks along the rugged, meandering D&MN mainline when Millen took inspection tours of the company's operations.[9]

Owned today by the Minnesota Transportation Museum in Minneapolis, John Millen's *Grand Marais* rail car still displays many of the niceties to which he obviously grew quite attached. Rich interior woodwork, stained glass and many fine furnishings that remain in immaculate condition attest to the style which Millen enjoyed and the care given the car by his successors, the Minneapolis, Northfield and Southern Railroad, which was acquired by the Soo Line in 1983. From 1957 until 1983, the car sat on the lakeshore near Walker, Minnesota, and served as a company retreat for officers of the MN&S Railroad.

But Millen was considerably more than a big boy with an expensive toy, for he built the premier logging railroad of the Midwest and dreamed of taking his trackage right to the Canadian border, where he believed he'd be able to make a connection with a Canadian line that would make the D&NM a profitable international link between Duluth and the lucrative western Canada business.

Only rarely did logging railroads use the cut and fill method of leveling roadbeds commonly seen on more established railroads and typically did only what was absolutely essential in the way of road preparation – even to the point of laying temporary, almost unballasted spur line tracks for short-term traffic after freeze-up in swampy or other soft areas. But the D&NM's rail lines traversed the most difficult of conditions and scarcely a mile of track could be laid anywhere that did not involve bridging, corduroying, cribbing and, sometimes, all of the above.[10]

The mapped rights-of-way of the logging lines appear tortuous and to meander aimlessly. They were actually laid out with an eagle eye on the best stands of timber by men who had cut their logging

Steam loaders greatly reduced the manpower needed to load rail cars. A gang working with the loader typically loaded up to 30 rail cars a day. Here, the loader handles the logs to load two Russel cars simultaneously.

The pulpwood dock at Knife River was added to the Alger-Smith properties at Knife River, as the harvesting of wood for papermills added income for the railroad and logging company. However, lumber remained the staple product of the logging camps throughout the period that Alger-Smith was the "bull of the woods" in northeastern Minnesota.

teeth designing winter haul roads that sloped seemingly forever downhill, so that teams of horses could haul the gigantic sleigh-loads that have been recorded.

Yet, even the best of these practical surveyors couldn't fight the north shore's character and in just the first two miles of its mainline track out of the Knife River yard the outbound trains had to climb 200 feet and were forced to make two trips ("double the grade") to pull the empties to Kane Crossing at the top of the grade. Conversely, incoming trains had to stop at Kane and set special brake retaining devices to ensure they did not develop too much speed heading down into the yard. Similarly, loaded westbound trains had to double the grade on a 4.5 mile section of track near Alger north of Two Harbors, where the mainline passed under the D&IR mainline.[11]

Despite the challenges posed by this rugged terrain, by 190l the D&NM had 46 miles of mainline track and was already pushing into the area north and east of Split Rock. In 1902, two spur lines were built off the D&IR's Drummond Branch into the Highland Lake area to fill a special order for long timbers to be used as pilings for the Chicago, Milwaukee and St. Paul Railroad's ore dock in Escanaba, Michigan.

That same year, the Alger-Smith bought 13 miles of railway that the Mitchell-McClure Lumber Company had laid northeast from the Wales Branch of the D&IR north of Alger. In that transaction, Alger-Smith also acquired the Mitchell-McClure sawmill in Duluth, the rolling stock of the railroad and 60 million board feet of standing pine accessible by the railroad. Originally, Alger-Smith contemplated routing its mainline on a portion of the Mitchell-McClure line it had purchased, but opted instead to treat that roadway as an extensive spur into its Greenwood Lake stumpage and to build its mainline farther south and closer to Lake Superior, from which it ran spurs in a jumble of configurations to its timber properties.

In addition to investing in timber, mills and railroading, Alger-Smith also invested in the latest logging equipment, like steam-powered loaders that would load 30 carloads of logs a day and replaced three work gangs, each of which consisted of a team of horses and four or five workmen.[12]

Northwest of Encampment Island, the D&NM crossed the tracks of the Estate of Thomas Nestor, another large, interesting Michigan firm (see discussion later in this chapter) that logged for almost a decade in the Gooseberry River watershed using a two-pronged rail system that reached well back into the forests from its landing at the mouth of the Gooseberry. The Nestor line crossed the D&NM just east of Alger and again northwest of Split Rock. Somewhat later in the area of the Alger crossing, the

D&NM built an interchange with the Virginia & Rainy Lake Lumber Company's landlocked short line railroad and may have also done some freight business with the Nestor in this vicinity. The V&RL used its own rolling stock and rail line to deliver logs that were destined for the company's Duluth sawmill over the D&NM and the D&IR lines.

Since the D&NM crossed most of the great fishing steams of the north shore, it began running the occasional summer excursion train for fishermen, offering stops at a number of rivers like the Knife, Stewart, Encampment, Gooseberry and Split Rock. As a common carrier freight and passenger line, by 1909 it was running a mixed train from Knife River to Finland, offering service to settlers along the way. Since the only competition to the railroad was boat transportation, and that only during the open water season, train service made settlement of inland areas along the D&NM route somewhat easier and had the advantage of being available on a year-round basis.

In 1909, Alger-Smith cemented its claim as the bull of the north woods by buying a tract of timber in Cook County from the Akeley and Sprague lumber firm that was estimated to contain a billion board feet of the best remaining white pine in Minnesota. This purchase gave the company enough stumpage to occupy its logging crews for at least 10 years and continue to deliver as many as 15 trainloads of logs a day to the Knife River yards. The company had also become serious about harvesting pulpwood and built the concrete dock that is still visible at Knife River to receive coal and to load boats with wood destined for paper mills farther down the Great Lakes.

By 1910, mainline trackage had been pushed into the Manitou River watershed about 12 miles north of Little Marais, although most of the logging was actually taking place a few miles back in the Lax Lake, Finland and Maple (on the east branch of the Baptism River) areas. So efficient were the company's logging operations that the best timber in this entire stumpage area only occupied the crews for about three years, when their focus of logging switched to the Manitou and Cramer area in about 1912. Pulpwood and other products continued to be harvested in the areas vacated by the logging camps, but the lumberjacks moved on to new stands of big pine and worked four years in the Cramer area, before that pinery was finished. The camps then moved to the area of Cascade and Little Cascade lakes in 1916, where they found enough timber for another four year supply as the railroad laid its

Duluth & Northern Minnesota president John Millen continued to dream of a connection into Canada via the Port Arthur, Duluth & Western (the PeeDee*) Railway at Mineral Center near Gunflint Lake, but his death in 1916 precluded reaching that goal. The D&NM would also die five years later.* THUNDER BAY HISTORICAL MUSEUM

The camp blacksmith was key in the efficient operation of a logging operation. Capable of making virtually anything needed in the woods, the blacksmith also shoed the horses, making it possible for them to pull enormous loads on roads that were glare ice.

final mainline trackage to milepost 99.25 and ran a 10- to 12-mile spur to the Brule Lake area to finish the pine there.[13]

As previously noted, President John Millen planned to push his railroad to the Canadian border at Gunflint Lake, where he envisioned connecting with the Port Arthur, Duluth and Western (PeeDee) Railway, which was built in 1893 from Port Arthur (now Thunder Bay, Ontario) to serve the shortlived Paulson iron mining venture in that area.

Millen believed the rail connection would develop good business between the ports at Duluth and Port Arthur/Fort William and western Canada. In 1912, he seriously considered ordering six large new locomotives to handle traffic on that route, but never got beyond planning. The Duluth, Winnipeg and Pacific completed a railway to International Falls/Fort Francis in 1912 and tied Duluth to the Canadian rail system at that location, rather than the Port Arthur/Fort William connection that Millen had envisioned.

Nonetheless, miscellaneous business on the D&NM was brisk, registering a high of 423,340 tons of freight and 14,863 passengers in 1918. Although this was nice added business, this local traffic was hardly at a level that would support an unsubsidized railroad operation and, for a number of years, the cost of operating and maintaining the ever-longer mainline out of Knife River had been increasing.

By the time of his death in 1916, Millen had apparently given up his dream of linking up with a Canadian railway, advocating instead that Alger-Smith build a line into Grand Marais and sell or abandon that long twisting mainline back to its yards and docks at the Knife. Since the company had considerable timber remaining in Cook County, a sawmill in Grand Marais would cut transportation expenses drastically and the harbor would provide good shipping for both incoming and outgoing cargoes. By that time, the eastern terminus of the mainline was only perhaps 14 miles as the crow flies from that harbor city and spurs extended as

Sunday in the logging camps were traditionally reserved for the 'jacks to do their laundry and take care of other personal tasks. Here, the loggers are boiling their clothes to rid them of soil and, no doubt, bugs of one type or another.

close as Devil Track Lake, where a launch was used to raft logs to a hoist and car loading area. The new rail line, mill and dock advocated by Millen would enable Alger-Smith to continue working its way north and east in the last of the big white pine timber stands that had sustained and been so profitable to the company for nearly four decades.

Although it's unclear how heavily Millen's death weighed in their decision, by 1916 or 1917 other interests had gained the attention of the company's principals. They were acquiring large timber holdings in Alabama and Florida, as well as investing in the neophyte auto industry in their hometown of Detroit. By 1919, the last of the timber was being loaded at Cascade and Alger-Smith's time of being the bull of the north woods abruptly came to an end when the decision was made to terminate the Minnesota operations. The Minnesota Railroad and Warehouse Commission ruled that the railroad must continue freight and passenger service for the settlers along its mainline, but that would prove to be only a temporary ruling.

In 1921, the D&NM received permission to abandon the rail line entirely and its assets were sold to an R. Waldron of Duluth, who was reported to be president of a group that planned to use the mainline as the route of the Duluth & Ontario, which would complete the line into Fort William that Millen had dreamed of. That plan was shortlived, however, and the line was sold to the General Logging Company of Cloquet, which took up all the spur line rails, the mainline track from Knife River to milepost 69.5, about seven miles north of Cramer and used the salvaged rail to construct a new mainline track that connected with the Duluth & Northeastern mainline at Hornby/Cascade Junction. The D&NM mainline from Milepost 69.5 to Cascade became part of the General Logging mainline as it stretched eastward to cut the pine lying north and east of the Cascade Lakes area to Clearwater and Rose lakes at the northern boundary of the state. By 1938, General Logging was finished and the last vestiges of the Alger-Smith Railroad were removed from the local scene and sold as scrap for the war effort.[14]

This rather ignoble end to what is unquestionably Minnesota's most colorful, successful common carrier logging railroad seems disquieting even today, but was a real thunderclap to the residents of Knife River. From a huge enterprise with hundreds of miles of rail lines, hundreds of rail cars, a dozen or more locomotives and hundreds of workers in the woods, rail and yard jobs, little but the wandering rights-of-way remained within a span of only three years. Yet, at the time, that was the way of the woods. Every consideration turned on the bottom line and for the Alger-Smith there was greater profit to be made elsewhere.

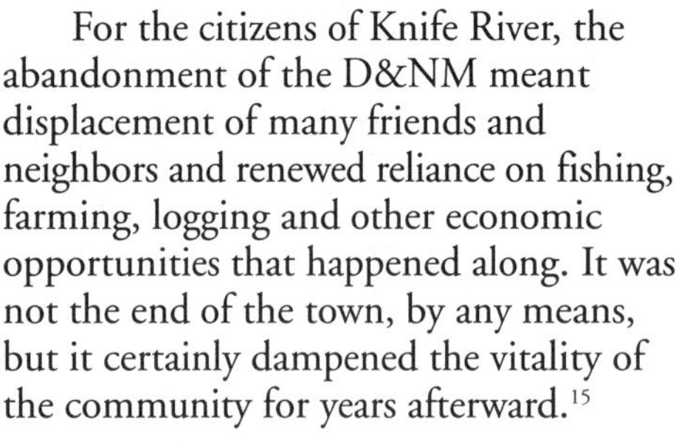

For the citizens of Knife River, the abandonment of the D&NM meant displacement of many friends and neighbors and renewed reliance on fishing, farming, logging and other economic opportunities that happened along. It was not the end of the town, by any means, but it certainly dampened the vitality of the community for years afterward.[15]

Split Rock

The Alger-Smith was not the only major Lake County logging endeavor. The same year that Alger-Smith settled at Knife River (1899), the Merrill & Ring Lumber Company of Duluth formed the Split Rock Lumber Company to cut the 200 million board feet of timber it had purchased in that river's watershed. The parent company had a huge mill complex on St. Louis Bay in Duluth capable of cutting upward of 40 million board feet of pine per year. The stumpage at Split Rock would constitute a sizable percentage of that mill's production over the next seven years. The Split Rock laid track for a railroad, with an unloading trestle and other facilities at the mouth of the Split Rock River. The company pushed the railroad inland for about 10 miles as logging continued along the two arms of its Y-shaped rail line following the river.

In an effort to avoid state and local property taxes on its log yard, rafting facilities, terminal and shops, Merrill & Ring incorporated the first couple of miles inland from the river mouth as the Split Rock & Northern Railroad and designated it a common carrier, despite the fact that it was not connected with any other railroad and never served any purpose other than hauling logs and company supplies. The company apparently believed that this ruse would place the most valuable of its assets under state railroad earnings tax in lieu of property taxes, but local officials didn't fall for the ploy and assessed property taxes totaling $1,500 for the three years of 1903-06.

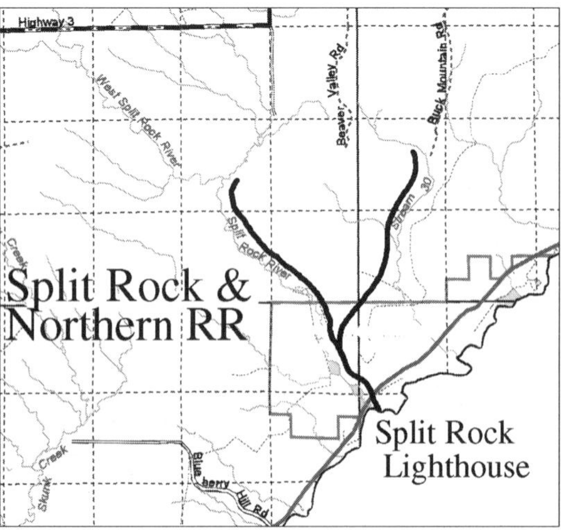

At the shoreline of Lake Superior, Split Rock operated a rail-to-raft operation to move the logs from its camps to the mill. Logs were hauled out onto a trestle over a pool that was dammed at the river mouth and were dumped into the water there. Cribbing held them in that location until rafting booms were formed to receive them on the lake. The logs were then sluiced out of the river into the booms, formed up into rafts and towed by the company's big, ocean-type tug *Gladiator* to the Merrill & Ring mill in western Duluth.

The Split Rock operations were so immense that seven years were all that was required to mop up the last of the 200 million feet of big pine in 1906 and cease operations at the end of that logging season. A few of the pilings for the rail trestle are still visible at the mouth of the Split Rock River.[16]

Gooseberry

The earlier mentioned logging firm with the odd name of Estate of Thomas Nestor also used a rail-to-rafting operation in the Gooseberry River watershed from 1900 to 1909, while also concurrently logging a large timber holding in the area of Grand Marais and rafting those logs from the harbor there.

The company name accurately represented the company's situation, since Thomas Nestor had established a large sawmill and logging operation at Baraga, Michigan, in 1881-82, after operating other lumbering endeavors in Michigan. Nestor's mill was rated at 40 million board feet and 6 million shingles a year, with a transportation fleet that included two steam barges and two tow barges, each capable of hauling a million board feet of lumber. In addition, a huge barge, the *Keweenaw*, was towed by the steam barges and added substantially to the lumber footages delivered by those vessels.

With this operation up and running successfully, Thomas Nestor died

Haul roads required constant work, including plowing the deep snow out of the roadway. After plowing, an ice road would require a liberal sprinkling with the water sleigh. After freezing, the ice would then be rutted, using special cutting equipment to create the tracks that the log sleigh runners would follow.

suddenly in 1890 at Baraga, with an estate valued at $3 million. The business was carried on jointly by his sons and a brother as the Estate of Thomas Nestor, encompassing logging in Wisconsin and Minnesota, as well as the Baraga mill and timber camps in that area. The scale of the Nestor operation was such that, in 1895, with no logging yet taking place in the Gooseberry pinery, the firm shipped 50 million board feet of lumber.

In 1900, the Nestor company paid $1.25 million for the entire north shore timber holdings and the sawmill that had been owned and operated by the firm of Knight and Vilas of Ashland, Wisconsin. Since the timber in the Gooseberry watershed was estimated to total 250 million board feet of pine and was valued at $4 per thousand board feet, the sawmill facilities were acquired for $250,000.

The records would seem to indicate, however, that at least the Vilas portion of that transaction may have only included the mill and the timber rights, since the land that Gooseberry Falls State Park now occupies was part of 30,000 acres of cutover land administered by the estate of former Wisconsin Senator William F. Vilas. Senator Vilas apparently believed that such logged-over land had value after the timber was harvested and had apparently profited by selling such cutover land to farmers and other developers after the pine was gone.

Interestingly, the Nestor acquisition was backed by the huge Calumet & Hecla Copper Company of Calumet, Michigan, which utilized enormous amounts of underground mining timbers, railroad ties and other lumber products. Since the Nestors' huge sawmill at Baraga, Michigan, was located only a short distance from mines operated by C&H on the Keweenaw Peninsula, the company was no doubt a valued supplier. The financial relationship likely cemented a supply of timber for the mines, while the Nestors' own capital could be invested in quickly starting their logging operation in this new territory.

Within a year, the company had a major logging operation on the Gooseberry and continued logging that watershed until 1909, pushing its two-pronged railroad northward and inland from its rafting yard at the mouth of the Gooseberry. In nine years of operation, the western branch stretched to within a couple of miles of the present DM&IR track north of Alger Crossing. The longer eastern arm of the Nestor railroad bore north and eastward to a crossing with the Alger line west of where the Silver Bay

Airport is now located on Highway 3. This arm of the Nestor would later provide some of the right of way for Alger-Smith's D&NM Greenwood Lake spur.[17]

While the Nestor and Split Rock logging operations were relatively shortlived, the rafts these operations floated became familiar sights on Lake Superior. The Nestor holds the distinction of having assembled and towed the largest log raft ever floated on Lake Superior – 6 million board feet – in 1901, the year after it opened the Gooseberry operation. The following winter, the company had 14 miles of rail and 800 men in five camps. By spring, 50 million feet of logs were banked at the mouth of the river to be towed to the Ashland or Baraga sawmills.

While there is some speculation that the Nestor railroad may have been a narrow-gauge operation, Todd Lindahl's research shows that the Nestor operation rented equipment from other railroads – which makes the narrow-gauge theory unlikely.

As previously mentioned, the firm of Mitchell-McClure was an early 1890s logger of Lake County pine in the Castle Danger area, rafting the logs from that location to their huge sawmill in Duluth. But the Castle Danger operation was relatively small in size and was done near the lakeshore, even while the company was building an elaborate rail system to haul logs from its larger holdings in Carlton County.

By 1901, however, with 60 million feet of pine stumpage east of the D&IR Wales line, Mitchell-McClure connected a spur from York on the D&IR and laid 13 miles of rail eastward into the forest. It would be the last hurrah for this old-line Duluth logging company, however, for Alger-Smith bought the entire company for

Equipping the Logging Railroads

Todd Lindahl has extensively researched and published a considerable amount of material about railroading in northeastern Minnesota. He says the early Duluth & Iron Range (later the DM&IR) Railroad operation included not only the haulage of logs for various companies in its service area, but also the rental of track and other equipment to the logging companies.

"As the D&IR replaced the original 60-pound rail (60 pounds to each three feet of length) with heavier 70-, 80-, 90- and 100-pound rail, the company held onto the old rail," Todd says. "The same was true as they replaced the older G and H class locomotives with bigger engines. When a logging company needed to build a rail spur, the D&IR would rent the equipment to the loggers at so much cost per length of rail plus the cost of renting any other equipment needed. Since a lot of those renters were tying into the D&IR for final haulage, it worked out well for both the logging companies and the D&IR."

Todd goes on to say that the smaller equipment being replaced by the D&IR was exactly what the logging operators needed, since the lighter rail was easier to handle and move around and was adequate for the logging trains. The smaller engines also worked well on the sometimes hastily built spur operations, since log trains were not nearly as heavy as the ore trains.

"After the ore shipping season was over, the train crews were pretty much laid off and some of them got jobs operating on the logging roads," Todd explains, while noting that some crewmen preferred going south when their work ended. "I guess you'd call them the first snow birds."

While the iron ore railroad preferred to keep older equipment and rent it to operators, the fate of the earliest and most famous of the D&IR locomotives differed.

"The Scott Holsten (later Scott Graff) Company was an early logging operator north of town and rented the 3-Spot for a while, but that ended when it was sold to the Alger-Smith in 1899. With a 2-6-0 drive wheel configuration, the 3-Spot was almost perfect on a logging railroad and Alger-Smith's Duluth & Northern Minnesota used it for a number of years in both summer construction and winter log hauling. It was scrapped as the Alger operations started slowing down, but the D&IR rescued it, rebuilt it and it ended up as a museum display."

Another time that use of outdated D&IR equipment didn't work quite perfectly had the Alger-Smith D&NM buying standard wheel trucks from cast-off D&IR ore cars to replace the 19-inch wheels on their Russel log cars, which the D&IR encouraged because the log cars would match up better with D&IR equipment that hauled the Alger-Smith logs from Knife River to Duluth.

"The 30-inch wheels changed the center of gravity on the log cars," Todd says. "That made them top heavy when loaded and they had a tendency to topple off the tracks, so that didn't work out so well." [18] ▲

$750,000, including stumpage, the new rail spur, the large Duluth sawmill and the rolling stock of the railroad. This rather low price may have reflected the desire by the principal investors in Mitchell-McClure to abandon logging in this area.

And, although railroads provided the means for the long haul from the woods to the sawmills of western Duluth, Robert Silver, who grew up in the Cramer area and now resides on Highway 61 in Schroeder, may be one of the last people who can testify to the use of an ice road and sleigh haulage of logs.

His particular memory was of a nine-mile ice haul road that followed the Caribou River Valley northward, where Alger-Smith was logging. His information was that this was the only such ice haul road used in the Alger-Smith Minnesota operations, but they were certainly used in many other companies' logging operations, often stretching for miles in downhill grades that allowed two- or four-horse teams to transport enormous loads of logs to river banks or train loading landings.

"This road was cleared 25 feet wide or so and there were six bridges across the Caribou on the ice road and two bridges across the Caribou on logging roads that joined the ice road. These branch logging roads were not iced, but were real good roads.They used 16-foot bunks (the cross-members of the sleighs, on which the lowest layer of logs was laid) ... so wherever there were turn-outs (where loaded sleighs could pass empties), the road had to be 40-or-so-feet wide." Silver stated.

Saying that Dick Coolidge of Knife River (the Knife River history shows only an A. Coolidge, a timber cruiser) was camp foreman for the large camp located on the Caribou in Section 23 where the ice road met a rail spur pushed into the landing from south of Cramer, Silver remembers later talking with one of the teamsters who drove a four-horse team on the sleigh road.

"He said the year they logged the Caribou Valley was a terrible snow winter. He said that after one terrific storm, they put 18 teams of horses on the snowplow trying to get the ice road cleared of snow. After the snow was cleared, there was the chore of hooking three teams onto the rutter and recutting the ruts for the sleigh runners. Of course, after the ruts were cut, (they) were continually hauling water with the tank sleighs, which were pulled by two teams. They naturally were going downhill loaded, but it took two good teams to pull the empty tank back up to their loading point."

Silver also remembered seeing the rutter lying near the old ice road until the years eventually rotted it away.

"The cutter was constructed of hewn 12-inch-by-12-inch birch timbers and the two outside timbers were approximately 20 feet long.... On either side was a cutter that was adjustable by a heavy threaded screw affair."

Silver went on to say that the ruts were cut between six and eight inches deep and that the entire machine, with its adjustable cutting apparatus, had been made by the camp blacksmith and woodworkers.[19]

Swallow & Hopkins and St. Croix lumber companies and Tomahawk Timber are discussed in Chapter 9 on the Winton, Section 30 and northern Lake County area, as is the DM&IR Forest Center rail line. North Star Timber Co. spur from Whyte on the D&IR Wales Branch (completed in 1917) east of Greenwood Lake to Isabella and the Scott Graff Lumber Co. spur off the Wales Branch to a few miles north of Greenwood Lake are discussed in Chapter 7 on Brimson-Toimi.

Knife River's Heyday

With the activity surrounding the arrival of the Alger-Smith Logging Company's Duluth & Northern Minnesota Railroad in 1898, the tiny settlement of Knife River entered its most active, glamorous period, serving as the company town for the railroad from 1898 until it shut down in 1919.

Prior to the Alger-Smith, as noted earlier, the area had first experienced a mini-boom in 1855, based on copper found in the rock formations in the area. Further exploration and a small mining endeavor proved that there was very little copper of commercial value. A bit later, an 1857 settlement named Buchanen was established just to the west of present Knife River. This townsite thrived for a short while, but was abandoned when the federal land office at the site was closed during one of the many economic depressions that marked that period.

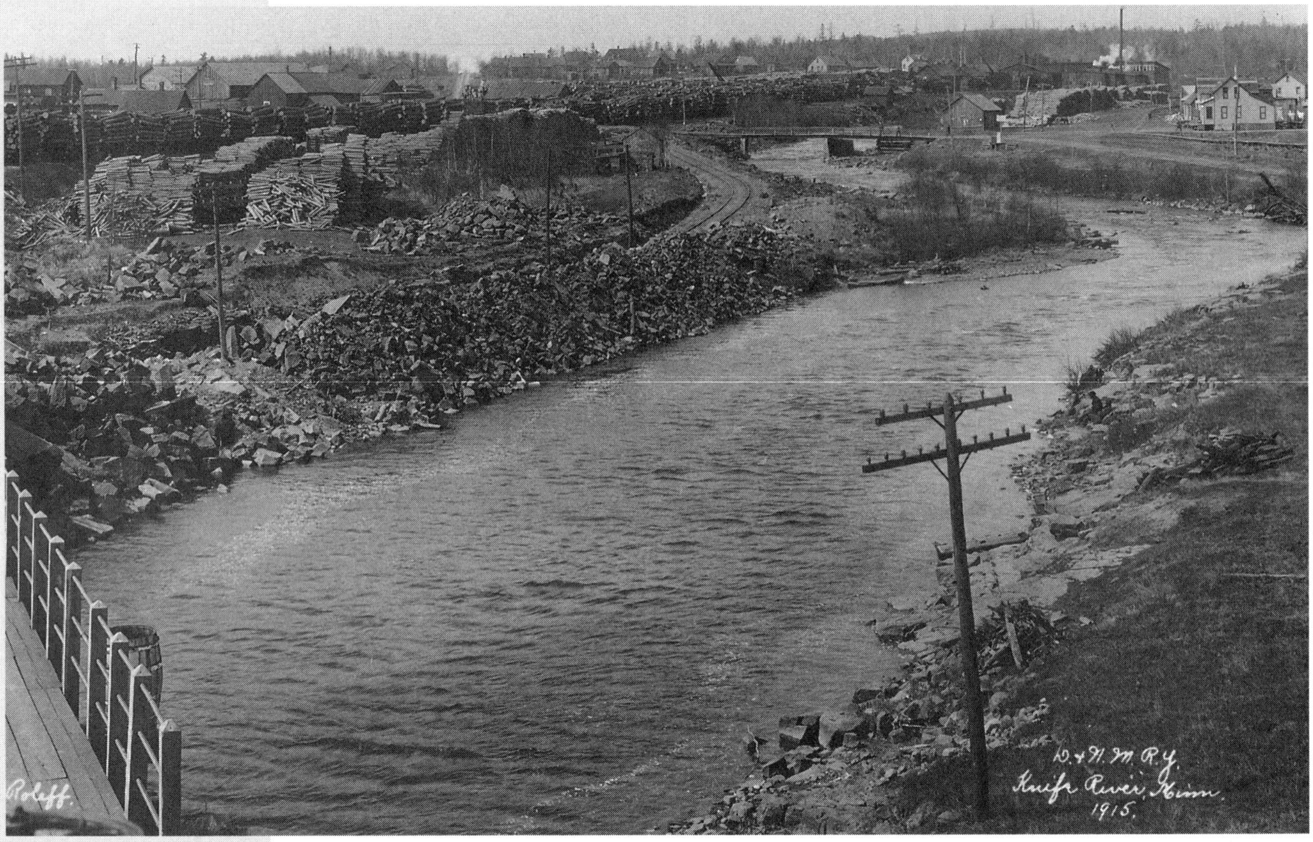

Following arrival of the Alger-Smith Duluth & Northern Minnesota Railroad, the tiny settlement Knife River boomed and remained an important railroad center for more than 22 years. As the terminus of the D&NM, it was the point at which the log cars were transferred to the D&IR Lake Line for delivery to the Duluth sawmill, but was also a transfer station for passengers wishing to travel eastward to points like Lax Lake, Finland and Cramer.

Captain Charles Anderson, a Norwegian seaman born in Oslo in 1840, and his wife, Serene, are recorded as the first permanent settlers in what would become Knife River. He is reported to have served in the U.S. Navy during the Civil War, attaining the rank of captain. After the war, he moved to Holland, Michigan, bought a lumber schooner and engaged in shipping wherever there was wood to be transported on the Great Lakes.

Likely, his wide-ranging voyages for lumber cargoes first led him to the attractive little cove protected by Knife Island at the mouth of the Knife River. In 1869, he purchased a sizable tract of forested lakeshore land on the eastern side of that river, built a log home there and moved his wife and three children to the site.

As the Booth Packing Company of Duluth began settling fishermen on Lake Superior shores, Captain Anderson sold small plots of his lakeshore to fellow Scandinavian fishermen for homes and fishing sites. Mons Jensen is recorded as the first of these fishermen and would later buy the original log house built on the property by Captain Anderson. Jensen was apparently shortly followed to the townsite by John Erickson, John Sandwick, Ole Barbo, Dave Lewis, Chris Roske and the Mindestrom, Hansen, Ojard and Bugge families. The family of Mr. and Mrs. John Mindestrom is recorded as arriving in 1884 with eight children.

When the Duluth & Iron Range Railroad built its Lake Line from Two Harbors to Duluth in 1886, some settlers at Knife River found employment opportunities on work crews, while others discovered ways to earn income by dealing with the workmen on the railroad, but this situation was relatively shortlived and the Knife River residents then returned to fishing, logging and clearing their land.

With the arrival of the railroad, the lakeshore settlers were no longer captives of boat shipping to move their fish and other produce to market and, although the Booth boats did continue to serve the townsite for several decades, the D&IR became an immediate and important means of transportation for Knife River area settlers and opened an easy commute to either Two Harbors or Duluth for both business and pleasure.

Even with D&IR rail service, development at the townsite remained rather stagnant for another 10 years or so – although Captain Anderson calculated that there were enough people to support the town's first saloon, which he opened during this period. His wife ran a boardinghouse for two years after the Alger-Smith railroad boom began in 1897 and he also operated a hotel in the same building as the saloon.[20]

Company attorneys initiated condemnation proceedings on December 13, 1898, in District Court at Two Harbors for a piece of land that was owned by Thomas Hillhouse, John C. TenEyck and Emma, William and Charles Paul. Captain Anderson also is reported to have sold some of his property to the railroad. These properties apparently became the foundation of the Alger-Smith D&NM Railroad holdings, which were to grow into the most extensive logging railroad in Minnesota – if not the entire Midwest.

As might be expected, the once-placid Knife River end of the railroad immediately experienced a frantic building boom, as the D&NM not only constructed its railyard, shops, warehouses and other facilities, but also struggled to provide housing for the families of workers it employed in its operations. It's recorded that builders worked long hours to keep up with all of the construction that was required as people flooded into the area to find jobs. In addition, a mountain of company freight was moving into the town – everything from materials required to build a railroad to food, snuff, clothing, pens and ink for the Johnny Inkslingers and every other article required to supply the lumber camps out in the woods.

The railroad shops were located on the south side of the river about a half mile upstream from the lakeshore in the general vicinity where the Highway 61 expressway now passes the townsite.

By the end of its second year of operations, Alger-Smith had extended the mainline railroad 15 miles north and east of Knife River. Its camps, yard, landing operations and the railroad had hundreds of men working – although former employees remembered that pay was a bit skimpy, even compared to wages for similar occupations at other companies. Ralph Anderson, a grandson of Captain Anderson and a youthful hostler on the D&NM, remembered in an interview that wages for a section hand were $1.75 a day, just slightly more than had been paid to similar employees when the D&IR was built years earlier in the mid-1880s.[21]

Having said that, however, it must be noted that, with the exception of World War I, there never seems to have been a shortage of manpower to work the railroad or lumber camps. And the employees and officials of Alger-Smith were not the only beneficiaries from this rush of logging.

As noted earlier, the Duluth & Iron Range Railroad quickly changed their role as strictly an iron ore railroad and became a major force as a logging railroad. As such, the railroad was able to keep a good number of its railroad personnel and equipment working year-round, since the shipping season for ore was the warmer months and winter was the season of heaviest logging activity. The D&IR also rented a good deal of the older, lighter rail and equipment that became obsolete in the iron ore operations to logging companies for spur lines and rolling stock. This provided an income from engines and other equipment that would otherwise have been sold or scrapped and provided logging companies with the kind of equipment and rail that worked best for them.

Approaching one of the three bridges spanning the Knife River in the first few miles of trackage, this D&NM log train heads for home as brake retainers restrain its speed on the downhill grade.

1585. Log Train on Duluth and Northern Minnesota, Knife River, Minn.

Merchants also found it profitable to set up business as the D&NM was getting up and running. Captain Anderson, the pioneer settler who opened the first saloon, also operated a hotel at the same location, but would shut down his business when it became apparent that Prohibition would become the law of the land at the end of the second decade of the 1900s.

A large logging and railroad operation requires a sizable number of men moving into and out of the woods. Jack Pepper's Hotel at Knife River likely saw a good deal of that transient traffic. Note the Fitger's Beer sign on the cornerpost of the porch.

Perhaps the best known and most successful of the early retailers at Knife River was Archie McPhee, who arrived from Michigan with the first wave of Alger-Smith employees. While it is unknown if he was encouraged by the company or not, within a year he had established the first general store in Knife River. Archie and his establishment became a favorite with virtually the entire town. Extending credit with a somewhat open hand, he also had access to the railroad telephone lines and would take orders from and ship out supplies by train to settlers all along the ever expanding line of D&NM tracks.

As perhaps the most successful merchant in the town during the boom years, Archie profited throughout the period the Alger Line operated, selling his business to Arnold Wiley and Sig Erickson in the early 1920s after Alger-Smith shut down. They maintained the business, with an annex on the building also serving as the post office for several years. McPhee's storekeeping experience was not retired when he sold the business and he is reported to have moved to California, where he opened another store.

Jack Pepper built a hotel bearing his name next to the tracks, which passed directly in front of his building. He operated there until 1911, when his hotel burned and took the tracks with it – forcing the D&NM to reroute on D&IR trackage until rebuilding could be finished.

Shortly after McPhee left town, Martin Bugge, another storekeeper, who was located a couple of blocks away, also disposed of his business. His nephew Wesley indicates that Martin joined McPhee in business in California, but went broke there.[22] The Volstead Act went into effect in 1920 as Alger-Smith was shutting down the last of its operation, casting a real pall over the businesses in Knife River. Captain Anderson had already shut down his saloon and hotel and the building was purchased by Bill Kendall, who used it as a warehouse. Many of the other business buildings from this boom period were simply abandoned or were converted to other uses.

As might be expected in a town where hundreds of men were shuttled to and from logging camps, a number of early businesses were operated that would not, perhaps, bear too close a scrutiny – however the descendants of the early pioneers stated that the town was mainly a peaceful and orderly place. As was common in boomtowns, a number of boardinghouses and hotels accommodated those who did not have more permanent housing.

An interesting side note to the movement of men in and out of logging camps on the railroad is that lumberjacks leaving the woods were not allowed in the passenger cars operated by the logging railroad, since the 'jacks were usually infested with lice and the railroad management wanted to protect their paying customers from the possibility of being exposed to this nuisance.

Settling In – The West

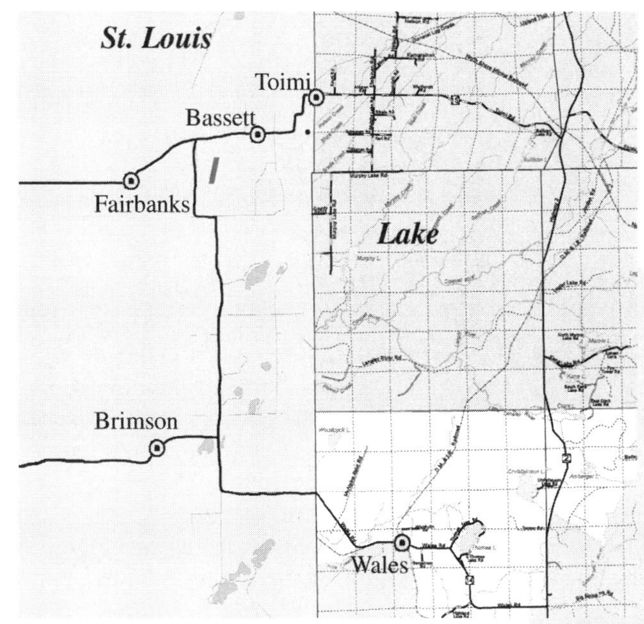

Brimson-Toimi Area

Undoubtedly, the early isolation and the large rural area that we call Brimson-Toimi makes it a bit problematic to tell exactly where the spirit of Brimson leaves off and that of Toimi begins, but the St. Louis/Lake County line is, at least, a geographical boundary, with the Toimi community solidly based in Lake and Brimson in Ault Township of St. Louis County.

Though technically not part of Lake County, Brimson has always been economically associated with Two Harbors, since the early construction of the Duluth & Iron Range Railroad through the area made a commute to Two Harbors for business or pleasure relatively easy. From there, one could catch a train for Duluth and make connections for anywhere in the world.

Arthur Wolf was the first station master at Brimson Depot, built in 1884 and first called Cloquet River. The name would later be changed to honor Walter Brimson, an earlier Duluth & Iron Range Railroad superintendent. A Mr. Quigley was listed as first postmaster, but early records show that there were no settlers in the greater Brimson-Toimi area as late as 1890 – other than those who worked for or settled immediately beside the railroad tracks, making distribution of mail considerably easier than it would be a few years later, when settlers scattered widely in the area.

Surprisingly, given the preponderance of Finns in the area, the early 1900s census reports for the Brimson-Toimi area through the 1920 census enumerate few, if any, Finnish settlers. Each, however, lists Russian and Swedish settlers. A substantial number of family names that appear in public records prior to 1920 strongly suggest Finnish origins.

After 1920, censuses would show many Finns in Ault, Fairbanks, Bassett townships and the Toimi area. This is probably explained by the fact that Finland did not declare independence from Russia until 1917 and was only organized and recognized as an independent republic in 1919. Those earlier settlers may, thus, have correctly listed their birthplace as "Russia," even though they were from the area that later became Finland. It is also true that some "Swedes" enumerated in the census reports likely came from Finland, since a fair number of Swedish people did remain there and spoke Finnish, while retaining their Swedish identity after Russia took over the Finnish territory in the early 1800s.[1]

The Brimson-Toimi Legacy, a history compiled by citizens of the area, records that many of the earliest settlers, circa 1900, walked upward of 12 tortuous miles from the Fairbanks station into the area that became Toimi, often carrying all of their belongings by hand and back muscle. It's

As shown here, Brimson is officially in St. Louis County, but much of its history has been tied to Two Harbors by the railroad. Toimi, on the other hand, is firmly within Lake County.

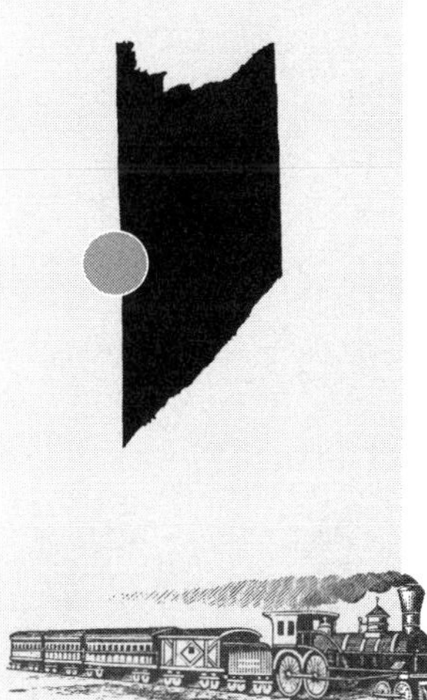

also interesting that these early Finnish settlers are said to have used the voyageur portaging technique of moving as much as they could handle for a quarter to a half-mile, setting that load down and going back for another load. Thus, by the half-mile traverse, their goods and belongings were moved to their new homesite.

Alvin Kuchta is shown as an early settler who worked for the D&IR Railroad and first lived near Milepost 50, about a mile north of the Highway 44 crossing. He would later move to Breda and take a homestead there. His son, William, is recorded as the first white child born at Cloquet River, before that name was changed to Brimson. Another early railroad employee was John Bodey, who lived with his family at Milepost 49 by about 1890 and worked with his son at the control block system for train control. Vestiges of the Milepost 49 operations are said to be still visible from the tracks south of the Highway 44 crossing.[2]

The George Ault family, for whom Ault Township in St. Louis County is named, originally lived east of Indian Lake, but moved to the Brimson Depot in 1903, when he was appointed depot agent. By that time, Betsy Highland, a widow with five sons and a daughter, was already serving as Brimson postmaster and would occupy that position from 1902 until her death in 1926. She had earlier run the boardinghouse for section crews and bought the early Brimson store that was originally opened by Gust Tuura, had the building moved to the west side of the railroad tracks and ran it as the post office and store for nearly a quarter century.

By the time the earlier settlers moved into the Brimson-Toimi area in the early 1900s, the logging companies had already cut much of the huge virgin white and red pine from the land, leaving mainly cutover land, second-growth and scrub timber for the settlers. The first timber was apparently cut in about 1880 and driven down the Cloquet River, utilizing a system of dams at strategic locations to impound enough water during spring runoff to keep the logs moving downstream during the river drives – the last of which is reported to have taken place in 1924. The earliest logging efforts were likely relatively small, compared to the huge operations that would be carried out later in the 1890s, when rail transportation became the preferred method of delivering logs from Lake County's rugged terrain to the huge sawmills at Cloquet and western Duluth.

Somewhat later, Oliver Iron Mining Company, a division of U.S. Steel Corporation, which owned enormous acreages of timber in the area, built a sawmill and logging headquarters on the railroad near Indian Lake. The lake served as the holding pond for the logs and it's reported that there are still a fair number of visible "deadhead" logs in the water from that period.

The Oliver sawmill produced mining timbers, railroad ties and other lumber for Oliver's vast mining holdings on the Mesabi and Vermilion iron ranges. That iron ore was an important part of U.S. Steel Corporation's assets when the company was formed in 1901 by merging a number of the largest steel companies into a single entity. U.S. Steel also acquired both the D&IR and the Duluth, Missabe and Northern Railroads in that merger. The two railroads were later merged to become the Duluth, Missabe and Iron Range (DM&IR) Railroad of modern times.

In 1906, a station house was constructed at Breda, where freight had previously been simply dropped along the tracks for retrieval and transport by whatever means were possible – oxen, horse, boat or manpower. Cattle chutes were located on the rail line at Brimson and Rollins for handling the horses and cattle that the logging companies shipped into their camps. Both locations also became important centers for shipping logs and lumber to market.

Later, the presence of the huge blackened pine stumps left by the logging companies raised the resentment of the Finnish settlers toward the companies, which had profited handsomely and then simply abandoned the wasteland they created.[3]

But these isolated settlers were not without their own means of getting satisfaction, according to an account in Irja (Laaksonen) Beckman's book, *Echoes from the Past*, which tells the story of her family's arrival in the Petrell (sometimes spelled Petrel) area in 1912 and much of what happened in the community thereafter.[4]

The Laaksonen family arrived in the Brimson-Toimi community in 1912 and put down deep roots on the homestead near Petrell. Daughter Irja Beckman recalled that her mother and the children were quite disappointed with the small two-story house that existed on the place.

"Some (logging) company holdings still had a few stands of virgin pine," Beckman relates. "One year, the settlers went en masse and cut down the trees (my father among them). They imported a sawmill to saw it into lumber. Not one of them, honest to the core as they were, felt that he was doing anything wrong. Instead they felt they were righting what they felt was an injustice – the scarcity of timber on their homestead claims.

"An effort was made to trace the trespass, but proved unsuccessful, in spite of a distinct sleigh track which led right through a farmer's yard. When questioned, he played dumb, knowing very well what happened to the logs, for had he not been a party to the trespass himself?"

Irja also noted that fish and game enforcement was a bit scanty in the area, while stating that both fish and game were plentiful and provided a sizable amount of the early settlers' diet.

"It was not an easy matter for a game warden to make a raid," she writes. "If he should step off the train some day, a human grapevine would have passed the word around before he got very far. It was one for all and all for one.

"Once a game warden did get off the train at Fairbanks. He stopped at the store, inquiring about the settlers in the hinterland. The storekeeper told him, 'If I were you, I wouldn't attempt to go into the interior alone. Who knows, you may not return.' The game warden took the next train back."

But her book also makes it clear that there was not a lot of what we would consider common comforts or conveniences, for she relates that when her family moved to their homestead in 1912, the train was met at Breda Station by an earlier settler, Mr. Palomaki, who guided the family on a mile-long trek through wilderness to Breda Lake, then rowed them a mile or so across to Petrell Creek and about three miles upriver, then guided them another mile or so to the homestead.

Once there, she says her mother and the children were considerably disappointed in the small two-story house, with a single room on each floor. Although she notes that there was a somewhat passable road beside the farmstead and a schoolhouse about a quarter of a mile away, the best of the road was apparently quite a short route, for she says she later took a ride in a wagon with a neighbor lady to the store located in the lower level of Petrell Hall. Shortly after leaving the homestead, the road abruptly became an obstacle course of stumps and huge boulders that had not

yet been removed from the right of way and bounced the wagon so roughly she was lucky not to be thrown out. The store was credited as being the first cooperative store in the area and supplies were hauled eight miles from the Brimson Depot by horse and wagon, likely on roads not much better than the one she describes.[5]

Roads were definitely one of the major concerns of the early settlers and improvement to logging tote roads soon became a focus of the pioneers. In fact, the early minutes of the various township boards all show the road and bridge fund being financed at two, three and four times the level of money allocated to other projects funded by the general fund. Those funds would buy a fair amount of work, too, since laborers on Ault Township roadwork earned $1.75 to $2 a day in 1909. A decade or so later, a man and his team of horses earned 40 cents an hour, but only after he may have already driven the team for a couple of hours to get to the jobsite by daylight.

One of the earliest roads was a rough logging trail that ran west from Brimson to a dam on the west branch of the Cloquet River, with an eastern leg running around the north end of Indian Lake and south of George Lake. By 1910, the eastern leg was apparently good enough that Harry Skinner could transport the lumber for a large Sears, Roebuck & Company house from the depot to the south side of George Lake, where it was erected. Here, Skinner, a conductor for the D&IR, is credited as starting a large farming operation, with hired hands caring for cattle, sheep, horses and other livestock and the vegetables and other crops he sold to the logging camps. About this same time, Emil Johnson and Clint Howell were also cultivating vegetables for the logging camps.[6]

Despite these tales of early agricultural success, Irja Beckman records that farming in the area was certainly no guarantee of prosperity, stating that frost could strike even in midsummer and that chilly windless evenings usually found the settlers setting bonfires around their small rocky fields and fanning the warmth of those fires with gunny sacks to keep their potatoes and other vegetables from frost damage. The effort would be a nightlong ordeal that she credits with saving many a potato crop.

Weather wasn't the only hardship on farmers, for the area was so rocky that Finnish people commonly referred to it as "Kivi Kontri," meaning "rock country" or "land of rocks."

Putting up ice was a winter activity that assured that rural families would have a way to keep perishables from spoiling. It also allowed them to occasionally make ice cream from the real cream produced by their cows.

That early services and conveniences in the area were crude is beyond question. In *The Brimson-Toimi Legacy*, Martin Tommila, an early resident, remembered, "The roads were questionable at best. During the winter season until 1930, snow removal was done by hitching two or more teams of horses to a wooden plow. We can well picture the results. Much traveling by individuals was done on skis."

While amenities were not abundant, the neighborhood did have the railroad for contact with the "outside" and nearly all the early settlers remembered the warmth of community get-togethers, with dancing, entertainment and plenty of food and coffee. Schools were among the first organized community efforts, although Irja Beckman notes that few of the early teachers stayed much more than one school year, with some leaving almost immediately upon discovering the isolation of their appointed teacherage.[7]

One service that was provided early and continuously was mail dropped from trains at the Brimson and the Fairbanks railway stations. It was then delivered to various other distribution points by mail carriers, the earliest of whom, Kalle Aho, is reported to have first hauled the mail out of Brimson by following a trail marked with blazes on trees. Subsequently, Jacob Viitanen hauled the mail with a horse-drawn wagon from the Brimson station to a post office located in the Nick Kylen home, which also housed a small store.

In the Toimi area, the first post office was opened in a sauna owned by Kalle Ranta. The mail had to be picked up at Fairbanks and hauled to the post office, where settlers took turns picking it up and distributing it in their immediate neighborhoods. Three rings of families would carry the mail three times a week, delivering it to points where neighbors living farther away could pick it up. Later, Matt Justinus Beck became postmaster and worked from his home. The office then moved to the Finnish Supply Co. in Bassett and a route was again maintained along which residents brought mail to central locations for pick up by other families.

Since far and away the largest percentage of homesteaders in the area were Finnish after 1910-1915, the early mail carriers were mostly Finnish and that continued to be true through much of the later period as well.

In a short column she wrote, former Toimi resident Donna Carlson recorded that her uncle, Victor Harju, delivered mail on foot in the Toimi community. "His starting point was his homestead on the Murphy River and back again. When you realize that Fairbanks, where he picked up the mail, was approximately 20 miles away, the enormity of those treks was truly impressive."

She also records that a trip to pick up supplies at Fairbanks was a daylong affair, starting in the dark of early morning, with a kerosene lantern for light, and arrival back home after dark, again using the lantern to light the pathway. The earlier settlers were restricted on these trips to what they were able to carry on their backs, since roads were non-existent.[8]

By the early 1920s, trucks had been driven into the community from Duluth over the Brimson-Kelsey Road (Route 547) and were used to haul mail, but winter delivery was still accomplished using a team of bronco horses, according to the area history. How long that remained true is not recorded, although it had no doubt ended by the time that motorized snowplowing began in 1930. Although numerous residents are listed as carriers and postmasters, the family of Arne Rinne, who won the contract for mail service in 1947, without question holds the longevity record, with three generations of the family serving as mail carriers continuously since 1947. As this is written, a daughter-in-law, Joyce Beck Rinne, whose father, Verner Beck, served as carrier from 1935 to 1939, continues to deliver in the community, although that trip now entails driving to Two Harbors to pick up mail for delivery on State Road 2 and through the Brimson-Toimi area.

As important as early mail service was to the early residents of the community, the stringing of wires from home to home may have been a more momentous event – giving residents direct telephone connections to one another and to the outside world through a long distance hookup with the Duluth & Iron Range Railroad's lines at Fairbanks. The

He "Milked" North Star Timber

Eligible for the draft by 1942, Castle Danger native Richard Stone took a job driving trucks with the North Star Timber division of Kimberly-Clark that winter, working from a large camp at Avoy.

"The company had five camps scattered from Skibo across to State Road 2 north of the Erie Mining crossing," Richard remembers. "My job was to haul supplies from Duluth to whatever camp ordered them. Suppliers only handled certain items, so I'd pick up stuff all over Duluth – everything from hardware from Marshall Wells in Canal Park to meat, canned goods, tobacco – whatever was on the list. After I had everything, I'd head back to whatever camps had ordered the stuff and deliver it.

"These were really big camps with a lot of men and horses, so I made the trip every day. In the fall when they were stocking up for the winter, I hauled a truckload of canned milk every day for a week, just to supply the camps with that one item." ▶

Fairbanks Farmers Cooperative Telephone Association was chartered in 1916, with the official language being Finnish and each subscriber agreeing to pay 25 cents a month plus their long distance toll charges. Operators were expected to be able to translate freely from Finnish to English or vice versa and eight short rings on the telephone crank would call out virtually everyone within earshot of the jangling bell. The eight shorts were used in emergencies, as well as for general announcements of such events as meetings or the welcome relief of a dance or party to which the community was invited. Of course, the party line system also encouraged "rubbernecking" by the curious, the lonely or those who were simply bored on a long winter day.[9]

Each subscriber bought their own wooden telephone set, which was wall-mounted and featured a hand-crank magneto for ringing and dual batteries for voice transmission. The subscribers were also responsible for so many poles and a specific footage of line for the five circuit system.

This telephone system continued until 1950, when it was re-organized as

Originally called the Toimi Co-op, this store was later renamed Brimson Co-op Store No. 2 when the two groups united in 1946. Most of the country stores have long since closed. Hugo's at Rollins remains a vital part of the community life.

the Brimson Telephone Association, which then repaired and upgraded lines and equipment and continued in operation until 1966, when it was sold for $600 to Northland Consolidated Telephone Co. In 1972, that company was purchased by CONTEL Telephone, which installed new cable and established two-party lines. Single-party lines arrived in 1991, after GTE bought out CONTEL, at which time touch-tone dialing and other upgraded equipment were installed.

For the record, Keith Koski made the last hand-crank long distance call from the exchange on March 14, 1969. His call to Two Harbors officially ended the pioneer phone system, which shut down the following day, thus bringing to an end what is surely one of the most successful cooperative enterprises in the area.

Another "highlight" for the rural community was electrification that arrived in 1951 via Co-Op Light and Power Association of Lake County. Although it required dynamite to blast the holes in which to set the poles, Uno Hyopponen's pulpwood loader made an easier job of lifting and setting the poles in place for the highline. Permanent residences got first service, with seasonal homes receiving power somewhat later. With the coming of electricity, the Brimson-Toimi area held a "shindig" at Bassett Hall and, according to then Co-Op Light and Power manager Bill Himango, "There was a good turnout!"[10]

But, even though the coming of modern conveniences meant a better life for the settlers in the area, it remained remote through much of its history and was most easily accessed during the first 30 or 40 years by catching a train at either the Iron Range or Two Harbors ends of the railroad.

To offset this remoteness, stores scattered throughout the community offered a wide range of goods to those in their immediate vicinity. The earliest such establishment shown in the history of Brimson-Toimi was that of Gust Tuura, which was built at Brimson on the east side of the railroad tracks in the early 1900s. As noted earlier, it was purchased by Betsy Highland, moved across the tracks and also became the Brimson Post Office, with Betsy as postmaster until her death in 1926. A succession of owners kept the establishment open and operating until it burned in 1981 – which resulted in the organization of the Brimson Area Volunteer Fire Department in the fall of that year.

As would be expected in a heavily Finnish community, the cooperative movement began early in the community. The Finnish Supply Company was organized in 1908 with members of the consumer group buying $5 shares to raise a total of $125 to capitalize the venture. First housed in a one-room building and operating three days a week to allow the staff time to transport goods to restock shelves, the operation built a new two-story building in 1910 that included meeting rooms on the first floor. It continued to operate as a cooperative through good and bad times until 1934, when disagreements among members led to failure. Jacob Wesala bought the business and operated the store as a private business for several years.

Meanwhile, two other cooperative stores had been organized in the area, the first being the 1908 organization of a group buying club with headquarters in the basement of Petrell Hall. In 1913, the operation, called the Farmers Store Association, moved into its own building, but articles of incorporation and bylaws were not adopted until 1928. This store struggled through most of its history, with a relatively small population in its service area.

The second co-op store, Toimi Co-op, was organized in 1932 and would operate independently until 1946, when the Farmers Store and Toimi Co-op merged and were renamed Brimson Co-op Stores, with the Farmers Store becoming No. 1 and Toimi being named No. 2. The Toimi branch was closed in intervening years and Brimson Co-op Store No. 1 burned in 1958 – thus ending the community's efforts in cooperative retailing.

Another store was built in 1922 by Albin (Dick) and Blanche Hassel a few miles away at Rollins. That establishment also had a succession of owners who were apparently successful through the years. In 1934, along with other remodeling, Otto Wallin, a Duluth fireman who owned a cabin on Stone Lake, put in a couple of booths for the sale of beer and the rest, as they say, is history. In 1958, Hugo and the late Gladys Hellman bought the store, which became Hellmans' Store. Hugo logged and managed the store for nearly 30 years, selling it in 1987 to his youngest son, Kevin, and wife, Mary. They renamed the establishment Hugo's Bar, remodeling and enlarging it. It remains a business and social center of the community.

Community halls were likewise important in the early social life and development of Brimson-Toimi. The earliest, Petrell Hall, completed in 1913, was built of hand-hewn logs, with lumber for the roof and trimwork cut by hand by crews of volunteer laborers using a whip saw. Edwin Petrell donated a piece of his homestead for the site and was also the operator of the cooperative buying club in the lower level of the building that later became the Farmers Store Association. Many years of community activities occurred there before deterioration threatened the historic "log hall." By 1984, it was apparent that the hall had to either be razed or restored and a community effort resulted in renovation work that has saved the building.

The Toimi People's Hall was not as fortunate. Opened in 1924, the hall hosted most of the events occurring in the community. But years of age and weather led to leakage that rotted the joists and allowed the dance floor to sag. In addition, mud from heavy rains washed into the kitchen and destroyed a wall. By 1964, fewer and fewer people attending fewer and fewer events meant that ticket sales would not support maintenance and the Toimi Hall Company sold the building to Wayne Carlson for salvage. In 1983, he put the structure out of its dilapidated misery, collapsing the walls and roof of the 40-foot-by-80-foot building onto the dance floor. An interesting side note is that many mattresses were assembled in the hall during the 1930s, with a number of families from the area participating in this do-it-yourself effort.

In addition to the community halls, social life in the community also centered on the several schools that served educational needs and the two churches, the Toimi Finnish Evangelical Lutheran and the Bassett Congregational churches.

Throughout its history, timber has been a major resource of the Brimson-Toimi area. As noted earlier, the huge logging companies owned and removed much of the choice white pine, leaving the settlers with smaller, less desirable species like jack and red pine, balsam, aspen, birch and some stands of cedar, spruce or tamarack. The earliest pioneers often worked in company logging camps during the winter, returning to their homesteads to farm in warmer weather. Indeed, logging camps remained scattered through the area until quite recently, although their character changed through the years, as did the nature of the timber business and the people who worked in the business.

▶ *Richard spent the winter at this job and the following June was drafted. He served in the Army until 1946 – by which time logging had changed to more mechanized operations, with few of the large bunkhouse and cook shack camps to be found.*

"I'm glad I had a chance to live and work in the old style logging camps," he says of his pre-war logging job. "It was interesting and I like being able to say I was part of the last of the camps."[11] ▲

Although the Duluth Missabe & Iron Range railway has been the predominant railroad in the Brimson-Toimi through the years, several other rail lines were also important to the communities at various times.

Eddie Koski recalled that the Duluth & Northeastern Railroad ran from Cloquet to Hornby and that General Logging Company extended that rail line all the way to Clearwater and Rose lakes at the extreme northern edge of Minnesota in what is now the Boundary Waters Canoe Area Wilderness in Cook County.[12]

The General Logging Railroad provided employment for a number of area men, both in picking up the rail previously used on the Alger-Smith mainline and spurs all the way from the Hare Lake vicinity seven miles north of Cramer to Knife River, then laying that rail along the General Logging right of way from Hornby/Cascade Junction northeasterly through Whyte to tie into the former Alger-Smith Duluth & Northern Minnesota mainline at Milepost 69.5 at Hare Lake. General Logging used this line to haul logs to Cloquet for 14 years, finally lifting the track in 1941 to be sold as scrap for the war effort.

As was their habit wherever possible, the Alger-Smith D&NM built spurs off the Duluth & Iron Range to harvest pine at a couple of locations near Brimson-

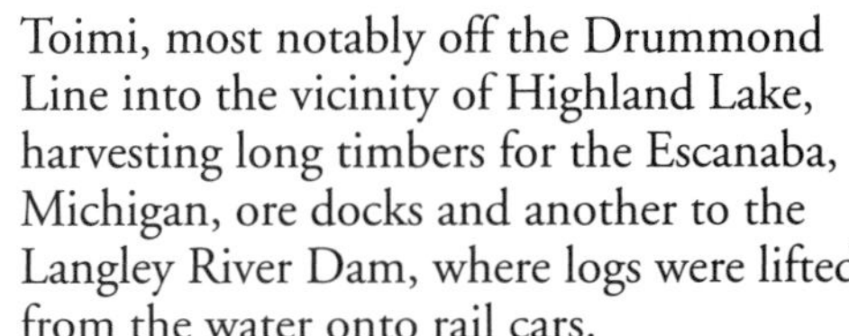

Toimi, most notably off the Drummond Line into the vicinity of Highland Lake, harvesting long timbers for the Escanaba, Michigan, ore docks and another to the Langley River Dam, where logs were lifted from the water onto rail cars.

The D&IR had, of course, been constructed as an iron ore railroad, adding early passenger and freight service, but by the latter 1890s the profits from hauling logs persuaded company officials to go heavily into that business, since iron ore traffic dropped to almost nothing in winter, when logging was at its peak.

Not only did the D&IR transfer all the timber that Alger-Smith railed to Knife River on into Duluth, but the company also served other logging interests working in proximity to its rails. The Wales Line was extended to Whyte in 1917 solely to service logging firms and that branch would be extended in the late 1940s all the way to Forest Center at Isabella Lake, where Tomahawk Timber Company built a settlement to serve its employees in the last large-scale logging operation in Lake County.

In addition to tying spurs of other companies into its mainline, the D&IR also occasionally built its own spurs to serve logging companies operating in a particular stand of pine. The iron ore railroad undoubtedly handled all of the timber products produced by its U.S. Steel Corporation companion company, Oliver Iron Mining Company, from huge timber holdings north and east of Brimson and the mill Oliver erected on the mainline near Indian Lake.

In addition to Oliver's Brimson-Toimi operations, Scott Graff Lumber Company is credited as having a spur from the D&IR Wales Line to the north of Greenwood Lake, a portion of which was later used for State Road 2 right of way. Alger-Smith also extended rail into the Greenwood area. Later, in the 1940s, North Star Timber, a subsidiary of Kimberly-Clark Company, had an operation in the area, with five large camps, and is reported to have used a rail spur running from Whyte to the Isabella area.

Petrell Hall was built by volunteer labor and the first of the cooperative buying groups set up a store in the lower level. Edwin Petrell donated the land for the hall, which was built of hand-hewn logs in 1913 and was substantially renovated in the mid-1980s.

While these logging companies did, indeed, log in the areas described, Frank King seems to indicate in his book *Minnesota Logging Railroads* that many of the rail spurs serving them in fact belonged either to the Alger-Smith or the D&IR/DM&IR.[13] In some other cases, the logging companies rented rail and other equipment from the Duluth & Iron Range.[14]

While the D&IR and DM&IR had employed people in the Brimson-Toimi community from 1884 onward, the arrival of Erie and Reserve mining companies in the early 1950s created new jobs that would prove to be attractive and relatively long-term for many area families. A number of men who had originally planned to work on the construction of the new mining railroads stayed on to become longtime employees and retire from those mining companies.

The logging tradition of the area remains to the present, although the large lumberjack camps and, later, the shacks of the "gypo" cutters are definitely long gone. Today, loggers work in "climate-controlled" equipment, turning out amounts of timber that old-timers would never have believed. One four-man operation using modern equipment may turn out from 30 to 45 cords of short wood a day – estimated to be the equivalent of what 40 to 50 men would have accomplished during the lumber boom.

At the outbreak of World War I, sons of the community volunteered for duty and served far and wide.

The Great Depression proved that the hardy settlers and their descendants were still able to live pretty well off the land. The Civilian Conservation Corp (CCC) Company 719 of Camp Charles on Sullivan Lake provided some local boys and men with jobs and income in the 1930s.

The CCC also commanded the muscle power that improved roads, strung 135 miles of telephone line, built 30 bridges and three dams, cut 130 miles of foot trails, improved a number of other facilities, planted new forest areas, fought fires that threatened forest areas and completed surveys that improved the state and federal information about the area.

J.C. "Buzz" Ryan of the Cloquet Valley State Forestry district was assigned to Camp Charles to plan and supervise needed projects, but the camp was commanded by U.S. Army 1st Lieutenant Grosvenor Charles, for whom it was named. Ryan's presence at the camp was especially remembered, since his wife, the former Luane Skinner, was a Brimson native and the projects he oversaw often involved work that was directed by area people. He would later write a number of short books about his experiences in northern Minnesota forestlands.

Another camp in the Brimson-Toimi community that provided needed employment was Camp Francis E. House on Lake George, sponsored by the

Camp Francis House on Lake George was a longtime summer vacation spot for hundreds of area children. Named for the president of the D&IR and supported by that company, the camp was sold to the Lutheran Church of America in 1962. A number of Brimson-Toimi people worked there through the years.

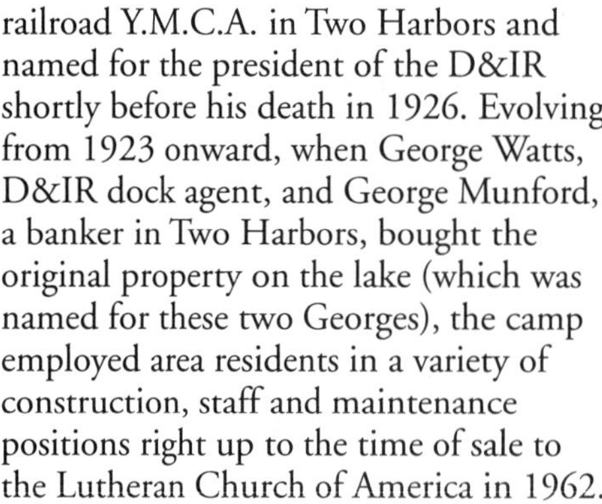

railroad Y.M.C.A. in Two Harbors and named for the president of the D&IR shortly before his death in 1926. Evolving from 1923 onward, when George Watts, D&IR dock agent, and George Munford, a banker in Two Harbors, bought the original property on the lake (which was named for these two Georges), the camp employed area residents in a variety of construction, staff and maintenance positions right up to the time of sale to the Lutheran Church of America in 1962.

Providing 39 years of summer fun and entertainment to decades of boys and girls, summer days at Camp House is a cherished memory for both the people who worked there and the kids who played there.

Arriving at Brimson depot by passenger train in earlier times, the campers were met by a truck to haul their luggage. Children who were deemed too small to make the three-mile trek from the depot to camp might also get to ride on the truck. The rest trudged along the dusty road and were undoubtedly elated to see the freshly painted, well maintained camp buildings nestled in the shady pines beside the clear blue water of the lake. For one week, this would be their home and playground.

A wide variety of activities kept the kids busy during their week at Camp House, but swimming was the keystone to all other activities and many expert swimmers learned the basic skills at camp that allowed them to earn certificates in advanced diving, swimming and life saving. The children's week at camp was also filled to overflowing with daily flag raising and lowering ceremonies, boating, archery, baseball, hiking, crafts, evening programs in the lodge and after-dark bonfires, where songs and ghost stories were enjoyed. Best Camper and Best Swimmer awards were remembered as the most coveted of the prizes given at the weekly Awards Night.

Four campgrounds operated by state or federal agencies entice anglers and campers to sample the hospitality of the Brimson-Toimi area, with the 25-site state-run Indian Lake Campground being one of the more popular facilities of local campers. Cadotte Lake and Sullivan Lake campgrounds also invite the public to put down roots for a night or two. Day trippers find the Salo Lake facility a nice place to launch and land boats. Development of the campgrounds was often undertaken under the guidance of the Brimson Sportsmen's Club.

Although the early settlers found the area trying, their devotion to their farms and homesteads remains in the community's residents today. While the population remains primarily rural and scattered, their loyalty to Brimson-Toimi, to one another and to the heritage of the community is as predominant as it was in those early days of stump pulling, rock picking and helping out a neighbor in need.[15]

Settling In – The East and North

Unlike southern and western Lake County, where the 1883-84 construction and opening of the Duluth & Iron Range Railroad provided hundreds of jobs almost instantly, development to the north and east (with the exception of Beaver Bay) was a bit later and a more laborious process that took a couple of decades to truly get under way. By 1900, there were settlers firmly established on the lakeshore and as far inland as Finland and Lax Lake – notably the Ben Fenstad Sr. fishing family at Little Marais, Esa Mantarri on an 1897 homestead in Finland, father Johannes and sons John, Eric and Axel Waxlax on Lax Lake homesteads as early as 1896 – as well as a scattering of fishermen at other locations all along the lakeshore from Knife River to Little Marais.

Written accounts place the arrival of Ben Fenstad Sr. at Little Marais in 1890. His oldest son, Alfred, is recorded as being born there on May 13, 1891. Ben Sr. had worked for the city of Duluth upon his 1883 arrival in the United States. His first wife and child died in childbirth during this time and he went back to Norway to marry his wife's cousin, Sirine, returning to Duluth to work on the city crew until the city cut back on its workforce during another of the frequent economic depressions of the period.[1]

By that time, Booth Packing Company of Duluth had scattered about 150 commercial fishermen along both the north and south shores of Lake Superior. Ben Sr. had worked as a fisherman in the old country and began fishing for Booth on the south shore, until he learned that he could obtain free land on the Minnesota shoreline under the homestead law, which allowed settlers to claim 160 acres after improving the property by building, clearing and living on it for five years.

"Homesteading" was particularly attractive to land-starved immigrants, who constituted the bulk of the settlers on Lake County homesteads. Ben looked around and staked his claim at Little Marais. With determination and a great deal of hard work, he was able not only to obtain title to the lakeshore land, but also to earn a living by selling his abundant catches of trout to Booth Fisheries. Herring would later become another important sale commodity, but had not emerged at that time.

The 149-foot freight and passenger boat SS *Hiram Dixon*, Booth's second company boat (the first being the tug *T.H. Camp*), made semi-weekly trips along the north shore to Port Arthur/Fort William, Ontario, and out to Isle Royale until 1902, when the Booth company

Pioneer homesteaders at Lax Lake in 1896 were Johannes Waxlax and his sons John, Eric and Axel. The men would work several years during the shipping seasons in Two Harbors to bring matriarch Wilhelmina and the rest of the family to their Lake County home.

Fenstad critter was likely love-lorn by the following spring, when she wandered 25 miles to Lutsen, where C.A.A. Nelson, the pioneering fisherman and founder of Lutsen Resort, found her and sent word to Ben Sr. to come on up the 25-mile trail to retrieve her.

Ben Sr. and Sirene raised seven sons and two daughters on their Little Marais homestead, its buildings clustered tightly on the lakeshore. In addition to a house that eventually became the largest on the shore with 10 rooms upstairs, the site consisted of the requisite fishhouse, a good-sized barn, an icehouse, a woodshed and a root cellar. As the largest house in the area, their home served not only the needs of the family, but was a gathering place for the community, served as the school for a short time and was home to early school teachers, as well as a stopping-place for others who needed board and room.[3]

The Fenstad family homestead at Little Marais clustered buildings tightly on the lakeshore, including the largest house for many years in the entire area. Operated first as a fishing site and farm, the property would evolve into a stopover for travelers. The house has since been renovated into the Stone Hearth Bed and Breakfast.

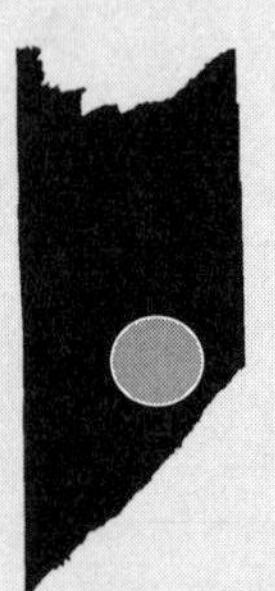

replaced it with the SS *America*. Stopping frequently to collect the catch of the fishermen and drop off passengers or whatever supplies the established families had ordered previously, after 1890 the boats also served as the mail vessels during the summer season, keeping the early settlers in communication with the rest of the world. Once the Fenstads were established there, Little Marais became an important landing place for many of the later homesteaders who pioneered on the shore or inland.

But, while regular service by Booth boats was available and certainly did yeomen's service for these early pioneers, one memoir about Ben Sr. indicated that it was not unusual for him to row his skiff the approximate 40 miles to Two Harbors to deliver fish and pick up supplies there. The trip would take several days, depending on the wind and weather, but was likely compensated by higher prices for his fish and lower costs for the supplies he bought there and transported himself.[2]

The family's first cow was delivered by the *Dixon*, forced to "walk the plank" into the lake and, with a rope around its neck, swim to shore behind the skiff. The milk, cream and butter she yielded were undoubtedly a treat for the growing family, but may have been shortlived, since there is no record of a bull being delivered and cows must bear a calf regularly to continue producing milk. Other early Lake County settlers remembered butchering their cows when they quit producing milk for lack of a breeding companion and, indeed, the

That the life of the fishing families was fraught with danger goes without saying and the published memoir about Ben Sr. records an instance in which he rowed his skiff out into the morning darkness to deliver fish to the *Dixon* and was caught in an off-land wind as he started rowing back to the homestead. It was obvious to Captain "Fog King" Hector that Ben would never be able to reach shore and he lifted Ben and his skiff aboard and continued along the shore to Duluth. On the return trip, he dropped Ben and his skiff off. Obviously, an anxious Sirine Fenstad, who had no way of knowing what had become of her husband, was overjoyed and relieved to discover that he had not simply disappeared into the lake.[4]

The Fenstad homestead was an early area school during the three summer months and later became a favored stopping place for the north shore mail carriers. When a complaint was registered that mail bags were being left overnight in an unauthorized place, the homestead was approved as a post office and Ben Sr. was named postmaster. He shortly petitioned to have the office designated as an International Post Office, which authorized him to issue money orders that could be mailed overseas.

As time passed, more and more people stopped for overnight stays, which Sirine provided for $1 and included the price of supper, a bed and breakfast. The idea of catering to tourists was solidly embedded by about 1912 and led to the renovation of the original house into the "House of Fenstad's," which joined C.A.A. Nelson's Lutsen property as an early north shore resort. It would later be renamed the Lakeside Inn and still operates as a public facility, now as the Stone Hearth Inn B&B. As long as Sirine had anything to say about it, no checks were accepted. Early in the hospitality business, she agreed to cash a visitor's check from her carefully hoarded cash reserves. Naturally, the check bounced, and it's recorded that her faith in checks did, too.

Ben and his sons grew increasingly dissatisfied with being at the mercy of fish wholesalers and by 1912 had started a mail order fish business out of Little Marais that shipped and mailed fish to all areas of the Midwest, with a money-back guarantee of satisfaction.[5]

An interesting offshoot of their mail order fish business was the establishment of the Lake Shore Rural Telephone Association in 1914, which built a telephone system that tied the established Lake Shore Telephone Company in the Grand Marais area to the Duluth & Iron Range Telephone system via the farmers' phone system in the Silver Creek community and provided long distance service to the north shore. The Fenstads loaned the Lake Shore Rural $1,000 for the project, but took no active part in its management.

Serving the area from east of Little Marais to the interchange with D&IR system, the Lakeshore Rural had 40 customers, each of whom bought a share of stock for $50. The Lake Shore Telephone Company at Grand Marais also numbered about 40 customers. Small switchboards were installed at Little Marais and Beaver Bay to forward calls, but switching was always a problem on this early system.

By 1920, the owner of the Grand Marais-based Lake Shore Telephone

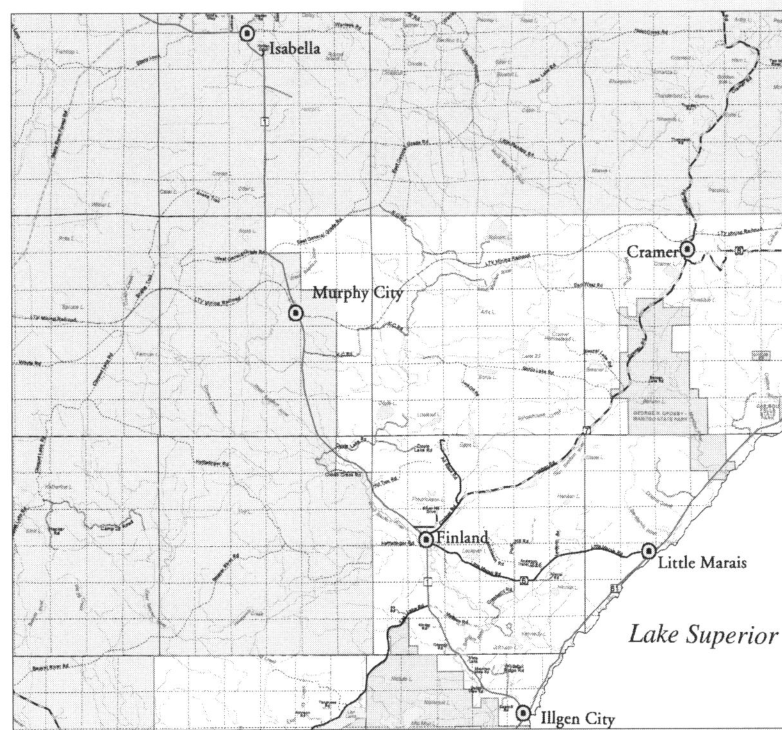

Company asked the Fenstads to buy the company for $7,000. The Fenstads did eventually agree to the purchase at a price of $3,500, but soon found that the rural company they had originally financed was keeping all of the money turned over by the D&IR for north shore long distance business. With half the total customers on the north shore, their new company was entitled to its share of the income generated by those customers.

The Fenstads were still owed the $1,000 they had loaned the Lake Shore Rural Telephone Association and the newly acquired telephone company was being subsidized with funds from their more successful fishing business. The brothers decided that the two businesses had to be separated and that the telephone business had to be the total responsibility of one of the brothers.

To determine who would take over their telephone company, the brothers drew straws, and Al, the loser, became the owner of the telephone business, which he held through a series of changes in business and telephone technology until 1928, when he sold his company to the Northern Telephone Company, which became part of Northwestern Bell Telephone Co. Al would continue to serve for many years as a manager for Northwestern Bell.[6]

Meantime, the other six brothers continued their fish and tourism businesses,

The 1909 Andrew Sonju homestead at Maple was home not only to the family, but to school teacher Nettie Roen as well.

although they, like most other commercial fishermen on Lake Superior, eventually found that fishing was no longer a viable occupation. To the day this account was written, however, the family's tradition for hospitality continues at Fenstad's Resort at Little Marais, as a fourth generation has begun to welcome customers.

Even as the Fenstad family fortunes gradually improved through the early years, the area was seeing more and more people arriving to take up claims on government land parcels.

Finns, in particular, found this rather rugged territory attractive and began claiming the interior land, although one of the earliest homesteaders was Joseph N. Cramer of Wayne County, Pennsylvania, who settled on Cramer Homestead Lake in 1905. He farmed, taught school at Maple and, a bit later, bought land and built a store and would lend his name to the townsite and post office at Cramer, when the Alger-Smith railroad arrived there in about 1910. His brothers, with the poetic names of Byron and Shakespear, joined him in the Cramer area and are also noted in early references. Joe would later buy and operate a large sawmill, after selling his store in about 1913, returning briefly to Pennsylvania, traveling to Montana and finally returning to his homestead on the lake bearing his name.[7]

Other early pioneer settlers in the area from the very early 1900s included Herman Lindstrom, Solomon, John and Arvo Haveri, John Koss, Charles Kennedy, Jacob Hangartner Jr., William Curley, Thomas Emerton, Charles Jentsch, David Crowley, Andrew and George Sonju, Wilpus Tikkanen, William Huuskonen, Evert Hakkarainen, the Andrew Beck, Otto Moisio and Alex Ruuska families, Adolph Leppanen, Valentine Ahlbeck, Joel and Edward Pelto, Edward J. and Henry Silver, John Kangas, Nils Egge, John and Mary Williamson, Jacob Mattson, John and Aina Harma. Although exact dates of arrival are uncertain for some of these settlers, most were likely established by 1904, since many of these names are recorded in the earliest township minutes.[8]

The township of Crystal Bay was organized on May 10, 1904, with supervisors being John Koss, David Crowley and Charles Kennedy, William Curley as clerk and Thomas Emerton, treasurer. Optimism no doubt ran high at this point, since the Minnesota Mining and Manufacturing (3M) Company of Two Harbors had established a mine and processing plant on the shore near what is now Illgen City.

3M's plans were to process corundum, which early explorers had reported in that area. The hard, abrasive, somewhat scarce mineral was in huge demand by manufacturers of equipment like grindstones, whetstones and sandpaper. When the reported corundum of Crystal Bay proved to actually be anorthosite, a rock with little or no commercial value, the 3M operation faltered. The mine and plant at Crystal Bay closed for good in 1906, but the company went on to much more prosperous times (see Chapter 2 for more on 3M).

Originally, Crystal Bay Township apparently included the Cramer area and a large area to the south of the present town line, but the Town of Cramer was organized as an independent township in July 1913. The southerly boundary of Crystal Bay Township is believed to have met Beaver Bay Township, but much of that territory ultimately became part of Lake County Unorganized Territory No. 1. The township is also reported to have originally included the Lake Superior shore, but at some point the easterly boundary was moved inland – perhaps at the time that Cramer Township was formed, since Robert Silver remembers that Cramer Township covered an area from the international border to the lakeshore and included Little Marais.

After organization, Crystal Bay township turned its attention immediately to establishing schools and building roads. One of the first acts of the board was appropriation of $200 to build a road and bridge over the Baptism River, as well as another $200 for a road to Pork Bay. At the next meeting, the board approved $100 (when available) for Andrew Sonju to build a road from Little Marais to Maple and at the December meeting the board approved $100 for William Curley to build roads from Crystal Bay eastward to Kennedy Landing and another payment of $350 was approved for Edward Pelto to build a road from Kennedy to the "state road."

Thus, the public roads were first roughed out, then succeeding yearly appropriations were approved to extend and refine the roads to handle the traffic of the time. From rock- and stump-pocked trails that were built strictly for horses and wagons or foot travel, the roads were graded and widened as cars, trucks and buses came into being. The state and Lake County also became involved in road construction and maintenance after the first few years.[9]

Similarly, classes for area children were initially held in makeshift facilities at various homes, sometimes with older teens of the community serving as teachers. From the earliest classes, Lake County School District No. 1 administered these scattered schools. First organized in 1859 at Beaver Bay with Gustav Wieland as chair, the district included all of Lake and an area of northern St. Louis County. It would be pared down to include only Lake County in 1866.

That administrative situation changed in 1912, when the county was divided between Lake County No. 1 and No. 2 school districts, with No. 1 continuing in the Beaver Bay area, but much of the rest of the county being taken over and administered from Two Harbors. Students in the western reaches of the county typically attended schools in the Ely district.

Since the only high school in the county was at Two Harbors, the school district provided room and board for rural students wishing to pursue a high school diploma and at least one written account states that the county superintendent discouraged students from distant schools from continuing beyond the eighth grade for that reason.

Within a few years, buildings were constructed to serve as schools in the Finland community and certified teachers became the norm in the classroom. Those teachers were usually responsible for all students enrolled in first through eighth grades and may have had only an eighth-grade education themselves. Many of the children had to learn English before going on with their lessons. In about 1905 at the Park Hill and Finland schools, Lempi Pelto from that area and Mary Lorntson of Beaver Bay were apparently the first teachers in the community. By 1910 five schools were located at Baptism River, Maple, Lindstrom, Little Marais and Crystal Bay (the latter two on the lake shore). Classes were being conducted in Isabella at the home of Herman Davidson and a new building would be opened for school there in 1913. The 72-mile trek required for superintendents Flynn or Campton to visit Isabella School included an 18-mile hike from Finland.

While early township officers were getting roads and schools under way and functional, everyone focused their attention on the hard work of making a

Sawbill or Bust

"Carol and I came up to Sawbill in about 1940 and I worked for Kenny Tomlinson in a large lumber camp that Tomlinson Brothers Lumber Company was operating there," says Bob Holden of Finland, who spent nearly 60 years logging in northern Lake County. "I drove a cat (crawler tractor) and drove a truck. We lived in a camp out in the woods for several years but moved into Sawbill after the school was built. Our oldest son, Roger, started school there, but he was the only one of our kids that went to that school."

Tomlinson had a number of large lumberyards across the upper Midwest, Bob says, so he later bought his own truck and hauled lumber from Sawbill to Whyte.

"Aspen box lumber was mostly what we were sawing," Bob says. "There wasn't all of the cardboard and other packing material we have today and the government needed a lot of boxes to ship supplies for the war. Aspen was perfect box wood because it wouldn't taint any food that was packed in the box. The government made the timber available to cut into box lumber and they paid pretty well for the wood, so that was mostly what we cut."

He reported for the draft several times during World War II, but was never taken ▶

Ed Silver, an early homesteader in the Cramer vicinity, gets ready to use his ox to "skid" a moose to his homestead.

few dollars of income to pay for the necessities – flour, spices, kerosene, sugar and other imperishable staples – which were delivered by the Booth boats to the lakeshore and laboriously lugged as far as 10 miles to homesteads in the Finland settlement. Enough food had to be stored by freeze-up to keep the family through the winter until the ice went out of Lake Superior in the spring, so large shipments and a good deal of backpacking were requirements of survival. Fish, game, wild berries and cultivated crops provided the basis of the diet in the earliest years. Only after the Alger-Smith Railroad arrived in the area in 1909-10 were supplies relatively easier to obtain for the settlers and the stores that served them.

But, in a memoir published in *How We Remember*, a collection compiled in 1995 by the Finland Centennial Committee, Elise Sonju Williams recorded that not every moment was devoted to work in these early days. She stated that the first dance in Crystal Bay Township was held at the Maple home of Andrew and Karoline Sonju, her parents. The dance area was the 12-foot-by-14-foot interior of their cabin, with Ole Sonju providing accordion music. She also indicates that later dances were held at the more spacious Koss and Fenstad homes. As many as 30 people often attended these social events.[10]

Andrew Beck is credited with having the first general store in Finland, operated at his homestead. His daughter, Hulda (Wilhunen), related in a 1958 memoir that when they arrived in the area in 1904, they stayed overnight at the home of a bachelor named Charles Jentsch, whom she claimed was the earliest area settler. She states that his cabin was about halfway from Crystal Bay to the Finland site and that he had a neighbor named Mike Schultz at that time. The Becks were headed to the Hakkarainen homestead, where they stayed for four months in a "10-by-12 foot" cabin with 12 people crowded into bunk beds inside. Hulda also stated that four of the adults, including her mother, later died of tuberculosis.

By the end of that summer, there were five cabins erected, making up the first settlement at what would later become Finland. The Becks returned to Duluth for the winter and the following spring backpacked all their household belongings, including a kitchen cookstove and Hulda's newborn brother, the 10 miles from Crystal Bay, where the *America* dropped them off to their homestead. Even after his wife was diagnosed with the aforementioned tuberculosis, it's likely that Andrew Beck struggled to hang on, but finally sold his homestead to Andrew Sonju in 1914 and disposed of the store inventory to the newly organized Co-operative Store. He moved first to Virginia and then to Two Harbors, where he operated a general store. Elvira, his wife, died in 1918.[11]

When the Alger-Smith Railroad crept into the community of Finland about 1907, the first choice of the company for a depot name was Beck, after the storekeeper, but Andrew objected, saying it should be named Finland for all the Finns living there. Thus, does the area's name actually predate the official name of the country by about 10 years, since Finland did not declare independence from Russia until 1917 and was recognized as a constitutional republic in 1919, when the name became official.

In about 1908, a Community Building was erected in Finland and an athletic club was formed that used the hall. Plays, Christmas parties, socials and dances were held in colder months, with picnics added during summers. Later, films would be shown there and, like a similar effort in Toimi Hall, a mattress-making project operated there in 1940 and 1941. In addition, a summer camp sponsored by the Co-op Store for area youth was held there in the 1930s.[12]

The slow but steady stream of settlers increased dramatically as the Alger-Smith's Duluth & Northern Minnesota mainline track wound its way inexorably through the area, moving steadily northeastward past Lax Lake through the Finland settlement, past Maple and into Cramer by 1910. Building dozens of miles of spur lines from this mainline to the logging camps in the vast stands of white pine, the company cut virtually township-sized swaths. The timber was loaded onto cars and hauled the 62 miles from Cramer to Knife River, where it was switched to the D&IR Lake Line for forwarding to Duluth.

More importantly, from the standpoint of settlers, the D&NM also served as a freight and passenger "common carrier," conveying people and goods to and from settlements along the way. With the railroad offering an inland alternative to boat transportation, more families moved more easily into areas that once required days of back-breaking packing of supplies from the shore of Lake Superior to their scattered homesteads. By this time, too, an expanding road system was making more of the territory accessible and the loggers left large areas of land relatively free of forest, although stumps and rocks definitely slowed down the development of farms in the area.[13]

In a 1999 memoir recorded by Robert H. Silver of the Schroeder area, the son of an early homesteader in the Cramer area, he states that his father, Edward, first arrived in the north shore area in 1900 and filed a 1902 claim at the Duluth land office for a quarter section (160 acres) on the then unnamed Caribou River about four miles northeast of the future Cramer townsite. The claim was proved-up and the patent issued in 1909. He also states that his uncle, Henry Silver, had filed on a claim adjacent to his father's and that they named the river the Caribou for an Ojibway trapper called Swamper Caribou, who trapped in the area each fall and winter and had a wigwam on the river.

After Joseph Cramer established his store at the location that would be named for him, he was appointed postmaster of the Cramer post office and served in that post for about three years, when he and wife, Amanda, sold the store to Silver's aunt and uncle, Mary and Joe Grabowski, who continued the business until Alger-Smith abandoned its railroad in 1921. Mary also served as the Cramer postmaster.

When the railroad reached the Cramer area, north shore settlers wanted access to the freight and passenger service it provided and work commenced to build a road from the Schroeder-Tofte area in Cook County to the railroad at Cramer. The road was pushed through to the Lake/Cook County line from the north shore and, after Cramer Township was organized in 1913, the town board funded completion of the road from the county line to Cramer. Silver indicates that Lake and Cook counties undoubtedly helped finance this road effort and that, in about 1917, the state highway department took on the job of maintaining the road from Two Harbors to Grand Marais, of which this section was a part. That inland route was called Highway 1 until the present Highway 61 was completed in about 1924.

From 1913 to 1920, the Cramer area served as an important waypoint on the railroad – not only for the Alger-Smith's own supplies and timber products, but for tons of herring and other goods that were shipped out. In fact, Silver remembers that it was a common winter sight to see dozens of bags of frozen "round" (uncleaned) herring lying in the snow beside the roadway near the Cramer townsite, because teams of horses were not able to pull a fully loaded sleigh up a hill and horseshoe curve in the roadway from the north shore. These sleighloads of fish were hauled about 10 miles from Schroeder and even farther from other shore locations.

From Milepost 63, a mile beyond Cramer, Alger-Smith's D&NM pushed an extensive system of spur lines north and

▶ because he and Carol had two or three children by that time and the government wasn't inclined to draft men with a number of dependents it would have to support. By the 1950s, he was working for Kimberly-Clark and operating a sawmill. With his own camp, sawmill and up to 30 employees, Bob turned over the truck driving to others and took up management of the operations. He shut down his sawmill after getting a contract to supply timber to Northwest Paper Company, which would later become part of Potlatch Corporation.

By the time he got the Northwest Paper contract, the work in the woods was increasingly mechanized, but both Bob and Alvin Jouppi of Isabella remembered with a certain grudging respect the so-called "gypo" cutters that worked the camps during the 1940s and early 1950s. Primarily bachelors and loners, they commonly lived one or two to a shack that might measure 10 feet square. The men were usually independent, tough and many were inclined to work only long enough to accumulate a stake that could be blown during a spree. A fair number are remembered as fellows who had a tough time adjusting to life after military service.

Alvin remembers, "It was usually when you were on a deadline to deliver timber ▶

The Cramer School served students for a number of years, likely opening when the Alger-Smith Railroad reached the area and settled a number of families at Milepost 63, which became known for a short time as Case. Later, children from the area attended school in Finland.

***Facing page:** The Axel Ruuska homestead was an early claim in the Isabella area. The photo is dated about 1925.*

west to serve its logging camps, as well as those of other companies like the Scott Graff Lumber Company, which had a large operation on Moose Lake and shipped all its timber on the D&NM. Silver states that there were repair shops, watering, coaling and other facilities at Milepost 63 and that a community called Case rose on the site to house workers and families during the relatively short time that site was active.[14]

Silver also notes that the spur system from Case stretched west as far as Dumbbell Lake (east of Isabella). Maps in Frank King's book, *Minnesota Logging Railroads,* confirm that this extensive D&NM spur system did indeed end within about two miles of Dumbbell at a location a mile or so west of Hoist Lake. If, as is often true, Hoist Lake was named by the early loggers for the function performed there, it may well have served as a staging and lift area to land floating logs and hoist them onto rail cars. In that case, the logs cut in the entire surrounding area were probably hauled by sleigh for distances of five miles or so and skidded onto the lake during winter for later retrieval and shipment.

For about a decade, the logging went on at a fierce pace, with as many as 15 log trains passing through Finland on busy days. Homesteaders with desirable timber on their acreage seldom saw appreciable income for their logs, since there was really little competition among the possible buyers, among which the Alger-Smith Company was primary. Adding further injury to that insult, fires in the slashings that the company left in logged-over areas frequently threatened or destroyed the homesteads of settlers, as well as bridges and other public structures. In fact, there is an intimation in some memoirs by early settlers that the logging companies may have intentionally torched some desirable stands of privately held timber to move the owners to sell quickly at whatever price was offered, since the scorched timber would deteriorate to worthlessness within a year or so and must be salvaged immediately – which the logging companies were obviously equipped to do.

Whether set intentionally, as the result of sparks from coal-fired locomotives or by lightning strikes, it is true that huge areas were burned. There are at least two

accounts of the monumental and weekslong battle waged in summer 1913 by original Lax Lake settler John Waxlax and his brother-in-law Fred Johnson to save the historic Waxlax homesteads from a huge fire that surrounded their properties. John had his family's most precious belongings stowed in two boats, ready to row to the center of the lake, should he not be able to fend off the conflagration threatening his homestead.

Fred Johnson's son, Anselm, remembered that they carried hundreds of gallons of lake water by shoulder yokes to fill barrels on the homesites. Soaking gunny sacks in the barrels, they beat back the fire time-after-time, stopping only for an hour or two of sleep when the fire had been beaten back. Eventually, the threat died down and John would go back to his work-a-day routine before establishing Lax Lake Resort in 1928.[15]

Despite such logging company hazards, the settlers were certainly not happy to see the logging die, for it was a momentous day when the last log train chugged down the mainline from Milepost 99.8 at Cascade in 1919. Although the D&NM was forced by the Minnesota Railroad & Warehouse Commission to continue passenger and freight service at that time, the service lasted only two years and all D&NM rail service was discontinued on July 21, 1921, forcing the settlers to again fall back upon their own ingenuity and resources when they had to travel. Luckily, by that time, roads and automobiles were becoming commonplace and a good deal of the original D&NM right of way was used for highways 4 and 7, with some of the numerous spur lines also used for roads or trails. Booth Fisheries was still operating the SS *America* as a freight and passenger vessel along the north shore, also giving settlers, particularly the fishing families, service between Duluth and Port Arthur/Fort William, Ontario.

Meanwhile, settlers continued to push farther and farther inland in the early years of the 1900s. Although original surveyors' notes from the Isabella area indicate that there were several settlers in the area when the survey was done in the 1890s, none of these early settlers seems to have stayed. Some speculation exists that these earliest "settlers" may have actually been bogus "entrymen" used by timber companies to acquire land cheaply.

Thus, when Matti Ruuska, Herman Norte (North), Antti Kokko and Kalle "Karl" Ahlbeck arrived in the area in September 1906, they became the first settlers to file homestead claims in the Isabella area. They were joined the following spring by Antti Erickson when they returned to the homesteads. Mrs. Matti Ruuska is believed to have also

▶ *that they decided to go get drunk and you just had to hope they got sick enough soon enough to come back so you could get the timber out."*

Bob says, "We had some cutters who didn't drink up everything they made, but a fair number did. They were paid for the amount of timber they cut, so they usually worked hard when they were cutting, but when they went drinking you might as well forget about them 'til they were out of money.

"In the 1950s, the logging camps changed a lot and we started to have quite a few families. Some of the gypos were still working, but they were pretty much a dying breed by then.

"The government was getting more involved in things like testing the water in the camps to be sure it was up to standards. We also had a company (Northwest) auditor check our books every month because we had a company checkbook for several years. They weren't so concerned about the dollars, but they wanted to make sure that all of the tax withholding payments, FICA, insurance requirements and other items were being taken care of. We never had any trouble with any of that and Northwest always seemed to able to get timber, so that worked out real well for us."

But as equipment replaced the gypos in the woods, the expenses skyrocketed, with some of the machinery ▶

arrived at the site at that time or sometime shortly thereafter, which would make her the first non-native woman at Isabella.[16]

Eric Grondahl and Mae Runnberg, the children of pioneer settlers Arthur Victor and Fiina Grondahl, remembered that Axel Ruuska also was an early settler and that, a bit later, the Lillback family set up a sawmill and shingle mill that supplied cedar shakes for roofing most of the homes in the entire area. Eric and Mae often walked four miles from their home to Redskin Lake to catch gunny sacks of northern pike. A five-mile hike to pick up the mail was their routine each Wednesday.[17]

Like most of the other early Isabella settlers, Eric and Mae's parents were Finnish immigrants and homesteaded by the Stony River in 1912. The Swedish surname was common in the area of Finland where they came from, which was quite near the Swedish border. The future nation of Finland had been controlled by Sweden for many years prior to the 1809 Russian takeover of the Finnish territory, and many Finns from that area were often referred to as Finn-Swedes.

By the time that Victor and Fiina Grondahl homesteaded in the community in 1912, they likely found not only the original settlers, but the Herman Davidson, Matt Tenkanen, K.W. Allen, Julius Ruuska, Albert Hendrickson and Victor Saine families settled, along with single settlers John Punkka, William Pulkinen, Victor Hill, Victor Hautanen, Esa Tapola, Gust Lillback, John Hopia, Hjalmer Mattson and Hilda Kotila. Nick Johnson would arrive later, as would several young women who married local bachelors and stayed on in the settlement.

Following their eighth-grade education at Isabella School, Eric and Mae attended Two Harbors High School, boarding with the Erickson family during the week for $20 a month and catching a ride to Little Marais to spend weekends with their parents. Often they arrived home in Isabella at 11 p.m. or later, after walking inland for several hours along the rough road.[18]

Although wresting a living from the stubborn Lake County soil was arduous, Isabella settlers did find that root crops like potatoes, rutabagas and beets would thrive in the short growing season – although preparing the soil for planting was always plagued by rocks, stumps and other obstacles. Since the growing season

The Nikula homestead stood about where the Apollo is now located in Finland and served as a "stopping off place" on the way to and from Isabella. This photo was taken about 1910 and shows John, Martha and Weikko Nikula in front of the log home.

was so short, settlers seemed always in a hurry to get their crops in – giving rise to the first name for the settlement, which was "Hurry Up." Where the name of Isabella originated is shrouded in the mists, but it is known that a vote was taken among residents and the rustic name of Hurry Up lost out to Isabella – although one old-timer refused to accept that vote and continued to refer to the settlement as Hurry Up until he died.[19]

While making a living from the land was proving to be difficult, the St. Croix Lumber Company of Winton began establishing logging camps on the Stony River, where steam haulers were used to deliver logs to the banks of the river for spring log drives. By that time, many settlers had begun to weary of the constant hardship of their lives. The camps provided winter employment for area men, paying real cash or trading provisions for their work. The camps also provided a market for any excess milk, eggs and other produce that the families were able to spare, above and beyond their own needs. Eric Grondahl remembered that his family sold milk for 10 cents a quart or 25 cents for a five-quart pail. With little more than such meager incentives, a number of the early families made the decision to stay on their land and tough out a living.[20]

St. Croix Lumber remained in the area until the early years of World War I and the Alger-Smith Company also had camps operating east of Dumbbell Lake at about the same time. Later, North Star Timber of Kimberly-Clark and Northwest Paper Company would operate large logging camps in the area and, during World War II, the arrival of Tomahawk Timber east of Birch Lake and its later establishment of Forest Center at Lake Isabella also spurred the economy of the area – although employing few local workers. Nearly all of Tomahawk's employees and pieceworkers came from central Wisconsin.

Meanwhile, trapping provided some income for a few of the families in the area, with the men often out on the traplines for a week or longer at a time. When the men were occupied in the logging camps or on the traplines, the women and children were responsible for keeping the homesteads operating. Milking, gathering eggs, feeding and cleaning the stalls of the animals would be carried out by older boys or girls, as would the carrying and stacking of firewood to warm the home and heat the cookstove. Shoveling snow from pathways between the various buildings would also consume time, since there always seemed to be abundant snowfalls.

Once there was a bit of stability in the hectic pace of getting a living, the settlers determined they needed a community hall and put up a building where they could gather for dances, programs, funerals and other events.The hall also served as the gathering place for members of the Socialist Party when it organized in the community. A strong movement among Finnish settlers in Lake County, the party had a number of units, espousing a better life for working people and maintaining a lending library of Finnish books.

The establishment of a cooperative store in the neighboring Finland area led to a shortlived branch of that store being organized in Isabella. After the Isabella branch closed, the Finland Co-op delivered to members in Isabella. Other independent stores were operated in the community by the Matt Tenkanens and, later, the John Lillbacks.

For years, the residents of Isabella, Finland and other communities had pressed for a good road to connect their communities. In 1920, gubernatorial candidate J.A.O. Preus made an arduous automobile trip from Ely to Isabella on a logging road built by St. Croix Lumber Co. He indicated that he knew Lake County could not afford to build a road across this long stretch of territory, promising that he would sponsor such a road at state expense if he were elected. Once he won the election, work started the following summer on what is now State Highway 1 to connect the north shore with Ely. Completed as a county road in 1923, the road almost immediately attracted fishermen and other tourists. When Trunk Highway 1 (now Highway 61) was officially opened and designated as the Lake Superior International Highway in 1925, northern and eastern Lake County truly became an attraction to motorized visitors. Serving those visitors began to emerge as a profitable industry.

By the late 1930s, Highway 2 connected to Highway 1 north from Two Harbors

▶ costing upward of $250,000. Bob remembers that he bought his first truck, an International semi tractor, for $2,400. Today, he says his son, Paul, drives a unit that he estimates cost more than $120,000.

"With prices like that, you have to keep producing the wood or you just won't make it," Bob says. The cost factor for new equipment is also the reason that many independent loggers choose to buy only used equipment that they can repair and operate themselves – thereby avoiding part of the enormous expense.

Reflecting on the future of the industry, Bob says that he is optimistic. In 1999, he saw the start of a harvest of red pine from lands that he logged when he first started in the Sawbill area.

"The areas that we logged were replanted and that pine is really nice – up to 18 inches on the butt," he said. "Aspen, of course, comes back after a cut even faster than pine and a lot of mills prefer it, so it seems like there'll always be a market and the forests will regenerate wood to fill the need.

"One other thing I know for sure is that if the paper companies owned all of the wood that was blown down in the Boundary Waters (in the July 4, 1999, wind storm), they'd demand that us contractors clean it up. It wouldn't just lay there and go to waste. We'd have to salvage it, if we wanted other work."[21] ▲

and the state assumed maintenance of Highway 1 as a state roadway connecting the north shore to Ely, improving and paving it.

As fishing, hunting and camping became more popular, it became apparent to Jack Crawford, an outsider, that the Isabella area needed accommodations for visitors. He selected the shore of Lake Gegoka to build Crawford Lodge. It would burn later, be rebuilt and is currently operating as National Forest Lodge in the same location.

After the major logging companies abandoned the area and before the new roadways were built, some families found life in Isabella too difficult and moved away. As recreation and independent logging became easier after construction

Chipping Out A Living

Alvin Jouppi describes his father, Eino, as being a truly entrepreneurial logger who also got involved in other moneymaking enterprises.

"Dad came up to Isabella in about 1940 from our home, which was east of Moose Lake. He was looking for smaller balsams that he could cut for Christmas trees that he sold on street corners in the Twin Cities and other places. The balsams here are the single needle variety that don't make nice Christmas trees, but Dad found 80 acres of nice aspen and birch across the road from the old section house that was owned by (early homesteader) John Punkka."

Thus, Eino joined the ranks of Isabella loggers and his family joined him after school let out in the following spring and each spring for several additional years, because no school operated in Isabella at that time.

"Dad set up a camp of gypo cutters. He always said he didn't want to feed anything when it wasn't working, so he used tractors instead of horses to skid the timber. He set up a sawmill and cut as much of the timber as possible into lumber, which was stacked, air-dried, planed and sold to customers in the whole area from Two Harbors to Ely. The pulpwood was hauled by truck to the railroad at Whyte."

By 1945, there were enough kids in the Isabella area to warrant re-opening the school. The Jouppi family moved to Isabella and the community would prove to be their permanent home.

In typical entrepreneurial style, when the first chainsaws arrived on the scene in about 1950 or 1951, Eino arranged to become a dealer for McCullough-brand saws, which were gear-driven and relatively heavy, but a welcome relief from the handwork that cutting had previously required. He would also disappear into the woods during the spring and fall to trap beaver. A lot of the old-timers in Isabella depended on trapping for part of their income and some of them would stay out for a month or more in what is now the Boundary Waters Canoe Area Wilderness. There would always be a number of game wardens looking for them, too.

Eventually Eino decided to cut out the middleman and became a buyer of furs from other trappers in the area.

"At the end of beaver season, he'd pack up the furs and go to New York to sell them," Alvin remembers. "He'd come back with a new car for himself and a fur coat for Mom."

Through experience, the Jouppis found that their best business bet was to focus on quality and to add value to the raw timber by careful sorting and special handling, rather than trying to be the biggest producer. They've also maintained control of costs by shopping for good used equipment and doing the repairs themselves. In at least one instance, they also found a way to turn timber that others discarded into a desirable product.

"Just before we shut down the sawmill in the 1960s, we were cutting cedar and the hollow logs of old-growth white pine that other mills wouldn't buy," Alvin says. "The cedar went mainly to canoemakers for cedar-strip canoes. With the hollow white pine, we quartered the log, then sawed lumber from each of the quarters and got really nice clear white pine lumber. It was more work, but we could make money because nobody else wanted the logs and we were adding value to wood that would probably be scrapped otherwise."

But Alvin says the nature of logging has changed through the years. "It's a hard business these days. If the mill yard is empty, the buyers know you, but if they've got wood, they don't. Buyers change and a new one may give you smaller contracts than you want. You have to stay on top of everything to stay in business.

"It helps that things just seem to come together sometimes, too," Alvin says. "About 12 years ago we were offered a contract to cut nice birch timber on a big parcel of privately owned land near Lake Superior. Birch wasn't a big seller at the time, but we were lucky that the Flambeau paper mill in Wisconsin started buying it and we've been able to get rid of all the wood we can cut that don't make veneer logs or bolts for lumber. You just have to have faith that some good things like that will come together."[22] ▲

Art Grondahl is pictured here with the cow Rillu and colt Timo. The sledge behind the horse was likely used to haul rocks from the field on the Stony River homestead.

Bottom: *Agriculture in Lake County has always been hard work, for both man and horse*

of better roads, other people moved in. Resorts opened on Grouse and Sand lakes and the "downtown" tavern operated by Joe Slogar of Ely opened. Chub Lake and the Knotted Pine taverns opened in 1934 and 1937 respectively.[23]

In 1954, independent developer Arthur G. Porter contracted with Edwin Nikula of the Finland area to build 10 homes at the site where the Erie Mining Company railroad would cross Highway 1 about midway between Isabella and Finland. Porter envisioned the settlement as a home for Erie railroad employees, but that plan would never develop and, since the townsite first opened for occupancy in 1957, the majority of the homes have been occupied by local non-Erie folks – a number of whom moved in from Forest Center after Tomahawk Timber Co. announced it was shutting down.

At the beginning of Erie's railroad construction work, the company built a school building that opened in December 1954 at Murphy City to serve the children of its construction workers. By the 1955 school year, 67 children were enrolled and the school employed two teachers, but in 1956 the enrollment plunged to only 12 children after construction workers and their families abandoned the area. The school then ran for several years as a one-room facility for kindergarten through fifth or sixth grades but was closed in 1963 and the students were bused to the newly completed Finland School. Briefly, in 1965, the school was reopened when the Isabella Job Corps Center started operation, but was closed permanently nine weeks later and the building was moved away by Erie Mining Co.[24]

Today, the cluster of homes at Murphy City is bounded to the north by forested area and on the south by the Erie mainline crossing. Only the similarity of the homes in this location marks this as a settlement that is different from those farther north and west that comprise Isabella – which at least one county resident has described as a state of mind, rather than a physical location.

Bonded naturally by the trails and roads they laboriously chopped out to connect them, the early settlers of the

:eam Hauler. A locomotive on runners, near Two Harbors, Minn.

The arrival of the St. Croix Lumber Company in the Isabella area gave the hard-pressed settlers a source of income. Many men went to work in the camps, where steam haulers like the one shown here were used to haul logs from cutting areas to the river banks for spring log drives.

Isabella, Finland, Little Marais and other areas in eastern Lake County typified the resiliency of pioneers – doing anything that was necessary to maintain the lives of their families.That the dreams of the original settlers did not always come true does not detract from the work and love they put into the land and the rearing of their families.

To some degree, that spirit remains in today's residents of the communities – massaging their sometimes isolated sites into homes where families learn the value of work and develop the rugged individualism fostered by their natural surroundings.

Isabella Job Corps and Wolf Ridge ELC

Excitement stirred the small population of Isabella in 1964-1965 as news surfaced that the federal government was planning a Job Corps Center on the side road to Mitawan Lake off of Highway 1.

An ambitious undertaking during the Great Society presidency of Lyndon B. Johnson, Job Corps was established in the early 1960s to provide educational, employment and life skills training for young men from deprived backgrounds. In a relatively short period, Job Corps training centers were hastily erected across the country in many federal forests or other locations where the enrollees received board, room and training.

Since they were nearly all in isolated locations, each Job Corps center was complete with recreational, educational, living and working facilities, as well as transportation to move the enrollees to work locations and for trips off the campus. While the Isabella center was pretty much a stick-built facility, some were constructed of modular units that could be quickly and easily assembled.

From the beginning, Job Corps was a federal program that raised controversy and the Isabella center was no exception. Lois Pelto, who lived in the Isabella area at the time, remembers that at first the residents did not take kindly to this project, fearing that the enrollees would be a problem for them and their families.

Despite protests in public meetings, the project moved ahead and the center was built and ready for occupancy by 1966. Lois also remembers that the end of the project was equally upsetting to many area residents, as many of the furnishings were simply taken out and buried.

By 1970, the Job Corps was winding down its operations at the Isabella center and a new, more long-lasting educational endeavor was about to unfold there. Jack Pichotta, an energetic, visionary social studies teacher who had organized a 1969 Earth Day program at Cloquet High School, met with a group of concerned educators in 1970 and hatched an ambitious outline to conduct environmental sessions for young people at the center.

By 1971, with a $280,000 federal grant in hand, Pichotta opened the former Job Corps center as the Isabella Environmental Learning Center, where the facilities provided shelter and kitchen facilities, but the natural surroundings of the center were the classroom, laboratory and lesson plans.

Focusing on groups of students from schools in a wide area of the Midwest, the center immerses students in an intense experience that often changes the way they look at our world. For a number of days, they are free of classroom routines and in touch with an environment that is totally foreign to many of them. The opportunity to paddle a canoe, use hand tools working with natural products or simply the chance to closely observe some facet of the natural surroundings provides excitement and a curiosity the students would not be likely to experience from mere classroom education.

As busloads of students and their teachers from often-distant locales travelled to the Isabella Environmental Learning Center, the staff was increased through the 17 years that it occupied the former Job Corps site. In 1980, the center was the first of its type to earn accreditation by the North Central Association of Colleges and Schools, gaining even greater credibility as *the* resource that teachers depended upon to provide this vital experience to students.

By the late 1980s, the center had outgrown the Isabella facilities and a new campus was built atop a ridgeline at Finland overlooking Lake Superior – adopting the new name of Wolf Ridge Environmental Learning Center when the staff moved in 1988. Here, surrounded by natural areas with the Baptism River flowing nearby, the new facilities attracted even greater attention from the educators of the Upper Midwest. Hundreds of pre-teen students are present each week during the school year and the Wolf Ridge staff also expands its offerings when schools are inactive to include a wide

Trapping also constituted a means of earning money for many settlers in the northern areas of Lake County. This settler has a nice collection of beaver hides curing as he prepares another skin for the drying rack.

The Isabella School served not only the educational needs of kids in the settlement, but was also used for other programs, gatherings and community events.

range of weekend and summer activities for adults, family groups and elderhostels for grandparents and their grandchildren to get to know one another better.

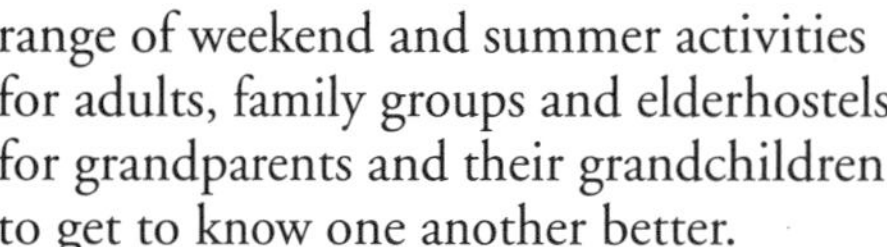

Employing 67 on staff, the center has a payroll of $1 million and hosts upwards of 16,000 people a year to a wide variety of educational and recreational activities – nearly always a combination of both.[25]

A Rural School Teacher's Memories

Sylvia Anderson Tucker grew up and received her first teaching assignment right out of high school in North Dakota. After a year of experience, she attended Spearfish (South Dakota) Teachers' College and received a teaching certificate. In late September 1920 she received a telegram from the superintendent of schools in Lake County offering a teaching job at Little Marais School, where her father had gone to join logging crews in the Cramer area.

"I took the train to Duluth," she recalled in an undated memoir. "At the old station where I left the train, I called Mrs. Lawrence (the superintendent) for further directions. Out on the depot platform, it was gloomy and drizzling and there was a loud noise at intervals that sounded like a monstrous cow bawling (obviously referring to Duluth's famous/infamous fog horn). Out in back was more water than I had seen in all my life."

Saying that her instructions were to board a logging train, she remembered, "We went northwest through heavy woods until we reached a certain trestle where I was to take another train to Finland (she is likely referring to Alger Crossing on the D&IR). I clambered down the bank to the track at right angles to the former one. After what seemed like a long time, I boarded the train and did reach Finland."

From the Alger-Smith Railroad station in Finland, she went to the post office, where Hilji Houle telephoned the Fenstads to come to pick her up. After a ride down the hill in a Model T Ford, she reached the Fenstad estate on the shore, where the teacherage was located. After a lesson in starting wood fires, since she had grown up using the lignite coal that is mined in North Dakota, she cleaned the school with the help of a couple of neighbor ladies, one of whom walked several miles to join the effort.

Opening school with Olaf, John and Arthur Fenstad and Mildred Connor as students, she remembered receiving $80 a month for teaching and $20 a month for janitorial service, which included getting wood into the building and carrying water. The school was a mile or so west of the Fenstad home, which is now the Stone

This little Isabella post office building on the grounds of the Whistle Inn was still in use in 1964.

Hearth Inn, and she found that an early piece of advice – get a pair of lumbermen's rubber boots – was particularly useful on the walk to the schoolhouse after the first snows arrived.

"Once in a while there would be a dance somewhere, such as Finland Hall, and we would pile into the Ford and go," Sylvia stated. "One dance was at Cramer Depot, hosted by the North Dakota people (she apparently does not include herself in that group by this time) and we went to that one."

After two terms, she resigned and enrolled in Duluth State Teachers' College (now University of Minnesota-Duluth) for a year, completing her coursework in September the following year. She was offered and accepted a teaching position at Thanksgiving at Thomasville School in Cook County, where her teacherage was a kitchen on the right and a bedroom on the left of the school entry. She received $100 a month and $20 for janitorial service. Eight students were enrolled at the school. She also remembers that several of the smaller students called her mama on occasion.

"One year, there was a forest fire up on the Sugar Loaf road.... There could be no concentration with smoke pouring over us, so we were all outside watching. The smoke diminished before it was time to go home."

Despite this close call, tragedy did strike. Sylvia recalled getting a telephone call before the children arrived one autumn asking her to send two students home immediately because their father had been shot in a hunting accident. He recovered. Another student died of a childhood disease during Christmas vacation.

Serving four years at this location, she remembered, "The picnic on the last day of school was a highlight of the year. Marion (Mickelson McKeever) still tells of how they looked forward to the big container of ice cream that was furnished by the teacher. We held the picnic at various pleasant spots. One was beside the Caribou River and the last one on the banks of the Little Marais Creek on my parents' place."

Like many of the early teachers, Sylvia found romance in the north woods, married and followed her Coast Guardsman husband, John Tucker, to several duty stations, before his retirement in Racine, Wisconsin.[26]

Settling In – The Northwest

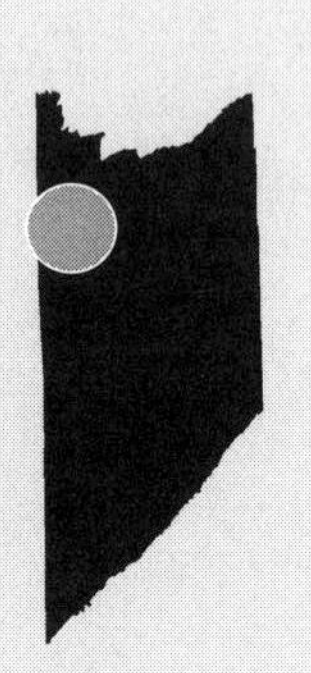

At the far western edge of Lake County in the early 1890s, the watersheds of the Kawishiwi and Shagawa rivers provided river access into Fall Lake from a large surrounding area, making river driving of logs possible from huge stands of prime white pine.

In 1893, Samuel Knox of Wisconsin, in partnership with R.V. Whiteside[1] and William Winton, began logging in the area and built a large lumber and lath mill on the west side of the peninsula of Fall Lake just across the county line in St. Louis County. Shortly thereafter, the Duluth & Iron Range Railroad laid a short extension of their trackage from the mines at Ely to the sawmill site. The town of Winton was born with some 25 homes, boarding houses to house workers and stables for the draft animals. It would be 1914, however, before the townsite just west of the Lake/St. Louis County line took the name of Winton to honor the partner in the lumber company.[2]

Between the years of 1896 and 1898, the Knox Lumber Company sawmill produced 15 million board feet of lumber a year, In 1899, the Knox interests sold their Winton operation to the St. Croix Lumber Company, owned by Terrinus Brothers of Stillwater, Minnesota. At the time of sale, the mill was enlarged to produce 50 million board feet per year and the company would be sold again to the Edward Hines Lumber Company of Chicago in about 1910 and was again reorganized, this time as the St. Croix Lumber & Manufacturing Co., which continued operations until 1922. The 24-year operation by the Knox and St. Croix companies produced an estimated one billion board feet of lumber, lath, box and other wood products from timber harvested on a huge scale in northern Lake and St. Louis counties.

In 1898, another enormous mill facility arrived on the shoreline of Fall Lake when Swallow & Hopkins Lumber Company, owned by George C. Swallow of Minneapolis and Louis J. Hopkins of Duluth, arrived at Winton and built a mill facility rated for 30-35 million board feet of lumber and lath per year. Located adjacent to and east of Knox's operation, this facility was just inside the Lake County line. In less than a quarter century, the two companies cut and processed an estimated 1.6 billion board feet of pine products. So large was the influence of these logging and mill operations that Winton's population swelled to an estimated 2,000 residents in 1914 – before rapidly plunging when the companies ended their operations shortly after 1920.

The Winton post office was opened in 1900 and a bit later a hospital was operated by a Dr. Metcalf. At the time the town reached maximum population, it supported seven saloons, wooden sidewalks, company stores, a fire department, a profusion of ethnic boarding houses and a Finn Hall where theatrics and gymnastics were showcased. It was also the first town to elect a woman mayor and clerk in 1921-22. It's recorded that there was an improved trail between Winton and the Section 30 townsite that arose at the Section 30 Mine. Wintonites often shopped at the Oppel Store there.

St. Croix's early logging was largely conducted in the area of Burntside Lake, the south shore of Fall Lake, the Fernberg

A view of the St. Croix Lumber Manufacturing Company sawmill facility just across the county line in St. Louis County at Winton. The original mill was built in 1893 by Knox Lumber Company.

and North Kashaway (now Kawishiwi) areas and the Stony River watershed. Most of its timber was pushed by river drives to the mill but, after 1911, the company expanded its logging east of Basswood Lake into the Kekekabic, Fraser and Thomas lakes area, purchasing rights on rail and water systems developed earlier in that area by Swallow & Hopkins.

Early in its operation, Swallow & Hopkins built two short rail spurs to connect the north end of Fall Lake with the nearby, but landlocked, Ella Hall and Mud lakes, where they began logging operations. Since Fall Lake is seven miles from north to south, where the mill was located, the logs were railed from the logging areas, dumped into Fall Lake then log booms were towed by steam launch from the north end of the lake to the mill. The company did all of its logging after freeze-up in the fall and spent the spring, summer and fall moving the timber to its mill, which operated only during the warmer months. S&H reportedly operated as many as 50 logging camps over the years and many of the lumberjacks were employed year-round, spending winters in the woods and summers working at the mill or on rail operations.

Once logging was completed in the area around Mud and Ella Hall lakes, the S&H rails were removed from the cutover area around Ella Hall and used to extend the Mud Lake line from the north end of Fall Lake to Hoist Bay on Basswood Lake, a distance of about four miles. The "Fourmile Portage" railroad connecting the two lakes opened in 1901. In 10 years, Swallow & Hopkins hauled more than 350 million board feet of logs over it.

As recorded in a 1952 memoir by G.H. Good, the former S&H general superintendent in the Winton area, and printed in Tauno Maki's collection entitled *Winton*,[3] the Fourmile Portage mini-railroad line operated with one primary locomotive that pulled 10 loaded Russel log cars between the lift-out on Hoist Bay and Fall Lake. A smaller engine was used for switching and other light duty such as pulling cars of freight or supplies from the D&IR switchyard in Winton onto a special barge for transport across Fall Lake and then across the portage line to Hoist Bay.

At first the logs on the S&H Fourmile Portage came mainly from the forests near Basswood Lake, but the company would

A second major lumber company mill was established at Winton in 1898 when Swallow & Hopkins erected this operation on the Lake County side of the county line.

continue acquiring stumpage and moving into new areas, eventually logging as far east as Knife and Kekekabic lakes. Over its history, Swallow & Hopkins owned about 200,000 acres of timber and water rights and their logging operations stretched across much of Lake County from west of Basswood Lake through many of the boundary waters lakes.

G.H. Good also noted that S&H built a series of dams to raise water levels, constructed sluiceways to channel logs to desirable waterways, deepened some water channels and sheared irregular shorelines with log booms to move the logs smoothly downstream from one interior lake to the next.

Many lakes had to be crossed without the benefit of flowing water for log driving. In those cases, the company constructed a large floating raft with a horizontal windlass in the center called a capstan. The horsepowered capstan was used to wind up a quarter of a mile of cable or rope attached to an anchor. Logs would be boomed, fastened to this raft and two men in a boat would row out the anchor and rope to the end of the line and drop the anchor. A horse would then walk round and round pulling the lever of the capstan to wind up the rope and pull the raft and boom to where the anchor lay. This would be repeated again and again until the logs reached a point where flowing water would again take over and move the logs downstream. Good noted that the system worked well when a following wind was blowing, but was considerably slowed by headwinds.

After 1902, the S&H logging operations had progressed north and east of Basswood Lake to a point that a steam-powered, cable-towed rail portage was built to move logs past Prairie Portage, a narrow 660-foot rocky obstacle that restricts the flow of water from Birch Lake westward into Basswood Lake. Otherwise, the logs were floated through the labyrinthine boundary waters from distant logging camps, then towed by steam launch down Basswood to the Fourmile Portage, again portaged by rail to Fall Lake, refloated and towed by launch to the mill. That such a system produced profits undoubtedly gives one a clear impression of the amount of profit that less cumbersome logging operations would yield.

As previously noted, after it finished cutting its timber east of Basswood, Swallow & Hopkins sold the Fourmile

Portage Railroad, waterway controls and the Prairie Portage operation to St. Croix Lumber in 1911 for $19,000. St. Croix continued to use it until about 1912 or 1913 to log stumpage it owned in the Kekekabic, Fraser and Thomas lakes area. After St. Croix shut down their north and eastern operations, the Fourmile right of way may have entered its most cherished period, serving for many years as the road that gave motorized access to Basswood Lake, where a number of large resorts and lodges were developed and attracted anglers and tourists.

After selling its first portage railroad to St. Croix in 1911, Swallow & Hopkins constructed a second portage line from Fall Lake to Jackfish Bay on Basswood to harvest its remaining stands of timber there and in the areas of Fourtown Lake and Horse Lake, for which this rail line was named. Despite these large cutting areas, the mill's production levels dropped during World War I and the business closed in 1922. The Horse Lake Line, however, was reported by Tauno Maki to have continued in use until 1940. The original Fourmile Portage remains the principal motorized pathway for anglers and paddlers taking boats and canoes into Basswood Lake.

By the early 1920s, the big push in the white pine forests of northern Lake County was reduced to the mopping up of scattered stands by the big logging companies, before abandoning the stumps and slashings to those with more permanent designs on the land. Swallow & Hopkins sold its operation in 1922 to the Cloquet Lumber Company, which moved the machinery elsewhere, but continued to use the rails of the Horse Lake Line. By 1923, St. Croix also called it quits and the boomtown of Winton saw most of its citizens pull up stakes and move elsewhere.

Despite the abandonment by loggers, the lakes and waterways of what would become the Boundary Waters Canoe Area (the word Wilderness was added in 1978) gained the increasing attention of outdoors enthusiasts. Between 1902 and 1908, more than one million acres of northeast Minnesota had been set aside and was officially designated as the Superior National Forest by President Theodore Roosevelt on February 13, 1909. That acreage would increase by hundreds

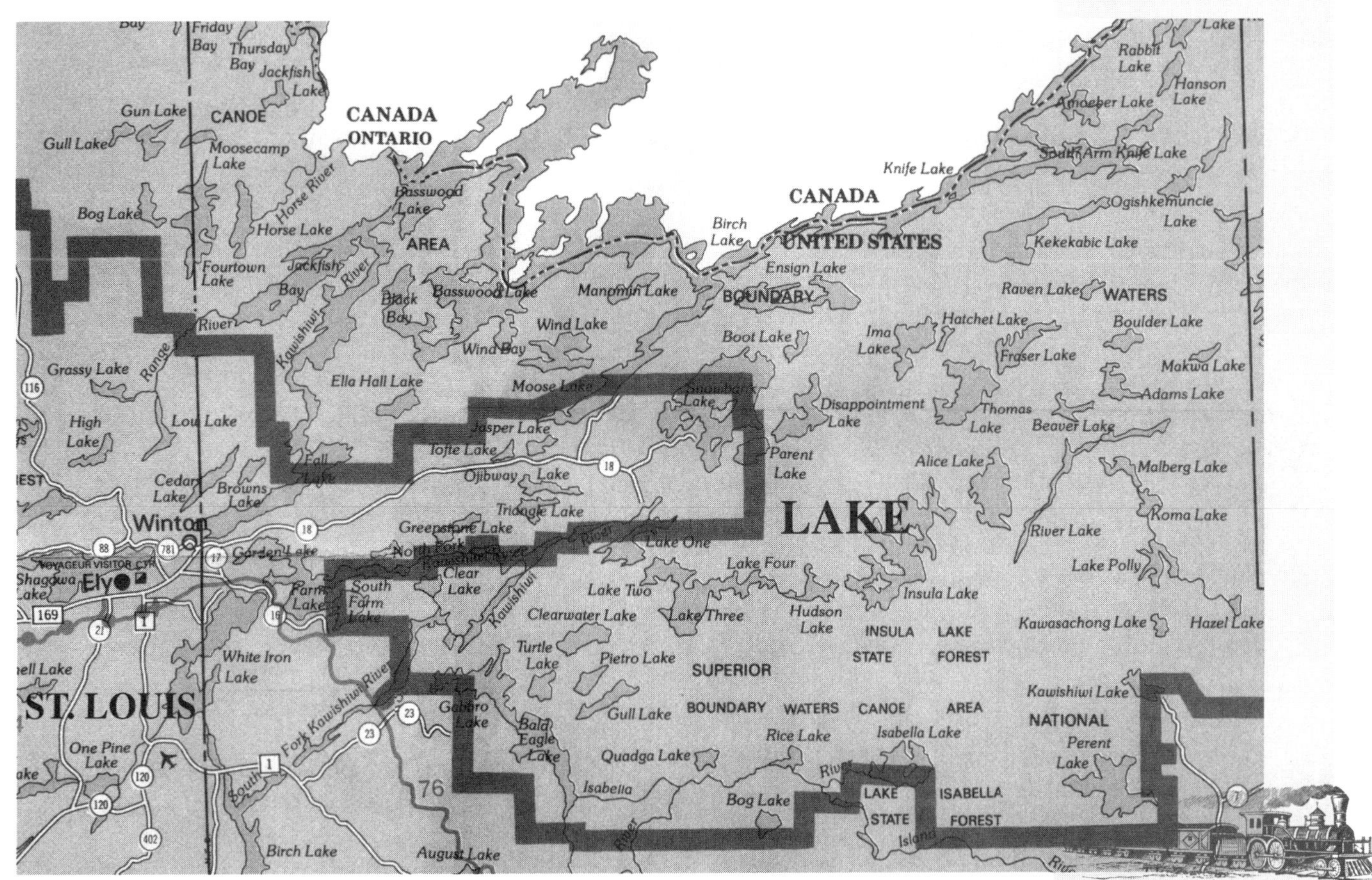

A huge area of what would later be included in the Boundary Waters Canoe Area Wilderness was logged by the two companies operating on the peninsula at the south end of Fall Lake. MINNESOTA DEPARTMENT OF NATURAL RESOURCES

of thousands of acres in succeeding years. At that time, the production of timber products and generation of hydro-electricity were the major considerations driving development of wild areas, but that attitude was about to change.[4]

Although a good deal of the area was already being logged or soon would be, the many lakes, rugged terrain and spectacular scenery of the boundary waters gave rise to more and more interest by tourists after World War I. That interest, in turn, led to requests for increased federal protection of the unique, scenic northern areas of Cook, Lake and St. Louis counties. By 1921, a Superior National Forest Recreation Association had been formed and voted to ask the Secretary of Agriculture to consider a thorough study of the Superior National Forest, keeping in mind all facets of development: "economic, recreational, scenic and aesthetic, with a view that its final development will give the highest possible service to all the people of the United States."

The choicest portions of the eventual BWCA from Saganaga to Basswood lakes would not become part of the Superior National Forest until 1936, but other areas of the BWCA had already been variously designated as Wilderness Area and Primitive Area at different times. After the 1936 addition of the spectacular boundary lands and waters between Basswood and Saganaga lakes, the entire area would shortly be designated the "Superior Roadless Primitive Area" in 1938, although there remained large areas of private ownership and large issues concerning usage of parcels within the entire area. Appropriations of $2.5 million in 1956 and $2 million in 1961 were aimed at settling the private ownership questions. More than two dozen privately owned resorts were bought by the federal government, essentially eliminating a sizable percentage of Lake County's tax base and prohibiting logging, motorized vehicles and boats, farming or virtually all other development in what makes up about a quarter of the land in Lake County.

In 1958, the name Boundary Waters Canoe Area was officially adopted and its status as a unit of the National Wilderness Preservation System was included in the 1964 Wilderness Act of Congress. Another act of Congress in 1978 expanded the BWCA area to 1.1 million acres, restricted motorboating and banned farming, mining, snowmobiling and logging, while adding the word "Wilderness" to the end of the previous name.

With logging now prohibited in this huge northern area and the removal of a number of once-popular resorts and lodges from lakes within the BWCAW, the focus of the area became "silent sport" tourism, with heavy emphasis on canoeing, camping, cross-country skiing or snowshoeing and other "wilderness experiences." The BWCAW continues to be an immensely popular tourism attraction and, despite a monstrous 1999 storm that blew down millions of trees and devastated thousands of acres of the wooded wilderness, will undoubtedly remain a popular and highly protected area.[5]

Meanwhile, a bit south of Winton in Section 30, a rich vein of iron ore had been discovered by a pair of timber cruisers/prospectors in 1883 and numerous legitimate and illegitimate claims were filed on the property. Before the legalities were settled, a million dollars and 15 years of litigation would be expended.[6]

Finally, in 1902, the U.S. Supreme Court settled the ownership disputes by ruling that the land belonged to Duluth's Eaton & Merritt Company, which was headed by Frank Eaton and Leonidas Merritt. Merritt was the oldest of the Merritt "Seven Iron Men" of Mesabi Iron Range fame. The Eaton & Merritt firm was originally formed to deal in timberlands and was highly successful in that endeavor, but Leonidas increasingly focused on the mineral prospects of the land they dealt in, using brothers and nephews to look over timber prospects but also to keep an eye out for the mineral riches that the family believed existed north of Duluth.

The Merritts' early interest in iron ore had led them to the Section 30 site in 1887 for exploration by John and Cassius Merritt. Their field notes and a map of compass dip needle readings appear in the book *Seven Iron Men*, which records the Merritts' history.[7]

Although the ownership disputes were ongoing at the time and despite the fact that the Merritt family had already lost control of the Mesabi mines and the

Duluth Missabe & Northern Railroad they had established in the early 1890s, diamond drilling by several firms began at Section 30 in about 1897 and continued for eight years.

After the ownership situation was settled, a road was built to the area in 1902 and encouraged more intensive exploratory drilling. By 1905, drill samples had delineated a solid body of ore measuring perhaps 365 by 1,000 feet and from 118 to 900 feet below the surface. The size and high quality of the ore made it a commercially viable lode and the owners proceeded to develop the site.

Merritt and Eaton first leased their property to a Sault Ste. Marie, Ontario, company, which soon gave up the lease. It was then taken over by Shagawa Mining Company. Proceeding to sink an exploratory shaft into the formation, that company began mining on the site in January 1906.

Driving the shaft downward at a rate of three feet a day with three shifts of workers, the Shagawa Company first found ore at 118 feet and four "drifts" (mining terminology for lateral or horizontal passageways in an underground mine) were pushed outward at that level. By May, 2,000 tons of high grade ore had been stockpiled and the shaft was at the 290-foot level, with other levels of drifts piercing the ore body at regular intervals.

Estimates were that the ore body contained 20 million tons of mineral, however, it appears that some dissension arose between the mining company and the fee owners of the ore body, for the Shagawa operation was shut down in January 1908 and pumping of the 700-foot-deep shaft ceased, letting water fill the shaft and drifts.[8]

Finally, in December 1908, George A. St. Clair took charge as manager on the site, putting things in order and overseeing plans to resume the mining that the Shagawa Company had abandoned. Leonidas and Bert Merritt, R.H. Fagan and Richard Whiteside[1] (all presumably either fee owners of the mining property or investors in the mining company) were reported to be making arrangements for work to resume. Mining Captain Alfred Holter was head of a 43-man mining crew and would remain in that capacity until 1916. W.G. St. Clair, a nephew of George, had been recruited in 1908 from Ishpeming, Michigan, to serve as superintendent of the operation, but his tenure was cut short in November 1910 when he accidentally stepped from the man-cage and fell 370 feet down the main shaft to his death.[9]

The Section 30 Mine was the only iron mining operation that shipped any significant amount of ore from Lake County. Located just inside Lake County, the mine turned out high quality Bessemer-grade ore from 1906 to 1923.

A substantial townsite developed near the Section 30 Mine to house workers and provide other services. The Hall, at center with two-toned roof, was a community center. The long building at center was a company bunkhouse and the house with the gabled roof was the Lamont Boarding House.

Section 30 Mining Company was chartered as a corporation in 1909 by George St. Clair, manager and president, Alfred Merritt, vice president, and A.W. Highfield, with headquarters in Duluth. Early in its history, the minelands were taxed by St. Louis County, which believed the property was inside its boundary. That controversy continued until the state Supreme Court ruled in 1912 that the mine was east of the boundary and therefore subject to taxation in Lake County.

The big mine pumps succeeded in dewatering the main shaft and two levels of drifts by March 1909 with another shaft opening a hundred yards to the east of the main shaft. That second shaft would become known as the Brown Pit. Drifts would interconnect the two shafts and each shaft would have its own stockpile area.[10] Yet farther east, the Bishop Pit would also be worked by Section 30 Mining Company, although that ore body was first homesteaded by a Tom Hyde, who sold to the Bishop Iron Company that became part of U.S. Steel Corporation in 1901.[11] The ore was, thus, apparently owned by U.S. Steel, but was likely insignificant to a company with many larger ore properties and was likely mined by the Section 30 company for a tonnage fee.

The *Ely Miner* newspaper carried a December 1909 story that George St. Clair had refused $1 million for 160 acres of the mining property, preferring to run the mine himself. Since the profit on a ton of the best ore delivered to Lake Erie was expected to be about $2.55, versus $1.25 in the ground, his refusal showed considerable optimism. That optimism, buoyed by the 67 percent iron content of the ore, was to prove profitable in the short term for St. Clair and the other investors. In fact, in 1916 the company boasted that it was shipping the highest grade iron ore of any property in Minnesota. That ore was destined for use in the Bessemer blast furnaces that produced the best iron products of that time.

By March 1910 Alfred Merritt, the third member of that family to get involved in the company, had arrived at the Section 30 site. A total of 140 men were producing 250 tons of ore a day, with expectations that the venture would produce 50,000 tons of ore that year. Construction of a rail extension from the Ely area to Section 30 was moving rapidly and tied the mine to the Duluth & Iron Range Railroad for delivery of the ore to Two Harbors.

The first train of ore was shipped June 7, 1910, consisting of 30 cars of 50 tons each for a total delivery of 1,500 long tons. Fee owners Richard Fagan, Leonidas Merritt, L.C. Harris and George Lonstorf were on the scene to help celebrate this event. By that time, 400 tons a day were being produced and this freshly dug ore was loaded directly onto ore cars, with 50,000

tons of ore that had been stockpiled the previous winter also being used to make up trains. By the end of the 1910 shipping season, 51,560 tons had been shipped from the Section 30 Mine.[12]

As work progressed, the mine would ship 157,344 tons in 1912; 136,359 tons in 1913; 85,943 tons in 1914; and 177,143 tons in 1915, with Zenith Furnace Company of Duluth taking 400 tons daily to fill 75 percent of their needs. Perhaps the apex of the mine's life occurred in 1916, when production reached 20,000 tons per month and resulted in sales of 300,000 tons, of which 226,089 tons were shipped. A 75-cent increase in the price per ton added to the profit column and raised expectations of a $3 per share dividend. Investors clamored to buy shares of the company, which were virtually unavailable.

But at the precise moment when success seemed certain, labor difficulties began to be felt, as the military conscription for World War I reduced the available manpower. Some of the remaining miners joined the Industrial Workers of the World (the so-called Wobblies), walked off the job and attempted to stop other workers from getting to work by gathering at mine entrances at the start of the work shifts. Other workers reportedly "hid out" to avoid being drafted for World War I duty. Despite these difficulties, the mine remained open and shipped 223,123 tons in 1917, but the next year managed to sell only 125,423 tons. Sales plummeted to 78,532 tons in 1919.

Despite a lack of laborers during the war and unrest among miners, those factors probably figured less prominently in the failure of the Section 30 Mine than did unfavorable conditions in the iron ore open market. Although high grade ore remained in the mine, the integration of ore supplies into fewer and fewer large corporations likely doomed this independent and seemingly successful private undertaking.

Plans to extend the life of the endeavor came to naught and the last gasp occurred in 1923, when a steam shovel loaded the last of the stockpiled ore and the mining lease expired. A total of 1,457,305 tons of ore had been shipped in 14 years, but the most easily mined ore was depleted and the entire operation simply closed up.[13]

A bit to the east of the Section 30 and Bishop pits of the Section 30 Mining Co., Chippewa Iron Mining Company also briefly tapped a Lake County iron ore deposit, with a Mr. Farnsworth reportedly the head of the mining operation. This was a separate operation from the Section 30 Mine, but the Chippewa company was also chartered in Duluth, with most stockholders being from Cincinnati, Ohio. While little was found about the operation beyond a brief mention in Winnifred Lomasney's unpublished manuscript[14] and two pages in Milt

The Bishop Pit became a second property worked by the Section 30 Mining Company. This photo shows the shaft for that mine.

Stenlund's booklet *Ghost Mines of the Ely Area,* the mine was started in 1917. Previous test drilling had proven the presence of iron ore assaying about 64 percent iron, which was in the Bessemer, or highest priced, category. By February 1918, a shaft had been sunk 100 feet and a drift was started laterally at that depth.[15]

By June 1919, ore was being stockpiled and the company expected to ship upward of 75,000 tons later that year. Work was under way to extend the D&IR Section 30 spur into the Chippewa mine. The primary shaft was 375 feet deep, with mining occurring in drifts at the 100-, 200- and 300-foot levels. Two shifts of workers spent 20 months developing the property, but in June 1920 the company informed the fee owners of the ore body that it was surrendering its 50-year lease, which was to pay the owners 60 cents a ton for the first five years and 62.5 cents a ton thereafter. The five fee owners, which included Oliver Iron Mining Company of U.S. Steel, were thunderstruck, since every indication up to that time was that the mine was a success and would be shipping ore after the shortest development period of any Vermilion Range property. Mining stopped and the equipment was removed to the La Rue Mine farther west on the Vermilion Range. Whether any of the Chippewa ore was ever shipped is an open question, although it would seem peculiar if it were not, given the extensive development effort and the amount of ore reportedly lifted to the surface.[16]

Most of the former miners of Section 30 gravitated to the Chandler, Pioneer, Zenith, Savoy or Sibley mines in the nearby Ely area, where jobs were available. Many moved the houses they had purchased cheaply from their former employer nearer to Ely. Others left the area for more distant promises, while a few stayed on, tenaciously clinging to the outdoor lifestyle they had learned to love. The sawmill workers from Winton moved on to jobs in timberlands of the western United States or utilized other skills to remain in this area.

After the boom ended, many early settlers in the northern and western portions of the county were left pretty much to wrest a living in whatever fashion presented itself. Guiding fishermen into the legendary lakes and wilderness area surrounding Ely-Winton became a summertime vocation for many of those who chose to stay.[17] And "wrest" is not too strong a word, for they had to be versatile in their skills, keen to the point of slyness, as strong and healthful as the native moose – with perhaps a trace of the playfulness of the river otter – to survive.

Once the logging boom in the northern areas of Lake County ended, commercial fishing became even more important for settlers on the shoreline of Lake Superior.

Smaller, independent logging camps provided mainly winter employment in the stands of timber left behind when the big companies abandoned the area. Some men would go on to establish their own logging businesses and the techniques and equipment they employed evolved into the mechanized industry we recognize today. A few farms were successful, but most of the county presented opportunity for what could only be termed subsistence farming that provided food for the

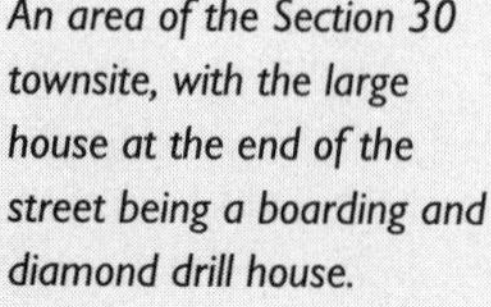

An area of the Section 30 townsite, with the large house at the end of the street being a boarding and diamond drill house.

family's table, with a bit left over to sell. Despite a vast acreage within the county that was available for homestead claims during the first three decades of the 20th century, at no time was more than perhaps 50,000 acres of agricultural land noted in Lake County and even those lands that were listed may have been inflated by rural folks who did some farming, but gained the majority of their income from other occupations.

Timber production remained an essential part of Lake County's economy after the 1920s' abandonment of the north woods by the huge logging companies. Companies like Tomlinson Brothers Lumber, Wheeler Lumber and Bridge, Northwest Paper Company (now Potlatch) and many independent producers like Cy Fortier of the Winton area continued to operate camps and produce vital timber products through World War II, but it would be the late 1940s before the county would again experience the excitement of a major logging boom.

During the 1940s, Tomahawk Kraft Paper (later Tomahawk Timber) Company of Central Wisconsin acquired timber rights on more than 150,000 acres of the Superior National Forest. After a few years of operating large traditional logging camps, Tomahawk decided to establish a settlement for employees and their families near Lake Isabella in the late 1940s and Forest Center was born.

The Duluth Missabe & Iron Range Railroad agreed to extend its rail line 49 miles from Whyte to Forest Center to ship the Tomahawk products, providing short-term construction employment for area residents and affording rail transportation for several logging interests along that trackage. Landings on this lengthy spur line were located at Jay See Landing, Isabella Station, Kelly, Sawbill, Wheeler and Martin landings, as well as the larger Forest Center operation.[18]

While a substantial percentage of the timber from this area of Lake County went to paper mills as wood pulp, a number of sawmills were active, including a large mill at Forest Center that produced lumber not only for Tomahawk's own needs, but commercially as well. Interestingly, according to Pat Thums, formerly of Forest Center and now Isabella, the Tomahawk mill employed mainly women in its sawmill operation, although Hilbert Butzke and his son served as the sawyers. Several other loggers like the Kainz Brothers, Bob Holden and Eino Jouppi also operated sawmills in the area for varying periods, in addition to cutting pulpwood.[19]

The construction of the DM&IR Forest Center rail line kicked off a bit of a boom in railroad construction over the next several years, as Reserve Mining Company would begin pushing its double-track mainline through Lake

The road to Winton from the Section 30 townsite was lined with a number of nice homes, many of which were later moved to Ely, after Section 30 failed and the miners accepted employment in the Ely mines.

County to Silver Bay in 1951 and Erie Mining Company's mainline track to Taconite Harbor was laid almost simultaneously. Each of the mining railroads provided substantial employment during construction and also enticed many local workers into permanent employment with the new mining companies.

In many ways, Tomahawk Timber's Lake County operations bridged the gap between the logging techniques of the earlier 1900s and modern mechanized logging. Forest Center certainly reflected this interim period. To house its workmen, Tomahawk constructed not only the traditional bunkhouses for bachelor lumberjacks, but as many as 53 family homes – referred to by the families as "our shacks," even though many were fully modern, two- and three-bedroom structures. The settlement had 23 such homes on its "main street."

Tomahawk also built a school for first through eighth-grade children in the community, as well as a post office, general store, recreation hall/roller rink and coffee shop. The company also provided the materials for the 1952 construction of St. John's Lutheran Church by parishioners at Forest Center. High school students caught a bus to attend Ely High School in the early years, but went to William Kelley High School in Silver Bay after that school opened in 1958.

Laying the track for the Forest Center line involved crossing long areas of muskeg and swampland. Often, the track crew found it necessary to blast out the muck before attempting to fill with gravel and crushed rock. FRANK KING COLLECTION, NE MINNESOTA HISTORICAL SOCIETY

A good deal of hand cutting was done in the early days of the Tomahawk operation, since power saws really weren't available or were so cumbersome and inefficient as to be nearly worthless until the mid-1950s. Also in those earliest days, horses provided a good deal of the power to move timber from the woodlots to landings where trucks could be loaded. As many as 112 horses were used to skid timber and other woodland tasks.

Later chainsaws and tractors would be incorporated when they became practical, although some cutters preferred and continued to use horses in their operations. The company constructed more than 50 miles of truck haul roads radiating from Forest Center, where it had an efficient operation unloading the trucks and loading railroad cars.[20]

Frank King, in his *Logging Railroads of Minnesota*, noted that the DM&IR reported that more than 5,000 carloads of timber products a year were moved on the Forest Center line during the early years and a former Tomahawk Timber official said that more than 90,000 cords of pulpwood were shipped annually in the early 1950s – a prodigious output, considering that the evolution to modern logging machinery was not really complete by that time. Still, over the life of the Tomahawk undertaking, a reported 650 million board feet of aspen, spruce and pine were harvested from an area stretching from Birch Lake near Babbitt to a huge area around the Forest Center settlement, much of which is now the BWCAW.

Up to 400 workers worked the northern forests in Tomahawk's 16- to 17-year operation. Most were paid on a piece-work basis, with a typical two-week paycheck in the early 1950s being around $65 to $80 after board was deducted, but increasing when better equipment like chainsaws and tractors became practical and allowed higher production rates per man.[21]

While the woodsmen could make decent pay most of the time, the company occasionally imposed quotas on the amount of wood they could cut. Lois Pelto remembered that their camp of about 18 men was told in 1915 that they would only be allowed production of 16 cords a week for one period of time. At the $7.50 they were paid per cord, the income for the entire camp would total $120 a week during the period the quota was in force – barely enough to cover cutting expenses and leaving little for groceries and other necessities.

Lois also remembers that life in the outlying camps was considerably more primitive than it was in Forest Center. The "shack" houses for the men and their families were 8 or 10 feet by 14 or 16 feet, with uninsulated walls and roofs. When winter temperatures dropped as low as 57 degrees below zero, the shelter provided in these "homes" was scanty indeed.

"All the heat just went right out the eaves and the walls were so cold you didn't want the blankets against them because they'd freeze," Lois remembered. "I carried all the water and washed laundry on a scrub board every day. I also baked six or eight loaves of bread every other day and cooked for a bachelor fellow who cut with my husband."

Lois said that, despite the bitter cold, the men seldom missed any work and that everyone remained in good health in their rustic camp.

"Many times when the men came back to camp from the woods, their clothes were solid white with ice and frost and the horses were the same way," Lois said. "Taking care of the horses was the first thing they had to do when they came in – then they could eat their supper and take care of anything else they had to do to get ready for the next day."

Ferdinand Thums, who settled in Isabella with his wife, Patricia, and their family after Forest Center closed in 1965, remembered that for the first year or two he used a bow saw (often referred to as a "Swede saw"), before the early Homelite-brand chainsaws became available.

Forest Center: The Village That Disappeared

Ferdinand and Pat Thums and Lois Pelto give a fairly clear and vivid picture of Forest Center, the company town built by Tomahawk Kraft Paper (later Timber) Company to house its workforce on the shorels of Isabella Lake from the late 1940s through the early 1960s.

Lois remembers the community as quite an improvement over the primitive remote camps she and her family inhabited for two winters when they first moved to northern Minnesota in 1957.

"The village had a laundry, school, coffee shop, store, church, all of the log and railroad yards and a good sized sawmill. All of the offices for the company were up on the hill and the village was down nearer the lake." Lois says. "When we moved into town from the Quadga Lake Camp, the company put all of us together, so we ended up living with people we already knew.

"In the remote camps, we lived in very primitive shacks that were maybe 10-by-14 feet, with no insulation and no running water or electricity. Some folks who moved into Forest Center would tack several of the shacks together and improve them, but we bought a trailer house, which was a lot nicer than anything you could make from the shacks."

In addition to the commercial and community properties, the village had upward of 50 homes, with electricity provided by a large generator, and a system of roads to shuttle the woodsmen to their work areas each morning.

Though it was a vibrant company community comprised mainly of central Wisconsinites that migrated to Tomahawk's northern Minnesota holdings, by 1964 the logging had apparently deteriorated.

"They (Tomahawk Timber) came to us (the wood cutters) and said if we'd take a cut in the price we were getting a cord, they'd be able to keep going," Ferdinand Thums remembers. "We said okay, but they still closed up a year or so afterward. We never did figure out what was going on, because there was still a lot of nice timber in the area, but it was right on the edge of the Boundary Waters (Canoe Area) and a lot of our cutting was going on in the BWCA. I'm pretty sure that had something to do with it."

Today, visitors in the area are unlikely to find any vestige that this once active little townsite ever existed. Forest Center was razed in 1965, with the buildings being either burned, buried or moved to other locations. The school proved to be one of the more migratory denizens of Forest Center, being first moved to Murphy City and then traveling on to Finland, where it now serves as the Recreation Center.

The former residents scattered somewhat, with a fair number migrating to the Knotted Pine area of Isabella, where most continued to work in the logging business and several went on to become independent loggers.

"We went up there last fall," Ferdy and Pat say. "The only thing we saw that we recognized easily was the big rock where the sawmill had been. The whole townsite was grown up with trees and the only way we even found where we lived was because the fellow who lived across the road from us had tied an orange marker ribbon to a tree in what had been his yard."[22] ▲

Although he quickly took a dislikeing to filing the finer teeth of the thin bow saw blades, he preferred that implement to the more cumbersome, troublesome crosscut saws used by some other cutters. He also remembered that the first of the chainsaws were heavy, smoky and required a fair amount of maintenance, but rapidly became the "bull of the woods," since cutters instantly found their production and income increased with this new tool.[23]

Although the operation was basically organized to produce pulpwood for its papermill in Tomahawk, Wisconsin, the company sawmill produced a considerable amount of lumber and, to keep both the sawmill humming and the railroad pulp cars moving, Ferdinand says the workers cut logs from any trees that had the correct dimensions, with pulpwood coming from smaller trees and the tops that remained after logs were selected.

The Tomahawk Timber operation was so large that the Superior National Forest established a separate ranger district, the "Halfway District," to manage that timber harvest. Over the life of the operation, Tomahawk set up six

Lois Pelto Memories of Forest Center

"Our first home in northern Minnesota was in a Northwest Paper Company logging camp near Wolf Lake about 35 miles southwest of Ely," says Lois Pelto, who settled there with her husband and 10-month-old daughter, Cherie, in a 10-foot-by-14-foot, primitive shack in September 1956. Having no electricity, outdoor toilets and a central outside well for water – when it wasn't frozen – presented challenges and an abundance of memories.

"Cherie was walking when we got to camp, which was called Palmquist Camp after the jobber who ran it. After the snow came, the roof leaked and water froze on the floor. Needless to say, my baby spent a lot of time sitting on the bed playing with her toys."

Lois and her family moved to the Northwest Paper Schreffler Camp near Bog Lake off the Tomahawk Trail 50 miles southeast of Ely in January 1957. The Northwest Paper headquarters and the Oppel and Carlson camps were nearby, in what is now the border area of the BWCAW.

Their new "home" was a 12-foot-by-16-foot structure located in a gravel pit – to avoid the muddy conditions that spring brought. Six men and one other woman, Vonda Schreffler, lived in the camp. Since Cherie wasn't potty trained, Lois spent a good deal of time each day carrying and heating wash water from a pump about two blocks away to do diapers and other laundry, scrubbing clothes by hand in a large tub on a metal washboard. After washing, the clothes were hung outside to freeze, then brought in and hung from indoor clotheslines strung from the log rafters of the shack to finish drying. They did have gas lamps and a gas refrigerator, but were regularly visited by wolves and, after spring thawing, bears.

Her oldest son was born in March 1957 at the Winton Hospital – the new Ely Hospital was not yet finished – and in April they again relocated, this time on the Little Isabella River near Bald Eagle Lake, where great fishing, huge blueberries and even bigger mosquitoes are remembered. After a year, her husband joined Tomahawk Timber Company, which assigned them to a camp at Quadga Lake consisting of 10-foot-by-14-foot shacks. Because they had a family, the company allowed them two shacks, which were placed in an L-shape so the doors would face one another, with an open platform between. One shack was used as the kitchen/living area and the other served as the sleeping room. The platform was hastily enclosed after Lois heard something walking on the platform and discovered huge wolf tracks in a dusting of snow on the deck separating her from the kids during their nap. In August 1958, her daughter Laurie was the 13th baby born in the new Ely Hospital.

While the remote camps were shantytowns in the strictest sense of the word, the village of Forest Center on Isabella Lake was a different story. She and her neighbors at Quadga were moved there in the spring of 1959 and she and her husband bought a 10-foot-by-50-foot trailer home that fall.

"The village had several sections and the company seemed to move people from the camps into the same area of the village, so neighbors stayed together," Lois remembers.

She immediately appreciated the electricity, indoor plumbing, the school for her kids, the nearby laundry, the monthly dances at the school and the neighborliness of the village. After the birth of another son in 1960 and a daughter 1961, they moved to Isabella, where a number of other Forest Center families were also relocating in the vicinity of the Knotted Pine Tavern.

She remembers that many of the Forest Center women worked at planting trees, picking princess pine and gathering pine cones to earn extra income. In the woods, the cutters earned piecework prices in the range of $7.50 a cord, so the women's added incomes were always welcome.[24] ▲

The rail yard at Forest Center was busy for many years after the D&IR pushed its railroad line from Whyte to the Lake Isabella town built by Tomahawk Timber Company for its work force. Up to 5,000 carloads of pulp were shipped on the line from the late 1940s until the company pulled out of the area in 1965. Forest Center's buildings were moved, razed or burned and nothing remains of the town. FRANK KING COLLECTION, NE MINNESOTA HISTORICAL SOCIETY

different camps, with Forest Center being largest and best known. But, like its predecessors from the earlier logging era, when the economics of longer hauls and less desirable timber caught up with the operation, Tomahawk warned its workers in 1964 to start thinking about other jobs. The entire operation was shut down in 1965, with the buildings being burned, buried or moved. Thus ended the last of the logging "boomtowns" of Lake County, although a fair number of the former Tomahawk workmen would stay in Lake County, particularly in the Isabella and Murphy City area, and would continue in the logging industry.[25]

The roads that had once served the boomtown communities of Winton, Section 30 and, to a lesser degree, Forest Center also opened access to many lakes that attracted hunters, anglers and other recreationally oriented visitors. Because the area to the north and east was already part of the Superior National Forest or became part of the BWCA after Tomahawk Timber built its roads and other access points, there was far less opportunity for private parties to develop lakeshore property in that area.

In the area east of Ely, however, cabins, cottages and resorts had been built on lakeshore parcels through the years. In fact, the exclusion from the BWCAW of White Iron, Farm, Garden lakes and a major portion of Fall Lake, as well as a rather incongruous strip of land along the Fernberg Road that jabs eastward into the BWCAW for about 18 miles, are all likely the result of earlier private development of properties in those excluded areas. Eventually many of the seasonal dwellings in these areas were expanded into or replaced by year-round residences, whose owners took up permanent residence in the "foreign" territory of Lake County, Minnesota.

While it's true that there has always been a county commissioner representing the residents of this far northern and western Lake County area, the focus for civic and social life has naturally tended to be nearby Ely. Their children attend school there, their shopping occurs there, they subscribe to the newspaper from Ely and they have a considerable drive when they need to attend to county or school business in Two Harbors. Indeed, to even make that trip, they have to go into Ely to pick up Highway 1, so it's little wonder that they often feel closer to their St. Louis County neighbors than they do with the workings of Lake County.

Developing Taconite and Parks

The development of Silver Bay as a company town for Reserve Mining (now Northshore Mining) Company in the mid-1950s created a major boom in both employment and land sales. While it is not recorded that any of the local landowners became ostentatiously wealthy by selling their property to the company, it is true that market prices were paid – unlike the earlier instance of the logging companies paying very little for the timber they purchased from some of the same local land-owning families.

The Reserve owner companies, Armco Steel and Republic Steel, spent hundreds of millions of dollars in constructing not only the massive lakeshore plant, but the primary crushers and the Peter Mitchell Mine at Babbitt. The construction of the mainline railroad from those facilities to Silver Bay also provided major employment for local residents, as well as the "imported" workers that streamed into the area. The mainline was originally built as a single rail operation, but a second track was added shortly after it opened. In addition, the company also developed the cities at each end of the operation that were needed to house the 2,500 employees and their families.

Much earlier in the history of this area of the north shore, work was completed in 1910 on the Split Rock Lighthouse. For decades, that important beacon warned ships away from the rocky shoreline that sank a number of ships, including the *Madeira* and *Lafayette* and severely damaged the *William Edenborn* in a single November storm in 1905.[1]

While the Split Rock Light did not provide significant employment to area settlers, it's attractive tower standing stalwartly atop the picturesque cliff provided a point of reference for boats passing that way and also gave numerous photographers a subject that nearly guaranteed them a monetary return. As it gained the public's affection, the lighthouse became a beacon that not only warned ships away from the north shore, but also drew attention to all the communities that were developing along that shore. As traffic increased along the shoreline when the International Highway made automobile travel possible in that corridor after 1924, the lighthouse and grounds were a favorite stop for motorists – also serving as a showplace for the U.S.

The wreck of the Lafayette *and a number of other ships along the north shore in 1905 raised awareness of the need for a lighthouse to guide ships away from the treacherous reefs and cliffs. Construction of Split Rock Lighthouse started in 1909 and was completed in 1910, when the light was dedicated.*

Coast Guard after that service took over operation in 1939.

The shoreline land where Reserve's huge plant would be built was settled in the early 1900s by a number of families, which included the Enok Edwardsens, Irma and Sievert Aakvik, Otto Rise, Simonsens, Oscar Pedersen and Petra and John Sorvik. All were involved in fishing, but also farmed to produce staples for their families. Gardens were tended, fodder and grain were harvested for the sheep, hogs and cattle that produced meat, wool and milk products that helped these settlers maintain good health and economic self-sufficiency. Since the men tended the nets, cleaned, packed and shipped the fish that gave them their main income, much of the work at the homestead was done by their wives and children.[2]

Nearby, of course, the long-established settlement at Beaver Bay provided mail service, shopping and other amenities for the scattered fishing families of the area, also serving as a social center for a considerable stretch of the shore. The families who remained there or settled after the Wieland brothers left in about 1883 – the Hangartners, Betzlers, Lorntsons, Slaters, Mattsons, Lovolds, Tates, Schaffs and others – were deeply ingrained by this point and only the rush of activity surrounding the early 1950s construction of Reserve Mining Company would disrupt their longtime stewardship of the homestead lands surrounding their townsite.

After road improvements opened the area to automotive traffic, the Beaver Bay Club, an exclusive enclave of summer homes owned by affluent Twin Cities residents, was established in May 1920, with Mrs. Henry "Ma" Slater as manager until her death in 1932. The club retains its exclusive nature to the present time. At about the same time that the Beaver Bay Club was being formed, Encampment Forest was developing farther to the west, serving the same purpose. Members of two branches of the Pillsbury family of Minneapolis are listed as important early members of both of these developments – with the "flour" Pillsburys at Beaver Bay and the "Munsingwear" Pillsburys at Encampment Forest.[3]

But despite such proximity to monied people, the residents of the north shore continued to pluck a living in whatever manner presented itself. Fishing was undoubtedly the mainstay for many, with logging also being an important source of income. The docks and railroad at Two Harbors also drew workers from a wide area during the shipping season – providing stable employment and wages that helped them maintain their scattered holdings.

Oscar Pedersen's Silver Bay Store was an early business enterprise that would lend its name to the city that was built in the 1950s when Reserve Mining Company was built.

In the 1920s, homesteader Oscar Pedersen opened and ran the Silver Bay Country Store on what would become the Reserve plantsite. After Pedersen's store had been open a while, he added cabins for tourists and Dorothy and Captain Nick Petersen, an ore boat captain, later opened and ran White Rock Cabins next door to Hjalmer Peterson's store about a mile west of Oscar's Silver Bay store. Captain Nick became legendary for sailing his ore boat between Pancake Island and the shoreline – a feat that did not necessarily endear him to his superiors.

The site got the name of Silver Bay when the captain of the SS *America* told Oscar Pedersen that the rocky shoreline had the appearance of silver. Pedersen liked that image and stuck the name on a small sign at his store. In about 1946, the Betzler family moved from the family's original homestead on the Beaver River (presently the Silver Bay Golf Course) into the store property and also operated tourist cabins.[4]

In an undated, unsigned transcript of a recorded interview with several members of the Betzler family, John said, "When

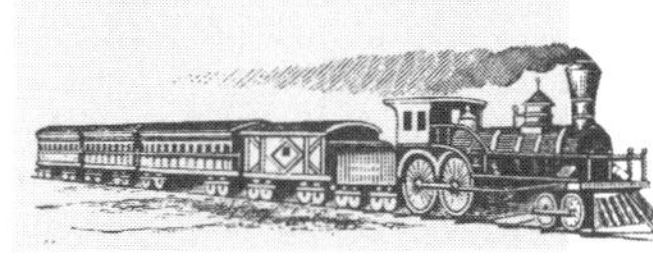

This and facing page: *The Pete Peterson homestead at Beaver Crossing dramatically shows conditions in which early settlers lived. The logged-over land was often rocky and inhospitable to farmers, yet many of the early settlers persisted and a few actually prospered.*

we first lived in Silver Bay, it was a three family community. Us and Swen Edwardsen across the road and the Jacobsen family.... There were summer homes along the shore. People from Minneapolis, Chicago and St. Louis lived in those at the time. So there were several different people who owned property and the Mattson family (also) owned quite a bit."

The Betzlers remembered attending school at Beaver Bay, in the building that would much later become the city's Green Door Bar and Liquor Store. The two-room elementary was characterized as quite a modern school, compared with some other schools in nearby settlements. Rosie especially remembered the school as being warm and clean with indoor plumbing, which was at that time a much appreciated novelty during cold weather.

Although the Betzlers were one of only three families in the immediate neighborhood, they remembered there were a number of fishing families scattered in both directions from their new homesite and that lakeshore resorts attracted many visitors to the area by that time.

Thus, there had been commerce on the townsite for several decades before the agents of the mining company began acquiring land in the latter 1940s. Prior to 1940, Reserve's owners had already arranged contracts on the vast mine property, but most of the serious effort to acquire the other property it would need occurred after World War II.

Once a flow sheet for the taconite processing operation had been tested and was in place and the land had been purchased, clearing for the lakeshore plant and the mainline railroad connecting the plant to the Babbitt mine began in 1951. This work provided a wide range of jobs for local residents, as well as attracting hundreds of workers from throughout the Midwest. Although bulldozers could be used in some areas of the plant and townsite development, some areas were so steep and cliffy that hand work was the only way to do the job. Rock was blasted to level portions of the plant site and other areas, like the new route of Highway 61 through the site inland from the lakeshore. The rock was also used to construct the two breakwaters that connected from the shoreline to Pellet (at that time unnamed) and Pancake islands.[5]

The steel companies contracted with a consortium that came to be known as Hunkin, Arundel and Dixon for construction of the facilities. Construction personnel filled every dwelling place on the north shore. Dormitory facilities offered housing to those bachelors or family men who were not accompanied by families and a sizable trailer camp near the plant also housed many workers and their families during the construction. The dormitory dwellers were fed in a large mess hall.

By the spring of 1952, more than 20 miles of railroad right of way had been cleared and the Highway 61 relocation was nearly complete above the plantsite. That first 20-mile segment of railroad provided a crucial link with the Duluth Missabe & Iron Range Railroad at Norshore Junction near the Jordan Crossing on State Highway 2. This junction would be critical in the construction, since it provided direct rail access to transport all of the equipment and other materials needed to build the huge plant on the lakeshore. By that fall, the harbor was more than half finished.

Over the 47-mile total length of the railroad, it rises about 900 feet in elevation between Silver Bay and Babbitt. Locomotives pull the empty cars up that long, gradual slope, but glide down the grade with loaded trains, each of which hauls about 8,000 tons of crude ore. Up to 10 trains a day were used when the full capacity of more than 10 million tons of pellets a year was being produced in the 1970s.

Throughout the summer of 1952, leveling of the plantsite went on 24 hours a day. Although the initial plant was built to produce only 3.5 million tons of pellets annually, the clearing encompassed the entire area that was planned for use when and if expansion increased that tonnage to 10 million tons per year.

The location of the townsite, while attractive in its amphitheater configuration, had only thin topsoil over rock ledge and required blasting in numerous areas to lay water and sewer lines. What scanty topsoil there was consisted largely of red clay and this created its own problems, as Jack Gralewski related in an interview. Jack served as a mechanic working on the equipment used by the townsite contractors.

"They were filling a kind of swampy area where the Campton School was going to be built and it was the middle of winter when the work was done. They pushed the clay into the hole and when it thawed out later they had a heckuva mess – just a muck hole. Naturally, it needed a lot of work before they started to build the school."[6]

That the building served for about 20 years as a school, later was rented and used for county and other offices and has since been converted into the Silver Bay Veterans Home probably tells us that the necessary initial work was done satisfactorily by the contractor. Unlike homes destined for Babbitt, Silver Bay's new homes could not be transported in prefabricated units on Highway 61, because several bridges restricted the size of the loads trucks could haul, so the houses were completely assembled at the site.

Even so, the townsite of one-story, story-and-a-half or two-story dwellings was assembled, offering the occupants a choice of basement or not. Included in the construction was the shopping center and other public facilities to make this a modern development. Although they could rent the houses reasonably from J.W. Galbreath and Company, many of the earliest residents

opted to purchase the new houses, with no money down and monthly payments as low as $65 per month.[7]

During the construction of the townsite, sod was purchased from farms in a wide area and hauled by a fleet of perhaps a dozen trucks, according to Gralewski. The late Les Hermans, who was a supervisor on the construction crew, laughed as he later admitted that there were times when as much as every other truckload of sod purchased for the townsite actually ended up being laid at the golf course, which was built on the former Betzler homestead as somewhat of a "moonlight" project of the townsite construction.

The new company that arose at Babbitt and Silver Bay was called the world's first commercial taconite production plant, but was, in fact, preceded by about 30 years by another plant that processed taconite ore at the Peter Mitchell minesite and shipped the iron ore through Two Harbors.

That earlier venture had been financed by investors like Bernard Baruch, Percy Rockefeller and others, but ultimately failed after only a couple of years, primarily because it was well ahead of its time. Ample natural ore was still being produced cheaply on the iron ranges. Adding to that marketing problem of the early endeavor, no really effective means of drilling blast holes in the hard, abrasive ore formation had yet been developed and, since drilling and blasting the solid ore body is the first step in the process to mine and upgrade the 25 to 35 percent iron content in taconite to a commercially viable iron content of about 65 percent, the investors abandoned the project in 1924, after shipping 150,000 tons of iron ore "sinter" through Two Harbors.

Taconite then remained a dead issue in the iron ore business until World War II virtually depleted the rich hematite ore of the Vermilion, Mesabi and Cuyuna iron ranges – except for the University of Minnesota school of mines team of "taconite scientists" and engineers led by Dr. Edward W. Davis. Dr. Davis, for whom the Silver Bay plant later would be named, worked with Reserve throughout its development, startup and later operation and spent the last years of his life in Silver Bay prior to his December 1973 death.

Davis and his team had worked years in developing a practical means of concentrating the iron ore that existed in the massive taconite ore body on the Mesabi Range. The processes that he and his researchers developed were first used and improved in the early Peter Mitchell plant and continued to evolve to form the basis for all later development of taconite ore.

The concentration of taconite involves several phases of crushing and grinding the crude ore to the fineness of talcum powder, at which point magnetic separators can remove the tiny iron particles from the waste rock and produce high-grade iron concentrate. The first plant in the Babbitt area shipped "sinter," an irregularly shaped mass of ore hardened by heating. After the failure of that plant, the Davis team determined that pelletizing the ore made it easier to handle and more desirable for use in modern blast furnaces. Pellets became the accepted product of all subsequent producers in the U.S. iron ore industry. The high-temperature firing of the iron ore pellets alters the iron particles from magnetic to non-magnetic hematite – the form of iron ore preferred by blast furnace operators.

Since drilling was a problem in the first taconite plant at Babbitt, Oglebay Norton and Company, which originally organized Reserve Mining Co. and served as operating or managing agent for the owner companies

through the development stages, assisted in the development of jet-piercing drills by Linde Air Products Company. Focusing high-temperature flame against the surface of the taconite rock, which created a spalling effect to pierce through the tough ore at a rate of 35 feet an hour, these newer model drills created blast holes much more rapidly and at lower cost than the rotary drills that had previously been used. Since drilling and blasting of the solid ore body is critical, these improved drilling techniques made a dramatic improvement in ore handling.

In 1948, Erie Mining Co. had started a pilot plant rated to produce 100,000 tons of pellets a year at Aurora and a year later Reserve opened its pilot plant at Babbitt to test various equipment and processing techniques in the resurrected 1920s plant building. Both the Erie and Reserve pilot plants used the DM&IR to move their pellets to Two Harbors for shipment to owner companies that were testing the product in their blast furnaces farther down the Great Lakes.

Early in the Reserve development phase, engineers determined that there would be a problem in obtaining enough water to process large amounts of ore at the Babbitt site, which sits at the top of the continental divide, with water quickly flowing away to either Hudson Bay or Lake Superior. The decision was made to build the main plant on Lake Superior, where the large volume of water required in the process would be easily accessible.

As it ultimately developed, Reserve Mining Company was designed to mine and do primary crushing of the taconite ore at its Babbitt mine location, transporting the crushed ore over its twin-track mainline railroad to Silver Bay for fine crushing, grinding, concentration, pelletizing and shipping. As designed, the initial Silver Bay plant was to produce 3,750,000 tons of high-grade iron ore annually, but by the second year the plant was already exceeding that tonnage by 250,000 tons a year. Silver Bay was also the site of the generating plant that supplied much of the electricity needed by the operation and, as noted earlier, the plant site and buildings were designed to be added onto when the need was such that an addition was logical.

Mine waste material, called tailings, was washed from the plantsite into Lake Superior by a sluiceway. Since about two-thirds of pit-grade ore becomes tailings, upward of 7.5 million tons of tailings a year were produced in the early stages of

HOUSING AREA
MAY 21, 1955
SILVER BAY, MINN

Of Hearings and Herrings: The Reserve Tailings Tale

The longtime litigation over Reserve Mining Company's permits to dispose of its tailings in Lake Superior became the most watched and one of the most prolonged lawsuits in north shore history. Jobs, the economy, the safety of the drinking water in several communities and the welfare of many families hinged on the outcome of those lawsuits.

From the beginning, Reserve's engineers and designers assured the public that the disposal of tailings into the lake would cause no problems in water quality, since the coarse tailings would create a density current that would pull the finely ground smaller particles (fines – about the consistency of talcum powder) to the bottom of a trench off the Reserve property, sealing them in place.

Some who heard that theory did not take it at face value. North shore fisherman Ragnvald Sve and son, Walter, of Split Rock River were two of many commercial fishermen who took it personally when Reserve Mining Company began disposing of tailings into Lake Superior in October 1955.

"My dad had been fishing from Split Rock since 1927 and I started when I was 16 years old in 1944," Walter remembers. "Up until about 1955 or '56, we also ran three deep sea fishing charter ▶

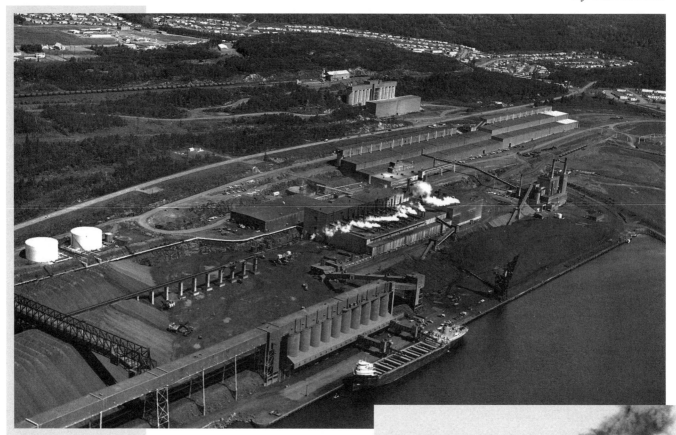

Republic and Armco Steel Companies finally decided that dwindling iron ore reserves on the nation's iron ranges necessitated a new source of iron ore. They invested hundreds of millions of dollars in building Reserve Mining Company, Silver Bay and Babbitt. ***Inset:*** *Although Reserve was dubbed the first taconite production plant, in fact an earlier company had used ore from the Peter Mitchell Mine and shipped upward of 150,000 tons of high grade iron sinter from Babbitt to Two Harbors.*

the Reserve plant development and more than 20 million tons would be produced each year after the expansion of the plant to produce 10 million tons of iron ore.

In contrast, Erie Mining, the second company to build a railroad across northern Lake County, would haul only its finished pellets from the company's plant at Hoyt Lakes to Taconite Harbor in Cook County. Although the processing of the ore at each plant was virtually identical, the notable difference of Erie's on-land tailings disposal basin would prove to be a difference that became critical in the future of Reserve Mining.

From the early days of the Reserve pilot tests, William M. "Doc" Kelley was credited by E.W. Davis with keeping the team of disparate engineers, scientists and other experts working in harmony and toward the common goal of developing good procedures to utilize taconite ore.

A Republic Steel Company vice president who rose through the ranks from apprentice machinist, Kelley spent his entire life in iron and steel production and seemed to revel in the tough role of developing, building, installing and maintaining new plants for the steel industry. Sixty years old when he arrived as vice president of the fledgling Reserve taconite project, the culmination of his career was to be the steady hand with which he guided the original research and his oversight of the construction and start-up of the huge commercial plant that resulted from that research.

As a 65-year-old, Kelley was named first president of Reserve, saw the project and the Silver Bay townsite through to success and, within a short time of the plant hitting its stride, he would quietly turn over his duties to Robert J. Linney, the second president of the corporation. But the memory of Kelley's professional and civic contributions to the area remains embedded in the consciousness of the north shore in the form of William M. Kelley High School at Silver Bay.

The actual construction of Reserve and Erie Mining companies occurred within a year or so of one another and created a huge boom in the area. Even vacationers to the north shore were caught up in the excitement and were welcomed at observation sites that let them view the development activities at both Silver Bay and Taconite Harbor, which is the shipping port and electrical generating site for Erie (later LTV Steel) Mining Co.

As might be expected with an entirely new technology and inexperienced workers at a huge operation like the Silver Bay Reserve mill, many obstacles had to be overcome in the start-up phase in 1955-56. Fine crushing of the hard, abrasive ore was the first major impediment to the smooth flow of ore through the operation and an additional line of fine crushers was installed by the end of 1956 to address that problem. The crushers then produced more dressed ore than the grinding mills and magnetic separators could handle. A two-foot extension in the length of the grinding mills solved that problem.

The quality of the early pellets was not satisfactory, producing an acceptable 64 percent iron, but upward of 15 percent fine materials (dust and the remnants of pellets that fell apart in handling), which the blast furnace operators found unacceptable. This problem was met with a series of improvements in the pelletizer that eventually led to less than 5 percent "fines."

As the pelletizer crews worked on the latter problem, the SS *C.L. Austin* arrived on April 6, 1956, to load 10,800 long tons (a long ton equals 2,200 pounds) of pellets from the large stockpile that had grown during the winter. The Wilson Transit Company ship was navigated into the harbor by Captain Peter J. Peterson in 45-mile-per-hour wind that was blowing a snowstorm. The ship left two days later bound for Republic Steel's furnace operation at South Chicago.

And, while all of the construction, organization and reconfiguring of the new taconite plant was taking place, the families in the company townsite were also seeing changes from the original ruggedness of life there. In 1954, it was officially announced that the original name chosen for the site by Oscar Pedersen would be retained for the townsite. On May 1, 1954, Mrs. Arnold Erickson, who ran the town's first post office from a house on the corner of Adams and Aiken Drive, received an official Postal Service cancellation stamp for "Silver Bay, Minnesota" and did a thriving business for several days postmarking the first post cards and other outgoing mail canceled with the name of the newest town in Minnesota.

The first church erected in the townsite was the Sychar Lutheran edifice, followed by the United Protestant and Catholic denominations. Clubs like Rotary, Jaycees, Veterans of Foreign Wars, Masons, Lions and others were organized.

The vote authorizing the incorporation of the Village of Silver Bay was held October 16, 1956, and the first election for public office was held November 27, with Len Brickles selected as mayor and Theodore Mathews, Roy Jacobson, Peter V. Bromme and Walter H. Frey elected to the council.

Meantime, many of the north shore's longtime residents found that the company offered not only steady work and wages, but that the area now had amenities they had not enjoyed in earlier days. A goodly contingent of construction and, later, plant employees carpooled from Finland, Isabella, Little Marais, Two Harbors and points farther away. Many newcomers to the area had moved to the new town site, while earlier residents used the security of a stable income to build additions to their homes. There seemed no end to the possibilities this huge new operation brought to the area.

All of the pellets produced at Reserve were divided equally by Armco and Republic steel companies, which underwrote the cost of construction and now received the pellets at the cost of production and shipping – which ran $10 to $20 per ton. At first, the pellets were simply dumped into the blast furnaces and mixed with natural ore.

Years earlier, the university taconite research team had predicted that pelletized iron ore would be an improved feed stock for blast furnaces, but, from the opening of the plant until 1960, the owner companies pretty well ignored that projection. By the end of the 1950s, the rich red natural ore was rapidly being depleted and the first tests to smelt blast

▶ *boats for trout fishermen, as well as our commercial nets, but the lampreys ruined trout fishing by about 1955."*

His father, Ragnvald, heard of meetings in St. Paul at which Reserve Mining's request for permits to dispose of tailings into the lake was being reviewed. Walter says, "Dad got Einer Edwardson from Silver Bay, Alvin Wick from Castle Danger and Paul Norby and Carl Erickson from Knife River to go to the meeting with him.

"The commercial fishermen knew the lake and told the people at the meeting that currents would move the fine tailings west and it would get into water plants like Two Harbors and Duluth. They were told they didn't know what they were talking about. Not many years later, filtering plants had to be built for those water systems."

Walter also says that herring fishing had remained good, even after the trout levels crashed when the lamprey invaded the lake, but that this would not last for long.

"Herring don't like dirty water and by August 27, 1956, the current had already carried dirty water past our place about 10 miles west of the plant and the herring moved farther and farther away from shore to avoid that water. Where we used to be able to see 50 or 60 feet down in the lake, the water clarity dropped to only a foot or so." ▶

furnace charges consisting only of pellets were undertaken at Armco's Bellefonte Furnace in Middletown, Ohio, during the summer of 1960.

Several 30-day test runs using pellets as the only furnace feed simply stunned the iron industry and proved the validity of the University of Minnesota team's predictions. The furnace was smelting 1,500 tons of pig iron a day from mixed ores, but poured 2,700 to 2,800 tons a day in the test runs using pellets only. Production estimates would later predict a 92 percent increase in production capacity per furnace-load of pellets, with a savings of up to 27 percent in energy consumption. The uniform size and shape of the pellets made such increases possible simply by increasing the amount of air blown through the blast furnace load.

Dr. Edward W. Davis of the University of Minnesota school of mines headed a research group that developed, tested and touted the use of the vast Mesabi deposits of taconite iron ore. Called the "father of taconite," he worked with any company that showed interest. The process he and his team developed to extract and concentrate the iron ore is still in use today. The plant at Silver Bay was officially named for him when it opened and he retired and made his home at Silver Bay until his 1973 death.

With the announcement of such dramatic superiority of pellets for blast furnace feed stock, the steel companies that owned Reserve almost immediately announced a $120 million expansion of the Silver Bay plant to double production to 9 million tons per year. Another wave of construction workers descended on the area and worked feverishly on the job. Increased capacity meant an increase in permanent jobs, as well, and the townsite was expanded to meet housing needs for these employees. The future economy of the north shore seemed as solid as the dense taconite ore on which much of that security depended.[8]

But this early impression of rock solid stability was more illusory than most economists would have suggested, for the future would conjure a mixture of public perception and legal entanglement that threatened the very existence of this major new industry in Lake County.

As described earlier, the decision to build the plant on Lake Superior had originally been made because the large volume of water needed in the process was doubtful at the Babbitt minesite. Lake Superior could supply that need with scarcely a ripple.

The bulk of the water that was taken from Lake Superior for use in the process would be returned to the lake as plant discharge containing the waste tailings. Hydrological studies of the time that were conducted for the company indicated that there would be little or no degradation of the water or the lake from the process, since the coarse, heavier tailings would settle relatively quickly from the water as a delta that would be little affected by wind or water movement. The finer waste material would be carried into and collect in a deep trough located a bit farther off shore from the plant. This deep deposition of "fines" theoretically shielded them from surface currents and turbulence that would stir them and cause muddy water.

Although skeptics of that theory came forward almost at once and dogged the company through much of its history, the Silver Bay plant continued to discharge its waste tailings into the lake until March 20, 1980, even after the major expansion in the early 1960s increased the ore production to more than 10 million tons per year and the tailings tonnage to more than 20 million tons per year.

Despite a widespread public relations campaign that touted the enormous economic benefits of taconite production to Minnesota and the Iron Range, as well as an aggressive housekeeping program that maintained nearly antiseptic conditions in the plantsite, continuing efforts to educate the public about environmental concerns and free plant tours for virtually anybody who showed up at the front door, many north shore visitors who passed the plant on Highway 61 viewed the operation as an intrusion on the pastoral lakeshore experience they were enjoying.

Then, a report in early 1969 that the company was causing extensive pollution led to a September 1969 lawsuit by the Sierra Club and the Minnesota Committee for Environmental Information demanding that state licensing groups hold hearings on supposed violations of state permits by Reserve. That litigation would stretch out for eight years, before the company was ordered in 1977 to quit dumping waste tailings into Lake Superior by April 15, 1980.[9]

Through much of that period, the company seemed to always be in headlines and endlessly involved in legal proceedings that carried the ultimate threat of shutting down the operation. For nearly the entire decade of the 1970s, Minnesotans continued to hear that the tailings from the mill contained minerals that resembled asbestos and therefore might be a hazard to public health. Other evidence was presented that refuted that claim.

Arguments raged back and forth, with experts on both sides, and Judge Myles Lord seemingly always in the center stirring things up, until he was thrown off the case in early 1976. Whatever the truth, the claim of asbestos contamination carried enough weight that several cities that used Lake Superior for drinking water added filters to block any such fibrous minerals from reaching consumers. A number of private owners of water wells like WDIO/WIRT-TV in Duluth also made complimentary well water available to people willing to travel to fill water containers from those wells.

Other allegations claimed that large areas of greenish water were being observed in the big lake. While the exact composition and source of this phenomena remained murky, there was the implication that something in the waste tailings was creating these areas of doubtful water quality.

Adding credibility to all these claims, the sheer volume of waste material – upward of 20 million tons per year – was a daunting statistic to envision for those unaccustomed to thinking in terms of such large volumes of material. Perhaps worse, from Reserve's public relations standpoint, the sometimes mountainous heap of pellets stockpiled during winter and visible from the highway reminded travelers that twice that volume of waste tailings had also been produced and dumped into the lake.

Ultimately, as a result of the 1977 court order and as part of an upgrade of the Silver Bay plant, the company began construction of an on-land tailing disposal basin at Milepost 7 of its railroad, thereby muting the most persistent complaint about its operation.

The building and operation of a tailing basin large enough to dump 20 million tons of waste per year is no simple matter, however, and Reserve faced special problems. With an uphill climb from the plant to the tailings basin, the operation involved pumping fine materials in a huge new pipeline system, with rail transport of coarser, partially dry waste tailings from the lakeshore plant up the grade to Milepost 7 and into the tailing basin area.

Dams and dikes had to be built to contain the water and tailings. Rail was laid to the basin site and pipeline and pumping stations were constructed. All of this construction, plus the additional cost of operating the disposal system day-to-day, added a major new expense to the cost of the pellets – just at a time when new South American iron ore mines meant that steel companies were demanding and getting lower prices on the ore they bought.

Ultimately, the overall $375 million cost of the tailing disposal basin and the upgrading of the plant resulted in an improved pellet product and the operation is still producing some of the best pellets in the world, but the added cost of building and operating the tailing disposal area may have been the straw that broke the camel's back, for Reserve's fortunes sagged during the mid-1980s and the facility was shut down in 1986 by the bankruptcy of LTV Steel Company, which had merged with Republic Steel in 1984 to become a half owner of Reserve.[10]

The failure of the mining company imposed hardship not only on the folks who depended on wages from the company, but for businesses and service providers in a large area of northeastern Minnesota. Despite the fact that a good many of the employees of the company had originally been "packsackers" from outside the area, many of them now found they did not want to leave the north shore, which had become home to them and their children. Employees with enough years of service were eligible to receive some pension but, for many, these payments were not enough to sustain them.

In the economic downshift after the plant shut down, some families did leave, but a sizable percentage hunkered down and did what they could to survive. Life might have dealt them hard times, but there were other options for some of the displaced workers seeking employment in the area, thanks in part to the economic

▶ *Walter says he was setting nets as much as seven miles out in the lake to find herring. In 1962 or 1963, Walter, his father and five commercial fishermen from Knife River attended a meeting to tell what was happening to the lake, but that officers from Reserve had the floor virtually the entire meeting. Disgusted, the Knife River contingent of fishermen decided leave late in the day and, when Reserve finally relinquished the floor, the chairman asked if anyone else cared to speak and was surprised when Ragnvald and Walter raised their hands.*

"Gee fellas," the chairman stated. "It's almost five o'clock. Can you hurry it up?"

After the Sves related their experience on Lake Superior, the meeting adjourned and nothing happened. "What we told them didn't mean nothing," Walter says with a note of disgust in his voice.

But their efforts did finally gain the attention of others and Milton Mattson of Beaver Bay remarked to them, "I think you Sves need some help on this Reserve thing," and organized the Save Lake Superior Association in 1969.

"We got a lot of members in the association right away because so many people could see that you couldn't keep polluting this beautiful lake like that," Walter says, also noting that ▶

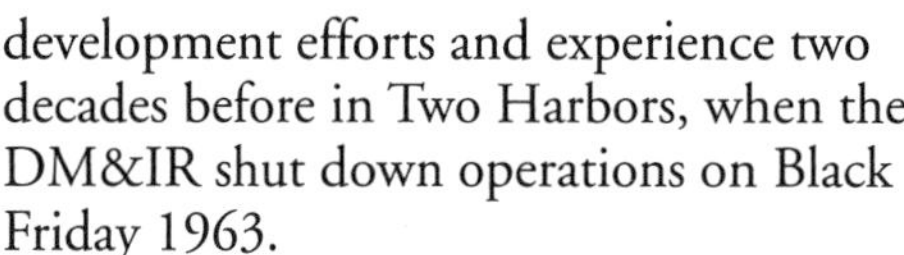

development efforts and experience two decades before in Two Harbors, when the DM&IR shut down operations on Black Friday 1963.

By this time, several successful companies were established in the Walter Norlen Industrial Park at Two Harbors and offered a scattering of jobs. With a wide range of job skills, the former Reserve employees became a pool of talent that these employers tapped. LaBounty Manufacturing was in a growth phase and hired some of the unemployed Reserve workers. Hahn Machinery, Northshore Steel and Two Harbors Machine Shop all used skilled workers. Louisiana Pacific Corporation was putting up a new plant to manufacture siding from processed aspen wood. Construction provided jobs for some of the former Reserve workers and a sizable permanent work force was hired when the plant went into production. Two Harbors Machine Shop in the downtown area was also putting up a new building in the Industrial Park.

Superior Shores was being developed as a new resort complex on Scenic Point just east of Two Harbors and needed workers with skills ranging from construction and woodworking to pool maintenance, housekeeping, food service, bartending and management.

Governmental units quickly stepped in to issue unemployment checks, aid in job searching and set up some "make work" projects. They also hired displaced Reserve workers whose skills matched the needs of their own permanent work crews. State, county, city and township officials scrambled to encourage development of businesses in the area to diversify employment for workers in Lake County. Tax Increment Financing, a program that waived some tax payments for a period of time to help cover start-up costs, was granted for some of the more promising developments. Silver Bay undertook development of its own Industrial Park, thereby posting notice that it intended to permanently cast off its role as a "company town" and seek a broader economic base.

While no single employer or development relieved the impact of the closure of Reserve Mining, the cumulative effect meant that many people who wanted to stay on the north shore were able to do so. Indeed, some of the employees who found other jobs during this period chose to remain in their new jobs when given the chance to return to the taconite plant after it was acquired by Cypress Minerals and reopened as Northshore Mining Company in 1989.

The reorganization of the taconite operation involved not only a multitude of financial arrangements, but major administrative changes like the elimination of union representation for employees and the introduction of management teams that gave employees a voice in the decision-making function.

As the first non-unionized iron producing facility in decades, the operation naturally came in for a good deal of skeptical interest and curiosity, but Cypress fashioned a package that enticed a sizable percentage of the former employees to return to the jobs they'd lost three years earlier. Even the specter of having no union backing did not dampen the enthusiasm at getting back to a familiar routine and regular paychecks that had been so unceremoniously interrupted.

In some ways, however, the veteran employees returning to the facilities found that the business had changed. Instead of measuring the plant's effectiveness primarily on the basis of maximum tonnages of homogeneous pellets it produced, the company now focused on a smaller volume of product, with the pellets increasingly tailored to the specifications of the buyers.

Cleveland Cliffs Corporation had been a bidder for the former Reserve Mining operation at the time that Cypress Minerals was awarded the bid by the court (Cliffs bid about $6 million more, in fact, than did Cypress). After the plant was operating, producing good pellets and had proven that it could operate efficiently, Cypress decided that this iron ore property did not really fit into its business very well, since the company was positioned to locate and develop mines to extract more exotic and profitable metals and minerals. Selling iron ore on the open market required an expertise and contacts that the company would need to either develop or contract for, and Cypress decided to shop for a buyer.

Cleveland Cliffs was already a major force in the Lake Superior iron business for nearly 150 years by that point, with ownership and/or management interests in the Tilden and Empire mines in upper Michigan and at LTV Steel Mining (formerly Erie Mining) in Hoyt Lakes, and Hibbing Taconite on Minnesota's Mesabi Range. As an original, unsuccessful bidder for the property, the company undoubtedly monitored the moves Cypress made at Northshore Mining and must have liked what it saw for, when the operation became available, Cliffs paid $66 million for the property that brought $53 million five years earlier, thereby boosting itself to the position of being the leading iron ore producer in North America.

The arrival of this old-line owner caused some speculation that the plant would revert to the rigid vertical management structure that had been in place prior to the Cypress era, but Cliffs assured employees it wanted to learn from their example. While some changes did take place, employees were largely comfortable that their voices were being heard in the decision-making process. By late 1999, Cliffs signed an agreement with the U.S. Steelworkers Union not to interfere with any effort to organize the Northshore workers, but there seemed little interest among the workers to move ahead in organizing a local at the company.

The future of the north shore plant continues to appear rosy at the start of the 21st century, with news headlines focused on the possibility that an addition to the Silver Bay plant would be built to produce up to 700,000 tons of direct reduced iron. Although direct reduction of iron ore into a more refined form of iron has been discussed on the Iron Range for years, shortly after Cleveland Cliffs took over Northshore, the company announced that it was moving into direct reduction, opting to put up the first plant in Trinidad. That plant was producing some product by the end of 1999, although it was not operating on a sustained basis in early 2000.

By late 1999, Cliffs and Northshore were into serious planning, analysis and environmental studies with various agencies to explore building a plant that was projected to increase employment by perhaps 200 to 350 people. The pig iron product would serve primarily electric arc steel furnace operators that have traditionally depended on scrap metal as feedstock in their operations.

Whatever the outcome of those studies, the fact that the corporate officers were moving ahead in their planning demonstrates the confidence that the company has in the skills, talent, work ethic and reliability of the people who built, operated and stayed in the area for the long haul, even when times looked grim.

Meanwhile, traffic on Highway 61 continues to increase and Split Rock Lighthouse State Park and Historic Site has a significant amount of that traffic stopping to experience a spirit of the north shore that seemed uniquely captured on the site. To serve that traffic, both the state park and the historical site expanded facilities, with additional parking and a new interpretative center adding many displays and exhibits to the lighthouse facilities. Additional acreage was added to the park when 80 acres that include the Gold Rock property was contributed by the Minnesota Parks and Trails Council in 1998.

Operated jointly by the Minnesota Historical Society and the Minnesota state parks system, Split Rock remains one of the most visited sites in Minnesota and provides jobs for a number of seasonal local employees who range from groundskeepers to historical interpreters during summers.

Nearby, the quaint village of Beaver Bay continued to be a favorite stop for many of the travelers on Highway 61. Shops that had once served a seasonal trickle of buyers adapted to meet the needs of many more tourists on a year-round basis. New businesses came to life. A small shopping center was built and immediately occupied by a variety of stores.

To the east of Silver Bay, Palisade Head is another north shore attraction that many visitors stop to enjoy again and again. Nearby, the evolution of the relatively small Baptism River State Park into Tettegouche State Park took place over a number of years as land was added through donations by the Parks and Trails Council, 3M Corporation and The Nature Conservancy. In 1994, the site of the original 3M quarry and plantsite at Crystal Bay was dedicated, giving the park a spectacular piece of Lake Superior shoreline. At that ceremony, a total of about 580 acres of property was added to the park by 3M and the cooperating organizations.

▶ his brothers Leonard and Floyd worked at Reserve. Since so many families depended on the company for a livelihood, Leonard and Floyd took a good deal of chaffing from other employees about the family's position.

Federal Judge Miles Lord closed the plant for two days in April 1974, citing the company for "substantially endangering the health of the people" in five communities, including Two Harbors and Duluth – as the testimony of the fishermen at the original meeting predicted. By 1976, Lord was tossed off the case, but his replacement, Judge Edward Devitt, socked Reserve with $1.1 million in fines for violating state pollution permits, willful disobedience and bad faith conduct.

Within a year, Judge Devitt also ordered Reserve to stop the Lake Superior tailings disposal operation by April 15, 1980. Work began in June 1977 to move tailings disposal on-land to meet that order – while the company also engineered changes inside the plant that would make its pellets more desirable on the iron ore market.

"When the tailings started going to the Reserve tailing basin at Milepost 7, the water in Lake Superior cleared up fairly fast and we started catching herring near here within about five years," Walter says. "We didn't really do any herring fishing from 1964 to 1990, ▶

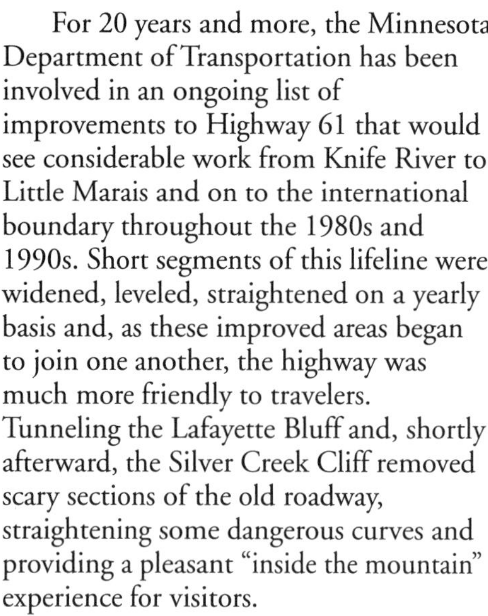

For 20 years and more, the Minnesota Department of Transportation has been involved in an ongoing list of improvements to Highway 61 that would see considerable work from Knife River to Little Marais and on to the international boundary throughout the 1980s and 1990s. Short segments of this lifeline were widened, leveled, straightened on a yearly basis and, as these improved areas began to join one another, the highway was much more friendly to travelers. Tunneling the Lafayette Bluff and, shortly afterward, the Silver Creek Cliff removed scary sections of the old roadway, straightening some dangerous curves and providing a pleasant "inside the mountain" experience for visitors.

The graceful, but aged Gooseberry River Bridge was replaced by a modern structure opened in 1998 that maintained the original bridge's classic arch. The sharp S-curve at the eastern end of that new structure was realigned in spring and summer 2000. To make way for that work, the former Gooseberry Falls State Park headquarters building built by the Civilian Conservation Corps during the Depression was abandoned and a new facility opened in the fall of 1997, with expanded space and facilities.

Cove Point Lodge at Beaver Bay opened its doors in the fall of 1995 on 150 acres of privately owned lakeshore near Beaver Bay and has become a favored accommodation for many travelers and visitors on Minnesota's north shore. This large, new development continues to add features that bolster to its reputation for a fine experience.

In late May 2000, LTV Steel Company announced that it was shutting down its LTV (formerly Erie) Steel Mining operation at Hoyt Lakes, casting a dark shadow over the future of the employees and the tax base that the company's railroad and power line provide to Lake County. While the announcement appears to be the final blow to that operation, only time will tell if this bell tolls a death knell or a wake up call for the oldish operation that has provided employment for residents in both the eastern and western reaches of northern Lake County. Some point out that the LTV mainline track and Taconite Harbor power plant and loading docks remain valuable properties and may yet be resuscitated by other interests. As with most historical documents, this story remains to have an ending written as this book goes to press.

A Tale of Two Attractions

Two of the earliest attractions on Minnesota's north shore continue to gain in popularity, as both Gooseberry Falls State Park and the Split Rock Lighthouse Historic Site and State Park see increased numbers of visitors each year.

In the early 1900s, when travel still depended on the ships and railroads that served the area, Lake County's rivers and wilderness were already a well-known outdoorsmen's paradise, offering abundant fishing, hunting and other outdoors experiences.

The Duluth & Northern Minnesota (Alger Line) offered Duluth and other sportsmen special weekend trips along the railroad rights of way to fish the Knife, Stewart, Baptism and other really productive angling rivers that the railroad crossed.

But those trips by rail or boat would prove to be a transitory mode of transportation, for the end of the Alger Line in 1921 and the construction of the International Highway (Route 61) in the 1920s saw automobiles become *the only* mode of travel for north shore travelers who could afford "any old Ford" – and highways would far outstrip anything the railroads and boats had offered.

Started in 1909 and commissioned in July 1910, Split Rock Lighthouse immediately became an attraction for passengers on the SS *America* and for photographers seeking a fresh site to imprint on post cards. A bit more than a decade later, the lighthouse site became a rest stop for highway travelers after the new lakeshore highway was opened.

Lee Radzak, manager of the Split Rock Lighthouse Historical Site, said, "Not long after the highway came through and travelers began to stop in, the keepers were instructed to dress in their uniforms on Sunday and to guide tourists through the site. The Lighthouse Service saw this as a showplace and even back in 1936 they estimated they had 100,000 people stopping here that year."[11]

With the solid evidence of a high level of interest in the north shore proven at

Split Rock Lighthouse Station, it's little wonder that local folks kicked off an effort in the 1920s to save the property adjacent to the new highway bridge over the Gooseberry River, with its spectacular view of the waterfalls on each side the bridge.

As he did so many times in the early days of the Two Harbors area, Thomas Owens again came to the forefront of an effort to promote a public facility at Gooseberry Falls. An admirer of the property formerly occupied by the Estate of Thomas Nestor Logging Company, Owens used his position as superintendent of the Duluth & Iron Range Railroad and as president of the Lake Superior International Highway Association to promote efforts to have the falls of the Gooseberry River preserved as a site for public enjoyment.

The property at that time was part of a 30,000-acre tract owned by the estate of former Wisconsin Senator William F. Vilas. Trustees of that estate were charged with managing it to benefit the University of Wisconsin. Those trustees were at first suspicious of plans to create a park on the Gooseberry River, but had begun to change their minds by the early 1930s.

It would be the Minnesota Highway Department's need for additional rights of way to widen the roadway and the original single lane bridge over the river that would serve as the means by which the state could acquire the 661 acres of land that became the park. By 1932, state officials and the trustees of the Vilas estate were in accord and the deal was struck in 1933 for both the rights of way and the park land.

Almost immediately, the Civilian Conservation Corps, a Great Depression works program for young men, moved a tent camp onto the river bank by the lower falls and the "boys" of Company 1720 began constructing permanent camp facilities upriver on the cliff above the upper falls. Once they completed the basic requirements for the camp, the tent unit moved out and Company 2710, the unit that actually did most of the work on the new park facilities, was activated.

The "boys" assigned to Company 2710 would be involved in a wide variety of activities, from brushing and clearing trails, removing debris left over from the logging days, blasting rock and masonry work involved in park buildings and other features. They were provided with most of the necessities and were expected to send at least half of their $30-a-month wage home for their families. They also had the opportunity to attend classes at "Gooseberry Falls University," a program affiliated with the University of Minnesota from Duluth.

Within a year, the CCCs had made major improvements, under the direct supervision of the National Park Service. With a careful eye to maintaining the natural features of the park land, native stone structures were planned and the massive stone structure known as the Concourse at the western embankment near the bridge was built specifically to accommodate automobile travelers with parking and viewing spaces.

Within two years, the campground, swimming and picnic areas were cleared, a number of buildings were completed, trails were extended in many directions and a host of other tasks were completed. Eventually, the construction crews built 13 stone buildings, eight "structures" and 65 "objects" of locally quarried red, blue, brown and black granite. The darker stone came from a site near East Beaver Bay, while the red granite was taken from an outcrop near the College of St. Scholastica in Duluth.

Although the park was recognized as a state facility virtually from the first day the land was acquired, it would be five years before all of the work was completed by the CCCs, who were also involved in a number of other projects like constructing the road into the Split Rock Lighthouse from the highway.[12]

As all of this activity was going on at Gooseberry, visitation at Split Rock Lighthouse was increasing and would take more and more time of the three keepers who were normally stationed there. After Coast Guard personnel began manning of the station in 1939, a lower ranking enlisted man was designated as a visitor host and tour guide to deal with the tourist traffic. Previously, that duty had been the responsibility of the head keeper, who decked out in his full-dress Lighthouse Service uniform on Sundays for the flow of visitors.

In 1942, Clyde Addams purchased the property between the highway and the

▶ *but we're doing all right again now."*

Meantime, with his fishing operation at a standstill by 1961, Walter went to work as a carpenter with Castle Danger contractor Richard Stone and would follow that trade for 30 years, until he retired and the herring fishing turned good again.

At 72 years of age, he is content to look back on a well-fought victory and to be back out on Lake Superior waters that are cleaner for that effort. Picking his nets in the early morning, he is again involved in dressing the finicky herring that the lake yields and peddling his catch to the numerous customers waiting to turn his catch into a delicious meal of fresh fillets or a memorable mound of fish cakes made from fresh-ground herring.

But don't expect to get those fish at the 2 to 3½ cents a pound he remembers receiving for the first fish he harvested in 1944. The days of many fishermen netting tons of herring are long gone on the north shore and the prices reflect that fact.[13] ▲

Hunting and other recreation have attracted people to northeastern Minnesota sites like this one near Gooseberry since it first was added to the United States.

lighthouse and established a gift shop within a few feet of the boundary of the station property, taking advantage of the traffic drawn to the site. Children of the keepers were often hired by Addams to work in the Split Rock Trading Post and the operation was successful for many years on the site, before the land was re-acquired in 1970 for inclusion in the Historic Site and State Park. The gift shop was moved to a parcel of private land on the highway and later took the name of the wrecked ore freighter, *Madeira*. The store was destroyed by fire in August 1999.

"The only time that we're aware of when visitors weren't welcome here was during World War II," manager Lee Radzak said. "In fact, the keepers were issued sidearms because there was a concern about spies and sabotage. The keepers welcomed the chance to show visitors around and show what they did. It was carefully maintained as a showcase and used for good public relations."

By 1961, the fog signal was discontinued and in 1968, the U.S. Coast Guard shut off the distinctive white flash of the light, which occurred every 9.5 seconds and was visible to mariners for 22 or more miles out over the big lake.

The federal government deeded the property to the Minnesota Department of Natural Resources in 1969, which operated the site and the adjacent Split Rock State Park until 1976, when the Minnesota Historical Society took over preservation and restoration of the 25-acre lighthouse site.[14]

In succeeding years, work on the historic site has focused on a two-pronged plan of action. First and foremost is the ongoing effort to restore and preserve the historic aspects of the site. Secondly, major planning and work resulted in the 1986 construction of a new building that welcomes visitors with easy parking, friendly, handicapped accessible rest rooms, an interpretative center and gift shop. An addition to that building was started in the fall of 2000 and will make the site even more attractive to visitors.

Today, the guides and re-enactors create an authentic experience of an earlier era when the site was almost as isolated as Siberia – a time when lamps were fueled by kerosene, a trip meant waterborne transportation and keepers continually worked to keep the lighthouse spruced up and ready to welcome the inspectors who arrived regularly with a sharp eye for any detail that wasn't up to par.

By the point when the Historical Society took over the lighthouse, the DNR was primarily interested in operating the state park that buffers the historic site. The park encompasses some 2,000 acres and has become a major north shore attraction for hikers, campers, nature fanciers and users of the water trail along the north shore.

Both Radzak and Gooseberry State Park manager Paul Sundberg expect increasing traffic in upcoming years at these two longtime tourist stops. The third state park, Tettegouche on the lakeshore at Baptism River, has also gained an enthusiastic audience, with unique features like the former site of the 3M "corundum" quarry and an historic set of buildings inland from the main buildings.

Two Harbors – Ups, Downs and Ups

Despite the death of 17 of its sons, along with thousands of other sons from the United States, Lake County's sacrifice in World War I did not apparently appease the world's rulers or its gods of war, for the recovery of Europe had barely started in the post-war period when Germany again began to make aggressive noises. Before that rumbling was over, 49 more Lake County residents would lose their lives.

Ultimately, the terms of the World War I peace treaty led to violent dissatisfaction among the German people, who elected Adolf Hitler as chancellor in 1933. A year later, this former corporal in the German Army would assume the dictatorship of Germany and lead his country into a series of adventures that were ever more provocative.

From 1934 onward, the world watched with increased foreboding as Hitler's forces became bolder and more aggressive in their invasion of neighboring land. In some cases, the excuse was made that the land had traditionally been German territory or was populated by Germanic people.

By the end of 1940, after the Panzer tanks, Luftwaffe air strikes and blitzkrieg tactics had subjugated not only so-called Germanic territories, but independent nations like Belgium, the Netherlands, Poland, Norway and France, it had become obvious that American participation in the war was inevitable. Well before the Japanese attacked Pearl Harbor on December 7, 1941, the United States was providing massive industrial aid to the nations resisting the forces of Hitler and his Axis allies, Italy and Japan.

The newly incorporated DM&IR Railroad was already registering massive iron ore tonnages in 1940, with the former D&IR Iron Range Division delivering a record 10.84 million tons through Two Harbors that year. The 1941 shipping season, which was pretty well finished before America entered the war in December, saw 15.1 million tons handled on the Iron Range Division and an aggregate total of 37.5 million tons by both divisions. In 1942, total tonnage would shoot upward to nearly 45 million tons and would remain above 40 million tons per year through the remainder of the war.[1]

Pearl Harbor was the catalyst that shattered the last vestiges of American "neutrality," unleashing America's wrath and mobilizing armed conflict wherever Hitler and his allies turned. Surely, the Axis leaders had underestimated or misunderstood the industrial and military capability of the United States, as well as the depth of this nation's commitment to world justice. Even before Pearl Harbor, more than 16 million men had registered for the draft in 1940 and many would shortly be called to active duty.

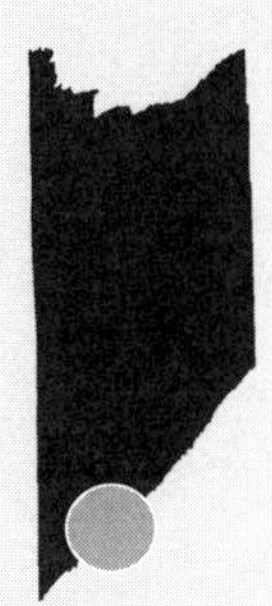

Though Beaver Bay was the first official county seat, the Lake County Courthouse has always been located at Two Harbors. Beaver Bay's county board meetings took place at residences or the school building. The county has been an important employer throughout its history.

The entry of the United States into the war had almost immediate results. Within five months of the December 10-11 declaration of war with Japan, Germany and Italy, the United States had landed the first American troops in Europe (Ireland), launched an April 18 retaliatory bombing strike on Tokyo from Navy aircraft carriers and recorded its first major naval victory over the Japanese in the battle of the Coral Sea on May 4-8. A month later (June 3-6) at Midway, naval ships would again intercept and pound the Japanese armada into retreat. By August, the full-blown invasion of Guadalcanal was under way and the first all-U.S. bombing attack against German territory struck Rouen, France, on August 17.[2]

On the home front, the young men who grew up in the harsh years of the Great Depression and found some rewards in the camps of the Civilian Conservation Corps were an important nucleus of draftees and recruits for the war effort. The CCC camps had been jointly operated by camp commanders who came from the military and civilian works administrators. The young men in those camps had, thus, been exposed to a bit of military discipline, had learned job skills and good work habits and were in good physical condition.

Most of the CCCers deeply appreciated the opportunities that the government had provided to them when times were tough and were ready to repay the government in whatever way they could. Within weeks of the declaration of war, thousands were enlisting or answering draft calls from Uncle Sam. The importance of their early presence in the ranks cannot be over-emphasized, for they needed a minimum of recruit training, knew how to live in an all-male fraternity, brought an important range of skills and experience to their military jobs, had learned the value of staying flexible and could adapt to a wide variety of situations.

The net cast by the military was wide and deep, however. Men and women of every class, skill, educational level or ethnic background were needed. Local draft boards quickly learned to turn a deaf ear to alibis, excuses or lies, although the patriotic fervor was such that even those who might be deferred for some reason often enlisted and served. Men subject to the draft had the option of signing up early in whatever service they preferred, whereas the draft exposed them to assignment in whatever service needed manpower.

The late Jim Swanson was a wheelman on an ore boat through the end of the season, when many of the sailors

The arrival of eight Mallet locomotives on the eastern branch of the DM&IR in 1941 came just in time to meet an enormous increase in ore shipments as the world went to war.

received notice they were being drafted into the Navy. Jim remembered that he and 52 other draftees were pulled out of the group of inductees at the Minneapolis screening center and were summarily assigned to the Marine Corps – based simply on their size. When they protested that they were drafted into the Navy, they were told that the Marine Corps is an arm of the Navy, and that explanation ended all conversation.

"The Marines were looking for guys who were big enough to lug around machine guns, ammunition and other heavy gear and we were the biggest guys in the group, so I ended up being a Marine machine gunner," he said, while indicating that he would have much preferred serving in the Navy. As a marine "grunt," he would serve honorably, if a bit grudgingly, through several of the island-hopping invasions in the Pacific that typified the Marine Corps' participation in World War II, but also recalled that of the 53 Minnesota men drafted into the Marine Corps, only 13 returned home after the war.

While men were subject to such vagaries in assignments under the Selective Service System, women could enter the military only by volunteering for service and increasing numbers did so as the war progressed – assuming more and more of the non-combat jobs. From drivers and ferry pilots of aircraft to nurses and supply personnel, women's roles in the military were important in freeing men to track down and defeat the Axis combat forces. Dorothy Huliares and Jean Bergman are recorded as the first women in Two Harbors to enlist in World War II, but they would be joined by a number of others before hostilities ceased.

Unlike World War I, the battlefields in this world war were truly global in scope. American troops were scattered all over the world and, wherever they and their Allied partners went, they exacted heavy tolls from the enemy.

While Allied forces in the Pacific hopscotched from island to island toward Japan's main door, the troops of the Allied nations pushed back the German forces in North Africa, invaded and overran Italy and turned their relentless gaze on the German forces entrenched and fortified in the heart of Europe. Only total victory would allow them to return home and get on with their lives, and there was nothing that would stop them from achieving that goal.

With Italy subdued and Japan defending its own backside, Hitler's forces were, in a sense, isolated in the Fortress

As more and more of the male employees of the railroad were drafted or enlisted in the military, women became a vital addition to the workforce on the railroad and docks. Although never glamorized like Rosie the Riveter, their efforts were certainly critical in keeping the trains moving and the iron ore flowing for the war effort.

Two Harbors' Leading Citizen

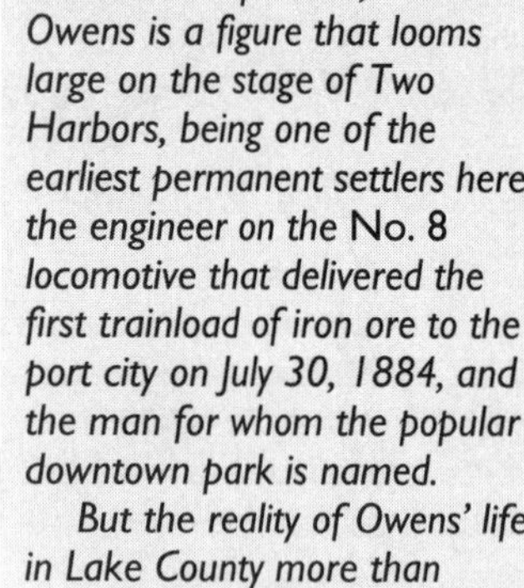

Thomas Owens was characterized in his 1944 obituary as "Two Harbors' First Citizen."

In an interview shortly before his death, Ebner Anderson said that T.O., as Thomas Owens was affectionately known in town and on the railroad, freely admitted to the company stenographers, "I didn't get the best education, so I'll tell you what I want to say and you take care of getting it right."

Despite that discrepancy and without question, Thomas Owens is a figure that looms large on the stage of Two Harbors, being one of the earliest permanent settlers here, the engineer on the No. 8 *locomotive that delivered the first trainload of iron ore to the port city on July 30, 1884, and the man for whom the popular downtown park is named.*

But the reality of Owens' life in Lake County more than equals the mythic aspects of his existence, for there seems little that happened in the early years of Two Harbors that he did not actively support and encourage.

From his position as the first locomotive engineer on the railroad, then as superintendent of the railroad from 1892 onward and as vice president/ superintendent from 1920 until the railroad was leased in 1931 and later merged to become the Duluth Missabe & Iron Range Railroad in 1938, T.O. was an unmatched booster of his town and area.

Over the years, he helped found the Lake County Fair Association, the Minnesota Arrowhead Association, Two Harbors Rotary Club and the Lake County Development Association. Other activities reported in various sources had him heading a group that lobbied to have Gooseberry Falls State Park established and he also spoke on behalf of the Rotarians in their successful effort to have the new north shore highway designated as the Lake Superior International Highway. He was an enthusiastic member of the Masonic Lodge.

Born September 28, 1856, in Oshkosh, Wisconsin, he learned railroading on Michigan's Marquette Iron Range, where he fired and learned the trade of engineer. He and wife, Sarah, were married in 1882 and had two daughters after their arrival in Two Harbors.

With a wide ranging curiosity, Owens got involved in many projects, including operating his farm, Bryn Dwr, near the rail track at the west end of Segog.

*Immigrating to Minnesota in 1883, he joined the early construction of the railroad, town and docks, also serving as an engineman when the now-historic 3-*Spot *locomotive was delivered by scow in dangerous seas that summer.*

But his rise to the top of the railroad hierarchy did not happen by magic. His first job in Two Harbors was unloading timber from boats. A note on an early photograph in what seems to be his own hand indicates that he was the carpenter who laid the first wooden sidewalk in front of the railroad offices, hotel and storehouse. Obviously, T.O. was a man of many talents.

In his 1934 speech on the 50th anniversary of the first iron ore shipped in Minnesota, Owens remembered his 1883 arrival aboard the side-wheel steamer Dove *at Agate Bay. "The boat came right to the gravel beach, where a plank was put out and we had a real landing like the 'Pilgrim Fathers.' We were greeted by the sight of men with wheelbarrows."*

Not long afterward, the sailing vessel Niagara *delivered the first load of rails.*

Likely tongue in cheek, Owens said, "John Shea, as foreman for the contractor, with a carry car and mule (the first motive power) supervised the laying of the first track." Shea would go on to a long career as a supervisor on the D&IR.

With tracks in place at Agate Bay, Owens and fellow engineman Henry Black could land the 3-Spot *at Agate Bay at the end of its harrowing trip from Duluth. The addition of the little locomotive was a significant event in the construction effort, since it made for easy delivery of men and material to the end of the ever lengthening tracks.*

Although his family home was on the 500 block of Second Avenue, T.O. also operated a farm in the countryside west of town in what is now Segog and it likely served as the inspiration for his efforts in organizing the county fair and the many years he served as its president.

On September 30, 1944, just days after his 88th birthday, Thomas Owens passed away after a brief illness. His wife had died three years earlier. A front page obituary was headlined "Two Harbors' First Citizen Passes On." ▲

Europe that their maniacal leader had concocted, facing a massive hostile force of Russian troops encroaching from the east and the combined forces of American, English and other Allied nations massed in England and threatening mainland Europe from just across the English Channel.[3]

As more and more men went to war, the DM&IR was hard pressed to keep its workforce equal to the task of delivering massive tonnages of ore. Despite moving laborers and apprentices quickly into skilled occupations, there were simply not enough men to fill the jobs. For the first time, women by the thousands entered the offices, factories and other workplaces vacated by men – and proved to be competent employees in nearly every job assigned them. Rosie the Riveter was the symbol of their effort, but women increasingly found that there were few jobs they could not handle – when given the chance.

Locally, ladies not only kept the home fires burning, but also kept the fires burning and the steam up in the locomotives that wailed their mournful song day and night in the countryside between the Iron Ranges and Two Harbors. Hundreds of thousands of tons of ore were dispatched by the dock crews to steel mills each week.

In 1940, the DM&IR had ordered eight new locomotives of the Mallet Yellowstone type from Baldwin Locomotive Works. Destined for use on the Iron Range Division trackage, which had considerably steeper grades than the Missabe Division, the first of these giants attracted a throng of interested spectators when it arrived in the spring of 1941, steaming in near perfection and hauling 9,000 tons per trip to increase the per-train ore tonnages by 25 percent. The wisdom of buying these locomotives became instantly clear, as tonnages of ore delivered at Two Harbors shot upward by nearly 50 percent to more than 15 million tons in 1941 and continued to average well above that tonnage through the duration of the war.[4]

The abundant supply of Minnesota iron ore was a crucial factor in the war effort, for from it were fashioned the tanks and ships, armaments and aircraft, mobile bridges and movie projectors, a wide assortment of automotive equipment, protection in the form of Quonset huts and combat helmets, pots and pans, wire, cable and a thousand varieties of cogs, gears and gizmos that flowed along the supply system to keep the armed forces moving. What did it matter that a salvageable landing craft lay abandoned on a beach after disgorging its troops and supplies? A new one would soon take its place from the factories that churned out a bewilderment of goods.

So massive was the consumption of iron ore in World War II that mines that had once been considered nearly inexhaustible had begun to scratch bottom by the end of the conflict. In comparison, the resources of the Axis nations were paltry to begin with and grew more so as continuous Allied bombing destroyed industrial centers and troop occupation stripped away land where some of those resources were located.

By the June 6, 1944, invasion of Europe at Normandy, it was clear to many that the Allies were in control – although you would have gotten an argument from the German and Japanese leadership – and the thousands of GI Joes in the trenches.

Perhaps it is only coincidence, but a day after the invasion started in France, the Two Harbors ore docks set a record by loading 198,040 tons of ore into 17 boats in a 24-hour period, a record that would stand for a number of years until much bigger ships and faster loading equipment came on the scene at Agate Bay.[5]

Following the invasion, an inexorable tightening of the noose around Germany continued, as the Allies broke free of the beachhead and pushed across France, sending German troops reeling backward or surrendering in droves. Allied Russian troops harried Germany's eastern areas and the surge in western Europe crossed the Rhine River in March 1945, striking into the heart of the German homeland. A bit more than a month later, the war in the European Theater ended with Germany's unconditional surrender on May 7.[6]

In the Pacific, troops commanded by General Douglas MacArthur landed at Leyte Gulf in October 1944, kicking off the reconquest of the Philippines. Castle Danger native Richard Stone was a driver in an infantry company during the

Arnold Pederson's Great Escape

By early 1944, the heavy bombers of the United States Eighth Army Air Force and England's Royal Air Force were hammering almost continuously at the German homeland, ferrying across Europe from bases in Great Britain. The damage the flyers inflicted on once fabled cities of the Reich can scarcely be described, although author Kurt Vonnegut gives a vivid picture in his novel Slaughterhouse Five *of the destruction rained on Dresden.*

As a flight engineer in the 452nd Bombardment Group of the Eighth Army Air Force, Arnold O. Pederson, the son of Knife River and Isle Royale fisherman Hans Pederson, was involved in the massive bombing of Germany. On February 8, 1944, his plane went down while on a bombing run en route to Frankfurt.

"We lost our No. 3 engine and couldn't feather it (the propeller)," Arnold says. As a result of the drag of the windmilling prop, their speed dropped and they couldn't keep up with the formation. They turned around and limped back toward England, but German fighters caught them and shot them down near Caen, France.

After bailing out of the plane, Arnold relates, "The Germans captured the rest of our crew and sent them to a prisoner of war camp, but I managed to hide from them and got picked up by French Resistance Forces."

The other members of his crew would spend 15 months in the POW camp, but Arnie spent more than a month in hiding under the French freedom fighters, moving frequently from one safe house to another. In the last location, he met Dave Goldberg and Gordon Crosby of the Royal Canadian Air Force and Neil Lathrop and Lowell Creason of the USAAF.

"Finally, they moved the five of us south to Toulouse, where an old man gave us a magazine with a note pinned to it with instructions. We were told to board an open car at the end of a train. Two young girls joined us and began berating us. While giving us a letter, they kept giving us hell. Lathrop read the letter, laughing to give the impression it was a joke.

"In the letter were five rail tickets and five bus tickets and it said, 'This train is going to St. Gaudens, but you must get off at Boussens. The Germans are checking all main line stations. You must tell the conductor to stop at Boussens, because it is not a regular stop. There will be two buses at Boussens, you take the bus to St. Girons. Good Luck.'"

Having evaded detection on the train, they boarded the buses and traveled to a point just outside St. Girons. They debarked and made contact with a young boy who led them into the woods, where they stayed until dark. They then trooped four hours to the foothills of the Pyrenees between France and Spain, where they stayed nine days with a young farmer and his wife.

"We were joined by a P-47 pilot and a Welshman who was an RAF pilot," Arnie says. "On April 7th, we started our crossing over the Pyrenees with about 24 men and two Spanish guides. About half of the group were French trying to get to Africa to join the Free French Forces.

"After three days of wandering, we discovered that we were lost and some wanted to return to St. Girons. Dave Goldberg, the RCAF man, told us we could do what we wanted, but that his Jewish last name meant he'd end up in a concentration camp and he was going on.

"The five of us in the original group and the P-47 and RAF pilots voted to go with him. One of the guides agreed to go with us and at 7 a.m. we left and crossed into Spain at about 3 p.m. Our guide seemed more familiar with the landscape and hid us with his Spanish friends for a week. They got us to the British Embassy in Barcelona. We were made British subjects and given British passports – which meant we were free to roam."

Saying that the passports were genuine and their new identity was legal, Arnold laughs and says, "We were told if any of us wanted to just disappear, we had the way to do it – but that no one ever had. It sure was nice to see a city with lights and I'm sure that a lot of money was exchanged with the locals to get us to Barcelona and then on to Gibraltar – but we had a ball for a week in Barcelona.

"On May 5, 1944, I arrived in Bristol, Wales, and returned to my unit. As I was going for a debriefing session, another crew passed me and recognized me as one of the crew from the downed bomber. They asked where I'd been and I laughed and told them, 'I spent a couple of weeks with two girls in Paris.' One of them said, 'Geez, Captain, we need to get shot down,'" he laughs.

But his face loses its grin when he talks warmly of the French people who faced certain death if they were caught helping Allied airmen, and the modern habit of badmouthing the French isn't tolerated by him.

"Nobody can say a bad word about the French when I'm around," he says with a certain ferocity. "They risked their lives to hide me and other airmen. Some of the people who helped me were caught later and killed by the Germans, so you better not run down the French people where I can hear you or you'll get a piece of my mind."[7] ▲

invasion and remembered waiting for days to land his truckload of barracks bags belonging to troops who had gone ashore. He also remembered that the troops discovered a fleet of automobiles that the Japanese had confiscated when they conquered the Philippines and that nearly every soldier commandeered one of the vehicles as their personal wheels – until the brass started to track down the original owners of those vehicles.[8]

A bit later, wading through the surf in suntans with a corncob pipe at a jaunty angle, MacArthur fulfilled his "I shall return" promise made to the Philippine people when he left the U.S. territory just ahead of victorious Japanese troops in March 1942.

The inexorable Allied invasion of island after island had placed Allied forces in command of Okinawa by June 1945, scarcely a three-hour flight to Tokyo for the heavy bombers. On March 10-11, 1945, U.S. air raids had virtually destroyed Tokyo, but Japanese resistance continued. After the bloody battle for Okinawa, U.S. leaders calculated that an invasion of the intractable Japanese island homeland would result in massive Allied casualties and deliberately opted to use the new, secret weapon developed by a bunch of eggheads whose secret work operated under the nickname of the Manhattan District.

Hiroshima and Nagasaki, Japan, were each destroyed by a single atomic blast on August 6 and 9, 1945, respectively. So devastating was the effect of the bombs on the Japanese cities that the Allied troops could scarcely believe their eyes when they arrived on the scene shortly afterward. Following those blasts, the Japanese immediately sued for peace, agreeing to surrender on August 14 and signing the unconditional surrender agreement aboard the USS *Missouri* in September.

Again, Richard Stone was on hand as part of the Allied occupation forces housed in Japanese troop barracks near Nagasaki and remembers the city as being nothing but rubble that was so contaminated that none of the Allied troops were allowed into the immediate blast area.[9]

Although 49 Lake County residents and a total of 670,846 Americans would not return from the war, survivors by the millions did flood happily back to civilian life after demobilization. Most were forever changed by their war experiences, but in some ways their tempering by the Great Depression and the Great War did not prepare them for the long period of productivity and prosperity that followed.

As the men returned to take up jobs they had vacated years before, the women who had replaced them were rather summarily thanked for their efforts, with the implication that they should return to their pre-war roles. Although most did, the war had largely erased the idea that there was a wide gap between "women's" and "men's" work, and it is almost certainly the legacy of Rosie the Riveter and her World War II sisters that the "equal opportunity" workplace has evolved in the years since.

While many returning veterans were content to go back to the jobs they left when they went off to war, the GI Bill gave them options. Suddenly, men who had planned to follow their fathers and grandfathers onto the railroad or the ore docks could envision enrolling in college or other educational institutions, receiving monthly payments to help with their education. The GI Bill also assured home loans under favorable conditions for those who had served.

These two provisions would have far-reaching results, as construction of new homes almost immediately spurred the post-war economy. Those homes needed a whole truckload of plumbing and electrical supplies, appliances, furniture and other items. Since automobile production had dropped to zero during the war, cars were needed to replace the aging pre-war models that had limped through the war on rationed gas and tires, which were often poor quality synthetic rubber and had been patched to the point of patching patches.

Under GI Bill educational benefits, thousands of veterans enrolled in schools to improve their job potential. Colleges and vocational schools churned out graduates with a wide range of skills. Those graduates would provide the technical expertise and leadership that resulted in prosperity and production that could have only been dreamed of only a few years before during the Great Depression.

Even though the war was over and the Two Harbors ore shipping tonnage dropped to about 14 million tons in 1946, that tonnage would rebound and average more than 15.35 million tons a year for the next 14 years – well above the levels posted before the war.[10]

The early 1950s would again find men in uniform, a fair number of whom had already served in World War II and were called up for their second term of warfare. The Korean War would claim eight Lake County citizens and seven more would lose their lives during the interminable Vietnam War. Although those wars ended with rather indeterminate results, veterans will always remember Korea as having exposed them to winter conditions that were as bad or worse than those in this area, with Vietnam being the direct opposite, but equally as miserably uncomfortable.

In the 1950s, the DM&IR modernized its operation by integrating diesel locomotives into its fleet. As high maintenance equipment, the steam locomotives gave way to more easily maintained diesel engines. The Two Harbors shops were shut down and shop personnel were transferred to Proctor or were laid off. The last big Mallet was retired in 1960, ending the reign of steam power on Minnesota's iron ore railroad.

By the mid-1950s, it was clear that the mines of the Vermilion Iron Range were reaching the end of their life and the DM&IR management had to make some decisions about their operations. Since virtually all of the Vermilion ore was shipped on the Two Harbors rail line, the depletion of those mines was of particular concern to personnel on that division.

The Iron Range Division hauled 10.5 million tons in 1961 and 11.75 million in 1962, compared with 7.9 million and 6.8 million tons the same years on the Missabe Division but, despite these favorable tonnages on the eastern branch, on a day that will forever be remembered as Black Friday in January 1963, the DM&IR announced that it was shutting down the Two Harbors docks, effectively closing all operations of the Iron Range Division. More than 150 senior employees were transferred to other DM&IR operations and another 100 were hired by Reserve Mining Company. Seemingly, the 80-year tradition of Two Harbors' railroading was dead.[11]

As gloom spread through the community that mid-winter of 1963, a small group of people determined that this would not be the death knell of their town. Noting that tourism had been a growing part of the area's economy for many years, they pointed to ways that this industry could become a larger factor in the economy. They encouraged businesses and governmental units to explore a wide variety of possibilities that would open the way for new businesses that were soon to locate and blossom there.

Luckily, a decade earlier, a fair number of Two Harborites had gone to work at Silver Bay when the townsite and Reserve Mining Company were being built in the mid-1950s, and many of them hired on with the company when Reserve began producing taconite pellets. Those jobs were secure, paid well and carpools were on the road in both directions during shift changes. This provided a stabilizing element in the uncertain Two Harbors economy of that moment.

The J.C. Campbell Company was a major lumber company in northeastern Minnesota since 1926 and had maintained a major presence in Lake County from about 1937 onward, with a large sawmill operation and several railroad spur lines at Whyte that had up to 250 people living there at times. The company's influence in the area was such that "Jay See Landing" is still noted on some maps along the former DM&IR Forest Center right of way and "J.C. Campbell Trail" is marked on the Lake County Emergency Services map off Highway 3 in the vicinity of London Crossing.

As the first company to announce after Black Friday that it was locating a new operation in the Two Harbors area, J.C. Campbell was a welcome addition when its sawmill and other facilities were built in Waldo in 1964. Purchasing 80 to 90 percent of its logs from the Superior National Forest and working with a number of area loggers, the company turned a large volume of timber into a range of lumber and pulp products, employing about 45 workers on a year-round basis. The company was sold to Midwest Timber in 1986, which continued the operation pretty much intact for 10 years, before selling it to Hedstrom Lumber Company of Grand Marais in September 1996. While some changes were made at the time of that sale, primarily involving larger and longer timber, the mill continues to produce a variety of lumber products and provides income for its 45 employees, as well as many loggers from a large area of upper Midwest forest lands.

Despite this promising start in attracting new business to town, a goodly group of doomsayers were counting Two Harbors down and out. Apparently, there was iron in Two Harbors' spine as well as the unused rails and docks of the city, however, for life did go on after the railroad shut down and Black Friday would ultimately prove to be a new beginning, rather than the end of Two Harbors.

Gradually, business and other community leaders came together as the Two Harbors Industrial Council and began to provide direction to the community's effort to refashion its economy. While they were involved in a number of development efforts, perhaps the most lasting influence was the development of the Walter Norlen Industrial Park, which immediately began attracting industrial development when property there became available in 1968.

Anchoring the First Avenue business district, the two banks continued to do brisk business and Sonju Motors proved that it could continue to bring in customers from a large area and compete in car sales. Across the street, the Ben Franklin Variety Store and Lauralee Department Store maintained their displays and kept a large selection of goods to meet many needs. Grocery ads continued to appear in the local newspaper. Falk's Pharmacy appeared to be prospering, along with Ray's Shoe Emporium, the Electric Shop/Gamble's Hardware, Nelson Brothers Clothing and the other downtown stores and businesses.

A couple of blocks north, Benna Motors was also competing nicely with Duluth and Iron Range dealers. Up on Seventh Avenue, the story was pretty much the same, as "the strip" provided businesses there with a continuing source of tourist dollars that helped bolster the local economy. The earlier move by the National Tea grocery store from First Avenue to Seventh Avenue provided another reason for travelers to stop uptown. Later the grocer would build a larger store on the southeast corner of the junction of State Road 2 and Seventh Avenue, which would be purchased by Super One.

In 1964, it was welcome news that Universal Fiberglass Corporation was locating a plant in the former locomotive repair shop and had a large contract to mold the bodies of three-wheeled "mailster" trucks for the U.S. Postal Service. Optimism ran high that these cheaper trucks would soon replace more conventional and expensive mail delivery vehicles. If so, the factory would be shipping trucks all over the country – providing needed jobs and a dose of hope in Two Harbors' struggling economy.

Those hopes suffered a setback in 1966 when the plant was destroyed by a fire, forcing the company to default on the postal contract. The death knell had already sounded over the enterprise, however, for the trucks proved to be top heavy and too unstable for regular mail delivery service. During its brief tenure, Universal had also molded fiberglass car fenders and canoes.

By that time, Abex Corporation had taken over the building that had formerly served as the railroad car repair shop, converting it into a foundry to produce large steel castings for the taconite industry, which needed a reliable source of replacement parts for the crushers and grinders used to reduce pit run taconite to talcum powder consistency. Crusher liners and mantles were continuously replaced and the location of the Abex foundry in Two Harbors seemed ideal, with Reserve just up the shore and Erie Mining Company a couple of hours away by truck at Hoyt Lakes.

Jack Gralewski of Two Harbors was an early employee at Abex and remembered that his job was operating a huge grinding machine to remove metal and finish the extremely hard manganese steel castings, which defied cutting with machine tools.[12]

"The grinding wheel must have been two feet in diameter and about three inches thick. The wheel spun at 1,900 rpms (revolutions per minute) to cut the

castings to the right tolerances. Sometimes we'd take as much as 250 or 300 pounds of steel from a casting to get it right. There was a quarter-inch-thick steel plate behind the grinding table that collected the grindings and sometimes we'd take off so much metal that the plate would be red hot from the heat of the grinder.

"When I first started cutting those crusher mantles and liners, I worked seven days a week many times and they seemed to want us to work all of the time. It was the only place I ever worked where they'd penalize you for not taking overtime, but they started to have union troubles and I left to take a job with the Lake County Road and Bridge (Highway) Department. Abex shut the whole place down shortly after that because of union troubles."

The Abex location would later house a foundry operated by J&J Castings for several years, but was closed for good in the late 1980s.

Although these two early and welcome employers failed after only a

The Day the Railroad Died

by Chris Blanchard

Mary Ann (Christensen) Habash grew up in Two Harbors, the daughter of Mr. and Mrs. Charles P. Christensen. Her father was a machinist and, later, a roundhouse foreman for the DM&IR. She vividly remembers the days when railroad work was in full swing and dominated the activities in town.

"The men returning from work at 3 p.m. when their shift was over wore shop caps, coveralls, bandannas around their necks and they all had lunch pails swinging at their sides. I also remember the women leaving the shop during World War II, when the men were off fighting. They looked like 'Rosie the Riveter' in their work clothes and wore bandannas that were knotted at the front around their heads, identifying them as women who were doing the jobs of men. As a child, I regarded them with awe."

Writing and performing music under the stage name of Chris Blanchard, Mary Ann says she wrote "The Day the Railroad Died" for her dad and her uncle, William Holden, a railroad engineer whose father was also a "hoghead." With many relatives employed on the railroad, Mary Ann quickly researched the material, produced and recorded the following verses shortly after Black Friday 1963, as a tribute to Two Harbors and to the men and women who dedicated their lives to the railroad.

For many, many years, I don't know just how long,
Two Harbors was a boomin' railroad town
But '63 brought misery
And the town is black with mourn
The great iron horse no more will trail
That long and lonesome steel rail
I sat and cried the day the railroad died.
Oh Lord, what will I do?

The hoghead[1] ran that iron horse
And, Lord, he ran her hard
She hauled those ore cars from the range
into the railroad yard
The tallow pot,[2] he sweat and fed
That demon coal and more
She needed fuel and fire and steam
to haul that iron ore.

The Mallet finally came to rest
Inside the railroad shop
The nut splitters[3] took good care of her
Amidst the laugh and talk
Of men with pride who did their work
And did it fast and well
No longer does the din ring out,
Since that black day of hell.

The slings of sledge on steel rails
Won't break the achin' backs
Of gandy dancers who used to lay
The glistenin' railroad tracks
My kith and kin were railroad folks
But now, our town's in dread
I tell you true, I don't know what I'll do
The Railroad is Dead!

No more to laugh or work with ore
How long can I be brave?
The legend of the railroad
Has settled in the grave
That was my life and now it's spent,
The Company said, "To spare expense"
I sat and cried the day the railroad died
Oh Lord ... what will I do?[13]

[1]Hoghead is railroad jargon for the engineer.
[2]Tallow pot was slang for the fireman, probably from the long spouted oil cans used to lubricate engine parts.
[3]Nut splitters was applied by railroaders to the mechanics and other repairmen. ▲

short while, the city had already entered a period of extraordinary entrepreneurship that would not only change the single-industry nature of the area's economy, but would lead to a situation in the early 1990s when businesses actually had difficulty hiring the skilled workers they needed.

Part of that story began a decade earlier just outside of Lake County in Ely.

In the early 1950s, area loggers were looking for ways to modernize their operations, which still depended to a large degree on horse and manpower to produce timber. Roy LaBounty, who started logging with brother Clarence in the Isabella area just after World War II, remembers designing and building several pieces of equipment like a slasher and loader to save labor in his own camp, but says that there was almost no equipment on the market that was specially designed to handle timber.

At about that time, Bob Larson, an Ely Oldsmobile dealer, was selling and delivering diesel generators to logging camps in the surrounding forestland. To make that job easier, Larson purchased a Swedish-built truck-mounted crane to handle the large generator units, but noticed that a few modifications on the crane would also make it practical as a loader on logging trucks.

Larson had a craftsman fabricate the necessary alterations and set up a plant to produce his "Hi-Bob" loader. He thus became the first manufacturer in the world to offer truck-mounted loaders to loggers. The Hi-Bob loader had hydraulic swing controls and a cable-controlled log grapple. Some of his earliest customers were cutting in Lake County and found this new equipment to be exactly what they needed at the time.

Ultimately, Larson moved the business to Ashland, Wisconsin, and ran into financial difficulty, but his introduction of this new equipment would have far-reaching effects for Lake County loggers – and in the local economy.

Already established by the 1963 railroad shut down, Ramey Manufacturing Company had opened in

Although Black Friday was traumatic, it kicked off a substantial effort to develop other commerce that would diversify the economics of Two Harbors' once-singleminded dependence on railroading and shipping. The groundbreaking ceremony for Walter Norlen Industrial Park in 1968 was a bellwether day in that effort. Within a year or two, firms were building facilities and locating in the new development. Groundbreakers were ***(left to right)*** *Ray Widen, Walter Norlen and Mayor David Battaglia.*

1954 as a welding shop at Fifth Avenue and Eighth Street in Two Harbors, but was soon involved in building truck-mounted loaders – the first two of which were built for loggers who went bankrupt.

Modeled on Larson's loaders, the earliest of the Ramey loaders also used a combination of hydraulic and cable-controls, but included modifications in the hydraulic system to eliminate oil leaks for which the Hi-Bob loader was notorious. Later, John "Boomer" Norlen, the Rameys' early sales distributor, came across a fully hydraulic Prentice loader on one of his sales trips. He told the Rameys about the new machine and he and Walt Ramey immediately went back that night to examine and sketch drawings of this innovation by flashlights. Using a few hasty sketches and notes, the Rameys would adapt their design into a fully hydraulic machine – making the grapple much more versatile and sensitive to the operator's control.

The interest in log loaders was intense and Rameys' experience in building loaders seemed promising. Despite setbacks, the company persisted in the business. A fire had destroyed their facility in 1958 and they moved to the southwest corner of Seventh Street and Seventh Avenue, where the business continued for four more years, before the Rameys moved to Duluth. Financial difficulties seemed to continuously dog the company and Mesabi Finance Company of Hibbing held a large note that it sold to Bartell Brothers of Duluth, who became the managing partners and made the Ramey loader the nucleus of Barko Hydraulics Inc. – the most widely recognized line of loaders of that time. Eventually, the company became a property of Pettibone Corporation.

Before Barko's success was assured, Kenneth Ramey bowed out and returned to Two Harbors in 1964, establishing Husky Hydraulics in a former Hamm's Beer warehouse on old Highway 61. Within a few years, that operation also began to encounter financial difficulty, but had attracted the attention of Standard Alliance Company, which took it over and erected the first building in the new Industrial Park, a year after the park was surveyed and platted in 1967. Husky was highly successful throughout the 1970s and into the 1980s, expanding its plant, keeping a sizable workforce employed and shipping equipment all over the United States and Canada.[14] The entire enterprise was sold in 1986 and moved to Alabama. A number of employees transferred with the company, but most returned to the northland within a year or two.

Once it was obvious that Husky Hydraulics was lost to Two Harbors, a small group of former Husky employees formed Minnesota Hydraulics and produced prototype log handling equipment under the "Black Bear" trademark. While the machines received high marks from those who witnessed their operation, the investors were unable to continue the operation to a point that it became profitable and went out of business within a year or so.

By 1966, construction of county arenas at Two Harbors and Silver Bay provided some jobs on the local scene and Northshore Steel had been chartered to manufacture structural and other metal products. Northshore opened its new building in the Industrial Park in 1969 and enlarged those facilities in 1973, employing up to 15 workers.

In 1969, David Coolidge started Two Harbors Machine Shop in the back room of the Beckman Pontiac garage building at 611 Second Avenue. At first doing custom and commercial fabricating, the business grew steadily and took over the rest of the building. Increasingly involved in producing hydraulic cylinders and other components for logging equipment, the business made a giant leap in 1979 when Canadian Harry Serson and Coolidge teamed up to begin production and sale of Serco-brand truck loaders. Operating at first in the Two Harbors Machine Shop's downtown location, the company soon outgrew the limited space of that building and built a new facility in the Industrial Park, where much of the fabrication work now takes place.

The businesspeople along Seventh Avenue had always viewed the stream of cars passing on the highway as an important factor in their business equation and took pains to stop a good share of the million tourists estimated to travel each year on Highway 61. Off-street parking and other amenities, upgrading facilities and providing better service, offering a mix of goods and services all continued to attract visitors. The municipal campground and golf course at the east end of town also attracted visitors and helped a number of the Seventh Avenue businesses.

The downtown businesses had traditionally relied more heavily on local shoppers and had been somewhat less dependent on tourism dollars. When they perceived that the Seventh Avenue businesses continued to prosper by catering to tourists, however, the downtown merchants took steps to also attract visitors. A storefront renovation project and other beautification improved the appearance of the businesses and the paving and landscaping of two large public parking areas to the south of First Avenue was a major improvement. Both the Moose and American Legion clubs had been longtime institutions downtown and would relocate to larger quarters there, with each of those

The Business of Black Friday

A lifelong resident and businessman in Two Harbors, John Emery Carlstrom was born September 30, 1917, on Eighth Avenue. His grandfather plastered the first house that was done in town, as well as the first Glass Block store in Duluth. His father and uncle continued in the plaster and stuccoing trade, but took time to create the "iron ball" located at Thomas Owens Park that commemorated the Two Harbors 50th anniversary of iron ore in 1934. The high grade ore used in that ball presented special challenges, since it was extremely dense and hard, adding to the difficulty of fashioning a perfectly round sphere.

Emery followed his father and grandfather into the stucco and plastering trade and remembers that Two Harbors was a bustling and prosperous town when all of the railroad facilities were operating full tilt. He says that at the end of the shift a parade of men walked out the gate in several directions, some stopping off at one of the several barbershops, dodging into a clothing or other retail store or, perhaps, stopping off at one of the several saloons along the way.

"The men wanted to be close to their jobs, so a lot of the houses in the downtown area are built on half-lots so more homes could go into that area. Sometimes they were so close together that we had trouble working between them when we were on a job," he remembers.

In addition to the shops, yards and docks, the railroad had a large pulpwood yard and ran the coal dock to supply fuel for heating and the steam equipment. Railroad officials also took an active part in most of the town's events, celebrations and civic activities.

In his career in the stucco and plastering trade, Emery worked far and wide in the northland, but decided as he got into his 40s that he wanted to be home more to help raise his daughter, Laura, and son, Lee. To make that possible, he and his wife decided to open Lauralee Department Store in space on First Avenue that had been vacated when the National Tea grocery moved to its new building on Seventh Avenue near Highway 2.

"We opened during the strike in 1959, so that was a lot of worry and sweating," he says. "After that, we did good business the next few years.

"We were on a buying trip to a show in Minneapolis when we heard about Black Friday in 1963. We were staying in the old Radisson Hotel downtown and Bill Reitan (a Two Harbors banker) and another fellow from Two Harbors came into the restaurant that morning and asked, 'Did you hear about Two Harbors?' and we told him no. He said, 'They're shutting the railroad down.'"

Noting that they always tried taking one or another of the clerks with them to buying shows, partly as a reward for good work, he says that the lady who was along on that trip started to cry when she heard the news.

"I thought about it a minute and said, 'We're not going to pay any attention to that at all. We'll just buy like we always do and hope for the best,' and that's what we did. It turned out well, too, because quite a few of the other merchants cut back or didn't buy any new inventory. Since we bought the same as always, we sold a lot of inventory that they didn't have."

While they weathered the immediate 1963 downturn successfully, Emery notes that they did not just rest on that success, getting involved in a wide range of activities to try and stimulate business during the remainder of the time they owned the store. From the annual spring cleanup of the downtown area to the renovation of store fronts and the placement of flower barrels at the front of their businesses, merchants were constantly looking for ways to attract customers and stimulate business. In 1980, the Carlstroms sold the store to John and Dory Pearson, who operated it until it closed in 1998.[15] ▲

projects improving the properties they occupied. The Legion Club celebrated the burning of their mortgage for the building and renovation in March 2000. An ongoing effort for several years was successful in getting state highway and other signage erected to direct visitors to the downtown waterfront area.

Meanwhile, local road and bridge contractor Roy LaBounty had created an attachment for his hydraulically operated excavator that made that machine much more versatile. His grapple made a wide variety of construction jobs far easier and by the time he retired as a contractor in 1972, he had a patent on the design and a plan to manufacture the machine and sell it to other contractors.

About the same time, Raymond Hahn, a successful logger in northern Lake and Cook counties, had built and tested a log processor that delimbed tree-length timber and cut it into the most profitable products the logger could sell.

By May 1973, Roy and Ray had determined there was a market for their inventions and, within weeks of one another, each started construction of buildings in the Industrial Park to house manufacturing plants for their machines. Both inventors had worked many years in the businesses for which their machines were created and thoroughly understood the business of their customers.

Through evolution, the original Hahn Harvester would be modified, improved, refined and new technology like computerization incorporated as it became practical. While the basic appearance and design of the Harvester did not change radically from year to year, such updating keeps it in demand among larger loggers who can invest in such technology. Most of the machines are destined for loggers far from the Two Harbors home of Hahn Machinery, but the benefit of those sales continues to be felt in the local economy through wages and other income. Although Ray has retired from the company, members of his family retain management of day-to-day operations and ownership remains in the family.

Although Ray Hahn created his first log harvester in Cook County, he chose Two Harbors when he established his Hahn Machinery Company to manufacture the automated Hahn Harvester.

An early LaBounty Manufacturing creation was the hydraulic grapple attachment that allowed contractors and other users to connect the equipment to their existing machinery for use in a variety of construction work. Later, LaBounty would patent a large shear that easily and safely cut up scrap metal and other debris.
LaBounty Manufacturing Division of Stanley Works

In contrast to the process of evolution of the Hahn Harvester, the LaBounty Manufacturing product line almost exploded in a seemingly endless stream of new products and innovative adaptations of existing products for new uses. As the grapple proved itself with contractors, customers queued up worldwide to describe other needs to Roy, his son and partner, Ken, and members of their sales staff. Their ideas were passed along to the company's designers, who created specifications for machines to meet the needs of those customers. A major breakthrough for the company was development of a large shear mechanism which could easily cut and handle large structural steel materials. The shear virtually eliminated the slower, more hazardous cutting with acetylene torches, which had been the only option previously available in the scrapping of large I-beams and similar heavy materials.

Knowing that contractors often face penalties if they fail to complete a job on time, Roy, Ken and the rest of the LaBounty staff made sure that orders were filled and on the way to the customer as quickly as possible. To make that possible, a large inventory of components and parts for the machines was manufactured and maintained, providing work for the crews during periods when orders dropped off a bit.

By the 1992 merger of LaBounty Manufacturing into Stanley Hydraulic Tools division of The Stanley Works Inc., the product line included almost 100 different models and sizes of grapples, shears, concrete pulverizers, product processors and other attachment equipment to serve businesses in recycling, demolition, salvage and construction. The innovative machines fabricated in Two Harbors made LaBounty Manufacturing a world leader in its field and by far the most successful locally founded and funded business.

At the time of the merger with Stanley, the company had sales of more than $27 million and a workforce of 280 employees, but a number of its closely guarded patents were expiring, making it possible for other manufacturers to copy

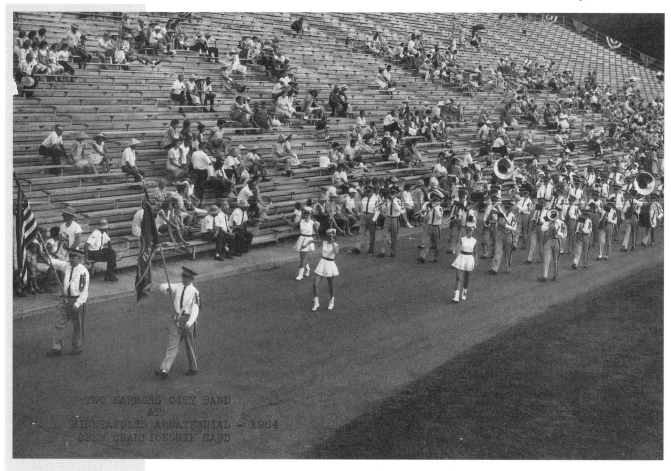

Despite the pall of Black Friday in 1964, the Two Harbors City Band continued its tradition of participating in the Minneapolis Aquatennial. This band took first place in the open class of competition that year.

the designs. Roy would stay on in a consulting basis with Stanley until retirement in 1997, but Ken and three partners, all formerly affiliated with LaBounty Manufacturing, established Genesis Equipment and Manufacturing in Superior, Wisconsin, a year or so before Roy's retirement. That company continues to offer a line of recycling and other equipment to contractors worldwide.[16]

While the railroad's seemingly disastrous Black Friday announcement precipitated much of the subsequent development and diversification effort, the DM&IR had a change of mind by 1966 and reactivated the Iron Range Division.

In his *Missabe Road* history of the DM&IR, Frank King indicates that the change of heart may have been spurred by the realization that the Two Harbors facilities would have several advantages over the Duluth-Superior ports when the huge ore boats were launched after the 1,000-foot Poe Lock opened at Sault Ste. Marie, Michigan, in 1968. Being much closer to deep water than the Duluth-Superior docks on St. Louis Bay, ships could run full speed ahead within a short distance of the harbor entry. Loading at Two Harbors also cut 40 miles or more from each trip, saving several hours of sailing on each voyage and many thousands of gallons of fuel during a season.

In addition to these favorable conditions for larger ships at Agate Bay, the location of the Minntac, Inland and Eveleth taconite plants on the eastern end of the Mesabi Range makes it economical for the pellets produced at those plants to be shipped through Two Harbors.

Thus, the trains and ships returned to Agate Bay. In 1978, the DM&IR and the city of Two Harbors cooperated in issuing bonds that allowed upgrading of the Two Harbors docks and storage facilities. In December 1978, Interlake Steamship Company's 1,000-foot *Mesabi Miner* ushered in a new era when it received the first cargo loaded by the new shiploader at Two Harbors.

With this major investment in modernization, optimism returned that the DM&IR is committed to its Two Harbors docks and railroad operations and will continue as an important element of the local economy – although it is never again likely to exercise the influence it once had, for a far smaller percentage of the population is dependent on railroad jobs and none of the senior management of the company is located here. The tonnage of iron ore shipped from Two Harbors has, however, stabilized at a respectable level and it seems likely that the tradition of Agate Bay as the "iron port" will continue for many years to come.

Construction of the Reserve tailing disposal basin and other upgrading of the plant during the late 1970s brought another rush of contractors and their employees to the area, reassuring Reserve employees who had almost continuously feared for their jobs for a decade, as lawsuits over disposal of tailings into Lake Superior dogged Reserve's every step. The optimism would prove shortlived, as the costs of that work eventually forced the company into bankruptcy. In a reversal of

Ebner H. Anderson's Good Job

"I was born June 16, 1908, in my parents' home at 421 Ninth Avenue in Two Harbors and still live there. My father arrived in 1904 and became a patrolman on the first police force after the city was incorporated in 1904 or 1905. My parents paid the builder $765 for our three-room house when it was finished.

"My first job was as a stenographer for the Duluth & Iron Range Railroad in the depot that became the Lake County Historical Museum. I was the fourth stenographer in the offices and my signal was four rings of the bell. I started on July 26, 1926, right out of high school and worked for the railroad until 1933, just before the merger that formed the Duluth Missabe & Iron Range Railroad.

"I often took dictation from Thomas Owens, who was superintendent of the D&IR and was later a vice president after the DM&IR was formed. He was a big man who talked real slow and he could never remember my name. He'd call me Ebenezer or Reuben or whatever happened to come to mind. He always said, "I didn't get the best education in the world, so I'll tell you what I want to write and you do the the letter." I'd take shorthand notes, type it up and usually I also signed it for him, if it was more or less routine business.

"Everybody was called by their first name in those days and Thomas Owens was always called T.O. In about 1930, he asked that I work on the book of rules for the railroad after the merger of the two railroads (the D&IR and Duluth Missabe & Northern). One of my jobs was to drive the car when the Two Harbors fellows had to travel to Proctor for a meeting. T.O. told me on one of those trips that I should be an engineer for the railroad. I asked why and he said, "I've been watching the speedometer all the way and you haven't changed speed by one mile an hour the whole trip." I think that was a pretty high compliment from him, because he was an engineer himself and brought the first trainload of ore into Two Harbors from Tower.

"I left the railroad in September 1933 and went to work for the first county welfare department during the Great Depression. They were looking for someone who had payroll experience and I had done payroll when I worked in Proctor, so they hired me. Ruth Ferguson was the first welfare director for the county, but she was gone before I went to work there. Agnes Hoff was the director when I started.

"I worked on accounts with the Civil Works Administration, which was a welfare program that involved work projects. In addition to payroll, I was also assignment officer and had to go to Finland, Toimi and Knife River every week to pay the workers, so I got to know everyone who was on the crews real well.

"Workers could earn up to $100 before their eligibility ended and they had to be laid off and we had to keep careful records to be sure we met the rules.

"Lake County was designated as a distressed area, so the county didn't pay any portion of the cost in those days. We had several federal and state programs that covered the costs and we even had a Feed Relief program for cattle up by the Big Noise curve. Cattle were shipped in from all over and fed up there. Vern Anderson was in charge of it.

"The railroad was pretty much shut down, of course, but an early government work program hired men to work on the first breakwater and the Civil Works Administration offered some short employment after it started. The railroad also tried to have one or two days of work a week for some of the men and the Proctor branch had a program that was called the extra gang to do some big jobs that paid wages to men.

"In 1948, I ran for county treasurer and held that position for six terms until 1975. I was never opposed for election – I guess nobody else wanted the job. When I retired, the county combined the auditor and treasurer's offices.

"All I ever wanted to do was a good job and I'm proud to say I think that's what I did.[17] ▲

the earlier economic difficulty in Two Harbors, by the time that Reserve actually shut down in 1986, a number of the Reserve workers would find jobs with the emerging businesses in Two Harbors.

My Merry Automobile

It seems ironic that a town built as the center of a railroad operation would evolve into a city of automobile enthusiasts, but such was the case with Two Harbors, as residents quickly embraced this new means of transportation when it became available. Shortly after completion of streets and roads that automobiles could navigate, businesses blossomed to sell, service and provide gasoline, tires and other accessories for the dozens of makes and models of automotive vehicles that soon flooded into the market.

The first cars and trucks were probably shipped into town by railroad and on the steamer *America* (which was, in fact, transporting a Model T Ford pickup truck the night it sank at Isle Royale in 1928) before roads were improved, but by the time the new lakeshore highway opened in 1924, there was so much demand for cars that several dealerships were already established and shoppers were able to "comparison shop" for exactly the make and model that suited their needs.

Perhaps the earliest dealership in the true meaning of the word was Olson and Falk Auto Company in 1919, selling Paige and Chevrolet automobiles and Republic and Chevrolet trucks. Earlier, Oscar Beckman had opened a garage next to the Beckman Brothers Livery and Boarding Stables in 1917. Originally, Beckman stored autos, but would become a Pontiac dealer later.

In the 1920s, the auto market boomed and several dealerships came to life. A Chevrolet-Buick dealership was opened on Seventh Avenue by David Elg and Wally Pearson. After a split in that partnership, Pearson would continue to deal in Chevies and Buicks, while Elg moved to the corner of Seventh Avenue and Seventh Street and sold Nash and Hupmobiles. Pearson Motor Company would later move to that location. Murphy and Anderson Auto sold Whippets and Willys Knights. Archie Murphy would later operate as an Oldsmobile dealer on the corner of First Avenue and Seventh Street. A Chrysler, Plymouth and International Truck sales operation owned by William and Herman Porger was located at 702 Seventh Avenue in the 1920s. Later Bacon Sales and Service would operate from that same location, before moving its Chrysler-

After shipping resumed at Agate Bay in 1966, improvement in the facilities and the arrival of ever larger boats made the docks an important part of the shipping industry. Here, an experiment in year-round shipping during the 1970s proved troublesome for the crew of the Presque Isle, *which arrived in midwinter with a thick coating of ice. The experiment was dropped shortly thereafter. Note the* Edna G. *steaming the hatches.*

The Minnesota Department of Natural Resources undertook major upgrading of Lighthouse Point in the mid-1980s, installing a nice boat launching ramp, parking, landscaping and other improvements.

Plymouth dealership to the Pearson building at Seventh and Seventh in the 1970s. Bacon would close in 1983 and the Chrysler line of cars came under the wing of Sonju Motors – which was already selling the General Motors line and has the distinction of being the oldest continuous auto dealer in the area.

Early in life, Alfred Sonju, the son of Maple/Finland pioneers Andrew and Karoline Sonju, displayed a talent for putting deals together that connected neighbors with equipment they needed.

After service in France during World War I, Alfred returned to Finland, married Mabel Jackson of Grand Marais in 1921 and spent three more years in the Finland area, before relocating in 1924 to Two Harbors. He opened Sonju Motors in 1925 as a dealer for Ford cars and trucks – although he would also continue to deal in miscellaneous other equipment for a number of years.

Through the late 1920s and the gloomy economy of the Great Depression, Alfred guided his company with the hard work and diligent respect for economy that his boyhood in the Finland area had taught him, keeping his business open 24 hours a day from 1931 to 1945 to provide extra services like towing, gas and storage of vehicles like Greyhound buses used along the north shore. Taxi service was added in 1941 and continued until 1954.

Competitors would come and go. He, the son of a father who farmed, logged, built roads, operated a store, served for a period of years as railroad depot agent and a postmaster, county commissioner for 17 years, early school board and town board member and community leader – he, Alfred, the son, would weather whatever came his way – although the Great Depression and, especially, the 1934 death of his father in a car accident must have surely been a trial for him.

Just as the worst of the Depression was passing and good times could be envisioned, Japan bombed Pearl Harbor and the United States entered World War II. Within a short while, Alfred's business encountered a new obstacle, as the building of civilian vehicles came to a standstill for the duration of the war. To

From a mere rut through the woods, improvements in Lake County roads have been ongoing and tireless. Often, an attraction like Gooseberry River would be cause for a road being built, but by the early 1920s, the state had completed its plan to build a modern highway the full length of the north shore. It was completed in stages and was dubbed the Lake Superior International Highway upon opening. The latest accomplishments include tunnels at Lafayette Bluff and Silver Creek Cliff and the new railroad bridge and underpass in Two Harbors.

make matters worse, his mechanics found fewer and fewer parts available to repair the aging vehicles that remained in use – many of which were built before the Great Depression – and gas and tires were rationed to the point that private owners were quite limited in their travels. A few vehicles were available for sale to governmental subdivisions or to people in vital industries, but that hardly constituted the amount of business he would otherwise have conducted.

An established and respected businessman in Two Harbors by this point, it was no doubt heartening to see full employment in town, with good wages flowing into the banks and businesses and the long line of workers walking by his business from the shops and yards at the beginning and end of the workday, but the salesman in Alfred surely felt a pang each time he was unable to fill a customer's need, for his business was built not only on good car deals, but on the service it could render to meet customers' needs.

That his competitors were in the same boat likely didn't help much, but at least he knew and had previously and personally done business with a great many customers, which gave him access to what business was possible.

With the end of World War II, business began to stream through the doors. People who had been driving the same patched-together car since the start of the Great Depression were now ready and able to purchase new automobiles. The car and truck business once again blossomed.

Of even more interest, daughter Phlaine married Adler Johnson, a star pre-war athlete at Two Harbors High School whose father had served as captain of the tug *Edna G.* A dashing ex-Navy pilot, Adler was taking business classes in college, would graduate and take a position with an international oil company for several years, before Alfred drily observed during a visit that he didn't know anything about his son-in-law's job, but knew for sure he'd be better off in the car business.

By that point, Phlaine and Adler were ready to return to their hometown and settled easily into the routine of being near family and lifelong friends. Learning the automobile business at the side of a master, Adler contributed to and witnessed Sonju Motors' expansion of sales to customers in Duluth, the Iron Range and all of northeastern Minnesota. At Alfred's retirement in 1966, Adler became president and served in that position until retirement in 1984, overseeing the move from First Avenue to the new building on Highway 61 in 1975 a month or two after Alfred's death. Sonju Motors also switched from Ford to General Motors products. Chrysler, Dodge and Plymouth lines were added in 1982, after Bacon Sales went out of business. At Adler's retirement, son Mark assumed the presidency until 1997, when he turned that responsibility over to brother Terry.

Through the years, competition came from a number of dealers like Beckman's Pontiac, Pearson's Auto Sales and Bacon Sales and Service, all of which thrived for varying periods, but it would be the original Martin Hill Terraplane franchise that was first taken over by a bank and then purchased by Benna Johnson that would go on to become the second large volume dealer that solidified Two Harbors' reputation as the car shopping mecca of the northland. Johnson, with wife Irene partnering as bookkeeper, bought a building on Third Avenue for his business and added adjacent properties as the business grew. He also added lines of cars as they became available, first taking on Hudson, then selling Plymouth and Dodge lines after 1946.

After Sonju Motors decided to switch its allegiance from Ford products to General Motors lines in 1966, Benna picked up the Ford/Mercury franchise and successfully operated with those lines. Thus, Benna Ford grew in sales and service volume, first from its original location on Third Avenue and then in the new facility it opened in 1995 at the west end of town. Meantime, the ownership changed to Benna's son, Robert, in 1969,

who in turn sold to David (his brother), Gary Ben Johnson, James Bangsund and Richard Kempfert in 1972, all longtime employees. In 1981, David Johnson sold out and moved from Two Harbors and David Houle was added to the owners list. In early 2000, the ownership again changed as a group of auto dealers took over that dealership.

While competition in sales and advertising by two large volume car dealers in the same small town might at first glance seem to be self defeating, it is more likely that this competition increased sales and awareness for both Sonju and Benna – since the continuing message to car shoppers through the years was that they had to check in Two Harbors to do a thorough price comparison.

And, once a sale was complete, out-of-town customers would also be returning to have warranty and other work done by their dealer – providing further opportunities for Two Harbors' businesses to benefit from the traffic the car business brought to town.

New Business and Growth

In the 1980s, the businesses already mentioned continued to provide a stimulus of employment and income, but the surge of new development would continue. Louisiana-Pacific Corporation built and opened its siding plant in the Industrial Park, providing loggers with an entirely new market for large amounts of timber and hiring a good-sized workforce – most of which came from the local area.

By 1984, the Pearson family had renovated its garage building at the corner of Seventh Avenue and Seventh Street into Harbor Landing Mall. That former site of Pearson Motors and, later, Bacon Auto Sales was transformed to house a variety of shops, adding to the mix of businesses along the Highway 61 strip.

But the Pearson family had plans for a far bigger development and had begun to lay the groundwork to bring those plans to reality. Located on the site of the family's venerable, but rustic, Scenic Point Resort, Superior Shores Resort and Conference Center started modestly enough, as several townhouses were built on the cliffy overlooks of the peninsula from 1983 to 1985. Mark Pearson seemed to be everywhere as he promoted the concept of a large, full-service tourism lodge and marina being constructed on a lakeshore-level area a short distance off Highway 61 on Flood Bay.

With persistence, a tax increment financing agreement and extension of the city sewer system to the property, permits were issued and work began on the central building, which included guest rooms, a bar and restaurant and an indoor pool. Construction of townhouses also continued and, once the hotel facility was open, the rental of townhouse units became part of that operation.

In May 1994, Blue Waters Development Corporation assumed management and controlling interest in Superior Shores, immediately planning the addition of a conference center, added lodging and a change in the floor plan to move the restaurant and bar upstairs to take advantage of the better view from that elevation. The work was completed and the new facilities opened to the public in May 1996.

By 1994, the Minnesota Department of Transportation (MNDOT) had completed the tunnel through Silver Creek Cliff, having earlier opened a tunnel through Lafayette Bluff to the east. Each of the projects provided employment for local workers and sub-contractors, with the blasting at Silver Cliff being a rather pronounced wake-me-up in Two Harbors for several months, but the project was completed well ahead of schedule and opened with a celebration that summer.

By the time the Silver Creek Cliff tunnel opened, the start of an enormous amount of activity was apparent to the west of the DM&IR underpass. Super One grocery had moved from its former location at Fourth Street and Seventh Avenue into a new store to the northwest of the railroad underpass, with the Pamida Store was located on the site – which had previously been undeveloped land. A Pizza Hut rose at the nearby highway intersection and a traffic light was installed to control the busy corner. The former Motel Two Harbors was razed and a new Country Inn by Carlson was built on that property east of the cemetery. A McDonald's restaurant opened adjacent to the property and the Milk House convenience store was built just east of Sonju Motors. Across the highway, an abandoned, dilapidated former chicken and ribs restaurant was renovated into the Subway sandwich shop.

At the west end of the cemetery, Lou's Fish House vacated its store at the vee where Highway 61 and County Road 11 merged in Segog, moving to a location on the east end of town. The former store was razed to make way for highway improvements.

Across the highway from the former Fish House, the Super America convenience store opened its doors and a new AmericInn motel was built a year or so later. Nearby, the Burger King also opened, turning this once-vacant area at the western end of town into a major development. The Minnesota Department of Transportation realigned the roadways and installed a traffic light at the corner of Highway 61 and County 11 to ensure that traffic flowed smoothly through the busy intersection.

At the east end of town, the city had continually added to and improved spaces in the Municipal Campgrounds, giving visitors added incentive to stop and stay a while. Across the highway, volunteers had completed a new golf clubhouse in 1993, replacing the picturesque but small and drafty original log clubhouse. The Two Harbors Curling Club constructed a new facility that tied into the golf clubhouse a couple of years later, replacing the original Curling Club, which had been up State Road 2 where the new fire hall is now located and was destroyed in a fire. Mounting pressure by golfers saw the expansion of the Lakeview Municipal Golf Course in 1996 from nine holes to a full 18-hole course and reopened in 1997 as Lakeview National Golf Course.

In 1999, another major Highway 61 project saw the demolition of the ancient railroad underpass that had always seemed

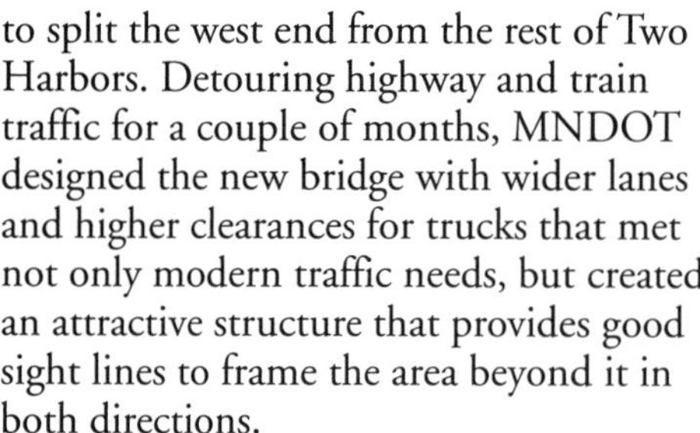

to split the west end from the rest of Two Harbors. Detouring highway and train traffic for a couple of months, MNDOT designed the new bridge with wider lanes and higher clearances for trucks that met not only modern traffic needs, but created an attractive structure that provides good sight lines to frame the area beyond it in both directions.

East of town a bit, the original rustic building of Betty's Pies, the longtime Stewart River favorite of sweetsters, was abandoned to make way for highway improvements. A new, modern structure, with expanded parking opened the spring of 2000. A few years previously, the site of the popular and historic Rustic Inn cafe at Castle Danger had been acquired to make way for highway improvements, but the building was moved a couple of hundred yards west, expanded and modernized and continues to be a favored stop for visitors.

Across the highway from the Rustic Inn, Star Harbor Resort had undergone improvements that included several new log rental units that quickly became a favorite with north shore visitors. In 1998, the property was acquired by a major developer of Lutsen-area lodging and dining facilities, was renamed and a large new facility now operates as Grand Superior Lodge, offering suites and guest rooms, casual and fine dining and a wide range of amenities.

In August 1999 the ownership of the Two Harbors Lighthouse was officially transferred to the Lake County Historical Society by the U.S. Coast Guard. Earlier that summer, the lighthouse was opened by the Lake County Historical Society as a bed-and-breakfast inn and enjoys a good measure of success, with guests year-round enjoying their up close and personal contact with Lake Superior and the old iron port on Agate Bay.

How will it be written?

Lake County continues to develop and serve as home to businesses and its people. Even in these modern times, many of the modern conveniences that we have known for years are just finding their way into the remote areas of the county. It truly is a wilderness in many respects, which excites some and entices others.

While the growth and development of Lake County in the past two decades has been steady and impressive, it goes without saying that the future will see changes that no one can anticipate. Just as the writers of earlier histories had no way of imagining the explosion of personal computers or connecting to the Internet via a local utility, there is simply no way of predicting what future historians will witness and record for their readers – or even if their efforts will be published or merely posted on that Internet.

Certainly, through the work of the Lake County Historical Society, the important events and the everyday lives of the people who make up this diverse community will continue to be documented. Their efforts will continue to provide material for writers, researchers and students as long as there is support for the society. Support includes not only funding, but donations of items and materials that reflect the lives of people living in Lake County, Minnesota – a county which began and continues to thrive by water and rail.

CHAPTER 12

Color Photo Appendix

*The oldest and newest towns in Lake County are located within a couple of miles of each other. Beaver Bay **(top)** was settled in 1856 and is the oldest continuous settlement on the north shore. Just to the east, Silver Bay, first occupied by three or four fishing families in the early 1900s, was named by store owner Oscar Pederson and became a company town in the 1950s when Reserve Mining Company was built.*

PAINTING FROM LCHS MUSEUM

SILVER BAY POSTCARD FROM JON ANDERSON COLLECTION

Top: *In stormy seas with an overloaded tow barge, the Duluth & Iron Range Railroad tug* Ella G. Stone *struggled from Duluth to Agate Bay to deliver the company's first locomotive, the* 3-Spot, *which hauled construction equipment while the railroad to Tower was being built. Later, it was purchased by the Alger-Smith Lumber Company and served that company's Duluth & Northern Minnesota Railroad for about 20 years. Rescued by the D&IR Railroad Veteran's Association, it was renovated and put on display as a museum piece* **(right). Bottom:** *The first trainload of rich Vermilion Iron Range ore was loaded and delivered to Two Harbors on July 31, 1884, with Locomotive* No. 8 *being operated by Thomas Owens, who went on to become superintendent and vice president of the railroad.*
THE *3-SPOT* PAINTING AND A PRINT OF THE ENGINE *NO. 8* FIRST ORE SHIPMENT ARE BOTH FROM THE LCHS COLLECTION.

The waterfront at Agate Bay was the scene of hustle and bustle throughout its history, with upward of 1,200 vessels a year transporting the iron ore and delivering the coal that fired steam engines and heating plants. These three-color postcards are likely from the 1920s and show various aspects of the harbor and city.
SHIP AND COAL DOCK POSTCARDS FROM THE JON ANDERSON COLLECTION
BOTTOM POSTCARD FROM KATHRYN LARSON COLLECTION

Although early travelers to Lake County locations either walked, rowed or sailed small boats, by the turn of the century they depended on steamships like the America *and railroad transport. That changed in the early 1920s, when the Lake Superior International Highway opened the lakeshore to motorists, whose numbers swelled by leaps and bounds. Obviously, Silver Creek Cliff was a popular spot on the north shore. The highway even offered motorists a pull-off area in the early 1940s when this postcard was produced, but that amenity fell victim to erosion later.*
AMERICA POSTCARD FROM JON ANDERSON COLLECTION
SILVER CLIFF POSTCARD FROM KATHRYN LARSON COLLECTION

SILVER CREEK CLIFF NEAR TWO HARBORS—NORTH SHORE OF LAKE SUPERIOR.

With the arrival of motorists along the International Highway, the beginnings of tourism came into play. Split Rock Lighthouse, an attraction for photographers from the time it was constructed in 1909, became a wildly popular stopping place for motorists after the highway reached the site in about 1923. Emil Edison's Campers Home Resort at Castle Danger is credited as being the first cabin resort on the north shore and he also opened a store and Edison's Cafe on the highway. The cafe was later named the Rustic Inn Cafe **(bottom)** *and has remained a popular eating spot for travelers – although it was moved west and enlarged in the mid-1990s to make room for highway improvements.*
POSTCARDS FROM KATHRYN LARSON COLLECTION

These scenes in Two Harbors show that the city was attractive to photographers and visitors, but the number of color postcards that have survived also probably points out that sale of the cards was a lucrative business for the companies that produced them. These photos appear to be from the 1940s. An interesting note on the "Lake County High School" postcard states that it was the only school in the state and one of only a few in the country to serve an entire county. That situation ended in the late 1950s when William Kelley High School in Silver Bay opened and began accepting students from the northern areas of the huge school district. Students in western Lake County have always attended school in Ely.
CITYSCAPE POSTCARDS FROM JON ANDERSON COLLECTION
SCHOOL POSTCARD FROM KATHRYN LARSON COLLECTION

3rd Avenue, Two Harbors, Minn.

101:—LAKE COUNTY HIGH SCHOOL, TWO HARBORS, MINN.

47756

While many improvements in public accommodations have taken place in Lake County through the years, two of the more notable projects were the upgrading of Lighthouse Point by the Minnesota DNR in 1985 and the replacement of the old underpass on Highway 61 by the state Department of Transportation in 1999. The grounds surrounding the lighthouse had been rutted and a two-track boat launch was so steep that it nearly defied use. Landscaping, paved parking, an easy launch site and benches invite public usage. Inset, a 1931 photo shows the narrow underpass that previously existed. The photo also records an ore train derailment that rained ore cars down on the highway, very narrowly missing Chester Holbeck ***(left)*** *as he drove a truck through the underpass.* DERAILMENT PHOTO FROM CHESTER HOLBECK COLLECTION

JUNE 1931

From hunting and fishing excursions to autumn color tours, Lake County's attractions have lured visitors for more than a century. Scenic and exciting locations like Palisade Head, Shovel Point or ***(facing page)*** *Gooseberry Falls have their own charms and man-made features like Knife River and Silver Bay (shown in Chapter 10) marinas attract visitors with other interests. A plan was also in the works to develop a marina inland at the northeastern end of Agate Bay and negotiations with the DM&IR Railroad seemed to be progressing the summer of 2000.*
GOOSEBERRY POSTCARD FROM THE KATHRYN LARSON COLLECTION

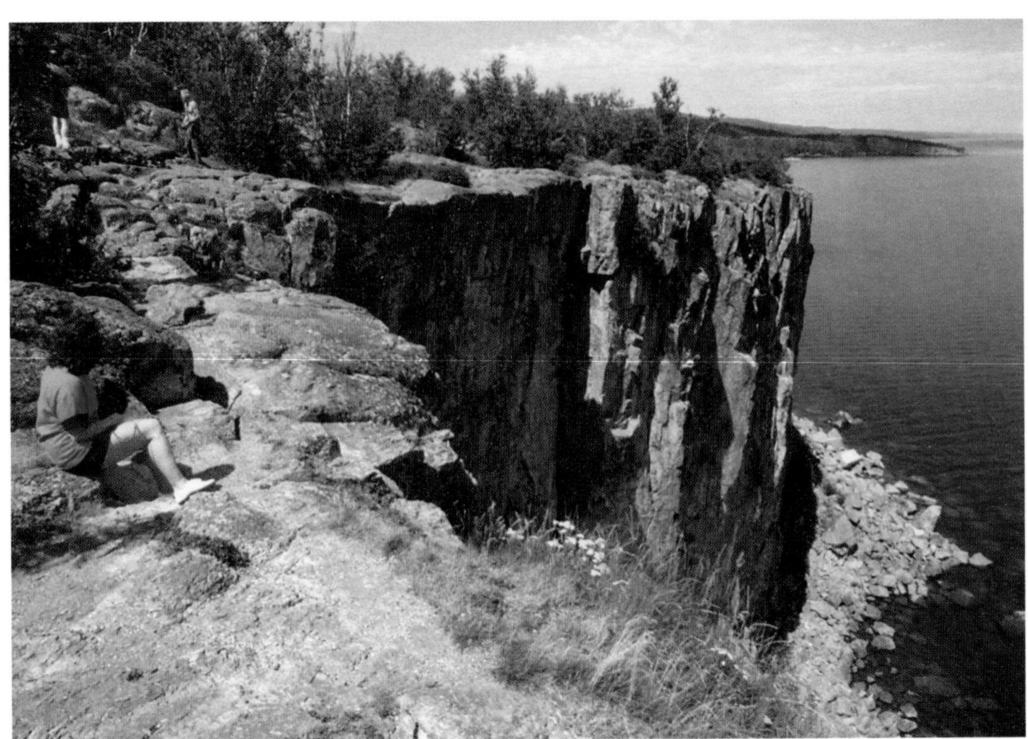

WATERFALL ON GOOSEBERRY RIVER,
LAKE SUPERIOR NORTH SHORE DRIVE,
NEAR TWO HARBORS, MINN.—60

The site of a substantial fishing economy through much of its history, Agate Bay's fishermen had abandoned their fish houses by the time that Grace Zemlin painted this scene, which hangs in the LCHS Museum **Bottom:** *In June 1985, all but one of the dilapidated fish houses on the east shore of the harbor were burned in an exercise for the city's firemen. The single remaining structure was destroyed in an unplanned fire a few years later.*
PHOTO FROM JON ANDERSON COLLECTION

The creation of LaBounty Manufacturing Company in 1972 by local contractor Roy LaBounty was a major boost to the area's economy, as the company went on to become a leading builder of a variety of construction and demolition attachments for hydraulic machinery and provided jobs for upward of 280 skilled employees. ***Bottom:*** *Progress comes in a multitude of forms and the evolution of Betty's Pies from a small summer roadside stand to a modern, four-season restaurant culminated in 2000, after planned highway improvements lopped a sizable piece from the front of the site.*
TOP PHOTO FROM LABOUNTY MANUFACTURING COLLECTION

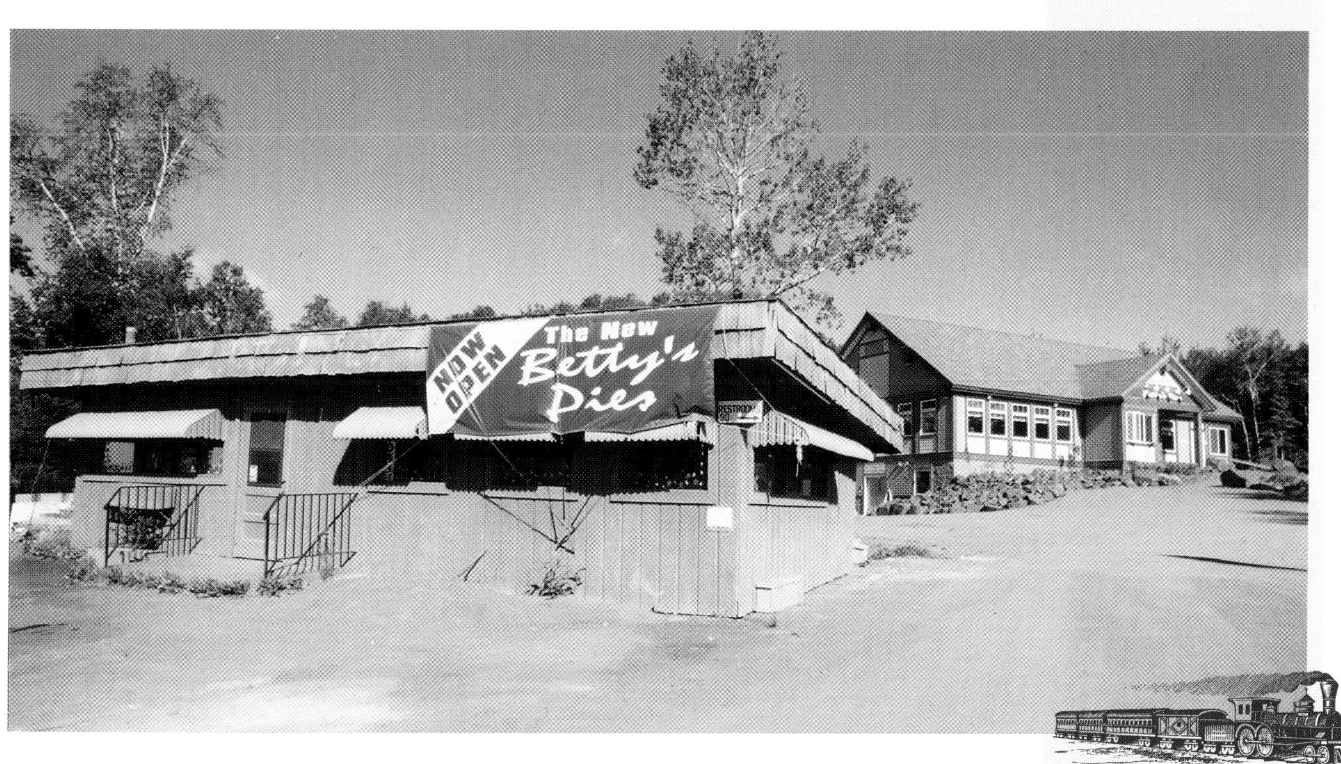

Through its first 75 years, the Lake County Historical Society has collected an impressive array of artifacts, many donated by the D&IR/DM&IR Railroad. The Depot Building, Mallet and 3-Spot locomotives, 3M Dwan Museum, tug Edna G. *and the Two Harbors Lighthouse are undoubtedly the most impressive of the LCHS displays, but the archives and collections contained in the museums are also a valuable resource for citizens tracing their family trees or seeking information about the past. The society is also the sponsor of this book through the generosity of a grant from Roy LaBounty.*

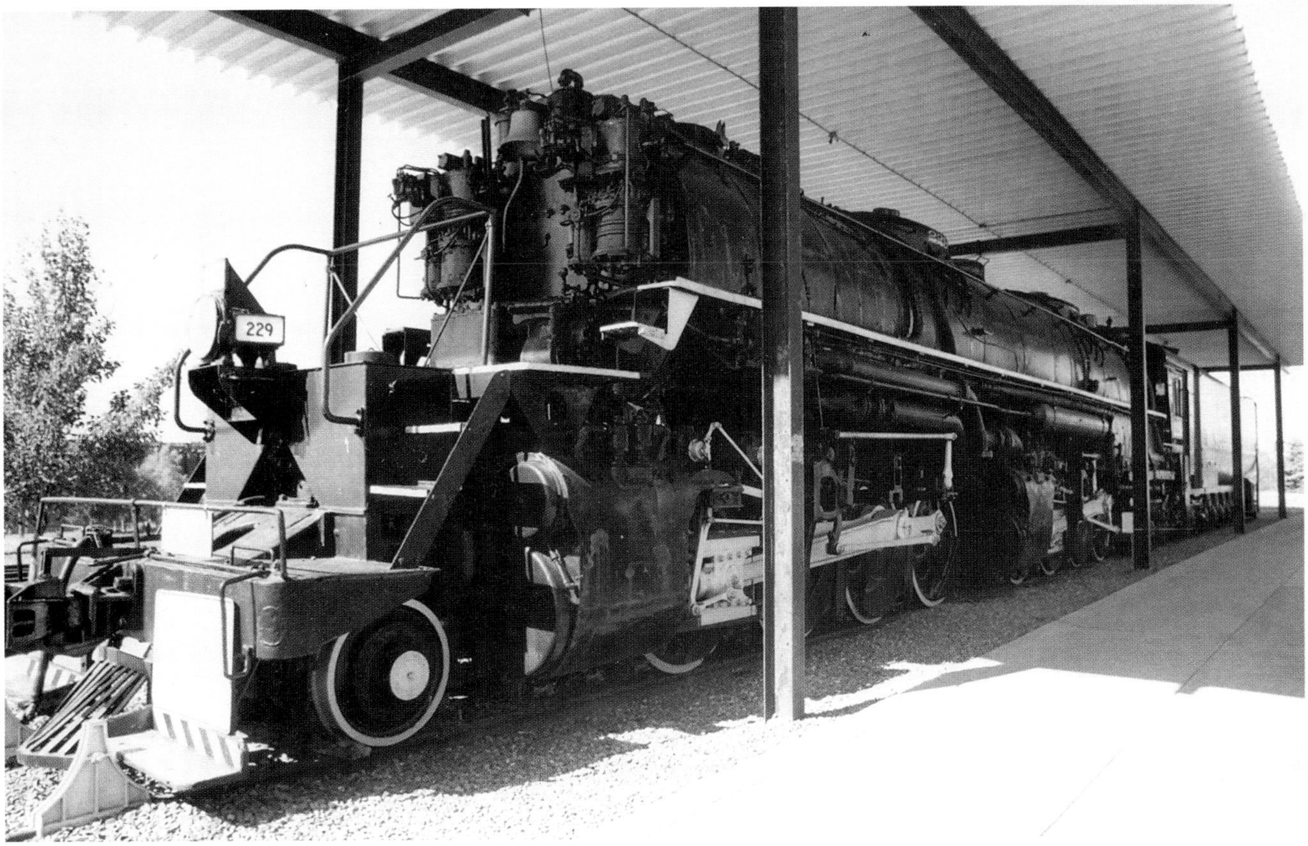
229

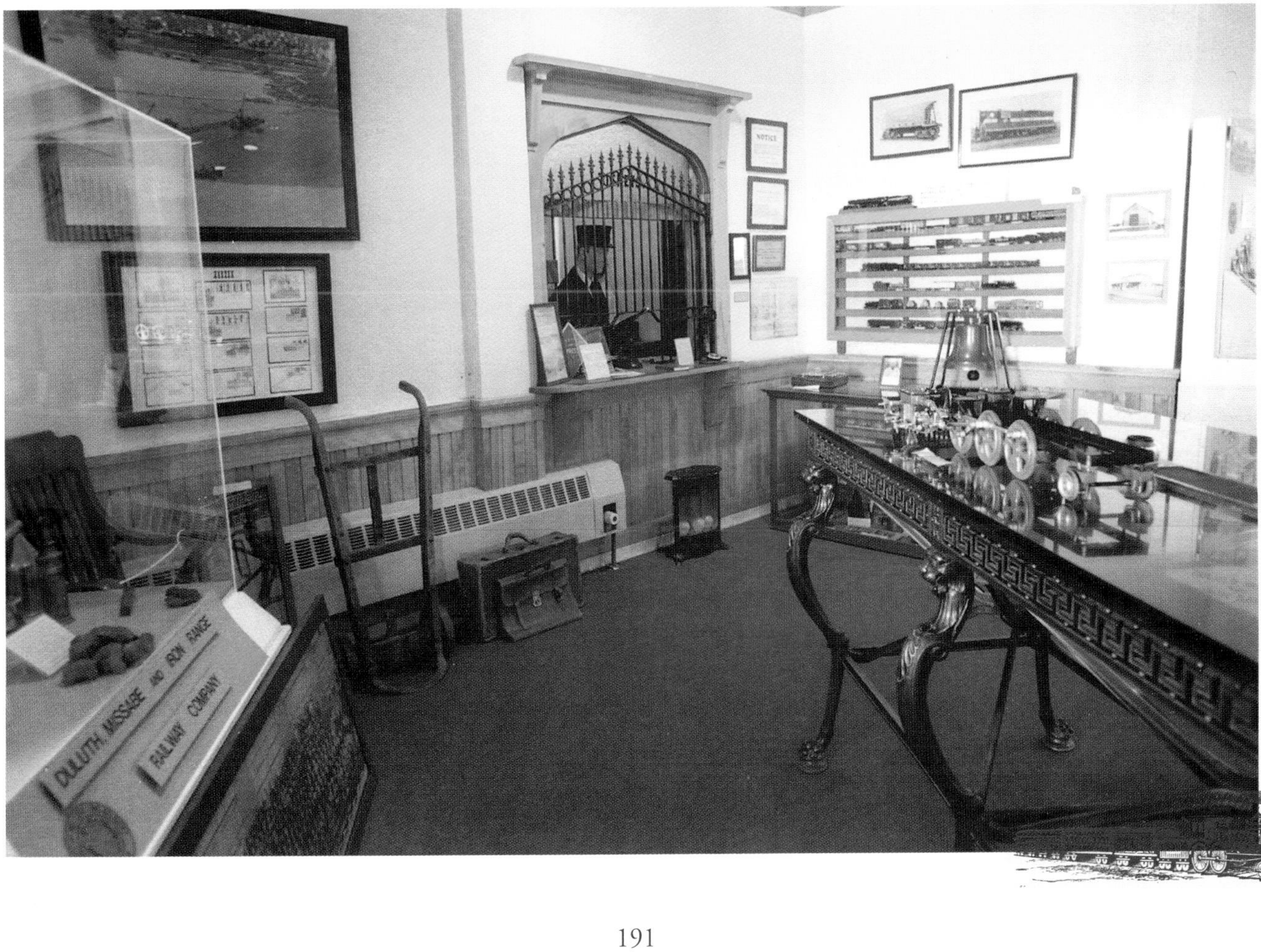
DULUTH, MISSABE AND IRON RANGE
RAILWAY COMPANY
NOTICE

While there are many attractions in Lake County, it is historically true that Lake Superior has always set the tone for much of what happens here. From shipping of iron ore at Two Harbors and Silver Bay to commercial and sport fishing, tourism and even the climate, the big lake is a constant presence and a great many attractions have been specifically created to give access to the lake-based activities. From upgrading of Lighthouse Point with visitor-friendly amenities and the Sonju Walking Trail to careful refurbishing of historic LCHS displays like the Crusader *fishing tug and the* Edna G., *which was the last hand-fired steam tug in operation on the Great Lakes, the waterfront of Lake Superior continues to draw well more than a million visitors a year, providing jobs and a stable economic benefit to the county.*

Two Harbors Lighthouse was officially acquired by the Lake County Historical Society on August 21, 1999, from the U.S. Coast Guard. Having opened as a bed-and-breakfast inn about a month earlier, renovation of the facilities on the lighthouse grounds continues. It is expected that this "new" attraction will continue to be one of the most popular stops along the north shore.

Endnotes

CHAPTER 1 [1-6]

[1]*Two Harbors, 100 Years, a Pictorial History*, Iron Ore Centennial Committee, 1984, Two Harbors, Minnesota, p. 7-10.

[2]Harrison, Redepenning, Hill et al., *The Paleo-Indians of Southern St. Louis County, Minnesota*, University of Minnesota, Duluth, Archaeometry Laboratory, 1995, Duluth, Minnesota, pp. 135-141.

[3]*Two Harbors, 100 Years*, p. 7.

[4]*Ibid.*, p. 8.

[5]*Ibid.*

[6]Grace Lee Nute, *Lake Superior*, Bobbs & Merrill Co., 1944, New York, NY, pp. 60-69.

[7]R.B. McLean, "Reminiscences of Early Days at the Head of the Lakes," *Lake Superior Magazine*, Volume 5 Issue 1 (Summer 1983), pp. 18-24.

[8]*Op. cit.*, Nute.

[9]*Two Harbors, 100 Years, Ibid.*

[10]*Two Harbors, 100 Years, Ibid.*

[11]Willis H. Raff, *Pioneers in the Wilderness: A History of Cook County*, Cook County Historical Society, 1981, pp. 45-47.

CHAPTER 2 [7-19]

[1]R.B. McLean,"Reminiscences of Early Days at the Head of the Lakes," Volume 5 Issue 1, *Lake Superior Magazine*, pp. 18-24.

[2]H.P. Wieland, "A Short History of the Wielands," manuscript dated Feb. 22, 1933, copy archived at Northeast Minnesota Historical Center.

[3]Fred W. Wieland, "Reminiscences of Early Beaver Bay," a letter to E.A. Schulze dated August 17, 1934, copy archived at Northeast Minnesota Historical Center.

[4]Jessie C. Davis, *Beaver Bay, Original North Shore Village*, 1968, St. Louis County Historical Society, Duluth, Minnesota, unnumbered.

[5]Henry P. Wieland, "Memoirs and Experiences at Beaver Bay and Duluth," undated 16-page manuscript from the archives of Northeast Minnesota Historical Center, p. 9.

[6]Helen Wieland Skillings, *We're Standing on Iron Ore: the story of the five Wieland Brothers 1856-1883*, St. Louis County Historical Society, Duluth, MN, 1972, p. 9.

[7]*Op. cit.*, Davis.

[8]*Op. cit.*, H.P. Wieland, *Short History*.

[9]*Op. cit.*, Davis.

[10]*Op. cit.*, Davis.

[11]*Op. cit.*, H.P. Wieland, "Memoirs."

[12]*Op. cit.*, F. Wieland, "Reminiscences."

[13]*Op. cit.*, Davis.

[14]*Op. cit.*, Davis.

[15]Carl A. Tate, "Memories," copy of undated typewritten and signed manuscript, Patricia Reed Collection, pp. 16-17.

[16]*Op. cit.*, F. Wieland, "Reminiscences."

[17]*Op. cit.*, Davis.

[18]H.P. Wieland, *Short History*.

[19]*Op. cit.*, Davis.

[20]Mrs. Elizabeth Hangartner, personal letter dated June 28, 1929, to New Ulm's Diamond Jubilee and Homecoming, Patricia Reed Collection.

[21]*Ibid.*

[22]Patricia Reed interview, videotaped 6/19/2000, LCHS archives.

[23]Elise Sonju Williams, *How We Remember: Stories and Recollections of Finland, Minnesota's First Century*, Finland, Minnesota, 1995, pp. 7-8.

CHAPTER 3 [20-32]

[1]Henry P. Wieland, "Memoirs and Experiences at Beaver Bay and Duluth," undated 16-page manuscript from the archives of Northeastern Minnesota Historical Center.

[2]William E. Scott, typewritten transcript of interview, circa 1950, conducted with Charles Saxton of Duluth, in "Early History, Volume II," LCHS archives.

[3]McLean, R.B., (1832-1922), "Reminiscences of Early Days at the Head of the Lakes," *Lake Superior Magazine* Vol. 5 Issue 1 (Summer 1983) pp. 18-24.

[4]*History of the Upper Mississippi Valley*, Minnesota Historical Society, 1881, p. 696.

[5]*Commemorative Biographical Record of the Upper Lake*, Chicago, Illinois, 1905, pp. 149-150. (Typewritten duplicate appears as p. 69, LCHS archival "Early History Volume II").

[6]*Op. cit.*, McLean.

[7]"John J. Hibbard," autobiographical account published in the August 11 and 18, 1939, *Duluth Free Press*, clipping in LCHS archives "Early History Vol. II."

[8]*Two Harbors, 100 Years, a Pictorial History*, Iron Ore Centennial Committee, 1984, Two Harbors, Minnesota, p. 15.

[9]Hal Bridges, *Iron Millionaire*, University of Pennsylvania Press, Philadelphia, Pennsylvania, 1952, pp.169.

[10]*Ibid.*

[11]*Ibid.*, p. 170.

[12]*Op. cit.*, *Commemorative Biographical Record of the Upper Lake.*

[13]*Op. cit.*, Bridges, p. 19.

CHAPTER 4 [33-44]

[1]Bridges, Hal, *Iron Millionaire: Life of Charlemagne Tower*, University of Pennsylvania Press, Philadelphia, PA, 1952.

[2]David A. Walker, *Iron Frontier: The Discovery and Early Development of Minnesota's Three Ranges*, Minnesota Historical Society, 1979, pp. 1-72.

CHAPTER 5 [45-78]

[1]*The Iron Frontier*, David A. Walker, Minnesota Historical Society, Minneapolis, Minnesota, 1979, p. 61.

[2]Frank King, *The Missabe Road*, Golden West Books, San Marino, California, 1972.

[3]*Op. cit.*, Walker.

[4]*Op. cit.*, King.

[5]Ebner Anderson interview, videotaped 2/2/2000, LCHS archives.

[6]Campman Anderson, "Early Pioneers of Silver Creek," copy of undated typed manuscript from Don Bolen.

[7]Ted Wahlberg interview, videotaped 2/2/2000, LCHS archives.

[8]*Ibid.*

[9]"Interview with Agnes Thorngren," untitled undated typed transcript, Patricia Reed Collection.

[10]Roy LaBounty interview, videotaped 2/2/2000, LCHS archives.

[11]Wesley Bugge interview, videotaped 3/27/2000, LCHS archives.

[12]*The Brand of the Tartan – the 3M Story*, Virginia Huck, Appleton-Century-Crofts Inc. and Minnesota Mining and Manufacturing Company, 1955.

[13]Alf Sandvik interview, videotaped 3/27/2000, LCHS archives.

[14]*Op. cit.,* Ebner Anderson interview.

[15]*In Faith and Love: the Centennial History of the Holy Spirit Parish, 1888-1988*, Two Harbors, Minnesota, 1988.

[16]John Gralewski interview, videotaped 2/2/2000, LCHS archives.

[17]"Ben Fenstad Sr., Early Fisherman at Little Marais," no author identified, *Silver Bay News*, August 26, 1958, p. 1.

[18]Ted Tofte, *Wonderland of the Herring Chokers*, Blackwater Press, 1982, pp. 5-9.

[19]Tom Sjoblom, *The Autobiography of a Herring Choker*, Bill Sjoblom's SJO-PRO TOURS, 1991.

[20]*Op. cit.,* Tofte.

[21]*Op. cit.,* Sjoblom.

[22]*Op. cit.,* Tofte.

[23]*Op. cit.,* Tofte.

[24]*Op. cit.,* Sjoblom.

[25]*Op. cit.,* Sjoblom.

[26]Walter Sve interview, videotaped 4/14/2000, LCHS archives.

[27]*Op. cit.,* Sjoblom.

CHAPTER 6 [79-98]

[1]Nute, Grace Lee, *Lake Superior*, 1944, Bobbs-Merrill Company, Indianapolis, Indiana and New York, New York, pp. 195-212.

[2]Frank King, *Logging Railroads of Minnesota*, Golden West Books, San Marino, California, 1981, p. 65 and on.

[3]*Op. cit.,* Nute.

[4]*Op. cit.,* King.

[5]Dan Minahan, Marilyn Lusk Kregear, et al., *Memoirs of Knife River*, published by descendants of original settlers, circa 1990.

[6]Todd Lindahl interview, videotaped 2/2/2000, LCHS archives.

[7]*Op. cit.,* King.

[8]"Memories of Ralph Anderson: Railroad Hostler," by Bonnie Tikkanen, *How We Remember*, Finland, Minnesota, Centennial Committee, 1995, p. 53.

[9]*Op. cit.,* Lindahl.

[10]*Op. cit.,* King.

[11]*Ibid.*

[12]*Ibid.*

[13]*Ibid.*

[14]*Ibid.*

[15]*Ibid.*

[16]*Ibid.*

[17]*Ibid.*

[18]*Op. cit.,* Lindahl interview.

[19]Robert Silver, untitled transcript of recorded memoirs, Schroeder (Minnesota) Historical Society archive, 1999.

[20]*Op. cit.,* Minahan, Kregear, et al.

[21]*Op. cit.,* Tikkanen, "Memories of Ralph Anderson," p. 53.

[22]Wesley Bugge interview, videotaped 3/27/2000, LCHS archives.

CHAPTER 7 [99-108]

[1]Elfie Rinne, editor, *The Brimson-Toimi Legacy*, Glensco Enterprise International, Iron, Minnesota, a Brimson-Toimi History Project Committee collaboration, 1995.

[2]*Ibid.*

[3]*Ibid.*

[4]Irja (Laaksonen) Beckman, *Echoes from the Past*, 1979, Parta Printers Inc., New York Mills, Minnesota.

[5]*Ibid.*

[6]*Op. cit.,* Rinne.

[7]*Op. cit.,* Beckman.

[8]*Op. cit.,* Rinne.

[9]*Op. cit.,* Rinne.

[10]*Op. cit.,* Rinne.

[11]Richard Stone interview, videotaped 3/27/2000, LCHS archives.

[12]*Op. cit.,* Rinne.

[13]Frank King, *Minnesota Logging Railroads*, 1981, Golden West Books, San Marino, California.

[14]Todd Lindahl interview, videotaped 3/27/2000, LCHS archives.

[15]*Op. cit.,* Rinne.

CHAPTER 8 [109-125]

[1]"Ben Fenstad Sr., Early Fisherman at Little Marais," *Silver Bay News*, August 28, 1958, no author noted.

[2]"An Interview with my Grandpa – Olaf Fenstad" by Tom Nikula, from *How We Remember: Stories and Recollections of Finland, Minnesota's First Century*, 1995, Finland Centennial Committee, pp 31-32.

[3]*Op. cit.,* "Ben Fenstad Sr."

[4]*Ibid.*

[5]Untitled typed manuscript about Alfred Fenstad and North Shore telephone systems, May 1956, Patricia Reed Collection.

[6]*Ibid.*

[7]Robert Silver, untitled transcript of taped memoirs, 1999, Schroeder Historical Society archive.

[8]*Keeping Our Heritage, Finland, Minnesota, 1895-1976*, Finland Schools Reunion Committee, 1976, pp. 7-25.

[9]*Ibid,* p. 29 and following.

[10]*Op. cit.,* "Memories of Elise Sonju Williams," *How We Remember*, pp. 7-8.

[11]*Op. cit., Keeping Our Heritage*, pp. 26-28.

[12]*Ibid.* pp. 45.

[13]*Op. cit.,* Silver transcript.

[14]*Op. cit.,* Silver transcript.

[15]*Op. cit.,* "An Interview with Anselm Johnson," *How We Remember*," pp. 18-19.

[16]Sue Sigel, editor, untitled, unpublished manuscript of the Isabella Community Council historical committee, 1999.

[17]*Op. cit.,* "Growing Up In Isabella: An Interview with Eric Grondahl and Mae Runnberg" by Bonnie Tikkanen, *How We Remember*, p. 45.

[18]*Ibid.*

[19]*Op. cit.,* Sigel.

[20]*Op. cit.,* "Growing up in Isabella."

[21]Robert Holden interview, videotaped 3/29/2000, LCHS archives.

[22]Alvin Jouppi interview, videotaped 4/31/2000, LCHS archives.

[23]*Op. cit.,* Sigel.

[24]*Op. cit.,* Sigel.

[25]Margaret Haapoja, "Forest of Dreams," *Lake Superior Magazine*, Vol. 15 Issue 3 (Oct./Nov. 1993), pp. 24-28.

[26]Sylvia Anderson Tucker, "Teaching on the North Shore," unpublished typed manuscript, Patricia Reed Collection.

CHAPTER 9 [126-139]

[1]Three sources refer to an R. Whiteside in the Ely-Winton area – Richard, Robert, Robert A., Robert B. and R.V. Whiteside. Whether these references are one person or, perhaps, brothers has not been determined, but Tauno Maki and J. William Trygg (see #2 and #3 below) agreed on the R.V. Whiteside name in this instance.

[2]Tauno Maki, *Winton, from Boom to Bust and Other Stories*, self-published collection of essays, historical sketches and miscellaneous materials, circa 1987, with Ely-Winton Historical Society.

[3]*Ibid.,* personal 1952 memoirs of G.H. Good, superintendent of Swallow & Hopkins Lumber and J. William Trygg of Ely.

[4]Mike Majeski and Barbara Soderburg for the U.S. Forest Service, *BWCAW*, 1993, U.S. Dept. of Agriculture, pp. 3-27.

[5]*Ibid.*

[6]Milt Stenlund, *Section 30: The Mine and Community*, Heritage North, Grand Rapids, Minnesota, undated, pp. 1-5.

[7]*Ibid.*

[8]*Ibid.*

[9]*Ibid,* p. 7.

[10]*Ibid,* p. 6.

[11]Winnifred Lomasney, "A Brief History of Section Thirty" unpublished essay manuscript, circa 1934, Alf Sandvik Collection.

[12]*Op. cit.,* Stenlund, pp. 6-11.

[13]*Ibid.*

[14]*Op. cit.,* Lomasney.

[15]Milt Stenlund, *Ghost Mines of the Ely Area (1882-1925)*, in cooperation with the Ely-Winton Historical Society, Ely, Minnesota, 1988, pp. 7-8.

[16]*Ibid.*

[17]*Op. cit.,* Maki.

[18]Frank King, *Minnesota Logging Railroads*, Golden West Books, San Marino, California, 1981.

[19]Lois Pelto interview, videotaped 2/27/2000; Ferdinand and Patricia Thums interview, videotaped 3/29/2000, LCHS archives.

[20]Lois Pelto manuscript and interview, videotaped 2/27/2000, LCHS archives.

[21]*Op. cit.,* Pelto and Thums.

[22]*Op. cit.,* Pelto and Thums.

[23]*Op. cit.,* Ferdinand Thums.

[24]*Op. cit.,* Pelto.

[25]*Op. cit.,* Pelto and Thums.

CHAPTER 10 [140-154]

[1]Lee Radzak interview, videotaped 4/14/2000, LCHS archives.

[2]Lorraine M. Rustari with Margaret Ness, "A Bit of Bay History," Bay Area Historical Society newsletter, Fall 1985.

[3]Jessie C. Davis, *Beaver Bay, Original North Shore Village*, 1968, St. Louis County Historical Society, Duluth, Minnesota, unnumbered.

[4]*Op. cit.,* Rustari-Ness.

[5]E.W. Davis, *Pioneering With Taconite*, Minnesota Historical Society, 1964, St. Paul, MN.

[6]John Gralewski interview, videotaped 2/2/2000, LCHS archives.

[7]*Op. cit.,* E.W. Davis.

[8]*Ibid.*

[9]Thomas R. Huffman, "Learn from Legacy of Reserve Mining," *Duluth News Tribune*, April 9, 2000, p. 21A.

[10]*Ibid.*

[11]*Op. cit.,* Radzak.

[12]Selected papers from Gooseberry Falls State Park archive.

[13]Walter Sve interview, videotaped 4/14/2000, LCHS archives.

[14]*Op. cit.,* Radzak.

CHAPTER 11 [155-178]

[1]Frank King, *The Missabe Road*, Golden West Books, San Marino, California, 1972.

[2]John W. Wright, editor, *2000 New York Times Almanac*, Penguin Reference Books, New York, NY, p. 91.

[3]*Ibid.*

[4]*Op. cit.,* King.

[5]*Two Harbors, 100 Years, a Pictorial History*, Iron Ore Centennial Committee, 1984, Two Harbors, Minnesota.

[6]*Op. cit.,* Wright.

[7]Arnold Pederson interview, 5/25/2000 by author.

[8]Richard Stone interview, videotaped 3/27/2000, LCHS archives.

[9]*Ibid.*

[10]*Op. cit.,* King.

[11]*Op. cit.,* King.

[12]Jack Gralewski interview, videotaped 2/2/2000, LCHS archives.

[13]Mary Ann (Christensen) Habash (writing and performing as Chris Blanchard) correspondence with author.

[14]*Op. cit., Two Harbors, 100 years.*

[15]Emery Carlstrom interview, videotaped 2/3/2000, LCHS archives.

[16]Lisbeth Boutang, "The Family LaBounty," *Lake Superior Magazine*, Vol. 15 Issue 3 (Jun./Jul. 1993), pp. 34-37, and personal interviews with Roy LaBounty by author.

[17]Ebner Anderson interview, videotaped 2/2/2000, LCHS archives.

Bibliography

Books

Beckman, Irja (Laaksonen). *Echoes from the Past.* New York Mills, Minnesota: Parta Printers Inc., 1979.

Bridges, Hal. *Iron Millionaire.* Philadelphia, Pennsylvania: University of Pennsylvania Press, 1952.

Commemorative Biographical Record of the Upper Lake. Chicago, Illinois: 1905. (Typewritten duplicate appears as page 69, Lake County Historical Society archival "Early History Volume II").

Davis, E.W. *Pioneering With Taconite.* St. Paul: Minnesota Historical Society, 1964.

Davis, Jessie C. *Beaver Bay, Original North Shore Village.* Duluth, Minnesota: St. Louis County Historical Society, 1968.

Harrison, Redepenning, Hill et al. *The Paleo-Indians of Southern St. Louis County, Minnesota.* Duluth, Minnesota: University of Minnesota-Duluth, Archaeometry Laboratory, 1995.

History of the Upper Mississippi Valley. St. Paul: Minnesota Historical Society, 1881.

How We Remember: Stories and Recollections of Finland, Minnesota's First Century. Finland, Minnesota: 1995.

In Faith and Love: the Centennial History of the Holy Spirit Parish, 1888-1988. Two Harbors, Minnesota: 1988.

Keeping Our Heritage, Finland, Minnesota, 1895-1976. Finland, Minnesota: Finland Schools Reunion Committee, 1976.

King, Frank. *Logging Railroads of Minnesota.* San Marino, California: Golden West Books, 1981.

King, Frank. *The Missabe Road.* San Marino, California: Golden West Books, 1972.

Majeski, Mike; and Barbara Soderburg. For the U.S. Forest Service, *BWCAW,* U.S. Dept. of Agriculture, 1993.

Maki,Tauno. *Winton, from Boom to Bust and Other Stories.* Self-published collection of essays, historical sketches and miscellaneous materials, with Ely-Winton Historical Society, circa 1987.

Minahan, Dan; Marilyn Lusk Kregear, et al. *Memoirs of Knife River.* Published by descendants of original settlers, circa 1990.

Nute, Grace Lee. *Lake Superior.* New York: Bobbs & Merrill Co., 1944.

Raff, Willis H. *Pioneers in the Wilderness: A History of Cook County.* Cook County Historical Society, 1981.

Rinne, Elfie, editor. *The Brimson-Toimi Legacy.* Iron, Minnesota: Glensco Enterprise International, a Brimson-Toimi History Project Committee collaboration, 1995.

Sjoblom, Tom. *The Autobiography of a Herring Choker.* Bill Sjoblom's SJO-PRO TOURS, 1991.

Skillings, Helen Wieland. *We're Standing on Iron Ore: the story of the five Wieland Brothers 1856-1883.* Duluth, Minnesota: St. Louis County Historical Society, 1972.

Stenlund, Milt. *Ghost Mines of the Ely Area (1882-1925).* Ely, Minnesota: in cooperation with the Ely-Winton Historical Society, 1988.

Stenlund, Milt. *Section 30: The Mine and Community.* Grand Rapids, Minnesota: Heritage North, undated.

Tofte, Ted. *Wonderland of the Herring Chokers.* Blackwater Press, 1982.

Two Harbors, 100 Years, a Pictorial History. Two Harbors, Minnesota: Iron Ore Centennial Committee, 1984.

Walker, David A. *Iron Frontier: The Discovery and Early Development of Minnesota's Three Ranges.* St. Paul: Minnesota Historical Society, 1979.

Wright John W., editor. *2000 New York Times Almanac.* New York: Penguin Reference Books.

Periodicals and Collections

Anderson, Campman. "Early Pioneers of Silver Creek." Copy of undated typed manuscript from Don Bolen.

Boutang, Lisbeth. "The Family LaBounty." *Lake Superior Magazine,* Vol. 15 Issue 3 (Jun./Jul. 1993).

Fenstad, Alfred. Untitled typed manuscript about North Shore telephone systems, May 1956, Patricia Reed Collection.

Haapoja, Margaret. "Forest of Dreams." *Lake Superior Magazine,* Vol. 15 Issue 3 (Oct./Nov. 1993).

Hangartner, Elizabeth. Personal letter dated June 28, 1929, to New Ulm's Diamond Jubilee and Homecoming, Patricia Reed Collection.

Hibbard, John J. *Duluth Free Press.* Autobiographical account published in August 11 and 18, 1939. Clipping in LCHS archives "Early History Vol. II."

Huffman, Thomas R. "Learn from Legacy of Reserve Mining." *Duluth News Tribune,* April 9, 2000.

Lomasney, Winnifred. "A Brief History of Section Thirty." Unpublished essay manuscript, circa 1934, Alf Sandvik Collection.

McLean, R.B. "Reminiscences of Early Days at the Head of the Lakes." *Lake Superior Magazine,* Vol. 5 Issue 1 (Summer 1983).

Rustari, Lorraine M.; Margaret Ness. "A Bit of Bay History." Bay Area Historical Society newsletter, Fall 1985.

Scott, William E. Typewritten transcript of interview, circa 1950, conducted with Charles Saxton of Duluth, in "Early History, Volume II," LCHS archives.

Selected papers from Gooseberry Falls State Park archive.

Sigel, Sue, editor. Untitled, unpublished manuscript of the Isabella Community Council Historical Committee, 1999.

Silver, Robert. Untitled transcript of recorded memoirs, Schroeder (Minnesota) Historical Society archive, 1999.

Tate, Carl A. "Memories." Copy of undated typewritten and signed manuscript, Patricia Reed Collection.

Thorngren, Agnes. Untitled undated typed transcript of interview, Patricia Reed Collection.

Tucker, Sylvia Anderson. "Teaching on the North Shore." Unpublished typed manuscript, Patricia Reed Collection.

Wieland, Fred W. "Reminiscences of Early Beaver Bay." Letter to E.A. Schulze dated August 17, 1934, copy archived at Northeast Minnesota Historical Center.

Wieland, H.P. "A Short History of the Wielands." Manuscript dated Feb. 22, 1933, copy archived at Northeast Minnesota Historical Center.

Wieland, Henry P. "Memoirs and Experiences at Beaver Bay and Duluth." Undated 16-page manuscript from the archives of Northeast Minnesota Historical Center.

Index

Boldface = Illustration

About the Author

Hugh E. Bishop

A resident of Two Harbors, Minnesota, since 1983, Hugh Bishop served as editor/publisher of the *Lake County News-Chronicle* for three years before moving on to magazine work in 1986. Previously, he had served as a public relations representative for Erie Mining Company at Hoyt Lakes, where frequent duties at Taconite Harbor first interested him in Lake Superior and Minnesota's north shore.

Thus, with a 25-year acquaintance in writing about northeastern Minnesota, he jumped at the chance to author this history when the Lake County Historical Society made the decision to move ahead on the project through the generosity of Roy LaBounty.

After finishing the text for this book, Bishop says, "This has really been a much larger and longer project than I ever anticipated. How did this area develop such a rich past, when way more than a third of its land is held as national forest and a designated wilderness? I hope that this book captures that story and leads some readers to search out the other historical efforts that are listed in the bibliography, for there is a good deal more localized history that goes into even greater detail than I could include here."

Bishop is senior writer at Lake Superior Port Cities Inc., regularly writes for *Lake Superior Magazine* and takes a good deal of pride in having been able to continue writing for a living for nearly 35 years in northern Minnesota. He and wife, Liz, have three children.